The Global Trading System

Kym Anderson is Professor of Economics and Executive Director of the Centre for International Economic Studies at the University of Adelaide, Australia. He was a WTO Dispute Settlement Panelist during 1996–2000.

Bernard Hoekman leads the International Trade Group at the World Bank in Washington, DC.

The editors worked together in the Economic Research and Analysis Division of the GATT Secretariat in Geneva during the latter years of the Uruguay Round. Both have authored and edited several books on trade policy and the global trading system.

Tauris Guides to Global Economic Issues

International Debt
S.E. Corbridge
ISBN 1 86064 274 8

The Global Trading System
K. Anderson and B. Hoekman
ISBN 1 86064 058 3

Global Transport Issues
R. Tolley and B. Turton
ISBN 1 86064 564 X

The Global Trading System

Edited by

Kym Anderson

Professor of Economics and Director, Centre for International Economic Studies, University of Adelaide

and

Bernard Hoekman

Senior Economist, International Trade Group, World Bank

Volume 2:
Core rules and procedures

I.B.Tauris *Publishers*
LONDON • NEW YORK

Published in 2002 by I.B.Tauris & Co. Ltd
6 Salem Road, London W2 4BU
175 Fifth Avenue, New York NY 10010

In the United States of America and in Canada distributed by
St Martin's Press, 175 Fifth Avenue, New York NY 10010

A full CIP record for this book is available from the British Library
A full CIP record for this book is available from the Library of Congress

ISBN 1 86064 058 3

Library of Congress catalog card number: available

Typeset by I.T.S., Edinburgh
Printed and bound in Great Britain by MPG Books Ltd, Bodmin, Cornwall

CONTENTS

Introduction to Volume 2: Core Rules and Procedures

Kym Anderson and Bernard Hoekman

Trading has been going on ever since humankind began seeking to improve well-being. It involves exchanging either endowments or the goods and services produced with them, including through specialization in production: between individuals within households or tribes, between households or tribes located within walking distance of each other, between rural and urban areas within nation states, between nation states and, for more than half a millennium, between continents. The Silk Road provided the first major inter-continental trade link, between Europe and Asia, but it was not until the expeditions of European mariners to the Americas, the Far East and Australasia from the middle of the past millennium that truly global trade began.

Anyone familiar with the history of international trade prior to the mid-twentieth century is acutely aware of its unruliness. Indeed it often took a war between nations before leaders would get together to develop a trade agreement. Even then it would typically be a limited bilateral agreement which, if it hurt other economies, could exacerbate tensions elsewhere. The recent popular history of the spice trade from 1553 to 1667 by Milton (1999) is a reminder of the brutal lawlessness with which international trade was conducted in centuries past. Certainly trade relations were relatively tranquil in the five decades to World War I, but they became unruly again in the interwar period.

When viewed from this historical perspective, the development of the modern global trading system since World War II has been both extremely rapid and far more successful than its planners dared hope for. The modern, legally binding, rules-based global trading system originated with the 1947 General Agreement on Tariffs and Trade (GATT). This was encapsulated in the World Trade Organization (WTO) that came into being in 1995 following the successful completion of the Uruguay Round of multilateral trade negotiations. Over that half-century international trade rose rapidly: more than one-fifth of global output is now exported, double the proportion of the 1950s. The GATT was a major contributor to that growth, as it proved to be a powerful vehicle through which nations were able to overcome domestic resistance to trade liberalization. GATT rules outlawing quantitative restrictions on trade, and successive GATT rounds of negotiations that resulted in cuts in bound tariffs on imports of manufactures by industrial countries led to tariffs coming down to 'nuisance' levels for many products. Manufacturing tariffs of OECD countries now average less than 4 per cent, compared with more than 40 per cent when the GATT was first signed in

1947 by the original 23 contracting parties (who at that time accounted for four-fifths of world trade). That membership, incidentally, has since grown to more than 140, with another 30 in the process of joining. Once the largest traders in that latter group accede, which include China and Taiwan (whose accession is imminent), as well as Russia, the WTO membership will account for more than 95 per cent of global international trade.

Appreciating the differences between the trading environment pre-GATT and today's system is an essential precursor to evaluating the latter. The GATT and now the WTO provide not only a set of multilateral rules and disciplines but also a forum to negotiate tariff reductions and rules changes, plus a legal mechanism to settle trade disputes that is recognized as an integral part of the world's body of international law. The WTO has added three other contributions to those of the earlier GATT: to monitor and report on trade and trade-related policy developments on a regular basis, thereby adding to policy transparency; to facilitate the fuller integration of developing and transition economies into the global trading system; and to improve cohesion between the WTO and other international economic agencies such as the World Bank and International Monetary Fund.

Superior though it is, the current system nonetheless still has plenty of room for improvement. Indeed much attention has been directed in recent years at its shortcomings. Among the issues that have focused attention are globalization, regional integration, noisy trade disputes across the North Atlantic and elsewhere, a perception by some that the system is unfair to developing countries, linkages between trade and other policy areas such as foreign investment or competition policy, and concerns about possible adverse impacts of trade on such things as inequality, poverty, the environment, labour standards, and food safety and security. These concerns were voiced loudly at the third WTO trade ministerial meeting in Seattle in late 1999, contributing to the postponing of the first comprehensive round of multilateral trade negotiations under WTO auspices.

There is thus a need for more-accessible information, knowledge and understanding of what the global trading system is about, how it evolved, how it works, why the world needs it, and what more it can, should, or should not try to do to make the world a more peaceful and prosperous place. These needs were accentuated at Seattle (and subsequently at other economic meetings of world leaders) where it was clear that many of the protesting groups knew little about the WTO and the workings of the rules-based global trading system, nor about what the world might be like without that institution and its rules and procedures.

There are a number of books on the GATT/WTO rules-based global trading system that are readily available.[1] The present set of readings is designed to complement those books with less-readily available journal articles and chapters from edited volumes. They come from the core trade disciplines of economics, law, and political science, but with an emphasis on the editors' profession of economics.[2] Our objective was to collect papers that have been cited often, provide a pertinent historical perspective, and/or address current and future issues that confront the trading system. Because of space constraints, quantitative ex ante and ex post assessments of the economic effects of trade reforms are explicitly excluded.[3] The selection is based on responses to a survey of around one hundred of our colleagues, whom we sincerely thank (with apologies for not being able to include more of their papers!). We also thank the original publishers of the included papers for permission to reproduce them in this collection. A list of the full set of papers in the four volumes, together with their original source, is provided in the Acknowledgements.

The present four-volume set has been prepared around the following topics: the genesis of the GATT; the rules and procedures embodied in the GATT (and, since its inception in 1995, the General Agreement on Trade in Services, or GATS); the exceptions to those rules; and the 'new' issues that confront the WTO membership in the twenty-first century as internationalization progresses further (the lowering of the transactions costs of doing business across national borders). Within each of the four volumes the readings appear in alphabetical order, since that makes them easier to find than if they were ordered chronologically or by sub-topics.

The rest of this chapter provides an introduction to the readings in the current volume, which cover the core rules and procedures of the GATT and now the WTO. As mentioned above, the key purposes of the WTO are to provide (i) a set of multilaterally agreed rules, (ii) a forum to negotiate changes in rules and reductions in trade-distorting measures, (iii) a legal mechanism to settle trade disputes, (iv) a system of monitoring and reporting regularly on trade and trade-related policy developments, and (v) ways to better integrate developing economies into the global trading system. How well do the GATT and now WTO rules and procedures contribute towards those objectives? We consider each of those five sub-topics in turn.

MFN AND OTHER CORE RULES

By and large, GATT's rules and procedures have been well suited to reducing trade conflicts, according to Conybeare (reading 4) but the rule that has been most contentious is the unconditional most-favoured-nation (MFN) clause – even though it is considered one of the fundamental pillars of the global trading system. One reason for the contention is that MFN need not lead to a government being willing to lower tariffs (at least directly), for in its unconditional form it requires a member to allow the same market access conditions as provided to its most favoured trading partner. Indeed in reading 3 by Caplin and Krishna, a game theoretic model is presented in which higher tariffs emerge from an MFN bargaining game. The key reason MFN is nonetheless revered is because it proscribes discrimination.

A forthright response to the standard criticisms of unconditional MFN is provided in reading 15 by Viner. He was writing in 1931 in the midst of the Great Depression in America, where reciprocal trade agreements or at most ones that contained conditional MFN clauses had been preferred by the US government. As Viner points out, conditional MFN (each trading partner gets MFN treatment for its exports only if it reciprocates with a similar degree of greater market access for US exports) may sound more equitable (less free riding) than if only the principal supplying country provides greater market access. But it works badly in practice: it increases the likelihood of trade diversion rather than trade creation; it lowers the tariff revenue collected in the importing country; and it is in any case equivalent (a) to an unconditional pledge when received from a country that practises unconditional MFN and (b) to no pledge at all when received from a country that is also only practising conditional MFN.

To explore this issue further, Ludema in reading 10 sets up a non-cooperative, dynamic bargaining game between three countries in which the choice between a bilateral agreement (in which only two countries make tariff reductions) and a multilateral agreement is endogenous. This enables him to address both the free-rider problem (in the presence of MFN) and the discriminatory coalition problem (in the absence of MFN) within a unifying framework. What he finds is that bargaining in the presence of MFN results in a mutually advantageous multilateral trade agreement that is Pareto efficient, and the free-rider problem does not arise.

In reading 13 by Schwartz and Sykes, the concept of MFN is explored in a political economy framework (positive as distinct from normative analysis). They search in vain for alternative solutions to the free-rider problem that MFN creates, and conclude that no alternative rule has the same ease of administration, or would do more to promote joint economic surplus on average. They also examine the exceptions to the MFN rule: GATT Articles XIX (often called the safeguards, escape or emergency protection clause) and XXIV (the clause permitting customs unions and free trade areas), and conclude that they represent a sophisticated balancing of the costs and benefits of the MFN obligation.

NEGOTIATING REDUCTIONS IN TRADE-DISTORTING MEASURES

The key to any negotiation is reciprocity, that is, an exchange of concessions that the parties would not want to make in isolation. Many economists puzzle over why bilateral or multilateral trade negotiations are necessary when standard trade theory tells us that (leaving aside the large-country case) a national economy benefits from unilateral reductions in its trade barriers. Winters in reading 17 explains that protectionism is mercantilist in that it stresses production and employment over consumption and leisure, with existing domestic producers carrying more weight politically than potential new domestic producers who in turn carry far more weight than foreign producers of the country's imports. Hence a national government considers it a 'concession' to reduce import restrictions that hurt its import-competing producers, and requires a similar 'concession' from its trading partner in the form of increased market access for its producers of exports before it will engage in trade liberalization. Having then exchanged such concessions, the liberalization agreement is enforced by the prospect of retaliatory denial of access to foreign markets. Hillman and Moser in reading 6 note that the gain to consumers and the increased efficiency of resource use from such trade liberalizations are almost incidental; it is the effect on producer returns and its impact in supplying the government with political support that dominates the government's calculus.

How can this potential gain from exchanging market access be made operational in the GATT's MFN environment, which implies free riding? The solution is the principal-supplier pattern of negotiation. Winters explains in reading 17 that if any concession that country A obtained from country B was to be made available to all of B's other trading partners, A's benefit from the concession relative to B's cost would be greatest if A were B's principal supplier of the good concerned. This clearly suits A, but it also suits B, for by these means B obtains the greatest leverage over A per unit of its own political cost. Similarly, A would offer concessions on B's principal exports, and so their talks would concern only mutual principal-supplier trade. Clearly, this process is more successful, the wider the range of sectors and issues on the table. Hence the pressure to avoid sector-specific talks and to strive for comprehensive, multi-issue rounds of negotiations. Finger (reading 5) was the first to quantify the extent to which concessions in GATT negotiations were 'internalized' by participants, showing that liberalization concessions often covered 90 per cent or more of the suppliers of the goods concerned.

Over the years, attempts have been made by governments to reduce the transactions costs associated with product-specific bid-offer or offer-request negotiations. Both Baldwin and Winters (readings 1 and 17) review past methods that have been used in negotiations and suggest superior ones. One obvious alternative approach is to agree on an across-the-board formulae-based cut in applied or bound tariffs. Reading 14 provides Stern's evaluation of some of those alternatives considered at the time of the Tokyo Round, and his suggestions of ways to quantify their effects. A problem with general formulae approaches is that they create incentives for participants to seek to exclude politically sensitive items. In practice, experience demonstrates that exception lists can become long, and that as much time is spent negotiating the exceptions as might have been spent on bid-offer negotiations. Baldwin and Clarke (reading 2) provide an analysis of the costs associated with the exceptions that were made to the formula approach used in the Tokyo Round. They show that in welfare terms the end result was inferior to what might have been obtained had the formula been applied without exception. They also show that formulae suggested by trading partners were generally superior in welfare terms for a country than the formulae proposed by the country itself.

SETTLING TRADE DISPUTES

A government is more likely to sign on to an international agreement the more confident it is that other signatories will honour their commitments. A dispute settlement procedure is one way to boost that confidence, but it simultaneously constrains one's own government's degrees of policy freedom. It is thus possible that the inclusion of a dispute settlement procedure in the GATT/WTO could result in higher rather than lower average trade barriers by inhibiting liberalization commitments from being made. Indeed some economists, using game theoretic modelling, have provided conditions under which that will occur. Their results challenged Kovenock and Thursby (see reading 8) to develop a class of bargaining models that include more realistic features of the global trading system. In particular, they incorporate the idea that GATT/WTO member countries feel an international obligation to support the global trading system (the political equivalent of living with one's conscience). In their modelling this takes the form of an implicit national cost if a member deviates from its trade agreements. This helps explain the fact that in practice much more cooperation is sustained (and much less retaliation is observed) than would be predicted by game theory. Even so, the experience under the GATT makes clear that the effectiveness of a dispute resolution mechanism depends on the procedures it adopts.

In the past, dissatisfaction with the GATT dispute settlement procedures led the USA in some cases to pursue unilateral retaliatory measures. In reading 12 Rhodes examines three such cases. She concludes that in those cases at least the US response had the desired effect, but she observes that some of the measures used (such as 'voluntary' export restraints) contradicted GATT rules. In reading 7 Jackson contrasts the experience under the pre-WTO procedures with what can be expected under the much-revised WTO procedures. The latter is a step towards a more rule-oriented system that should lead to quicker resolution and hence serve more as a deterrent to reneging on a member's obligations. It should also provide more predictability and reliability for entrepreneurs, and reduce greatly the felt need for governments to act unilaterally rather than through the WTO's dispute settlement body. As Jackson points out, though, there is the risk that the WTO will be seen as taking away too much national sovereignty, which could lead to a backlash by governments and the public against the WTO. This issue is addressed also in readings in Volume 4 of this collection, as 'new' issues confront the institution and its member states.

MONITORING POLICIES AFFECTING TRADE

Disputes and formal dispute settlement procedures are a last resort to enforce negotiated agreements. Often disputes can be defused through exchange of information and communication. Thus cooperation can be sustained and disputes avoided more easily the more countries and stakeholders have information on the policies maintained by their trading partners. One of the significant additions to the global trading system provided by the Uruguay Round was the agreement that members would notify the WTO Secretariat of changes in trade-related policies and would subject their policies to review on a regular basis. A trade policy review mechanism (TPRM) was introduced by the GATT Secretariat on a trial basis in 1989, and has continued ever since. The first decade of that experience is assessed in reading 9 by Laird.

The stated purpose of the TPRM is to improve adherence by members to the rules, disciplines and commitments made under WTO agreements, and thereby to the smoother functioning of the global trading system. Experience to date suggests it has done that and more. Each government comes under TPRM audit regularly (every two years for major economies, every four years for most others except the smallest which are every six years). This serves several purposes. It reminds governments of their obligation to continually notify WTO of changes in policies, and it provides trading partners with a stocktaking of current policies and changes over the review period. But perhaps most important of all is that notification and review bring transparency to the policy-making process within the national polity. Since there is typically under-investment in information about the adverse effects of protectionist policies (because of a free-rider problem of collective action by the consumers and others who are made harmed), this greater transparency reduces the probability that wasteful policies will be tolerated. The TPRM improves domestic economic governance also by encouraging other ministries to interact with their colleagues in the trade ministry in search of better policy coherence. Of particular importance has been the improvement in the use of macroeconomic policy measures rather than trade barriers for dealing with balance of payment problems in developing countries. And the absence of a link between the TPRM and dispute settlement in the WTO has ensured that the discussions of TPR reports have been more constructive than confrontational.

INTEGRATING DEVELOPING COUNTRIES INTO THE GLOBAL TRADING SYSTEM

Prior to the Uruguay Round, developing countries as a group had been fairly inactive participants in GATT activities. In the early post-war period the majority of them were busy trying to become independent of their former imperial masters. They perceived that as requiring their economies to become more self-sufficient by adopting import-substituting industrialization policies and restricting exports of primary products so as to encourage diversification of the economy beyond raw material production. Hence in the early GATT rounds of multilateral trade negotiations this group was not inclined to offer much in the way of industrial market access, and so received little in return. Reading 5 by Finger shows, for example, that the United States' commitments to market opening following the Dillon Round benefited developing countries hardly at all.

Developing countries also felt that equal treatment of unequals was unjust. As a consequence, this group demanded to be allowed exceptions to many of the obligations being negotiated under the GATT: not only fewer and slower tariff reductions but also tariff preferences and what became known generally as 'special and differential treatment'. In effect, as Wolf explains in reading 18, developing countries sought and received from industrial countries the right under GATT to hurt themselves economically. But in addition to hurting their own economies they also weakened the global trading system. It was only after the high domestic costs of their inward-looking policies became clearly evident that this group began to consider the virtues of more-open policy regimes. McMillan argues in reading 11 that developing countries would do themselves and the trading system a service by refraining from seeking the goodwill of industrial countries in the form of preferences and derogations from core WTO rules and instead playing the main game, that, is, seeking access to industrial country markets in return for opening up their own markets. In reading 16 Winters provides some suggestions as to how such negotiations could be conducted given the presence of many non-tariff barriers inhibiting North-South trade. Certainly some progress was made during the Uruguay Round, but the impact is only just beginning to be felt and, as some of the readings in Volume 3 make clear, there is still a long way to go before the developing economies (and those in transition from socialism) are fully integrated into what could then truly be called a global trading system.

NOTES

1. See, for example, Diebold (1952), Curzon (1965), Jackson (1969, 1997), Dam (1970), Hudec (1975, 1987, 1993), Tumlir (1985), Winham (1992), Davey, Jackson and Sykes (1995), Hoekman and Kostecki (2001), and Trebilcock and Howse (1999). A new one by economic theorists is due shortly (Bagwell and Staiger, 2002). The legal texts of the GATT/WTO rules are collected in WTO (1995a), while GATT legal case history is summarized in WTO (1995b). Detailed negotiating histories of the Uruguay Round can be found in Stewart (1993, 1999) and Croome (1998).
2. A lawyer's collection is available in Howse (1997).
3. See, for example, Deardorff and Stern (1981) on the Tokyo Round and Martin and Winters (1996) on the Uruguay Round of GATT negotiations.

REFERENCES

Bagwell, Kyle and Robert W. Staiger (2002), *The Economics of the World Trading System*, Cambridge, Massachussetts: MIT Press (forthcoming).

Croome, John (1998), *Reshaping the World Trading System: A History of the Uruguay Round* (revised edition), Geneva: World Trade Organization.

Curzon, Gerard (1965), *Multilateral Commercial Diplomacy*, London: Michael Joseph.

Dam, Kenneth W. (1970), *The GATT: Law and International Economic Relations*, Chicago: University of Chicago Press.

Davey, William, John H. Jackson and Alan Sykes (1995), *Legal Problems of International Economic Relations*, St. Paul: West Publishing Co.

Deardorff, Allan V. and Robert Stern (1981), 'A Disaggregated Model of World Production and Trade: An Estimate of the Impact of the Tokyo Round', *Journal of Policy Modeling* 3(2): 127–52.

Hoekman, Bernard and Michel Kostecki (2001), *The Political Economy of the World Trading System: The WTO and Beyond*, London and New York: Oxford University Press.

Howse, Robert (ed.) (1997), *The World Trading System* (4 vols of readings), London: Routledge.

Hudec, Robert E. (1975), *The GATT Legal System and World Trade Diplomacy (2nd edition)*, Salem, New Hampshire: Butterworth.

Hudec, Robert E. (1987), *GATT and the Developing Countries*, Aldershot: Gower for the Trade Policy Research Centre.

Hudec, Robert E. (1993), *Enforcing International Trade Law: The Evolution of the Modern GATT Legal System*, Salem, New Hampshire: Butterworth.

Jackson, John H. (1969), *World Trade and the Law of GATT*, Indianapolis, Indiana: Bobbs-Merrill.

Jackson, John H. (1997), *The World Trading System: Law and Policy of International Economic Relations (2nd edition)*, Cambridge, Massachussetts: MIT Press.

Martin, Will and L. Alan Winters (eds.) (1996), *The Uruguay Round and the Developing Countries*, Cambridge and New York: Cambridge University Press.

Milton, Giles (1999), *Nathaniel's Nutmeg*, London: Sceptre (Hodder and Stoughton).
Stewart, Terence (1993), *The GATT Uruguay Round, A Negotiating History (1986–1992)*, Volumes I to III.
Stewart, Terence (1999), *The GATT Uruguay Round, A Negotiating History (1986–1992)*, Volume IV.
Trebilcock, Michael J. and Robert Howse (1999), *The Regulation of International Trade (2nd edition)*, London and New York: Routledge.
Tumlir, Jan (1985), *Protectionism: Trade Policy in Democratic Societies*, Washington D.C.: American Enterprise Institute.
Winham, Gilbert R. (1992), *The Evolution of International Trade Agreements*, Toronto: University of Toronto Press.
WTO (1995a), *The Results of the Uruguay Round of Multilateral Trade Negotiations: The Legal Texts*, Geneva: World Trade Organization.
WTO (1995b), *Analytical Index: Guide to GATT Law and Practice*, Vols. I and II, Geneva: World Trade Organization.

Acknowledgements

The publishers and editors are grateful for permission to use copyright material.

VOLUME 1: GENESIS OF THE GATT

1. Bagwell, Kyle and Robert W. Staiger (1999), 'An Economic Theory of GATT', *American Economic Review* 89(1): 215–48, March. Nashville, Tennessee: American Economic Association
2. Corden, W. Max (1987), 'On Making Rules for the International Trading System', Ch. 10 in Robert Stern (ed.), *U.S. Trade Policies in a Changing World Economy*, pp. 413–26. Cambridge, Massachusetts: MIT Press.
3. Deardorff, Alan V. (1996), 'An Economist's Overview of the World Trade Organization', in Gordon Flake and Florence Myeong-Hwa Lowe-Lee (eds), *The Emerging WTO System and Perspectives From East Asia*, Washington, D.C.: Korea Economic Institute of America.
4. Diebold, William, Jr. (1952), *The End of the ITO*, Essays in International Finance No. 16, pp.1–37. Princeton, New Jersey: International Finance Section, Department of Economics and Social Institutions, Princeton University Press.
5. Eichengreen, Barry and Marc Uzan (1993), 'The 1933 World Economic Conference as an Instance of Failed International Cooperation', Ch. 6 in Peter Evans, Harold Jacobson and Robert Putnam (eds), *Double-Edged Diplomacy: International Bargaining and Domestic Politics,* pp. 171–206. Berkeley: University of California Press.
6. Finger, J. Michael (1991), 'The GATT as an International Discipline Over Trade Restrictions: A Public Choice Approach', Ch. 7 in Roland Vaubel and Thomas Willett (eds), *The Political Economy of International Organizations: A Public Choice Approach*, pp. 125–41. Boulder, Colorado: Westview Press.
7. Goldstein, Judith (1993), 'Creating the GATT Rules: Politics, Institutions and American Policy', Ch. 6 in J. Ruggie (ed.), *Multilateralism Matters: The Theory and Praxis of an Institutional Form*, pp.201–32. New York: Columbia University Press.
8. Hungerford, Thomas L. (1991), 'GATT: A Cooperative Equilibrium in a Noncooperative Trading Regime?' *Journal of International Economics* 31: 357–69. Elsevier Science Publishers.

9. IRWIN, DOUGLAS A. (1993), 'Multilateral and Bilateral Trade Policies in the World Trading System: An Historical Perspective', Ch. 4 in Jaime De Melo and Arvind Panagariya (eds), *New Dimensions in Regional Integration*, pp.90–119. Cambridge and New York: Cambridge University Press.
10. IRWIN, DOUGLAS A. (1995), 'The GATT in Historical Perspective', *American Economic Review* 85(2): 323–8, May. Nashville, Tennessee: American Economic Association.
11. JOHNSON, HARRY G. (1965), 'An Economic Theory of Protectionism, Tariff Bargaining and the Formation of Customs Unions', *Journal of Political Economy* 73(3): 256–83, June. Chicago: University of Chicago Press.
12. KINDLEBERGER, CHARLES P. (1951), 'Group Behaviour and International Trade', *Journal of Political Economy* 59(1): 30–46, February. Chicago: University of Chicago Press.
13. KINDLEBERGER, CHARLES P. (1989), 'Commercial Policy Between the Wars', Ch. 2 in Peter Mathias and Sidney Pollard (eds), *The Cambridge Economic History of Europe, Vol. 8*, pp. 161–96. Cambridge: Cambridge University Press.
14. MEADE, JAMES (1942), 'A Proposal for an International Commercial Union', British War Cabinet paper reproduced in *The World Economy* 10: 399–407, 1987, and in Susan Meade (ed.), *The Collected Papers of James Meade, Volume III: International Economics*, London: Unwin Hyman, 1988.
15. STAIGER, ROBERT AND GUIDO TABELLINI (1999), 'Do GATT Rules Help Governments Make Domestic Commitments?' *Economics and Politics* 11(2): 109–44, July. Oxford: Blackwell.
16. UNITED STATES TARIFF COMMISSION (1919), *Reciprocity and Commercial Treaties*, pp.17–48 & 9–14. Washington, D.C.: Government Printing Office.
17. VINER, JACOB (1924), "The Most-Favored-Nation Clause in American Commercial Treaties', *Journal of Political Economy* 32(1), February, pp.17–39. University of Chicago Press. (Reprinted as Ch. 1 in his *International Economics: Studies by Jacob Viner*, Glencoe, Illinois: The Free Press.)

VOLUME 2: CORE RULES AND PROCEDURES

1. BALDWIN, ROBERT (1986), 'Toward More Efficient Procedures for Multilateral Trade Negotiations', *Aussenwirtschaft* 41: 379–94. *The Swiss Review of International Economic Relations.* Swiss Institute for Research in International Economics, University of St Gallen, Switzerland.
2. BALDWIN, ROBERT E. AND RICHARD N. CLARKE (1988), 'Game-Modeling Multilateral Trade Negotiations', *Journal of Policy Modeling* 9: 257–84. Elsevier.© Society for Policy Modeling 1987.
3. CAPLIN, A. AND KARLA KRISHNA (1988), 'Tariffs and the Most-Favored-Nation Clause: A Game Theoretic Approach', *Seoul Journal of Economics* 1(3): 267–89.
4. CONYBEARE, H.A.C. (1988), 'Managing International Trade Conflicts: Explanations and Prescription', *Journal of International Affairs* 42(1): 75–91.© Trustees of Columbia University in the City of New York.
5. FINGER, J. MICHAEL (1974), 'GATT Tariff Concessions and the Exports of

Developing Countries – United States Concessions at the Dillon Round', *Economic Journal* 84(335): 566–75, September. Oxford: Blackwell.

6. HILLMAN, ARYE AND PETER MOSER (1995), 'Trade Liberalization as Politically Optimal Exchange of Market Access', in M. Canzoneri, Wilfred Ethier and Vittorio Grilli (eds), *The New Transatlantic Economy*, Cambridge and New York: Cambridge University Press.
7. JACKSON, JOHN H. (1998), 'Designing and Implementing Effective Dispute Settlement Procedures: WTO Dispute Settlement, Appraisal and Prospects', Ch. 5 in Anne O. Krueger (ed.), *The WTO as an International Organization*, pp.161–80. Chicago: University of Chicago Press.
8. KOVENOCK, DAN AND MARIE THURSBY (1992), 'GATT, Dispute Settlement and Cooperation', *Economics and Politics* 4(2): 151–70, July. Oxford: Blackwell.
9. LAIRD, SAM (1999), 'The WTO's Trade Policy Review Mechanism – From Through the Looking Glass', *The World Economy* 22(6): 741–64, August. Oxford: Blackwell.
10. LUDEMA, RODNEY D. (1991), 'International Trade Bargaining and the Most-Favored-Nation Clause', *Economics and Politics* 3(1): 1–20, March. Oxford: Blackwell.
11. MCMILLAN, JOHN (1989), 'A Game-Theoretic View of International Trade Negotiations: Implications for the Developing Countries', Ch. 2 in John Whalley (ed.), *Rules, Power and Credibility*, pp. 26–44. London: University of Western Ontario.
12. RHODES, CAROLYN (1989), 'Reciprocity in Trade: The Utility of a Bargaining Strategy', *International Organization* 43(2): 273–99.©1989 World Peace Foundation and the Massachusetts Institute of Technology.
13. SCHWARTZ, WARREN F. AND ALAN O. SYKES (1996), 'Toward a Positive Theory of the Most-Favored-Nation Obligation and Its Exceptions in the WTO/ GATT System', *International Review of Law and Economics* 16(1): 27–51, March. Elsevier Science.
14. STERN, ROBERT M. (1976), 'Evaluating Alternative Formulae for Reducing Industrial Tariffs', *Journal of World Trade Law* 10(1): 50–64.
15. VINER, JACOB (1931), 'The Most-Favored-Nation Clause', *Index* 6, pp.94–108. Stockholm: Svenska Handelsbanken, January. (Reprinted as Ch. 5 in his *International Economics: Studies by Jacob Viner*, Glencoe IL: The Free Press.)
16. WINTERS, L. ALAN (1987), 'Negotiating the Abolition of Non-Tariff Barriers', *Oxford Economic Papers* 39: 465–80. Oxford: Oxford University Press.
17. WINTERS, L. ALAN (1987), 'Reciprocity', Ch. 7 in J. Michael Finger, and Andrzej Olechowski (eds), *The Uruguay Round: A Handbook on the Multilateral Trade Negotiations*, pp. 45–51. Washington, D.C.: The World Bank.
18. WOLF, MARTIN (1984), 'Two-Edged Sword: Demands of Developing Countries and the Trading System', Ch. 9 in Jagdish Bhagwati and John Gerard Ruggie (eds), *Power, Passions, and Purpose: Prospects for North-South Negotiations*, pp. 201–29. Cambridge, Massachussetts: MIT Press.

VOLUME 3: EXCEPTIONS TO THE CORE RULES

1. ANDERSON, KYM (2001), 'Bringing Discipline to Agricultural Policy via WTO', Ch. 3 in Bernard Hoekman and Will Martin (eds), *Developing Countries and the WTO: A Pro-active Agenda*, Oxford: Blackwell.
2. FINGER, J. MICHAEL (1991), 'Development Economics and the General Agreement on Tariffs and Trade', Ch. 13 in Jaime De Melo and Andre Sapir (eds), *Trade Theory and Economic Reform: North, South, and East: Essays in Honor of Bela Balassa*, pp. 203–23. Oxford: Blackwell.
3. FINGER, J. MICHAEL, H. KEITH HALL AND DOUGLAS R. NELSON (1982), 'The Political Economy of Administered Protection', *American Economic Review* 72(3): 452–66, June. Nashville, Tennessee: American Economic Association.
4. FINGER, J. MICHAEL AND L. ALAN WINTERS (1998), 'What Can the WTO Do for Developing Countries?' Ch. 14 in Anne O. Krueger (ed.), *The WTO as an International Organization*, pp. 365–93. Chicago: University of Chicago Press.
5. HIGGOTT, RICHARD A. AND ANDREW F. COOPER (1990), 'Middle Power Leadership and Coalition Building: Australia, the Cairns Group and the Uruguay Round of Trade Negotiations', *International Organization* 44(4): 589–632, Autumn. ©1990 World Peace Foundation and the Massachusetts Institute of Technology.
6. HOEKMAN, BERNARD (1996), 'Assessing the General Agreement on Trade in Services', Ch. 4 in Will Martin and L. Alan Winters (eds), *The Uruguay Round and the Developing Countries*, pp. 88–123. Cambridge and New York: Cambridge University Press.
7. INGCO, MERLINDA D. (1996), 'Tariffication in the Uruguay Round: How Much Liberalisation?' *The World Economy* 19(4): 425–46, July. Oxford: Blackwell.
8. KAHLER, MILES AND JOHN ODELL (1988), 'Developing Country Coalition-Building and International Trade Negotiations', Ch. 8 in John Whalley (ed.), *Rules, Power and Credibility*, pp.149–67. London: University of Western Ontario.
9. MESSERLIN, PATRICK A. (1989), 'The EC Antidumping Regulations: A First Economic Appraisal, 1980–85', *Weltwirtschaftliches Archiv*, 125(3): 563–87.
10. MICHALOPOULOS, CONSTANTINE (1999), 'The Developing Countries' Participation in the WTO', *The World Economy*, 22(1): 117–43, January. Oxford: Blackwell.
11. SAMPSON, GARY AND RICHARD H. SNAPE (1985), 'Identifying the Issues in Trade in Services', *The World Economy*, 8: 171–81. Oxford: Blackwell.
12. SNAPE, RICHARD H. (1991), 'International Regulation of Subsidies', *The World Economy,* 14: 139–64. Oxford: Blackwell.
13. SNAPE, RICHARD H. (1992), 'History and Economics of GATT's Article XXIV', Ch. 12 in Kym Anderson and Richard Blackhurst (eds), *Regional Integration and the Global Trading System*, pp.273–91. London: Harvester Wheatsheaf and New York: St Martin's Press.
14. WINTERS, L. ALAN (1998), 'Regionalism versus Multilateralism', in Richard Baldwin, David Cole, Andre Sapir and Anthony Venables (eds), *Regional Integration*, pp. 1–39. Cambridge and New York: Cambridge University Press.

15. Wolf, Martin (1990), 'How to Cut the Textile Knot: Alternative Paths to Liberalization of the MFA', Ch. 9 in Carl Hamilton (ed.), *Textiles Trade and the Developing Countries: Elimination of the MFA in the 1990s*, pp. 215–37. Washington, D.C.: World Bank.

VOLUME 4: 'NEW' ISSUES FOR THE WTO

1. Anderson, Kym (1998), 'Environmental and Labor Standards: What Role for the WTO?' Ch. 8 in Anne O. Krueger (ed.), *The WTO as an International Organization*, pp. 231–55. Chicago: University of Chicago Press.
2. Bhagwati, Jagdish N. (1994), 'Fair Trade, Reciprocity and Harmonization: The New Challenge to the Theory and Policy of Free Trade', Ch. 13 in Alan V. Deardorff and Robert M. Stern (eds), *Analytical and Negotiating Issues in the Global Trading System*, pp.547–61. Ann Arbor: University of Michigan Press.
3. Bhagwati, Jagdish N. and T.N. Srinivasan (1996), 'Trade and the Environment: Does Environmental Diversity Detract from the Case for Free Trade?' Ch. 4 in Jagdish N. Bhagwati and Robert E. Hudec (eds), *Fair Trade and Harmonization: Prerequisites for Free Trade? Vol. 1: Economic Analysis*, pp. 159–99. Cambridge, Massachusetts: MIT Press.
4. Brown, Drusilla K., Alan V. Deardorff and Robert M. Stern (1996), 'International Labor Standards and Trade: A Theoretical Analysis', Ch. 5 in Jagdish N. Bhagwati and Robert E. Hudec (eds), *Fair Trade and Harmonization: Prerequisites for Free Trade? Vol. 1: Economic Analysis*, pp. 227–80. Cambridge, Massachusetts: MIT Press.
5. Davidow, Joel (1981), 'The Seeking of a World Competition Code: Quixotic Quest?' pp. 361–403 in Oscar Schachter and Robert Hellawell (eds), *Competition in International Business*, New York: Columbia University Press.
6. Deardorff, Alan V. (1992), 'Welfare Effects of Global Patent Protection', *Economica* 59: 35–51, February. Oxford: Blackwell.
7. Hamilton, Bob and John Whalley (1984), 'Efficiency and Distributional Implications of Global Restrictions on Labour Mobility', *Journal of Development Economics* 14: 61–75. Elsevier Science Publishers.
8. Hoekman, Bernard (1997), 'Competition Policy and the Global Trading System', *The World Economy* 20(4): 383–406, July. Oxford: Blackwell.
9. McCulloch, Rachel and Robert Owen (1983), 'Linking Negotiations on Trade and Foreign Direct Investment', Ch. 14 in Charles Kindleberger and David Audretsch (eds), *The Multinational Corporation in the 1980s*, pp. 334–58. Cambridge, Massachusetts: MIT Press.
10. Nogues, Julio (1990), 'Patents and Pharmaceutical Drugs: Understanding the Pressures on Developing Countries', *Journal of World Trade* 24(6): 81–104.
11. Palmeter, David (1999), 'National Sovereignty and the World Trade Organization', *Journal of World Intellectual Property* 2(1): 77–91. Geneva, Switzerland: Werner Publishing Company.
12. Sykes, Alan O. (1999), 'Regulatory Protectionism and the Law of

International Trade', *University of Chicago Law Review* 66(1): 1–46, Winter. ©1999 University of Chicago.

13. TUSSIE, DIANA (1994), 'The Policy Harmonization Debate: What Can Developing Countries Gain From Multilateral Negotiations?' *UNCTAD Review* 5: 1–8. Geneva and New York: United Nations.
14. VOGEL, DAVID (1997), 'Trouble for Us and Trouble for Them: Social Regulations as Trade Barriers', Ch. 3 in Pietro Nivola (ed.), *Comparative Disadvantages: Social Regulations and the Global Economy*, pp. 98–145. Washington, D.C.: Brookings Institution.
15. WILLIAMSON, JEFFREY G. (1998), 'Globalization, Labor Markets and Policy Backlash', *Journal of Economic Perspectives* 12(4): 51–72, Fall. Nashville, Tennessee: American Economic Association.

1. Toward More Efficient Procedures for Multilateral Trade Negotiations

R. E. Baldwin

1. EARLY NEGOTIATING TECHNIQUES

THE FIRST MULTILATERAL TARIFF negotiation occurred in 1947, while international discussions were still going on over the specific provisions to be included in the ill-fated International Trade Organization (ITO). Political leaders in most countries wanted to reduce the high tariff barriers erected during the early 1930s as soon as possible, and therefore decided not to wait until the ITO was approved. Fortunately, as part of the agreement reached, namely, the General Agreement on Tariffs and Trade (GATT), the negotiators approved most of the articles in the commercial policy part of the ITO draft that covered «good» international behavior with regard to various nontariff trade matters.

The negotiating technique followed initially was similar to that developed by U.S. negotiators in the 1930s and early 1940s under the Trade Agreements Act of 1934. It was shaped by the need to satisfy several constraints. First, unilateral tariff cuts were ruled out on the grounds that the already unfavorable unemployment situation of the 1930s would be exacerbated. This meant that bilateral or multilateral negotiations were necessary to achieve the politically required rough balance of changes in the value of total exports and imports. A multilateral approach in which the participants would follow a simple tariff-reducing rule was given some consideration, but it was rejected on grounds that insufficient attention would be devoted to the problems of individual import-sensitive industries (Hawkins and Norwood, 1963, p. 75). A multilateral approach based on item-by-item negotiations was also ruled out as being impractical due to the complexity of negotiating simultaneously with many countries on many items (Hawkins and Norwood, p. 74).

Another important constraint was that the negotiating procedure had to be consistent with the most-favored-nation principle adopted by the United States in 1923 and very firmly held by the architects of the trade liberalization movement. However, this requirement, coupled with a bilateral, item-by-item approach raised the «free rider» problem. If two countries, A and B, reciprocally cut their duties on many items and extended these cuts to all countries, other nations which export the same products to A and B would be reluctant to cut their own duties on items of export interest to A and B, since they already would enjoy greater market access to these two countries. The solution devised to meet this negotiating problem was to utilize the principal-supplier rule, under which two countries exchange offer and request lists on tariff items for which each is *the* (or at least *a*) principal export supplier of the other country. This supposedly enables the most-favored-nation principle (MFN) to be followed by all countries and yet still keeps to acceptable levels the «free rides» gained by those that do not want to make major concessions themselves. These latter countries do not receive concessions on their major export products.

It was recognized that this technique did not fully resolve the «free rider» problem, however. Suppose a small country was heavily reliant on one or two items for most of its export earnings from large countries but was not the principal supplier of these items to the large countries. After the large countries negotiated with their principal suppliers of these goods, the small country would have little incentive to open up its own markets to the large countries. One method used by large countries to deal with this problem was to cut their duties somewhat in negotiations with their principal suppliers, but then cut these duties still further in negotiations with non-principal suppliers for whom concessions on the items were important. The cuts were, of course, always extended to all countries each time. Another technique sometimes followed when there were distinguishable country differences in the quality of a product covered by a single tariff rate was to establish separate tariff lines for each variety and then negotiate separately with the principal supplier of each.

Following the principal-supplier rule and at the same time requiring at least a rough balance of concessions bilaterally limited the scope of the negotiations. Mutual concessions tended to be made on lists of items whose total export values were approximately the same. Consequently, in situations where the export values of principally supplied items differed significantly between two countries, tariff-reducing negotiations were never held on some items. Of course, one way this can be handled is for each country to cut duties on all principally supplied items but for the larger exporter in value terms to cut duties by a smaller percentage. But even if this is followed, the resulting cuts are likely to be less than what is politically possible.

The five multilateral negotiations held from 1947 until the Kennedy Round in 1962 were essentially a series of simultaneous bilateral negotiations.[1] Country teams were formed to exchange offer and request lists with each other and conduct reciprocal negotiations. Participants were expected to take into consideration the indirect benefits they received from the negotiations between other governments in determining when a balance of concessions with their trading partners had been reached. However, this was done after a series of tentative pairwise agreements had already been reached and thus did not significantly alter the essentially bilateral nature of the negotiations. The main multilateral feature of the negotiation was that the agreements between the various pairs of countries were combined into a single agreement between all the participants at the end of the negotiations.

Using a linear programming approach applied to actual 1964 trade and tariff data for dutiable imports of non-agricultural goods and assuming a reasonable set of import demand elasticities, Baldwin and Lage (1971) compared the trade-expansionary effects of a maximum 50% cut from a bilateral versus a multilateral balancing requirement for a group of six major participants in the Kennedy Round, namely, the United States, the European Free Trade Area, Japan, and

Canada. They found that if a multilateral approach had been followed, using the constraint that the change in a group's total imports from the others cannot exceed its change in total exports to the others by more than 20%, the maximum increase in world trade would have been $5.91 billion. However, with the constraint that no group's change in imports from any other group could exceed its change in exports to that group by more than 20%, the maximum increase in world trade permissible under these conditions would have been only $.35 billion. As might be expected, a bilateral balancing requirement significantly limits the permissible increase in world trade.

2. THE KENNEDY AND TOKYO ROUNDS OF NEGOTIATIONS

2.1 Tariff Negotiating Strategies and Methods in the Kennedy Round

One criticism of the item-by-item approach, the validity of which became more and more apparent during the negotiations of 1950s, is that the difficulties faced by each individual industry tend to receive too much attention compared with the potential national benefits of broad duty reductions. Adjustments in economically inefficient but politically powerful sectors tend to be postponed indefinitely so that protection remains high in a number of important industries.

The extent of duty cuts in the four GATT tariff-reducing rounds that followed the 1947 negotiations illustrates the difficulty of going much beyond duty-cutting in industries not faced with significant import competition. In most industrial counties at the end of World War II there were still many high-duty sectors that had received their protection as a consequence of the general protectionist trend of the 1930s rather than because of any import competition problem they faced. In the initial postwar trade-liberalizing negotiations, it was not very difficult politically to reduce these duties significantly. The average cut in all U.S. duties in the 1947 negotiations was 21.1%. It was difficult politically to continue this pace of liberalization. In the next four rounds between 1949 and 1962 the average U.S. cuts amounted to only 1.9%, 3.0%, and 2.4%, respectively.

After the European Economic Community adopted a common external tariff schedule by averaging the tariffs of its six members, Community trade officials became increasingly concerned about the difference between their industry profile of tariffs and the duty profiles of the United States, Japan, and the United Kingdom. The averaging process tended to yield a pattern of Community tariff rates that was mainly in the 10% to 20% range, whereas many U.S., Japanese, and U.K. tariffs remained above 30%. There was concern that this divergent structure would cause a significant amount of trade to be diverted from these other major import markets to the Community. Thus, Community trade officials favored a negotiating approach that would bring about significant cuts in the high-duty items of the United States, Japan, and the United Kingdom. To implement this objective the EEC proposed an across-the-board tariff cut of 20% at the outset of the Dillon Round in 1960.

The United States did not accept the Community's formula approach in the Dillon Round, but in the Kennedy Round (1962–67) American officials did move to a position of favoring a general tariff-cutting rule rather than an item-by-item approach. President Kennedy wanted a deep average cut in tariffs for both international political and domestic economic reasons. He believed that such a cut would not only strengthen political ties among the nations of the non-communist world but would also reduce the degree of trade diversion away from American suppliers and to suppliers within the Community. This diversion was being brought about by the elimination of duties within the Community. Consequently, U.S. trade negotiators proposed an across-the-board 50% reduction at the outset of the Kennedy Round in 1962.

By this time, however, the Community did not want just a uniform percentage cut in all manufacturing tariffs but a cutting rule that would bring about a larger percentage reduction in high-duty items than in low-duty items. Consequently, Community negotiators countered the U.S. proposal for a 50% general cut with one based on the concept of *écrêtement* or «depeaking» that would reduce tariffs on manufactured goods by 50% of the *difference* between their existing levels and 10%. Duties on semi-manufactures and raw materials were to be cut 50% of the difference between their existing rates and 5% and zero, respectively.[2]

The United States vigorously opposed the Community's depeaking proposal on the grounds that there would be an average cut of only about 15%, even before any exceptions. The U.S. proposal for a 50% cutting rule was finally accepted but with the qualification that in cases where there were «significant disparities in tariff levels» the tariff rules would be based upon «special rules of general and automatic application.»[3] The term «significant» was defined as «meaningful in trade terms», and the purpose of the special rules was to «reduce such disparities.»

Despite lengthy negotiations, the participants were unable to agree on a simple formula that would reduce staff disparities. The Community's suggestion was to define a disparity as existing for a country if the duty on a manufactured item in one or more of the so-called reference countries, namely, the United States, the United Kingdom, and Japan, was at least twice as high as the duty on the same item in the country and at the same time exceeded this latter duty by at least 10 percentage points. On items satisfying these criteria the reference country would cut its duties by 50%, while the country claiming the disparity would cut its duty on the item by only about 25%.

The problem with this proposal was that it tended to hurt third countries. Take the case of watches. U.S. tariffs on watches were over 50% whereas watch duties in the EEC were around 15%. Furthermore, Switzerland, which was the major watch exporter, maintained duties of only about 5%. Thus, both the Community and Switzerland could claim a disparity against the United States and thereby only cut their watch duties by 25%. But this would mean that Switzerland would only gain a 25% cut in one of its major export markets, namely, the EEC. Without such a rule the Swiss would receive a 50% cut from the EEC as well as from the U.S. Because of the opposition of such third countries to the Community's proposal, a general disparities rule was never adopted. Instead, the EEC dealt with major disparities bilaterally on the case-by-case basis.

A key feature of the Kennedy Round was that trade ministers agreed at the outset there would be «a bare minimum» of exceptions to the linear cutting rule.

At the time that the 50% cutting rule was being agreed on, tough political decisions were being made within each country on the particular items to be excepted. In the United States, for example, President Kennedy gave approval to the exceptions list near the beginning of the negotiations. Each country also had to justify any exceptions at the time it submitted its list of items on which it was willing to make cuts. Consequently, the initial exceptions were quite modest for most countries and mainly confined to declining industries or ones where national security considerations seemed important.

There was, however, another constraint that had to be satisfied for each participant, namely, the achievement of reciprocity. While not explicitly stated, it seemed to be accepted that reciprocity between two countries would be achieved if both countries cut all duties by the full formula. However, exceptions to the full cut gave others the right to consider pull-backs from their initial offers if they did not think a balance of concessions had been achieved.

Once each country tabled its exceptions, the process of achieving reciprocity proceeded in a manner similar to the old item-by-item method. After examining other countries' exceptions lists, each of the participants that had accepted the formula approach prepared request lists of products on which they asked for greater tariff reductions from various other participants. They also prepared and circulated indicative lists of items on which they would withdraw their initial offers either partially or fully if their requests for further concessions were not satisfied. Some further liberalizing offers were forthcoming in the Kennedy Round as a result of this negotiating process. However, the United States had tabled a smaller exceptions list than the EEC or Japan, and U.S. negotiators felt that these participants had to be much more forthcoming for a satisfactory balance of concessions to be reached.

Such further significant liberalization did not occur and after presenting its indicative withdrawal list in November 1966, the United States in March 1967 formally withdrew many items from its list of products subject to the full 50% cutting rule. For example, the initial set of offers included a 50% cut on all cotton textiles. However, because others did not offer to cut to this extent in this sector, the U.S. announced it was reducing the cuts in this area to about 20%. Reductions in initial offers were also made on man-made fibers, steel, machinery, electronic products, and agricultural goods. After others responded to U.S. withdrawals, the U.S. removed still more items from its offer list when it presented its final offers in May 1967. About 10% of all dutiable items were withdrawn from the U.S. offer list during the final stages of the negotiations.

2.2 The Tokyo Round

The Tokyo Round of tariff negotiations differed in a number of important respects from the Kennedy Round. First, the United States agreed to a duty-cutting rule that reduced higher duty rates by a greater percentage than lower rates. Initially, the United States suggested a uniform 60% cutting rule, but in the face of considerable resistance to this formula by the Community and other participants, American negotiators formally proposed a rule that gave a modest degree of harmonization up to 6.67% and then became linear at 60% thereafter. The EEC harmonization proposal was to cut each duty by a percentage equal to the level of the duty rate itself. This process was to be repeated four times. The Japanese and Canadians also proposed cutting rules that reduced high duties more in percentage terms than low ones.

As in the Kennedy Round the United States objected vigorously to the EEC formula on the grounds that the modest level of average duty reduction it produced (about 25%) was hardly worth the effort of a major multilateral negotiation. The Community was equally adamant that the U.S. formula would not produce tariff harmonization.[4] Discussions among the major participants led to agreement on the need for a cutting rule that produced a significant degree of both tariff harmonization and average duty reduction. The compromise formula accepted was proposed by the Swiss. Each duty rate would be cut by a rate equal to $x/(x + .14)$, where x is the existing rate of duty. A 14% duty would, for example, be cut by 50%.[5]

Another important feature of the Tokyo Round was that the duty-cutting formula was negotiated mainly by the trade ministers from the various countries and did not involve detailed high-level political decisions concerning just what the exceptions to the cutting rule would be. Indeed, the ministerial meeting opening the negotiations did not resolve to minimize exceptions to the extent that the conference opening the Kennedy Round had. As a consequence, in a country such as the United States the internal negotiations over the tariff-cutting rule were quite separate from those over the particular items to be excepted from full cuts.

In making its initial offer the European Community applied the Swiss formula to all dutiable manufactured items. In contrast, the original offers of the United States and other industrial nations included a significant number of exceptions, e.g., the United States excluded all footwear from cuts. However, the United States as well as Japan and Canada also offered many greater-than-formula cuts in order to obtain the overall average cut of about 40% that had been agreed by some participants. In making these greater-than-formula cuts U.S. negotiators stated that they would be implemented only if other countries made equivalent concessions. The EEC responded by stating that it would not give credit in its reciprocity calculations for such cuts that often worked against the harmonization objective. Consequently, in April 1978, only three months after making its initial offers, the EEC announced a list of tentative withdrawals aimed at yielding a better balance of concessions. Community negotiators did emphasize, however, that they would restore items to the list if other countries were more forthcoming.

Apparently, sufficient improvement in the offers of others did not occur and in July 1979 the Community made these withdrawals as part of their formal offer list. A rough comparison of the Community's initial and July offers indicates that about 20% of all its tariff items were withdrawn from full formula cuts at this time. In February 1979 the United States announced it would withdraw its greater-than-formula reductions at the end of the month and did so with regard to most cuts when other countries failed to come up with satisfactory additional cuts. In making its final offers in March 1979, the EEC exempted another 15% of its tariff items from full formula cuts. The United States also pulled back still more in announcing its final offers in April 1979.

2.3 Nontariff Negotiation

Although U.S. trade officials had the authority to negotiate on nontariff trade barriers or distortions during the Kennedy Round, they made only conservative use of this authority. Negotiations in the tariff area, particularly on the disparities issue, were too time-consuming to permit much in the way of nontariff discussions. The main accomplishments in the nontariff area were the negotiation of an antidumping code, agreement on the abolition of the U.S. practice of valuing certain chemical products for customs purposes at their American Selling Price (ASP) rather than at their foreign price, and elimination of the discriminatory elements of certain road-use taxes in Europe. These agreements were never implemented, however, because the U.S. Congress thought that the Executive Branch had usurped the right of Congress to make laws on such matters.

In contrast, nontariff trade barrier (NTB) negotiations were a major part of the Tokyo Round. Committees were established to negotiate new codes of «good» international behavior with regard to subsidies, government procurement procedures, safeguards, customs valuation practices and technical barriers to trade. Any participant interested in these subjects could take part in the committee deliberations. There was considerable hope initially that sectoral negotiations covering all forms of trade-distorting measures in a particular industry would take place on a widespread basis, but in manufacturing, sector negotiations proved successful only in the aircraft industry.

One major objective of the United States was to curtail the use of government subsidies. U.S. industry officials believed that the far greater use of subsidies by foreign governments gave foreign exporters an unfair advantage not only in their own and U.S. markets, but in third markets as well. In contrast, other countries, such as the members of the European Community, favored the continued use of subsidies to promote economic adjustments as well as other social and economic goals. Due to these basic differences in views, the codes finally agreed on were very broadly worded and often included the language proposed by the disagreeing participants. Thus, depending on what part of the code was referred to, each participant could claim its viewpoint was upheld by the code. Since the dispute settlement part of each code was weak, the actual manner in which the codes have operated has done very little to strengthen international discipline in the NTB field.

Negotiations over nontariff barriers were most successful when they went beyond general declarations of good intentions and resulted in specific trade-liberalizing declarations by the participants. The government procurement code provides a good example of this. After agreeing upon the desirability of denying preferential treatment to domestic suppliers on non-military government contracts, the signatories negotiated on the particular agencies and products to be subject to nondiscriminatory bidding practices. The countries involved evaluated the degree to which the offers of other countries gave them reciprocity and, as in the case of tariff negotiations, then pressed for further offers or threatened to reduce the list of their agencies that would not discriminate against foreign suppliers unless these additional offers were forthcoming.

3. IMPROVING PROCEDURES FOR A NEW GATT NEGOTIATING ROUND

3.1 Tariffs and Nontariff Import Barriers

The extent of multilateral tariff reductions has been significantly limited not only because of industry-specific domestic political pressures for protection based on such reasons as national security or adjustment difficulties, but because of national negotiating objectives dealing with overall reciprocity and desired shifts in the level and profiles of other countries' tariff rates. The shift to formula approach, while still permitting formula exceptions, represented no effort to implement general negotiating objectives relating to tariff levels and profiles more fully and at the same time to satisfy politically powerful domestic sector demands for protection and achieve reciprocity. Yet, especially in the Tokyo Round where decisions concerning average tariff levels and profiles were first negotiated, then national decisions covering exceptions undertaken, and finally national judgements concerning reciprocity made, the outcome that emerged seemed to be much inferior to the optimum outcome that would satisfy each country's concerns with regard to all these elements in its objective negotiating function.

Using a game-theoretic approach, Baldwin and Clarke (1984) found that the Swiss formula produced a reasonably good compromise between the desire by the United States for a deep average cut in EEC tariffs and the EEC's desire for a significant reduction in the variance of U.S. tariff rates. EEC rates would have declined by an average of 39% under the Swiss cutting rule rather than by the 60% proposed by the United States, while the variance in U.S. rates would have been reduced even slightly more under this formula than under the cutting scheme proposed by the Community.[6] However, after U.S. exceptions were introduced and subsequent pull-backs by the EEC and the U.S. took place, the outcome was quite unsatisfactory. The actual average cut in EEC duties was only 26%, and the actual reduction in the variance in U.S. tariffs was only 34% in contrast to a variance reduction of 87% given by the Swiss cutting rule.

Thus it appears that failing to better integrate the formula negotiations, the process of determining exceptions and the attainment of reciprocity necessarily led to an inefficient negotiating outcome. Since the same type of negotiating game has been played several times by the main participants, all should understand what types of industries are most likely to be excepted by the various participants and how this is likely to affect the industry pattern of cuts as well as the average depth of tariff cuts. If such consequences are recognized at the time negotiations on a cutting rule are taking place, it may be possible to select a rule that better achieves the objectives of all. Similarly, the nature of withdrawals on reciprocity grounds should not come as a great surprise to any participant, given the long experience each has had with the others. Taking account of likely reciprocity-seeking behavior by other countries may lead a participant to modify its exceptions list and the type of cutting formula it initially seeks in order to more fully satisfy its own objective function, taking account of all elements of the negotiations.

The argument that the negotiations would simply be too complex and cumbersome in the absence of a sequential procedure no longer has much force, given the negotiating experience of the participants and, in particular, the existence of high-speed computers that can easily process the large amounts of data needed to develop information about the many interrelationships that exist. But having knowledgeable negotiators and an easily accessible database that provides trade and tariff data on other participants is not in itself enough. Pressure must also be applied to the negotiators to come up with more efficient results. There is an unfortunate tendency for negotiators not to try as hard as they might to improve everyone's position, once they think they have reached a compromise that they can declare represents a successful negotiation from an international political and domestic economic viewpoint.

One source of pressure for more efficient negotiating outcomes could be the smaller industrial countries which have long recognized the benefits of lower protection levels in the large industrial countries. The role of these countries in preventing the disparities issue from becoming a significant derogation to the 50% cutting rule during the Kennedy Round and in achieving a tariff-reducing rule in the Tokyo Round containing both significant harmonization and cutting elements was very important. These countries could also be mobilized to reduce the disintegration in the negotiations that seems to occur once a minimal success point is reached. A GATT negotiating committee could be formed to oversee the process by which country-specific requests for further improvements and threats of further withdrawals on reciprocity grounds are handled. It presumably would rely heavily on the Secretariat which would maintain a comprehensive databank and suggest possible compromises to the participants that would meet their particular concerns but also benefit other participants to a greater extent.

Such a group, along with the Secretariat, should also try to achieve a broader and more flexible view on the concept of reciprocity. Pull-backs on reciprocity grounds should be subject to a justification and consultation process, just as exceptions to the 50% cutting rule were in the Kennedy Round. Account should also be taken not just of bilateral benefits between principal suppliers but of indirect benefits resulting from cuts by other participants. It has long been recognized that these benefits should be counted, but the complexity of the negotiations prevented participants from doing so. However, with computers and a comprehensive GATT database available to all participants, such calculations could be easily carried out by individual countries or by the Secretariat for these countries. Furthermore, rather than pulling back offers on the grounds that reciprocity has not been achieved, countries should be urged to consider such alternatives as staging their cuts over a longer period than their trading partners, pressing for agreements on future reciprocity-yielding cuts by other countries within a given time period, saving the unfavorable balance for use in future negotiations, and proceeding with the cuts but making it clear that they may have to be withdrawn if injury-causing import increases occur as a result.

High-speed computers and a comprehensive database will enable the next negotiation to proceed in a manner that is less likely to result in a highly inefficient negotiating outcome than in the last two rounds. After agreeing in broad terms at a ministerial conference about the nature of the negotiations, for example, that a significant average cut will be sought that includes a major effort to reduce pockets of high tariffs and easily quantifiable nontariff protection, trade officials can initiate the negotiations by presenting country-specific request lists for reducing particular tariff and nontariff barriers. The items on which each country will request concessions from others will tend to be those on which domestic export interests believe a significant increase in foreign sales can occur if foreign barriers are lowered. Consequently, in considering whether concessions can be made on items requested by other countries, trade officials will be able to balance politically important export interests against politically important import-competing sectors. In recent negotiations trade officials have had to press within the government for liberalizing concessions by import-competing sectors without having specific export interests as allies in the political bargaining process. Moreover, once the list of exceptions has been agreed on domestically, it is very difficult to reduce the number of items covered even though a foreign concession is offered that not only makes such concessions worthwhile in national welfare terms but would make additional liberalization politically feasible in the absence of such an agreement.

But what if a particular participant decides not to be as forthcoming in its requests and possible offers as most of the other participants? Will this not reduce the level of concessions for all to the level of the country least desirous of liberalization? If the country is small, the problem can usually be handled by isolating it through the use of the principal-supplier rule or by subdividing tariff categories. However, if the country is a major trading power, the problem is more serious. But the procedure used to try to make this country more forthcoming in the negotiations can be the same one that has proven successful under the formula approach. With a mechanism that measures the benefits to all countries (and not just principal suppliers) of tariff concessions by a major trading power, the weight of the entire negotiating community can be brought to bear on the country favoring only a modest average reduction. Just as when broad tariff-cutting rules are being negotiated, the possibility of failure of the negotiations can be laid at the doorstep of such a country. If past experience is relevant, this pressure is likely to produce a more trade-liberalizing response.

Both goods and services should be covered in the negotiation, since there are important concession-balancing opportunities between goods and services. For example, if a developing country agrees to allow a certain number of additional foreign banks or insurance companies to operate in the country, it could be granted an increase in its foreign textile and apparel quotas or reduced tariffs on such labor-intensive items as jewelry, musical instruments, and sporting goods. Such trade-offs as liberalizing bidding on government contracts for a country in return for easing its domestic content requirements for foreign firms should also be explored.

3.2 Unfair Trade Practices

Although there is a need to reduce the many tariffs and easily quantifiable nontariff barriers that significantly restrict trade in goods and services, much of the pressure for further negotiations in recent years has been directed at reducing the use of so-called «unfair» trading practices such as domestic subsidies that artificially promote a country's exports or reduce its imports. As noted earlier, negotiations in such areas as domestic subsidies have not been very successful.

When there is no initial agreement concerning what «good» behavior should be, negotiations on codes of good behavior lead to vaguely worded rules that are difficult to implement, particularly when the dispute-settlement procedures and enforcement mechanisms are weak. This has very much been the case with the GATT.

What is needed in this area are comprehensive negotiations conducted in a manner similar to those for tariffs or for the particular products and agencies covered by the government procurement code. The aim for subsidies should be to phase out particular subsidies gradually, bind their levels for a specified period of time, or introduce export taxes to offset the export-subsidizing element of domestic aids. The incentives to bring another country to the bargaining table would be not only the willingness to reduce one's own subsidies but the threat of carrying out the countervailing duty procedures permitted under current GATT rules. Prime attention should be given to industry-specific subsidies, since these are not only the easiest to identify but are the type of subsidies that raise the greatest objections on the part of foreign producers.

Each country would first undertake a comprehensive evaluation of the subsidizing practices of other countries that it believes are causing material injury to its industries. It would then make specific requests of other countries concerning the reduction or offset of injury-causing subsidies. At the same time the country would announce the countervailing duty action it was prepared to initiate domestically if bilateral or multilateral negotiations were not successful. If past experience is any guide, most countries will enter into serious negotiations aimed at preventing the imposition of countervailing duties against their exports. Countries which believe their subsidies do not violate GATT rules could announce that they would either request the formation of a GATT panel of experts to make a decision on their contention or they would take appropriate unilateral action. With a large number of panel requests, significant progress could be made in establishing precedents and procedures in the panel decision-making process in the GATT. Other allegedly unfair trading practices such as various domestic rules that discriminate against foreigners are more difficult to handle, but the same general procedure could be tried. In these cases the threat of retaliatory discriminatory action would also be used to bring countries to the bargaining table.

The possible danger of a comprehensive negotiation on unfair trading practices is that the entire liberal international trading order could unravel. However, this is just what is happening under the piecemeal approach now being followed on the subsidy problem. If the current trend toward the breakdown of international trading discipline continues, many of the benefits of postwar international cooperation on trade matters are likely to be lost. However, if the entire problem is faced at one time, the need to preserve the existing order becomes more apparent to all and multilateral forces are likely to be marshalled for reaching a compromise that will permit more open trade within a framework that is regarded as fair.

NOTES

1 See Catudal, 1958.
2 Agricultural products were not covered by the formula.

3 Ministerial Resolution, *Bulletin*, U.S. Department of State, June 24, 1963.
4 Community officials stated that their objective was to reduce the differences in tariff structures or profiles among trading partners by cutting high duties by a greater percentage than low duties. They stressed that they did not seek to equalize customs duties for the same products.
5 Some countries used .16 or .15 for the constant term in the formula.
6 These calculations are obtained by applying the formula to the tariff and trade data for 22 sectors given in Alan V. Deardorff and Robert M. Stern. *An Economic Analysis of the Effects of the Tokyo Round of Multilateral Trade Negotiations of the United States and of the Other Major Industrialized Countries*, MTN Studies 5, Committee on Finance, U.S. Senate, Committee Print, CP 96–15, pp. 26–30 and p. 149.

REFERENCES

Baldwin, Robert E. and Gerald M. Lage, 1971. A Multilateral Model of Trade-Balancing Tariff Concessions. *The Review of Economics and Statistics*, 53-237-245.

Baldwin, Robert E. and Richard N. Clarke, 1984. Game-Modelling the Tokyo Round of Tariff Negotiations. Department of Economics, University of Wisconsin-Madison.

Catudal, Honore M., 1958. How a Trade Agreement is Made. *Bulletin*, U.S. Department of State.

Deardorff, Alan V. and Robert M. Stern, 1979. *An Economic Analysis of the Effects of the Tokyo Round of Multilateral Trade Negotiations on the United States and the Other Major Industrialized Countries*. MTN Studies 5, Committee on Finance, U.S. Senate, Committee Print, CP 96–15.

Hawkins, Harry C. and Janet L. Norwood, 1963. The Legislative Basis of United States Commercial Policy, in William B. Kelly, Jr. (ed.), *Studies in United States Commercial Policy*, University of North Carolina Press.

2. Game-Modeling Multilateral Trade Negotiations

R. E. Baldwin and R. N. Clarke

1. INTRODUCTION

Governments participating in trade-liberalizing negotiations invariably regard reductions of their own import barriers as concessions to other countries, and cuts in foreign import restrictions as gains for their own country. This attitude could be based on a view of international tariff-setting, first analyzed by Harry Johnson (1954), that countries impose optimal tariffs to improve their terms of trade and raise their welfare levels. Consequently, lowering duties from this equilibrium is likely to reduce a country's welfare by causing deterioration in its terms of trade. Alternatively, regarding tariff reductions as concessions could be justified on the basis of the recent analyses of tariff bargaining under imperfectly competitive conditions, such as that of Brander and Spencer (1981), in which countries impose duties to try to capture part of the rents earned by foreign firms operating in imperfectly competitive international markets. We believe a political economy explanation of this attitude toward trade concessions may be more plausible than a strictly economic interpretation. In the balance of this introduction, we explain why this approach is reasonable, and describe the several optimizing game models we construct to model the political economy of tariff-reducing trade negotiations.

Cheaper imports increase consumer welfare but may cause temporary unemployment and losses in particular industries. These latter impacts can reduce significantly the real income of employees and capital owners in these industries, while the gain to consumers is likely to be spread thinly over many individuals. With larger per-person income changes at stake, individuals in the import-impacted sectors are more likely than consumers to overcome the free-rider problem in organizing to raise the funds needed for effective lobbying. Even though the aggregate benefits to consumers exceed the aggregate losses to producers, individual consumers are not likely to consider it rational to contribute to an interest group seeking a liberal trade policy which, if adopted, would benefit them regardless of whether they contributed. Consequently, since elected officials risk losing votes and campaign-funding support if they initiate a duty-cutting exercise, it is quite understandable that government negotiators regard voluntary reductions in their own levels of protection as "concessions."

Yet political leaders who represent the nation as a whole also seem to believe that there are significant political and economic advantages associated with reciprocal trade-liberalizing negotiations. Rightly or wrongly, they tend to think that trade liberalization promotes better economic relations among nations and reduces political tensions. Furthermore, the correlation between economic prosperity and trade liberalization in the post-1945 period appears to have convinced most political leaders that general reductions of trade barriers promote overall prosperity for their nations. Therefore, they are sometimes prepared to accept the political risks of antagonizing organized groups representing import-competing sectors, and to engage in multilateral trade negotiations. At the same time, of course, they try to minimize political costs by stressing employment and profit benefits from increased export opportunities due to lower foreign trade barriers, by staging the cuts in tariffs and other barriers over an extended period, and by excluding certain industries from the liberalizing process. Understandably, each country's negotiators attempt to shape the rules and processes followed in the negotiations to enable them and their political superiors to claim that the gains from increased exports exceed the losses due to increased imports.

In the first five months of multilateral negotiations sponsored by the General Agreement on Tariffs and Trade (GATT) between 1947 and 1962, bargaining over reciprocal tariff cuts took the form of item-by-item negotiations. In the last two multilateral negotiations, the Kennedy (1962–1967) and Tokyo (1974–1979) Rounds, the participants replaced this cumbersome process with one in which the participating countries negotiate a tariff-cutting rule or formula that, with some exceptions, is to apply to all dutiable manufactured items.[1] In the Kennedy Round, U.S. negotiators proposed the rule that all duties be cut by 50% and, in effect, informed other participants that the United States would not participate in the negotiation unless this formula was adopted. In the Tokyo Round, negotiations on the duty-cutting rule were more open and flexible. The bargaining process evolved essentially into one between the United States and the European Community, with other participants acting as facilitators in reaching a formula acceptable to these two economic superpowers, as well as to themselves.

The process of bargaining over a tariff-cutting rule can be modelled as a game between several player-countries, with the Tokyo Round of multilateral trade negotiations serving as an example of a two-country game.[2] Each country has payoffs or levels of welfare that depend on characteristics of the negotiated structure of protection. We examine two different types of tariff equilibria. One, the noncooperative Nash-Gournot solution, assumes that each country considers only the direct impact of a proposed tariff schedule on itself and is not concerned about the level of welfare the tariff-cutting rule implies for the other participants. The other equilibrium is the Nash cooperative solution, which supposes that countries seek tariff schedules that maximize the joint welfare of the group, subject to certain minimum welfare levels for each country. Improvements in one country's welfare are, therefore, sought only to the extent that they improve the joint payoff.[3]

In the following section, the political-economic tariff goals of different countries, in particular the United States and the European Community, are presented and specified as components of an overall welfare function for each trading nation or bloc. The consistency of these goals is also analyzed. Section 3 uses these individual welfare functions to demonstrate the noncooperative Nash-Cournot and cooperative Nash bargaining equilibria. Several theoretical characteristics of these tariff equilibria are examined and related to observed characteristics of the tariff negotiations process. In Section 4, we estimate the relative weights that the U.S. and EC attached to the different components of their welfare functions, based on statements made by their representatives prior to and during the actual negotiating process. We further refine these weights using the two participants' sequentially suggested tariff-cutting rules as additional data. In Section 5, the theoretic game equilibria based on the estimated weights are compared with the tariff rates actually negotiated in the Tokyo Round of multilateral negotiations. We find that while either of our proposed negotiating game equilibria may track realistically the results of the formal negotiating process, later, more political intercessions caused the finally determined tariffs to be "less optimal." Concluding remarks are in Section 6.

2. TARIFFS AND WELFARE

During the early phases of negotiations, countries communicate to other participants the characteristics of the tariff schedule they see as most important to their negotiating goals. These characteristics can be combined into a utility function that cumulates the welfare benefits that a country receives from a particular set of tariff rates.[4]

For convenience, we display a model for two countries with k different product classifications. It is straightforward to extend this analysis to any finite number of country-players. Initially, each country has a k-vector of tariff rates for the set of product classifications:

$$t^0 = (t_1^0, \ldots, t_k^0)', \; s^0 = (s_1^0, \ldots, s_k^0)',$$ [5]

where t^0 represents country 1's initial tariff vector and s^0 represents country 2's initial tariff vector. Through negotiations, countries seek to establish new tariff vectors:

$$t^1 = (t_1^1, \ldots, t_k^1)',$$
$$s^1 = (s_1^1, \ldots, s_k^1)',$$

that better satisfy their welfare criteria for a desirable tariff structure.

The relative quantities of goods that each country imports of each product class are given by two additional k-vectors:

$$m = (m_1, \ldots, m_k)',$$
$$n = (n_1, \ldots, n_k)',$$

where m represents country 1's imports and n represents country 2's imports.

A vector component m_i is the fraction of country 1's total imports that are in product class i; similarly for country 2.[6] Although relative quantities of imports should change as tariffs shift from their initial to final levels, negotiators typically use the initial set of import values as fixed weights in evaluating different tariff-setting proposals. Consequently, we assume that each country's import bundle remains constant, although our analysis could be expanded to accommodate different initial and final import vectors.

We now examine and quantify several of the characteristics countries may desire in the structure of tariff rates.

A. Some countries, in particular, members of the European Community, are concerned about the variability of tariff rates across products. Though the average level of industrial tariffs in the Community is about the same as in the United States, Japan, and other developed countries, there is greater dispersion in U.S. and Japanese rates about their average levels than in the EC.[7] According to Community officials, reducing all tariff rates by, say, 50% still leaves a group of relatively high tariff items in countries such as the United States and Japan that are significantly protected. In other words, they seem to believe there is overkill in high tariff rates, and that these rates will still have a considerable protective effect even after a uniform percentage cut. They maintain it is necessary to reduce high duties by a greater percentage than low duties to eliminate this effect and to achieve reciprocity. Community negotiators also believe that higher percentage cuts are needed to correct for the diversion of third countries' exports from the Unites States to the Community caused by high U.S. rates.[8]

We measure the variability of a country's tariffs by the country's unweighted variance of different product class tariffs around their unweighted urban tariff, divided by a measure of the mean squared tariff rate desired for that country.[9] This measure of country 1's tariff variability is called A^1, and country 2's tariff variability is A_2:

$$A_1 = \frac{1}{(k-1)\bar{t}^{*2}} \sum_{i=1}^{k} \left(t_i^1 - \frac{1}{k} \sum_{j=1}^{k} t_j^1 \right)^2$$

$$= \frac{1}{(k-1)\bar{t}^{*2}} \left(t^1 - \frac{1}{k} ee' t^1 \right)' \left(t^1 - \frac{1}{k} ee' t^1 \right) \qquad (2.1)$$

$$= \frac{1}{(k-1)\bar{t}^{*2}} t^{1\prime} \left(I - \frac{1}{k} ee' \right) t^1,$$

$$A_2 = \frac{1}{(k-1)\bar{s}^{*2}} \sum_{i=1}^{k} \left(s_i^1 - \frac{1}{k} \sum_{j=1}^{k} s_j^1 \right)^2$$

$$= \frac{1}{(k-1)\bar{s}^{*2}} \left(s^1 - \frac{1}{k} ee' s^1 \right)' \left(s^1 - \frac{1}{k} ee' s^1 \right) \qquad (2.2)$$

$$= \frac{1}{(k-1)\bar{s}^{*2}} s^{1\prime} \left(I - \frac{1}{k} ee' \right) s^{1},$$

where e is a k-vector of 1's, $e = (1, \ldots, 1)'$, and $\bar{t}^*$ and $\bar{s}^*$ are the measures of unweighted average tariff rates desired for the United States and the European Community, respectively.[10] Note that since A_i increases a country i's tariff variability rises, countries seek to reduce the size of the A_i's. Thus, A_i can be considered a component of a negative utility function or "loss" function for each country's welfare. A country's aim, then, is to minimize its welfare loss.

B. Countries also have views concerning the optimum average level of tariffs. Government leaders who believe that lower tariffs promote economic efficiency and domestic growth will balance these goals against the greater political pressures brought by import-competing industries the deeper they cut the average duty. The United States pushed strongly for a deep average cut in the Kennedy and Tokyo Rounds to reduce the margin of preference provided to EC members selling within the Community compared with U.S. sales to the Community. Thus, an important goal of U.S. trade policy has been to reduce the disadvantage faced by imports from the United States that arose from the elimination of duties within the Community.

We assume that each country desires a certain percentage reduction in its own and other country's duty collections. Country 1 desires a reduction of $1-\delta_1$, and country 2 of $1-\delta_2$.[11] Thus if tariff collections are initially $\sum_{i=1}^{k} m_i t_i^0$ and $\sum_{i=1}^{k} n_i s_i^0$, country j would prefer these collections to be $\delta_j \sum_{i=1}^{k} m_i t_i^0$ and $\delta_j \sum_{i=1}^{k} n_i s_i^0$. Loss of welfare results if actual negotiated tariffs do not yield approximately these desired levels of collection. We assume that the amount of loss is proportional to the square of the divergence between desired and negotiated collections. Country 1's loss from not meeting its target reduction in own tariffs is denoted B_{11}. Its loss from country 2's tariff reduction not equalling country 1's desires is B_{12}. Country 2's loss on country 1's failure is B_{21}, and on its own divergence is B_{22}:

$$\begin{aligned} B_{11} &= \Big[\sum_{i=1}^{k} m_i t_i^1 - \delta_1 \sum_{i=1}^{k} m_i t_i^0\Big]^2 \\ &= [m'(t^1 - \delta_1 t^0)]' \, [m'(t^1 - \delta_1 t^0)], \end{aligned} \tag{2.3}$$

$$\begin{aligned} B_{12} &= \Big[\sum_{i=1}^{k} n_i s_i^1 - \delta_1 \sum_{i=1}^{k} n_i s_i^0\Big]^2 \\ &= [n'(s^1 - \delta_1 s^0)]' \, [n'(s^1 - \delta_1 s^0)], \end{aligned} \tag{2.4}$$

$$B_{21} = \Big[\sum_{i=1}^{k} m_i t_i^1 - \delta_2 \sum_{i=1}^{k} m_i t_i^0\Big]^2 \tag{2.5}$$

$$= [m'(t^1 - \delta_2 t^0)]' \; [m'(t^1 - \delta_2 t^0)],$$

$$B_{22} = [\sum_{i=1}^{k} n_i s_i^1 - \delta_2 \sum_{i=1}^{k} n_i s_i^0]^2$$

$$= [n'(s^1 - \delta_2 s^0)]' \; [n'(s^1 - \delta_2 s^0)]'. \qquad (2.6)$$

C. To gain domestic political support for the tariff rates agreed on in the tariff-bargaining process, negotiators must be able to claim that reciprocity (or better) is achieved with its trading partners. A commonly accepted standard for reciprocity is that the average duty cut, as measured by the percentage change in pre-cut and post-cut tariff revenues (based on the pre-cut import values), be the same among the major trading participants. Consequently, we shall assume that each country expects other countries to alter the import-weighted level of their tariffs to the same degree that it does. In our two-country model, we shall measure this difference in tariff cuts by the squared divergence between the percentage change in country 1's and country 2's import-weighted tariff levels, and call this C in Equation (2.7):

$$C = \left[\frac{\sum_{i=1}^{k} m_i(t_i^1 - t_i^0)}{\sum_{i=1}^{k} m_i t_i^0} - \frac{\sum_{i=1}^{k} n_i(s_i^1 - s_i^0)}{\sum_{i=1}^{k} n_i s_i^0} \right]^2 \qquad (2.7)$$

$$= \left[\frac{m'(t^1 - t^0)}{m't^0} - \frac{n'(s^1 - s^0)}{n's^0} \right]' \left[\frac{m'(t^1 - t^0)}{m't^0} - \frac{n'(s^1 - s^0)}{n's^0} \right].$$

D. Sometimes negotiators express a desire to have equal protective levels in each sector, thereby creating so-called "level playing field" in each broad industry grouping. This concept of sectoral negotiations is set forth as an objective in the U.S. Trade Act of 1974.[12] Lengthy negotiations on various nontariff issues, however, precluded extensive negotiations along these lines. Furthermore, the European Community was not very enthusiastic about sectoral negotiations and specifically stated that harmonization did not require an equalization of customs duties on the same products. Since this sectoral goal is likely to be relevant for future negotiations, we describe it in this outline of negotiating objectives, though we will not include it when we analyze the Tokyo Round empirically.

The intercountry similarity of product-class tariffs can be measured by the sum of squared deviations between countries' tariffs on individual product classes:

$$D = \frac{1}{k-1} \sum_{i=1}^{k} (t_i^1 - s_i^1)^2$$

$$= \frac{1}{k-1} (t^1 - s^1)' \, (t^1 - s^1). \qquad (2.8)$$

Each country would experience this loss if tariff schedules are not equivalent across products.

E. A country's overall welfare loss from failing to satisfy perfectly each of these criteria for a desirable tariff structure is a weighted sum of the individual losses listed above. Since the units of measurement for tariff variance, target cut, reciprocity, and sectoral pattern are not commensurate, and since countries may differ in their relative concern for each of these criteria, we allow the weights attached to different loss sources to vary among the criteria and over countries. Thus, we may denote country 1's and country 2's overall welfare loss from a new set of tariffs t^1 and s^1, when initial tariffs are t^0 and s^0, as

$$L_1(t^1, s^1) = a_1A_1 + a_2A_2 + b_1B_{11} + b_2B_{12} + cC + dD, \quad (2.9)$$
$$L_2(t^1, s^1) = \alpha_1A_1 + \alpha_2A_2 + \beta_2B_{21} + \beta_2B_{22} + \gamma C + \delta D, \quad (2.10)$$

The weights a_1, a_2, b_1, b_2, c, d and α_1, α_2, β_1, β_2, γ, δ for countries 1 and 2, respectively, are non-negative constants. Their relative values determine the differences in importance of individual criteria to a country and differences in interest across countries.

F. Each country wishes to choose a set of tariffs that minimize its welfare loss, $L_i(t^1,s^1)$. It is generally not possible, however, for a country to completely eliminate loss because minimization of one source of welfare loss may be inconsistent with minimizing another source. Before we examine, in the next section, how countries decide what is their overall most favorable tariff structure, we look at the compatibility of these several negotiating objectives.

Countries want to reduce the variance of their tariff rates over different product classes (i.e., minimize A_i). This variance can actually be reduced to zero by equalizing all of a country's individual tariff rates, i.e.,

$$t^1 = \bar{t}^1 = (\bar{t}^1_1, \ldots, \bar{t}^1_k)' = \bar{t}e \text{ and } s^1 = \bar{s}^1 = (\bar{s}^1_1, \ldots, \bar{s}^1_k)' = \bar{s}e.$$

Elimination of variance loss also does not conflict with achieving a target cut in own tariff collections, because constant tariff rates $\bar{t}$ and $\bar{s}$ can be selected so that each country's total tariff collections are reduced by $1 - \delta_i$ from their initial levels. To do this, country 1 can choose a constant tariff rates of $\bar{t}$, to:

$$\min_{\bar{t}} B_{11} = [m'(\bar{t}e - \delta_1 t^0)]' \, [m'(\bar{t}e - \delta_1 t^0)]$$
$$\Rightarrow e'mm'(\bar{t}e - \delta_1 t^0) = 0$$
$$\Rightarrow \bar{t} = \frac{\delta_1 e'mm't^0}{e'mm'e}.$$

If this $\bar{t}$ is substituted into B_{11}, then $B_{11} = 0$; hence there is no loss from failing to meet one's own target tariff cut. Substituting s for t and 2 for 1 repeats this proof for country 2. While it is feasible to select tariffs to minimize interproduct variance and also achieve a country's own desired cut, it will generally not be feasible for this policy to provide the foreign country with no loss as well. Unless the foreigner's desired tariff reduction of $1 - \delta_2$ equals the domestic country's desired reduction $1 - \delta_1$ exactly, the $\bar{t}$ selected by country 1 will not set $B_{21} = 0$.[13] Thus, the first source of conflict between country 1 and country 2 arises.

Criterion A, however, is completely compatible with criterion C (equiproportional reduction in tariff collections). Zero loss can be incurred by both countries if each sets its tariff rates constant at $\bar{t}$ and $\bar{s}$, respectively, such that

$$\bar{t}\,\frac{m'e}{m't^0} = \bar{s}\,\frac{n'e}{n's^0}.$$

Likewise, criterion D is compatible with A. No loss is incurred under criterion D if each country's tariff on a product class equals all other countries' tariffs on that product class, i.e., $t_i^1 = s_i^1$, $i = 1, \cdots, k$. Thus the choice of $\bar{t} = \bar{s}$ will ensure both zero variance on tariffs between product classes and equal tariffs on each product charged by each country.

Criterion B is completely compatible with criterion C. To satisfy B with no loss, we need t^1 and s^1 such that

$$m't^1 = \delta_1 m't^0,$$
$$n's^1 = \delta_2 n's^0,$$
$$\delta_1 = \delta_2 = \delta.$$

While satisfying C with no loss requires

$$\frac{m't^1}{m't^0} = \frac{n's^1}{n's^0}.$$

Substituting from the requirements of B, we get

$$\frac{\delta_1 m't^0}{m't^0} = \frac{\delta_2 n's^0}{n's^0}.$$

which is true if, as B also requires, $\delta_1 = \delta_2 = \delta$. Hence, any specific percentage reduction in tariffs can be reconciled with an equiproportionate reduction in collections across countries.

Condition D requires elimination of differences in the tariffs different countries change on product classes. This is achieved if $t^1 = s^1$. Equalization across countries of tariff schedules is also consistent with criterion B so long as $k \geq 2$.[14] To see this, note first that satisfying criterion D with zero loss requires a common tariff vector $u = t^1 = s^1$ across countries. To also satisfy B, we need

$$m'u = \delta m't^0,$$

$$n'u = \delta n's^0,$$

where δ is the common desired tariff depreciation factor needed for B to be internally consistent. The resulting system of equations,

$$\begin{bmatrix} m' \\ n' \end{bmatrix} u = \begin{bmatrix} \delta m't^0 \\ \delta n's^0 \end{bmatrix},$$

has at least one solution for u if dim m = dim $n = k$ equals or exceeds 2.

Criterion C, equiproportional change in countries' tariff collections, and criterion D, equal tariff rates across countries, are similarly consistent. Criterion D requires $u = t^1 = s^1$ and C requires:

$$\frac{m't^1}{m't^0} = \frac{n's^1}{n's^0} = 0.$$

Substituting, we get

$$\left(\frac{m'}{m't^0} - \frac{n'}{n's^0} \right) u = 0,$$

which may be solved for u.

As is evident, combinations of these criteria taken three at a time, or four at a time (as in the case of our full welfare loss function), are less likely to be mutually fulfilled. In the next section we indicate how equilibria in this mesh of conflicting interests may be identified.

3. GAME EQUILIBRIA

Each country's trade representative negotiates with other representatives to determine each country's tariff schedule. The institutional structure of these negotiations can vary. Depending on the character of these processes, several different definitions of a tariff equilibrium may be appropriate. In this section we describe two such equilibria and demonstrate how the optimal tariffs may be computed for each equilibrium.

We examine both the noncooperative Nash–Cournot equilibrium and the cooperative Nash equilibrium. These solutions to the tariff negotiation game differ largely in how much common ground is established between the countries prior to negotiation, and how much appreciation each country has for tariff adjustments that improve the welfare of other countries at the cost of some of their own welfare. We begin with the noncooperative equilibrium.

In a Nash–Cournot noncooperative game, negotiators are solely concerned with their own country's welfare, and refuse to grant concessions to other countries unless these actions also directly improve their own country's well-being. In this game, the only common ground established prior to negotiation is each country's announcement of its welfare loss function to the other participants. Each negotiator then makes and entertains proposals for new tariff schedules. A country only proposes tariffs that improve its own welfare – effects on other countries are ignored – and does not embrace another country's proposal unless this proposal directly improves its own welfare. Noncooperative Nash–Cournot equilibrium is reached when no country can make any further unilateral tariff changes that both directly improve its own welfare and do not harm other countries' welfare so as to incite them to take retaliatory actions that end up reducing the initial country's welfare.

A cooperative approach to negotiation results if countries are willing to trade off certain losses in their own welfare, provided that other countries receive larger gains in their welfare. This is in contrast to the zero trade-off that characterizes the noncooperative model. Nash cooperative bargaining equilibrium permits intercounty trade-offs by establishing a joint welfare criterion function. This welfare function is the product of the difference between each country's individual welfare that results from a proposed set of tariffs and a "security level" of welfare that the country could achieve in the absence of cooperatively determined tariff schedules. This security level might be the welfare level that is achieved in a noncooperative equilibrium, if this is the likely outcome should cooperative negotiations break down. Or, if countries agree to maintain their current tariff schedules when they cannot reach a new cooperative agreement, security levels could be countries' current welfare levels.

Using this cooperative world welfare function, proposed tariffs are evaluated based on the level of joint welfare they generate, subject to the proviso that acceptable tariff schedules must provide each participating country an individual welfare level that equals or exceeds its security level. The acceptable schedule that ranks highest in world welfare terms is then selected.

We now examine how optimal tariffs under these two equilibrium concepts may be computed. Using the noncooperative Nash–Cournot concept, countries try simultaneously to choose their tariffs to maximize their own welfare by minimizing their welfare loss:

$$\text{Country 1: } \min_{t^1} L_1(t^1, s^1), \tag{3.1}$$

$$\text{Country 2: } \min_{s^1} L_2(t^1, s^1), \tag{3.2}$$

where $L_1(t^1,s^1)$ and $L_2(t^1,s^1)$ are given in (2.9) and (2.10). This optimization is carried out by solving the following first-order conditions:

$$0 = \frac{\partial L_1}{\partial t^1} = a_1 \frac{\partial A_1}{\partial t^1} + a_2 \frac{\partial A_2}{\partial t^1} + b_1 \frac{\partial B_{11}}{\partial t^1} + b_2 \frac{\partial B_{12}}{\partial t^1} + c \frac{\partial C}{\partial t^1} + d \frac{\partial D}{\partial t^1}, \tag{3.3}$$

$$0 = \frac{\partial L_2}{\partial s^1} = \alpha_1 \frac{\partial A_1}{\partial s^1} + \alpha_2 \frac{\partial A_2}{\partial s^1} + \beta_1 \frac{\partial B_{21}}{\partial s^1} + \beta_2 \frac{\partial B_{22}}{\partial s^1} + \gamma \frac{\partial C}{\partial s^1} + \delta \frac{\partial D}{\partial s^1}. \tag{3.4}$$

Note that from (2.1), (2.2), (2.4), and (2.5) we know that

$$\frac{\partial A_1}{\partial s^1} = \frac{\partial A_2}{\partial t^1} = \frac{\partial B_{12}}{\partial t^1} = \frac{\partial B_{21}}{\partial s^1} = 0.$$

Using the derivatives

$$\frac{\partial A_1}{\partial t^1}, \frac{\partial A_2}{\partial s^1}, \frac{\partial B_{11}}{\partial t^1}, \frac{\partial B_{22}}{\partial s^1}, \frac{\partial C}{\partial t^1}, \frac{\partial C}{\partial s^1}, \frac{\partial D}{\partial t^1} \text{ and } \frac{\partial D}{\partial s^1},$$

from (2.1), (2.2), (2.3), (2.6), (2.7), and (2.8); rearranging terms and discarding superfluous constants, we can convert (3.3) and (3.4) to the system

$$\begin{bmatrix} a_1\left(\dfrac{I-ee'/k}{(k-1)\bar{t}^{*2}}\right) + \left(b_1 + \dfrac{c}{m't^0m't^0}\right)mm' + \dfrac{d}{k-1} & -cmn' - \dfrac{d}{k-1} \\ -\gamma nm' - \dfrac{\delta}{(k-1)} & \alpha_2\left(\dfrac{I-ee'/k}{(k-1)\bar{s}^{*2}}\right) + \left(\beta_2 + \dfrac{\gamma}{n's^0n's^0}\right)nn' + \dfrac{\delta}{k-1} \end{bmatrix} \begin{bmatrix} t^1 \\ s^1 \end{bmatrix}$$

$$= \begin{bmatrix} \delta_1 b_1 mm't^0 + c\left(\dfrac{mm't^0}{m't^0m't^0} - \dfrac{mn's^0}{m't^0n's^0}\right) \\ \delta_2\beta_2 nn's^0 + \gamma\left(\dfrac{nn's^0}{n's^0n's^0} - \dfrac{nm't^0}{m't^0n's^0}\right) \end{bmatrix}.$$

Call the left-hand matrix Q and the right-hand vector r. Unique noncooperative Nash-Cournot equilibrium tariff vectors ${}^{n}t^{1}$, ${}^{n}s^{1}$ exist if Q is nonsingular:

$$\begin{bmatrix} {}^{n}t^{1} \\ {}^{n}s^{1} \end{bmatrix} = Q^{-1}r. \tag{3.5}$$

Substituting these optimal tariffs into each country's welfare loss function, we can compute the countries' lowest amount of welfare loss under the non-cooperative Nash–Cournot equilibrium: $L^{1}({}^{n}t^{1}, {}^{n}s^{1})$ and $L_{2}({}^{n}t^{1}, {}^{n}s^{1})$.

To compute the cooperative Nash equilibrium, we first must determine the security levels of welfare loss, $\mathcal{J}_1$ and $\mathcal{J}_2$, that countries 1 and 2 can assure themselves of should cooperative negotiations fail. One possibility is that countries would revert to noncooperative Nash–Cournot behaviour that provides them with welfare losses of

$$\mathcal{J}_1 = L_1({}^{n}t^{1}, {}^{n}s^{1}) \tag{3.6}$$

and

$$\mathcal{J}_2 = L_2({}^{n}t^{1}, {}^{n}s^{1}). \tag{3.7}$$

A second possibility is that tariffs remain as previously; hence,

$$\mathcal{J}_1 = L_1(t^0,s^0) \tag{3.8}$$

and

$$\mathcal{J}_2 = L_2(t^0,s^0). \tag{3.9}$$

The joint world welfare loss function that the two countries both seek to minimize is now

$$L = [L_1(t^1, s^1) - \mathcal{J}_1][L_2(t^1, s^1) - \mathcal{J}_2], \tag{3.10}$$

subject to additional requirements that

$$L_1(t^1, s^1) \leq \mathcal{J}_1 \tag{3.11}$$

and

$$L_2(t^1,s^1) \leq \mathcal{J}_2. \tag{3.12}$$

Forming the Lagrangian

$$\mathcal{L} = L + \lambda_1(\mathcal{J}_1 - L_1) + \lambda_2(\mathcal{J}_2 - L_2),$$

and minimizing with respect to t^1 and s^1 yields the first order conditions:

$$\frac{\partial \mathcal{L}}{\partial t^1} = (L_2 - \mathcal{J}_2 - \lambda_1)\frac{\partial L_1}{\partial t^1} + (L_1 - \mathcal{J}_1 - \lambda_2)\frac{\partial L_2}{\partial t_1} = 0,$$

$$\frac{\partial \mathcal{L}}{\partial s^1} = (L_2 - \mathcal{J}_2 - \lambda_1)\frac{\partial L_1}{\partial s^1} + (L_1 - \mathcal{J}_1 - \lambda_2)\frac{\partial L_2}{\partial s^1} = 0,$$

$$\mathcal{J}_1 - L_1 \geq 0, \quad \lambda_1(\mathcal{J}_1 - L_1) = 0,$$
$$\mathrm{J}_2 - \mathrm{L}_2 \geq 0, \quad \lambda_2(\mathcal{J}_2 - L_2) = 0,$$
$$\lambda_1, \lambda_2 \geq 0.$$

Solving these equations produces the possibly non-unique set of cooperative Nash tariffs ${}^ct^1$, ${}^cs^1$. The welfare loss suffered by each country is now $L_1({}^ct^1, {}^cs^1)$ and $L_2({}^ct^1, {}^cs^1)$.

Before relating the above theoretical constructs to empirically implied welfare loss functions and their computed optimal tariffs, we make several comparisons between the character of cooperative versus noncooperative tariffs. The first point is that if security levels are the amounts of welfare loss each country would incur from noncooperative tariff setting, then each country achieves an equal or lower level of welfare loss by cooperating over not cooperating. This is illustrated in Figure 1. Point A represents the noncooperative security levels of $\mathcal{J}_1$ for country 1 and $\mathcal{J}_2$ for country 2. World iso-welfare loci are the rectangular hyperbolae radiating southwest from the security point A. The welfare loss possibility frontier indicates the minimum levels of loss that each country could achieve in tandem with the other country's given loss. The welfare allocation that minimizes the world welfare loss is indicated by point B: loss of L_1^B to country 1, and loss of L_2^B to country 2. Note that for such a point B to be superior to world welfare to security point A, it must provide both countries with at least as much welfare as their security level, i.e., $L_1^B \leq \mathcal{J}_1$, $L_2^B \leq \mathcal{J}_2$.

If the counties' security levels are poorer than their noncooperative losses, as might be the case if the original tariffs are retained, then it is possible that individual countries could do better or worse under cooperation that non-cooperative Nash–Cournot. Refer back to Figure 1. Suppose C represents the noncooperative welfare loss allocation of L_1^C to country 1 and L_2^C to country 2, while point A represents the security allocation of $\mathcal{J}_1$ and $\mathcal{J}_2$. The cooperative solution with respect to security allocation A is point B, which gives both countries less loss than security level A. But country 2 receives a better level of loss than it would receive under noncooperation, $L_2^B \leq L_2^C$, while country 1 receives a worse level of loss than cooperation, $L_1^B \geq L_1^C$. Note also that while the iso-loss curves tend to favor equal distributions of loss over unequal ones, it is still quite possible for losses to be more unequally borne under cooperation than noncooperation.

A final contrast between the character of optimal loss under cooperation versus noncooperation is that in the cooperative equilibrium, a greater percentage of a

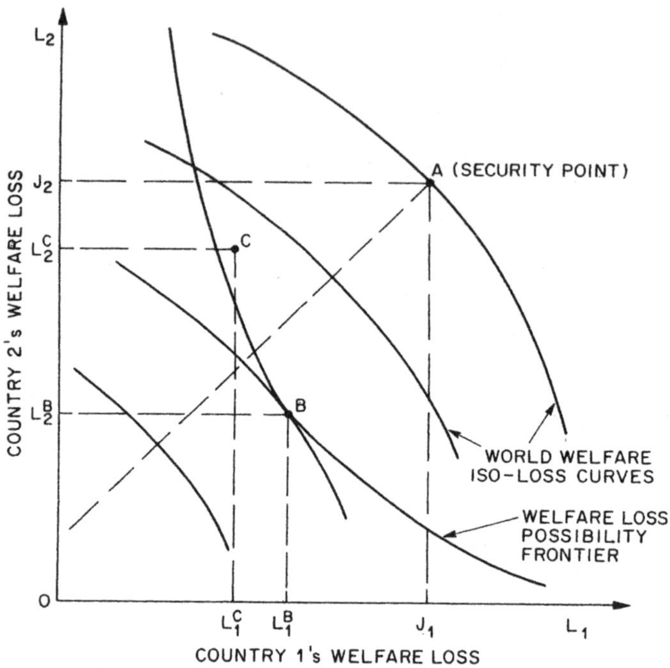

FIGURE 1 Cooperation versus noncooperation.

country's total loss will result from losses that the country has complete control over, e.g., interproduct tariff variance loss and target reduction loss (A_1 and B_1 for country 1, A_2 and B_2 for country 2), than will occur in the noncooperative equilibrium. This is because under cooperation, a country is willing to accept more personally avoidable loss if it means that other countries' welfare improves significantly.

4. SELECTING THE WEIGHTS FOR THE WELFARE LOSS FUNCTIONS

In the preceding section, three characteristics of the tariff-cutting rule to be negotiated in the Tokyo Round were singled out as being important elements of the tariff-reducing goals of the United States and the European Community: 1) the effect of cutting formula on the degree of dispersion among duty rates in each country; 2) the depth of the average cut produced by the cutting rule; and 3) the relationship between average cuts in the two trading blocs.

At the outset of the Tokyo Round negotiations, the weighted average of U.S. tariff rates over 22 ISIC product classes was 4.8%, while the EC's weighted average tariff rate over the same sectors was 7.0%.[15] While the average level of U.S. tariff protection was somewhat lower than the level in the European Community, tariff rates in the United States were more variable across product classes. The unweighted variances of the initial rate structures of the United States and the Community were 33.18 and 13.50, respectively.

The United States was strongly in favor of a deep average cut. The European Community appeared to attach less importance to this feature of a tariff-cutting rule, strongly favoring a harmonization of tariff rates over different products, while U.S. negotiators did not appear to be particularly concerned about the variation of tariff rates. As in previous negotiations, each country wanted the average tariff reduction of the other to be approximately the same as its own average cut.

The foregoing suggests that $1 - \delta_1$, the United States' desired tariff cut, was greater than $1 - \delta_2$, the tariff cut desired by the European Community. Furthermore, it suggests that the sum of the welfare weights that the United States attached to interproduct variance, i.e., $a_1 + a_2$, was lower than the sum of the weights that the Community attached to this feature of a cutting rule, i.e., $\alpha_1 + \alpha_2$. Statements by the negotiators representing the two trading powers also indicate that the sum of the weights placed by the United States on the target average duty reduction, i.e., $b_1 + b_2$, was high compared to the European Community's weighting of this characteristic, i.e., $\beta_1 + \beta_2$. Furthermore, given the mercantilistic outlook of the negotiators, one can infer that each country was more interested in reductions in the other country's variance and average cut than in its own, i.e., $a_1 \leq a_2$, $b_1 \leq b_2$ and $\alpha_1 > \alpha_2$, $\beta_1 > \beta_2$. Each country also expected the average tariff reduction of the other to be approximately the same as its own average cut.

Additional information about the weights on the welfare loss functions is revealed by the sequence of proposals for a tariff-cutting rule. One expects that the rules first proposed by the United States and European Community would yield the proposer a lower welfare loss than would the rule proposed by its trading partner. The rule finally settled on, however, should represent a compromise between these welfare outcomes.

The first serious discussion of specific formulas occurred at a May 1975 GATT meeting at which delegations presented suggestions for a cutting rule.[16] The United States proposed a 60% across-the-board cut in tariffs. The European Community proposed cutting the tariff on each item by the level of the tariff on the item and repeating this several times. Japan proposed reducing all duties by a fixed percentage, such as 60%, and then adding a constant number of percentage points, such as three, to the result. The Japanese proposal also included a 5% tariff-level floor below which no duties would be cut.

Here was little further progress in settling on a formula until March 1976, when the United States formally proposed a cutting rule of $y = 1.5x + 50$, where y is the percentage by which the tariff is cut, x is the initial percentage tariff rate, and the constant term, 50%, is the uniform element in the formula. The United States also imposed a 60% cut ceiling on all rates currently over 5%, since the U.S. law that gave authority to reduce tariffs contained such a ceiling. This formula reduced U.S. weighted average rates by 58%, from 4.8% to 2.0%, and reduced EC weighted average rates by 60%, from 7.0% to 2.8%. The variance in unweighted U.S. rates decreased from 33.18 to 5.41 under this formula, while that of the European Community declined from 13.50 to 2.02. The reaction of the Community and the other participants to this U.S. formula was generally negative on the grounds that the formula produced insufficient harmonization of tariffs. They pointed out that it was essentially the old 60%-cut proposal of the United States, since it became a linear-cut rule of 60% for all rates initially above 6.67%.

The Community made its proposal for a cutting rule in July 1976. The formula was $y = x$ repeated four times, where y is the percentage reduction and x is the percentage tariff on an item. Hence if an item had an initial tariff of 20%, this figure would be cut by 20% down to 16%, the 16% reduced by 16% down to 13.44%, the 13.44% reduced by 13.44% down to 11.63%, and finally the 11.63% reduced by 11.63% down to 10.28%. This cutting rule decreased the weighted average tariff levels of the United States and the European Community to 3.4% and 4.7%, respectively, or by 29% and 33%, and their unweighted variance to 4.37 and 3.34, respectively. The reaction of the United States and the other participants to this EC formula was also generally critical, this time on the grounds that the formula did not produce a deep enough average cut. It was pointed out that, even before any exceptions, the formula gave only a 33% average cut in the EC's own tariff schedule. The U.S. formula, in contrast, gave an average cut of 60%.

Summing up the accomplishments of the March 1976 meetings, the chairman of the negotiating group, the Director-General of the GATT, stated that a consensus appeared to be emerging that the tariff-cutting plan should contain an important element of harmonization and aim at a significant reduction in duties.

Japan and Switzerland took on the task of trying to come up with a compromise formula that would meet these objectives, and they both suggested new formulas at the next meeting in October 1976. The Swiss formula was $y = 100x/(14 + x)$, where y is the percentage cut and x is the existing percentage duty. A 14% tariff, for example, would be reduced 50% under this formula. The Japanese formula was $y = 100(0.7 - 3.5/x)$, where y is the percentage tariff, 0.7 is the uniform element in the cutting formula, and 3.5 is the term that produces the harmonization. A 14% tariff would be cut 45 percent under the Japanese cutting rule. The Japanese proposal also called for no reduction in tariffs that were currently 5% or less.

The Community's initial reaction to both proposals was generally favorable, noting in particular that both formulas contained an element of harmonization. The United States expressed interest in the two formulas, with a preference for the Swiss formula because it gave a greater average duty reduction for the major trading countries than did the Japanese formula. The U.S. delegation also objected to the 5% tariff floor in the Japanese cutting rule, which would have unacceptably excluded fully 17% of all developed-country tariffs. The final outcome of the negotiations was that the participants agreed on the Swiss formula.[17] This rule

TABLE 1 *Characteristics of Average Tariff Rates and Variances (in percent)*

	U.S.		EC	
	Mean (weighted)	Variance (unweighted)	Mean (weighted)	Variance (unweighted)
Pre-negotiation	4.8	33.18	7.0	13.50
U.S.-proposed formula	2.0	5.41	2.8	2.02
EC-proposed formula	3.4	4.37	4.7	3.34
Swiss-proposed formula	3.1	4.35	4.3	2.55
Actual	3.3	22.03	5.2	10.38

cut U.S.-weighted average tariffs by 35% to 3.1% and EC=weighted average tariffs by 39% to 4.3%. The unweighted tariff variance in the two countries was reduced to 4.35 for the United States and to 2.55 for the Community. Interestingly, the variance for U.S. rates – the main concern of the European Community – was reduced slightly more under this formula than under the Community's own suggested formula. But in agreeing to this cutting rule, the Community had to accept a considerably deeper average cut in its rates than under its own formula. The United States, for its part, seemed quite willing to trade the deeper reduction in its variance for a deeper average cut in the EC's rates. The means and variances for the United States and the European Community under the Swiss formula and under the other proposed cutting rules are given in Table 1.

Besides satisfying the conditions previously set forth concerning the relative magnitude of the weights on the different welfare components and on the relative size of the weights of foreign versus domestic welfare components, the weights selected should, as noted above, yield a "reasonable" progression of welfare losses from the actual sequence of negotiating proposals. Specifically, the welfare loss for the United States should be less under the U.S. formula than under the EC formula, and the Community's loss under its proposed rule should be less than under the U.S. formula. Finally, the Swiss formula should give an intermediate loss position for both countries. Consequently, the determination of the weights involved, first, arbitrarily selecting a set of weights that satisfy the conditions imposed concerning the relative magnitude of the weights attached to a particular welfare component and the respective evaluations by the two trading partners of changes in their own versus the other's welfare, and then varying these weights, still satisfying the imposed conditions, until the resulting welfare losses under the U.S., EC, and Swiss formulas conformed to the relationships stated above.

A set of weights that yields these relationships when inserted into the overall welfare loss Equations (2.9) and (2.10) is as follows:

$$L_1(t^1,s^1) = 0.03A_1 + 0.80A_2 + 1000B_{11} + 4000B_{12} + 50C \qquad (4.1)$$

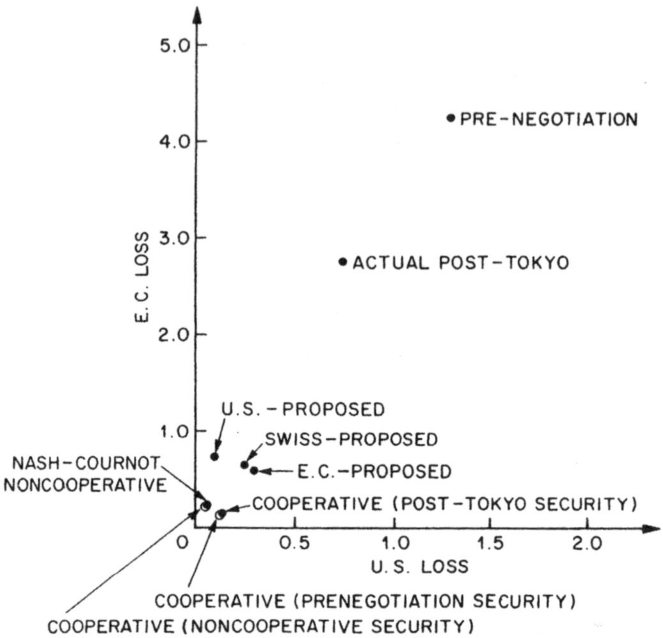

FIGURE 2 U.S. and E.C. welfare losses.

and

$$L_2(t^1,s^1) = 0.80A_1 + 0.10A_2 + 3000B_{21} + 500B_{22} + 50C, \tag{4.2}$$

where $\delta_1 = 0.40$ and $\delta_2 = 0.68$.[18]

The resulting losses for the United States and the European Community under the three tariff-cutting rules and under the initial set of tariff rates are plotted in Figure 2.

5. CALCULATED GAME-THEORETIC EQUILIBRIA AND THEIR RELATIONSHIP TO FORMULA AND ACTUAL TARIFFS

Using the welfare weights selected in the previous section, we next compute the theoretic noncooperative and cooperative equilibria. To compute the cooperative equilibrium, we alternatively use the initial tariffs, the actual post-Tokyo Round tariffs, and the noncooperative Nash-Cournot optimum tariffs as security levels. Table 2 lists the home and foreign welfare losses of the United States for the three components of the loss function (together with the overall loss) for these four equilibria as well as for the three proposed cutting formulas, the initial tariffs, and the actual post-Tokyo Round rates. Table 3 gives the same information

TABLE 2 *U.S. Welfare Losses*[a]

Tariff structure	a_1A_1	a_2A_2	b_1B_{11}	b_2B_{12}	CC	Sum
Pre-negotiation	0.1533	0.4250	0.1175	0.6079	0.0000	1.3037
U.S.-proposed	0.0237	0.0630	0.0002	0.0004	0.0044	0.0916
EC-proposed	0.0203	0.1040	0.0340	0.1201	0.0198	0.2981
Swiss-proposed	0.0200	0.0793	0.0219	0.0703	0.0680	0.2595
Actual post-Tokyo	0.0972	0.3100	0.0239	0.2013	0.1124	0.7448
Noncooperative optimum	0.0055	0.0267	0.0051	0.0284	0.0000	0.0658
Cooperative optimum (prenegotiation security)	0.0011	0.0461	0.0142	0.0612	0.0001	0.1227
Cooperative optimum (noncooperative security)	0.0010	0.0318	0.0173	0.0154	0.0002	0.0658
Cooperative optimum (post-Tokyo security)	0.0011	0.0464	0.0142	0.0636	0.0001	0.1254

[a] a_1A_1 = U.S. loss from U.S. tariff variability, a_2A_2 = U.S. loss from EC tariff variability, b_1B_{11} = U.S. loss from U.S. tariff reduction, b_2B_{12} = U.S. loss from EC tariff reduction, cC = U.S. loss from unequal tariff reduction, and Sum = overall U.S. loss.

TABLE 3 *EC Welfare Losses*[a]

Tariff structure	$\alpha_1 A_1$	$\alpha_2 A_2$	$\beta_1 B_{21}$	$\beta_2 B_{22}$	γC	Sum
Pre-negotiation	4.0868	0.0531	0.1003	0.0216	0.0000	4.2618
U.S.-proposed	0.6327	0.0079	0.0742	0.0163	0.0044	0.7354
EC-proposed	0.5402	0.0130	0.0339	0.0016	0.0198	0.6084
Swiss-proposed	0.5343	0.0099	0.0247	0.0031	0.0680	0.6400
Actual post-Tokyo	2.5916	0.0387	0.0211	0.0018	0.1124	2.7656
Noncooperative optimum	0.1470	0.0033	0.0749	0.0086	0.0000	0.2339
Cooperative optimum (prenegotiation security)	0.0283	0.0058	0.0837	0.0056	0.0001	0.1228
Cooperative optimum (noncooperative security)	0.0277	0.0040	0.1893	0.0127	0.0002	0.2339
Cooperative optimum (post-Tokyo security)	0.0306	0.0058	0.0819	0.0055	0.0001	0.1239

[a] $\alpha_1 A_1$ = EC loss from U.S. tariff variability, $\alpha_2 A_2$ = EC loss from EC tariff variability, $\beta_1 B_{21}$ = EC loss from U.S. tariff reduction, $\beta_2 B_{22}$ = EC loss from EC tariff reduction, γC = EC loss from unequal tariff reduction, and Sum = overall EC loss.

for the European Community. By comparing the weighted loss components with others in the same row, it is possible to see how under a particular tariff structure, loss in one area, e.g., domestic variability, compares with loss in another area, e.g., reciprocity. By comparing entries in the same column but different rows, one can see how different proposed tariff structures affect loss in any particular category. The four theoretic tariff equilibria and the actual post-Tokyo Round overall losses for the two trading blocs are also displayed in Figure 2.

The overall welfare losses of the United States and the European Community are lower under the noncooperative Nash-Cournot and all the cooperative solutions than under the Swiss formula. The noncooperative and cooperative solutions are also better for the European Community than either their own proposed cutting rule or the rule set forth by the United States. In the U.S. case, the noncooperative solution and the cooperative one using the noncooperative solution as the security point are better than all the proposed formulas, but the cutting rule proposed by the United States is better for the United States than the other two cooperative solutions. While all of the proposed formulas generate welfare losses that are relatively "close" to the game-theoretic losses, the actual post-Tokyo Round rates yield welfare losses for both the United States and the Community that are much greater than for all the game-theoretic solutions and the proposed cutting formulas. This suggests that while game models may be successful at predicting the outcome of formal GATT negotiations, they are less accurate in describing the subsequent, more political, process of requesting exceptions from the general formula. The welfare losses under the actual rates, however, do pass the test of reasonableness, yielding welfare losses to both trading blocs that are less than in the pre-Tokyo Round situation.

Mis-specification of the negotiating model, both in selecting the welfare functions and equilibrium concept, and incorrect empirical selection of weights may explain the failure of this model to predict precisely the actual negotiated tariffs. There is another plausible reason, however. To appreciate why the actual welfare losses for the two trading blocs are greater than the outcomes would have been if any of the formulas had been implemented or plausible game-theoretic behavior had been followed, it is necessary to understand that there were essentially two distinct parts to the negotiations in the Tokyo and Kennedy Rounds. The first part, at which the cutting rule was negotiated, was conducted by the countries' chief negotiators with comparatively little political pressure from particular economic sectors. Perceived national goals, such as achieving a deep average cut in others' tariff rates or a significant reduction in the variance in their rates, dominated the negotiating issues. The working hypothesis was that there would be a minimum of tariff item exceptions from the generally agreed cut.

Once the cutting formula was agreed on, the second stage of the negotiations began, determining the specific items to be excluded from formula tariff reductions and achieving overall reciprocity with other major trading partners. The internal process of determining exceptions involved a much broader group of interests than deciding on the more general formulas to propose. Particular industries and labor organizations now brought strong political pressure on members of Congress, Cabinet officials, and the President to exclude their sectors from any cut, or at least from the full formula cut.

Governments vary greatly in their ability and willingness to withstand these pressures. In the Kennedy Round, for example, President Kennedy's strong support for a deep average cut enabled U.S. negotiators to stand up quite successfully to these lobbying pressures and to keep the initial exceptions to a minimum; EC and Japanese negotiators were less successful. In the Tokyo Round, the Community's initial offer list contained no exceptions to the Swiss cutting rule, whereas there were many exceptions in the initial U.S. offer list. In order to produce a significant average cut despite these exceptions, the United States actually offered cuts of more than 60% on many items with rates of 5% or less. (The 1974 Trade Act permitted cuts of up to 100% on this group of rates.)

After the initial sets of formal offers in January 1978, countries attempted to improve the offers of others by requesting specific additions to the offer lists. After this stage, which was only partially successful, the process of pulling back to achieve reciprocity began. For example, in April 1978 the European Community announced that, in view of the exceptions of the other countries and its unwillingness to give compensation for greater-than-formula cuts, it would withdraw formula cuts either partially or totally on a specified list of products unless the exceptions of others were withdrawn. Apparently this announcement produced few tangible results, and in July they formally withdrew these items from formula cuts. A rough sampling from their initial and July 1978 offers indicates that about one-fifth of the tariff items were withdrawn from the full formula cut at this time.

In February 1979 the United States announced it would withdraw its greater-than-formula cuts at the end of the month, and this was done. Then in March 1979 the Community presented its final offer list, which involved a further pull-back in order to achieve what it regarded as reciprocity. A rough estimate of the extent of this additional pullback is that it involved another 15% of all tariff items.

On reading the relevant GATT documents and talking with individuals who were directly involved in the negotiations, one concludes that neither the participants nor the GATT Secretariat made sufficient efforts to minimize the pull-backs designed to achieve reciprocity for the individual participants. Many of the pull-backs in both the Kennedy and Tokyo Rounds were on items on which there was not much domestic political pressure for less-than-formula cuts, and hence, were made for reciprocity purposes only. It almost seemed that the negotiators were content to call what had been achieved a great success and to conclude the long process of negotiation as quickly as possible. The main point to emphasize is that the process of determining exceptions and achieving reciprocity resulted in a considerably different outcome than would have occurred if the cutting rules were followed strictly.

6. CONCLUSIONS

Using actual trade and tariff data for the United States and the European Community, this paper indicates how a multilateral trade negotiation such as the Tokyo Round, which in its first stage seeks to achieve agreement on a general tariff-cutting formula, can be interpreted as an effort by the participants to minimize individual, multidimensional welfare loss functions, each component weighted differently for the two trading blocs. The different components and specific weights on these components were selected on the basis of the negotiators' statements as to what their objectives were and what would give a logical sequence of welfare changes as various formulas were proposed. Using these weights, the Nash-Cournot noncooperative equilibrium and three separate Nash cooperative equilibria, differing only in their security points, were calculated.

These welfare outcomes were compared with those given by the initial and final tariff rates, using the same weights. While the final set of rates improved the welfare position of both the United States and the European Community as compared to their initial positions, the final outcome was inferior to that given by the various formulas or the different game-theoretic outcomes. It was noted that the second stage of a negotiation, where exceptions are determined and pull-backs to achieve perceived reciprocity are made, is likely to result in such an inferior outcome. Various welfare considerations dealing with the weights placed on individual sectors that are not included in our model could also account for this result. In any event, thinking about trade negotiations in the terms outlined in this paper would seem to be useful for improving the negotiating process in the future, especially with regard to minimizing pull-backs for reciprocity purposes.

NOTES

We are indebted to Bih Jane Liu for expert research help and to Marie Thursby for valuable comments. This paper does not necessarily reflect the views of the U.S. Department of Justice or AT&T Bell Laboratories.

1 The procedure for determining what items would not be subject to the tariff-cutting rule and what withdrawals would be made in response to other countries' exceptions was similar to traditional item-by-item negotiations.

2 Others who recently have analyzed the tariff-bargaining process in game-theoretic terms include Brander and Spencer (1981), Mayer (1981), Riezman (1982), and Thursby and Jensen (1983).

3 For a discussion of each of these game solution concepts, see Chapters 2, 3, and 5 in Friedman (1986).

4 Whether these publicly suggested tariff characteristics are an accurate indicator of a country's true preferences is investigated later by using numerical examples to evaluate how closely the actual proposed and negotiated tariffs compare to the ones that would be optimally implied by the professed considerations.

5 A prime indicates a transposed vector.

6 It is also possible to interpret m_i and n_i entries as actual dollar values of imports in product class i, if country 1 and country 2 have equal total amounts of imports.

7 The EC's lower degree of dispersion is the result of the simple averaging of country rates on tariff items that was performed when the Community was formed.

8 Community officials first made these points in the Kennedy Round and repeated them in the Tokyo Round. See Baldwin (1965).

9 The purpose of this variance normalization is to make the variability measure less sensitive to the absolute level of tariffs.

10 These measures are computed as follows:

$$\bar{t}^* = \frac{\delta_1}{k} \sum_{j=1}^{k} t_i^0 \qquad \text{and } \bar{s}^* = \frac{\delta_2}{k} \sum_{j=1}^{k} s_i^0.$$

Factors δ_1 and δ_2 are the fractions of initial average tariff rates desired by the U.S. and EC. They are explained at greater length two paragraphs below.

11 Reducing tariffs below these desired levels would increase a country's welfare loss in the view of its political leaders, due to pressures from industries injured by such cuts. Desired percentage increases would be denoted by negative δ_i's.

12 See the Trade Act of 1974, P.L. 93–618, 93rd Congress, H.R. 10710, Sec. 102.

13 Note that, similarly, if country 2 selects *s* to minimize interproduct variance and achieve its desired cut of $1 - \delta_2$, then if $\delta_1 \neq \delta_2$, $B_{12} \neq 0$ and country 1 will suffer a loss.

14 Or more generally, the number of individual product class tariffs equals or exceeds the number of countries whose schedules must be equalized.

15 These averages are calculated by summing the tariff revenue from each sector and dividing by the total value of imports in the 22 sectors. The tariff and trade data used in the analysis are taken from Deardorff and Stern (1979).

16 For a brief history of the Tokyo Round negotiations, see the Director-General of General Agreement on Tariffs and Trade (1979). In addition to this source, the following description is based on other GATT documents and on conversations with some of those who were involved in the negotiations.

17 Some countries, such as the European Community, used 16 as the constant term in this formula, while the United State and some others used 14 as the constant term.

18 Experimentation with other sets of weights indicates that minor variations in any of the weights still permit the overall set to satisfy the imposed conditions and generate the same results. It should be remembered that, since the measurement units of variability *A*, target cut *B*, and reciprocity *C* are different, no inference can be drawn about the relative magnitudes of weight across different classes of loss. Comparisons are only valid between foreign and domestic loss.

REFERENCES

Baldwin, Robert E. (1965) Tariff-Cutting Techniques in the Kennedy Round. In *Trade, Growth, and the Balance of Payments* (R. E. Caves, H. G. Johnson, and P. B. Kenen, Eds.). Chicago: Rand McNally.

Brander, James A., and Spencer, Barbara J. (1981) Tariffs and Extraction of Foreign Monopoly Rents Under Potential Entry, *Canadian Journal of Economics* XIV (3):371–389.

Deardorff, Alan V., and Stern, Robert M. (1979) *An Economic Analysis of the Effects of the Tokyo Round of Multilateral Trade Negotiations on the United States and Other Major Industrialized Countries*, MTN Study 5. Washington, D.C.: Committee on Finance, U.S. Senate.

Director-General of General Agreement on Tariffs and Trade (GATT) (1979) *The Tokyo Round of Multilateral Trade Negotiations*. Geneva: General Agreement on Tariffs and Trade.

Friedman, James W. (1986) *Game Theory with Applications to Economics*. New York: Oxford University Press.

Johnson, Harry J. (1954) Optimum Tariffs and Retaliation, *Review of Economic Studies* XXI(2) (55):142–153.

Mayer, Wolfgang (1981) Theoretical Conditions on Negotiated Tariff Adjustments, *Oxford Economic Papers* 33:135–153.

Riezman, R. (1982) Tariff Retaliation from a Strategic Viewpoint, *Southern Economic Journal* 48:583–593.

Thursby, Marie, and Jensen, R. (1983) A Conjectural Variation Approach to Strategic Tariff Equilibria, *Journal of International Economics* 14:145–161.

3. Tariffs and the Most-Favored-Nation Clause: A Game Theoretic Approach

A. Caplin and K. Krishna

I. INTRODUCTION

The Most-Favored-Nation Clause (MFNC) has a long history in trade agreements. According to a country most-favored-nation treatment consists of offering the country a tariff rate at least as low as that offered to any other country on the same commodity. As early as 1226, Emperor Frederick II extended to Marseilles the same trade privileges previously granted Pisa and Genoa.[1] In 1692, a treaty between Denmark and the Hanse Cities used the term "Most-Favored-Nation." In the early seventeenth century, most European countries insisted on mutual MFN status. More recently, the MFN clause has come into prominence since the articles of GATT require that signatories extend MFN status to all members.[2]

Eminent trade theorists such as Viner (1924, 1936, and 1950) and Johnson (1965) and more recently Baldwin and Murray (1977) and Finger (1979) have analyzed the MFNC. But there has been little recent work on the economic effects of the MFNC: notable exceptions are Gruenspecht (1985), and Fries (1987). In contrast, there has been a good deal of interest in MFN from a legal standpoint. Jackson, *et al.* (1985) is a useful guide to this work. In addition, there has been a good deal of work on customs unions, which is related to the role of the MFN – see Corden (1985) for a useful survey. A selective discussion of the literature appears in the next section.

While the older work on the MFNC contains a number of interesting ideas, they need a more formal theoretical and empirical basis. In addition, a consolidation of previous work and extensions in an explicitly game-theoretic direction seems worthwhile. This is especially so in light of the upcoming GATT negotiations regarding GATT and the lack of recent attention paid to such issues by trade theorists.

Section II presents a brief historical survey and summary of previous research. In Section III we provide a simple model which illustrates the role of the MFNC in a non-cooperative tariff-setting game. We find that the MFNC may raise *all* tariffs, and harm welfare. The model suggests ways in which institutional arrangements might foster trade liberalization. In Section IV, we consider the role of the MFNC in a static model of tariff bargaining. We show that there may be good reason to expect negotiated tariffs to rise in the presence of the MFNC in such a setting. In Section V we consider simple dynamic models of non-cooperative bargaining. This analysis suggests that the MFNC alters the power structure in negotiations. Section VI concludes.

II. A SURVEY OF THE LITERATURE

In this section we discuss previous literature on the MFNC. We divide our survey into: (1) the effects of the MFNC on the costs and benefits of negotiations, (2) a discussion of the unconditional as opposed to the conditional MFNC, and (3) the strategic effects of the MFNC.

1. Costs and Benefits of Negotiations

A good deal of attention has been focused on trade treaties as an attempt to obtain some of the benefits of free trade. The costs of a sequence of bilateral treaties or multilateral negotiations which reduce tariffs are thought of as being greater than those of treaties concluded with a single country and extended to all countries via mutual MFN clauses. For this reason, the MFNC is thought of as reducing the cost of negotiations.

However, the MFNC also has an effect on the benefits of negotiation. Under the MFNC, a free rider problem develops. This is because costs, both direct negotiation costs and the cost of reducing tariffs, fall on the negotiating countries, while benefits accrue to all countries with MFN status.

The free rider problem is less severe for commodities in which the pattern of trade is highly concentrated. For this reason, products on which concessions are granted are selected so that the partners involved in the negotiations are the principal traders. In the limit, goods can be defined in so narrow a manner as to make the MFNC irrelevant. The classic example of this is the following extract from a German–Swiss treaty of 1904 (quoted in Curzon 1976, p. 60, and Viner 1931, p. 101). Tariff concessions were granted on "Large dapple mountain cattle or brown cattle reared at a spot at least 300 metres above sea level and having at least one month's grazing each year at a spot at least 800 metres above sea level." By defining the items on which tariff reductions are obtained in a narrow way, the benefits of negotiation can be "internalized." However, the cost of this procedure is that the fraction of imports "covered" by negotiation falls. To the extent that such narrow definitions in contracts are too costly for universal application and implementation, product selection cannot eliminate the free rider problem, as pointed out by Johnson (1965).

This is the focus of Finger (1979), who looks at the extent to which the positive externality of concessions being generalized to third parties has been "internalized" by such means as product selection. He also examines the cost of such internalization in terms of "coverage." He finds that there is evidence of an internalization-coverage trade-off, both at a bilateral and multilateral level, and analyzes the extent of the trade-off in successive rounds of negotiations. Table 1, which summarizes some of his work, is derived from Table 1 in Finger (1979).

Finger estimates the percentage of imports on which tariff reductions and bindings are negotiated and which originated in the participating countries at a bilateral and multilateral level. This is given in rows (3) and (4) of Table 1. He compares these numbers to the dutiable imports from participants as a percentage of dutiable imports from all countries, the second row of Table 1. The difference

TABLE 1 *Internalization and Coverage in U.S. Negotiations across the Rounds*

(1)	Concession imports as percentage of total imports	78	39	7	9	12	46
(2)	Dutiable imports from participants as percentage of imports from all countries	65	6	34	67	66	72
Percentage of concession imports originating in participating countries:[1]							
(3)	Bilateral	n.a.	16	56	74	69	n.a.
(4)	Multilateral	76	18	62	89	96	94
(5)	Bilateral internalization = (3)–(2)	n.a.	10	22	7	3	n.a.
(6)	Multilateral internationalization = (4)–(2)	11	12	28	22	30	22
ROUNDS		Geneva (1947)	Annecy (1949)	Torquay (1951)	Geneva (1956)	Dillon (1960–61)	Kennedy (1964–67)

[1]The denominator of both is the value of U.S. imports on which the U.S. made concessions. The numerator in the bilateral measure is the value of U.S. imports on which the U.S. made concessions which originated from the country with whom the concession was negotiated. The numerator of the multilateral measure includes in addition imports from other participating countries as well.

between the two, given in rows (5) and (6) of Table 1, indicates the degree to which product selection internalized the benefits of U.S. concessions to countries that granted concessions to the U.S. at a bilateral and multilateral level. As expected, the latter is uniformly larger than the former in all rounds. However, the cost of this is a low value of coverage, i.e., of concession imports as a percentage of total imports given in the first row of Table 1.

Also notice the shift from bilateral internalization to multilateral internalization as is evident after the Tokyo Round when bilateral internalization fell sharply from 22 to 7, but the multilateral figure fell only from 28 to 22. This is evidence of more multilateral bargaining in later rounds.

Johnson (1965) also looks at the free rider problem and the MFNC but from a slightly different perspective. Johnson postulates a "preference for industrial production" in the countries concerned and explores the implications of this postulate.

2. MFNC takes on Two Forms: the Unconditional Form and the Conditional Form

In the conditional version (CMFNC), *A* extends to *C* all concessions granted by treaty to *B*, only if *C* matches the concessions made by *B* to *A*. The conditional form was used by the U.S. in nearly all commercial treaties until 1923, when President Harding approved the adoption of the unconditional form in U.S. trade treaties. During the same period, most European countries used the unconditional form.

Use of CMFNC was the subject of considerable debate in the U.S. in the 1930s. In a series of articles, Viner (1924, 1931, 1936) argued against the CMFNC, and in favor of the MFNC. He had a number of points to make.

(a) Trade creation vs. trade diversion: He argued in favor of the MFNC on the grounds that the unconditional extension of negotiated tariff reductions reduced the possibility of "trade diversion" and increased that of "trade creation" (Viner 1931, p. 97).

(b) Adverse revenue effects: He also argued that bilateral agreements on tariff reduction with a *small* supplier of the import would merely lead to a transfer of tariff revenue from the treasury to the producers in the small supplying country with no gain to domestic consumers since the *small* supplier has, by definition, no impact on the world price.[3]

(c) Finally, Viner argued that:

> The conditional pledge is to all intents and purposes equivalent to no pledge at all when it is received from a country all of whose pledges and whose practice is conditional [e.g., the U.S.], and is in its mode of operation identical with the unconditional pledge when it is received from a country whose pledges or whose practice is unconditional [e.g., France or Britain.] (Viner 1936, p. 88)

The first assertion is straightforward; the CMFNC only guarantees the extension of concessions granted to a third party on "payment" of equivalent compensation; but it is up to the grantor of concessions to determine what is meant by "equivalent." "No country ever derived any advantage from a conditional pledge by the United States, except in a few minor instances as the result of inadvertence on the part of the drafters of the pledge" (Viner, *ibid.*). The second becomes obvious on a little reflection. Say France has a CMFNC with the U.S., and an UMFNC with Britain. It exchanges concessions with Spain; these are automatically extended without compensation to Britain. But if Britain received the concessions gratuitously, then the U.S. is also entitled to receive them free, by virtue of her CMFN status. By this means the U.S. apparently was granted all concessions negotiated between Europeans before 1914, without having to give anything in return. The CMFNC is thus empty in two ways. First, if used by a country which has an MFNC with any other country, it cannot be truly conditional. Second, if used as the basis of negotiation with all countries, it can be empty of content.

3. Strategic Effects

If all other countries operate on an MFNC basis, it is in the interest of a single country to operate on a CMFNC basis. This is ruled out by GATT for good reason. This is precisely what the U.S. did prior to 1923. Although this was to the short run benefit of the U.S., it was not necessarily to its long-run benefit as argued by Viner.

> The United States . . . has been one important commercial nation, with the exception since 1918 of vanquished Germany, which has not been reasonably certain of being given equality of treatment in tariff matters by the rest of the Western World . . . The conditional practice, instead of operating, as its supporters contended, to gain specially advantageous conditions for American commerce, failed to secure for it mere equality of treatment with the commerce of other nations. (Viner 1923, p. 37)[4]

One reason Viner gives for this is simply that European irritation with America led them to discriminate openly against it (Viner 1924, p. 37). A more theoretical argument against searching for bilateral reciprocity (by means of the CMFNC) is that treaties are harder to negotiate: for if "the country receiving the concession does not also receive a pledge of most-favored-nation treatment, it is not likely to place a high value on the concession, since not only may it later be extended to other countries, but in subsequent negotiations other countries may be given even greater concessions on the same items, with the result that the original concessions becomes totally useless" (Viner 1936, p. 83). In this view the MFNC's importance is as a commitment against future discrimination, rather than as a vehicle for ensuring present equality of treatment.

The MFNC says nothing about the *level* at which tariffs are set. It has also been noted that the provision may inhibit reductions in tariffs. For example, Curzon (1965, p. 59) points out that:

> With the rapid decline of trade after 1929 it [the MFNC] lost most of its effectiveness as an agent of freer trade, however. During this period the argument was that tariff concessions could not be granted to individual countries with whom one would have liked to make bilateral concessions because the clause in treaties with third parties spread these concessions to other countries unwilling to "pay" for them. Instead of some concessions between parts of countries the fear of unrequited benefits for third parties led to a freezing of the then existing situation or even to increase in tariffs equally and indiscriminately applied to everyone. The most-favored-nation clause, under these circumstances, reinforced protectionist tendencies.

More recently, Gruenspecht (1985) points out that the MFNC put constraints on a government's ability to strategically tax and subsidize its exports,[5] since it cannot choose discriminatory levels of these instruments. Hence, given the tax/subsidy policies of other governments, the MFNC reduces a country's welfare. However, since the equilibrium itself changes, it may raise or lower equilibrium welfare.

In contrast to Gruenspecht, we do not focus on imperfect competition in the product market, but on the effects of institutions, such as the MFNC, on the equilibrium levels of tariffs with competitive product markets. Hence, we focus more explicitly on the game-theoretic effects of the MFNC. Recent work along related lines by Fries (1987) focuses on the use of MFNC as a device for preventing discrimination, in a world where the discriminatory outcome is Pareto dominated.

Despite the acknowledgment of possible drawbacks of the MFNC in GATT, the general presumption in the literature is that the MFNC in GATT has been a major force behind trade liberalization.[6] Recently there has been considerable attention paid to the part played by GATT and the MFNC in facilitating trade liberalization.[7] Yet, little formal analysis using simple game-theoretic tools has been attempted.

III. NON-COOPERATIVE OPTIMAL TARIFFS

We provide a benchmark analysis of a world with asymmetric optimal tariffs. In the absence of cooperation, countries set tariffs to trade-off domestic consumer surplus and tariff revenue: non-zero tariffs are a reflection of market power on the demand side of the market. Here, we find that the most-favored-nation clause may raise the equilibrium value of all tariffs, but with ambiguous effects on welfare. Further analysis of our asymmetric general equilibrium framework should clarify how the impact of MFN depends on preferences and on technological factors.

For the MFN clause to have any impact, it is necessary that each country have at least two external trading partners. Hence a 3-country world is the simplest possible benchmark. We model the commodities subject to MFN as three distinct varieties, and include a numeraire good. Each country is endowed with one unit of one variety of good, along with a fixed amount of the numeraire commodity. The numeraire is assumed to be freely tradeable among countries, and is not subject to tariffs.

Overall, our model is designed to have a "representative agent" structure: utility functions U^j and endowments W_j of the distinct countries $j = A$, B and C are related in cycle fashion, as recorded in equation (1).

$$\begin{aligned} U^A(x_1, x_2, x_3, x_N) &= d\ln x_2 + \ln x_3 + x_N \,;\; W^A = (1, 0, 0, I), \\ U^B(x_1, x_2, x_3, x_N) &= d\ln x_3 + \ln x_1 + x_N \,;\; W^B = (0, 1, 0, I), \\ U^C(x_1, x_2, x_3, x_N) &= d\ln x_1 + \ln x_2 + x_N \,;\; W^C = (0, 0, 1, I), \end{aligned} \tag{1}$$

Goods 1 to 3 are modelled as distinct varieties of a single commodity, which enter utility functions in a separable manner. The utility parameter $d>1$ reflects the underlying asymmetry of the model: each country places greater weight on one of its two imports, and chooses distinct optimal tariffs. In other respects, the model is designed for simplicity: endowments and preferences dictate that A exports good 1 to B and C, B exports good 2 to A and C, and C exports good 3 to A and B. In addition, we assume that the endowment of the non-traded good, I, is "large" so that in the equilibria studied below, income is sufficient to purchase commodities to the point where the marginal utility of additional income is unity. Finally, the presence of the freely traded numeraire allows us to normalize consumer prices, p, so that $p_N^A = p_N^B = p_N^C = 1$.

We study two distinct tariff-setting regimes. In the first regime, each country sets two distinct and valorem tariff rates to maximize domestic welfare, taking other tariffs as given. In the second regime, countries are bound by MFN to set a single tariff rate. We begin with some general statements that apply to the model regardless of whether or not the MFN clause is in effect. Note that throughout the analysis we disallowed domestic tax and subsidy schemes other than tariffs.

The first observation is that in equilibrium the price that exporters receive must be independent of the export market. The implications for equilibrium prices are recorded in equation (2), where we have introduced the notation q_i to stand for the export price of good i, and the change of variable $z_i^j = \dfrac{1}{1 + t_i^j}$ to represent the ad valorem tariff of country j on good i.

$$\begin{aligned} q_1, &= z_1^B p_1^B = z_1^C p_1^C \\ q_2, &= z_2^A p_2^A = z_2^C p_2^C \\ q_3, &= z_3^A p_3^A = z_3^B p_3^B \end{aligned} \tag{2}$$

Equation (3) records tariff revenue for country B on commodity 1: analogous formula apply to all imports.

$$TR_1^B = t_1^B x_1^B q_1 = (1-z_1^B)p_1^B x_1^B = (1-z_1^B)d. \tag{3}$$

The first substitution in equation (3) follows from equation (3), while setting p_1^B $x_1^B = 1$ results from the Cobb-Douglas form of the demand function, together with requirements that I be sufficiently large to warrant the unit marginal utility of income. Equation (2) together with the Cobb-Douglas demand functions allow us to summarize the dependence of equilibrium prices on tariff rates in the simple form of equation (4),

$$\begin{aligned} q_1 &= dz_1^C + z_1^B \\ q_2 &= dz_2^A + z_2^C \\ q_3 &= dz_3^B + z_3^A \end{aligned} \tag{4}$$

The implications of equation (4) or tariff rates depend on whether or not the MFN clause is in effect. If not, country A has two instruments z_2^A and z_3^A with which to influence welfare, where

$$U^A(z_2^A, z_3^A) = dln\left[\frac{dz_2^A}{dz_2^A + z_2^C}\right] + ln\left[\frac{z_3^A}{dz_3^B + z_3^A}\right] \tag{5}$$
$$+[\, I + d(z_1^C - z_2^A) + (z_1^B - z_3^A)]$$

The first two terms in (5) represent consumption of goods 2 and 3, while the final term represents tariff revenue, and income from endowments. The first order (and sufficient) conditions for optimal tariffs yield the two equation system,

$$\begin{aligned} z_2^C &= z_2^A\,(dz_2^A + z_2^C) \\ dz_3^B &= z_3^A\,(dz_3^B + z_3^A) \end{aligned} \tag{6}$$

Consider symmetric optimal tariffs, so that $z_2^A = z_3^B = z_1^C = \hat{z}_d$, and $z_3^A = z_1^B = z_2^C = \hat{z}_1$. In this case, (6) has the unique solution,

$$(\hat{z}_1, \hat{z}_d) = \left[\frac{\sqrt{d}}{\sqrt{d}+1}, \frac{1}{\sqrt{d}+1} \right], \text{ or} \tag{7}$$

$$(\hat{t}_1, \hat{t}_d) = \left[\frac{1}{\sqrt{d}}, \sqrt{d} \right]$$

Equation (7) confirms that without MFN countries will choose discriminatory optimal tariffs. Specifically, the tariff is higher on the commodity for which the country has the more intense preference: there is an incentive to raise the tariff in line with the degree of monopoly power on the demand side of the market.

With countries sharing mutual MFN status, country A has only one instrument, $z_2^A = z_3^A = z^A$. The first order condition for A's optimal tariff is,

$$\frac{d(z^C + z^B)}{z^A(dz^A + z^C)} = d + 1. \tag{8}$$

At a symmetric optimum, $z^A = z^B = z^C = \hat{z}$ yielding,

$$\hat{z} = \frac{2d}{(d+1^2)} \text{ or } \hat{t} = \frac{1+d^2}{2d}. \tag{9}$$

A comparison between equations (7) and (9) reveals that the MFN clause raises tariff revenue and may actually result in a uniform tariff rate in *excess* of the maximum rate in the absence of MFN. To verify the increase in tariff revenue, let TR^M and TR^N respectively denote the revenues with and without MFN. Direct computations reveal,

$$TR^M - TR^N = (\sqrt{d}-1) + \left[\frac{d-1}{d+1} \right] \tag{10}$$

$$\sim 1 - \frac{\sqrt{d}+1}{\sqrt{d}+1} > 0, \text{ for } d > 1.$$

Equation (10) also shows that MFN causes a greater increase in tariff revenue as d rises. A comparison between $\hat{t}$ and $\hat{t}_d$, the higher of the two non-MFN tariff rates, further highlights the role of d,

$$\hat{t} > \hat{t}_d \Leftrightarrow 1 + d^2 > 2d^{3/2}. \tag{11}$$

Equation (11) shows that $\hat{t}$ exceeds $\hat{t}_d$ for all values of d exceeding a critical value d_c, with $3 < d_c < 4$: with highly asymmetric preferences MFN unambiguously raises tariff rates. Note that the alternate case in which MFN lies below $\hat{t}_1$ is impossible,

$$'\hat{t} - \hat{t}_1 = \frac{1+d^2 - 2\sqrt{d}}{2d} > \frac{(1-\sqrt{d}\,)^2}{2d} > 0, \text{ all } d > 1. \tag{12}$$

Paradoxically, while MFN may raise all tariff rates, it also raises welfare. The representative utility levels with and without MFN satisfy,

$$U^M = dln\left[\frac{d}{d+1}\right] + ln\left[\frac{1}{d+1}\right] + I \text{ and} \tag{13}$$

$$U^N = dln\left[\frac{\sqrt{d}}{\sqrt{d}+1}\right] + ln\left[\frac{1}{\sqrt{d}+1}\right] + I$$

so that $U^M > U^N$. The explanation is straightforward: in a symmetric equilibrium the only unknown is the proportion of the exported commodity which goes to the country with the high preference parameter. When tariffs are set separately, countries set higher tariffs on the commodities in which they have greater influence on the demand side of the market, and hence import relatively less of their favored commodity than in the free trade equilibrium. Here, MFN has the beneficial effect of preventing measures which discriminate against the more favored import, restoring the free trade equilibrium.

In a model with production, or with domestic consumption of the export commodity, the MFN-inspired increases in tariff rates will lower the volume of world trade, and have an offsetting effect on welfare. Consider a variant of the above model with domestic demand for the endowment commodity, as specified for country A in (14) below.

$$U^A(x_1, x_2, x_3, x_N) = lnx_1 + dlnx_2 + lnx_3 + x_N. \tag{14}$$

The analogous adjustments are made for countries B and C. Equation (15) expresses the equilibrium condition for good 1.

$$q_1 = 1 + dz_1^C + z_1^B. \tag{15}$$

The first order conditions for symmetric optimal tariffs in the absence of MFN become,

$$z_1(1 + dz_d + z_1) = 1 + dz_d \tag{16}$$

$$z_d(1 + dz_d + z_1) = 1 + z_1.$$

The following rearrangement is useful

$$z_1 + z_1^2 = z_d + dz_d^2 \tag{17}$$
$$dz_d(1 - z_1) = z_1(1 - z_d).$$

As before, (17) shows that the optimal tariff is higher for the preferred commodity. Manipulation shows that with $d = \dfrac{(a-1)(a^2-3a+1)}{2a-1}$,

$$z_1 = \frac{a-1}{a} \tag{18}$$
$$z_d = \frac{2a-1}{a(a-1)},$$

any $a > 1$.

By comparison, the first order condition with MFN can be rearranged to,

$$z^2(d + 1)^2 - z(d - 1) - (d + 1) = 0. \tag{19}$$

Formulae (18) and (19) can be used to show that in the presence of domestic consumption of the export commodity, MFN may raise all tariffs *and* lower welfare when preferences are asymmetric. Note first that the consumption vectors in a symmetric equilibrium with and without MFN, x^M and x^N respectively, obey

$$X^N = \left[\frac{1}{1+dz_d+z_1}, \frac{dz_d}{1+dz_d+z_1}, \frac{z_1}{1+dz_d+z_1}, I\right] \text{ and}$$
$$X^M = \left[\frac{1}{1+dz+z}, \frac{dz}{1+dz+z}, \frac{z}{1+dz+z}, I\right] \tag{20}$$

with the first commodity representing the export commodity, and the second representing the commodity with preference parameter d. From (18) it is clear that without MFN as d rises, so z_l heads to unity, and consumption of the commodities with the same preference parameter heads to equality. In addition the product dz_d comes to approximate the value of a (recall $d = [\frac{a-1}{2a-1}][a^2 - 3a + 1]$) as before. With MFN, equation (19) shows that as d rises, so dz approaches $\frac{a}{\sqrt{2}}$ so that for high d both imports are reduced by MFN.

Consider a numerical example with $d = 15$ so that with MFN $z \approx \frac{2.16\sqrt{16}}{2.16^2} = \frac{1}{4}$ (from the quadratic formula applied to (19)). This results in utility,

$$ln \frac{z}{(1+dz+z)^2} + d\, ln \frac{dz}{1+dz+z} \approx ln \frac{1}{100} + 15\, ln \frac{3}{4}. \tag{21}$$

Without MFN, $d = 15$ corresponds to $a \approx \frac{15}{2}$, so that $dz_d \approx 4$ and $z_1 \approx \frac{13}{15}$ (from (8)); and

$$ln \frac{z_1}{(1+dz_d+z_1)^2} + d\, ln \frac{dz_d}{1+dz_d+z_1} > ln \frac{1}{45} + 15\, ln \frac{3}{4}, \tag{22}$$

exceeding the MFN value.

Overall, for high d, MFN damages welfare in two ways. First the country chooses to levy high tariffs on both commodities, forcing consumption of the one it favors less toward zero. Even for the commodity it prefers, the tariff rate is higher with MFN: hence consumption is shifted still further toward the domestic product.

IV. INSTITUTIONAL VARIATIONS

The model of the previous section suggests that although the MFNC is a simple way of changing the institutional structure within which tariffs are set, and thus the equilibrium level of tariffs – it may well raise all tariffs. The natural question to ask then is whether other institutional structures are suggested by the model which would reduce the levels of tariffs in equilibrium.

Suppose that each country could set different tariffs on the two countries from which it imports but that countries have agreed to link the tariffs they set on a particular variety of the goods. In particular, suppose that a unit increase in country *A*'s tariff on Variety 2 is linked to a γ decrease in country *C*'s tariff, and vice versa, so that

$$\frac{dz_2^C}{dz_2^A} = \frac{dz_3^B}{dz_3^A} - \gamma .$$

In this case, the first order conditions for *A*'s optimal tariffs are,

$$z_2^C + \gamma\, z_2^A = z_2^A(dz_2^A + z_2^C), \text{ and}$$

$$d(z_3^B + \gamma\, z_3^A) = z_3^A(dz_3^B + z_3^A). \tag{23}$$

At a symmetric solution, $z_2^A = z_3^B = z_d$, and $z_3^A = z_2^C = z$, yielding

$$(a)\ z_1 + \gamma\, z_d = z_d(dz_d + z_l), \text{ and}$$

$$(b)\ d(z_d + \gamma\, z_l) = z_l(dz_d + z_l). \qquad (24)$$

Consider the graphs of 24 (*a*) and 24 (*b*) in (z_1, z_d) space. It can be shown that for $\gamma \geq 0$ the equations have a unique non-zero solution, with $0 < z_d < z_1$. It is also straightforward to verify that both graphs shift out as γ increases and have positive slope where they intercept. Hence increases in γ change both tariffs in the same direction. Finally with $\gamma = 1$, $\hat{z}_1 = \dfrac{1+d}{2}$ and $\hat{z}_d = \dfrac{1+d}{2d}$, both of which lie above their values when $\gamma = 0$. Hence an increase in γ raises both equilibrium levels of z, lowering optimal tariffs.

The reason for this reduction in tariffs is that the institutional arrangement inhibits each country's monopoly power. An increase in *A*'s tariff on good 2 reduces the *world* price of good 2 less if it is accompanied by a simultaneous reduction of *C*'s tariff on the same good. However, if $\gamma < 0$, the arrangement would increase each country's monopoly power and would raise tariffs by the same arguments.

It is also easy to verify that an arrangement which linked the level of z_2^A positively to z_1^B and z_3^A to z_1^C would also have a similar effect. In this case tariff increases by a country on its imports would be discouraged since they would automatically lead to tariff increases on its exports.

The preceding analysis suggests that it may be useful to think of rules or agreements as cooperatively setting the environment within which countries behave non-cooperatively. Of course, the politics of such agreements are likely to be very complicated and for this reason our analysis should be interpreted with a great deal of caution.

V. MFN AND BARGAINING

In practice, tariff-setting frequently involves cooperative elements, with deals struck in either bilateral or multilateral negotiations. In the remaining models we analyze the impact of the MFN clause in a number of different bargaining contexts, which idealize different aspects of tariff-bargaining. As will be seen, the role of MFN varies with the institutional setting within which tariff bargains arise. Hence arguments that MFN was beneficial prior to the GATT agreements need not imply that it aids the GATT bargaining process.

Throughout our analysis, we maintain that tariff bargains between two countries are honored, unless the same parties agree later to alter the terms of the bargain. In practice, there may be little or no reason to honor past agreements as circumstances change. In this case, a vital function of an international trading arrangement is to punish violators. The MFN clause may play a role in such punishments. While this is an interesting possibility, it does not appear that the existing GATT arrangements provide clear punishments: disputes are resolved by intricate bargaining procedures, rather than by strict application of GATT codes. Nevertheless, the topic is sufficiently important to warrant further attention.

The model of this section is of an essentially static nature, and captures the free-rider aspects of bargaining under MFN. The need to lower tariffs to more than one country represents an externality which is not captured in simple bilateral bargains. As a result a simultaneous round of bilateral bargains may be less effective at lowering tariffs with MFN than without. The model appears most relevant to the pre-Tokyo Round GATT negotiations, which were conducted on bilateral lines.

In Section VI we turn to dynamic bargains in which countries may bargain sequentially. In these dynamic models, the MFN clause may have more subtle and interesting effects, such as altering the balance of power in negotiations, and making the order of negotiation a key strategic variable.

There is a simple observation which illustrates the difficulties in providing a general bargaining-theoretic rationale for MFN. There is a grand utility possibility frontier available to countries using all the commercial trading instruments at their disposal, such as tariffs. If we view the bargaining process as yielding efficient outcomes, as for example with the Nash bargaining solution, then MFN simply limits the tools available to different countries, shifting in the utility possibility frontier. Hence the most positive aspects of MFN can only be illustrated when the bargaining process absent-MFN yields inefficient outcomes. It is for this reason that dynamic analyses, in which issues of time-consistency may arise, appear promising as settings in which MFN may aid efficiency.

A. Simultaneous Bilateral Bargains

As in Section III, we present the simplest "representative agent" structure with sufficient heterogeneity for MFN to have an impact. Here, it is convenient to maintain all variables as powers of 2: there are 4 countries, A through D, and 8 commodities x_1 through x_8. The commodity flows between countries are schematically recorded in Figure 1. It is convenient to use simple reduced-form utility functions which record that optimal tariffs on imports are positive, while countries like tariffs on their exports to be reduced to zero. Equation (25) records country A's utility function as it depends on the ad valorem tariff rates on A's imports and exports.

$$U^A(t_1, t_4, t_5, t_8) = -\{(t_4, - T)^2 + (t_8 - T)^2 + t_1^2 + t_5^2\} . \tag{25}$$

Other countries have analogous utility functions.

The non-cooperative outcome has all tariffs at level T, with welfare $-2T^2$. The symmetric welfare optimum has tariffs at level $T/2$, with welfare $-T^2$. We consider two alternative bargaining structures, with and without MFN. In both cases bargains are bilateral. Within MFN, A and B negotiate over (t_1, t_8), B and C negotiate over (t_2, t_7), C and D over (t_3, t_8) and A and D over (t_4, t_5). With MFN, each country j sets a single tariff rate t^j and so can take part in only one bargain: we let A and B bargain over (t^A, t^B), and C D over (t^C, t^D).

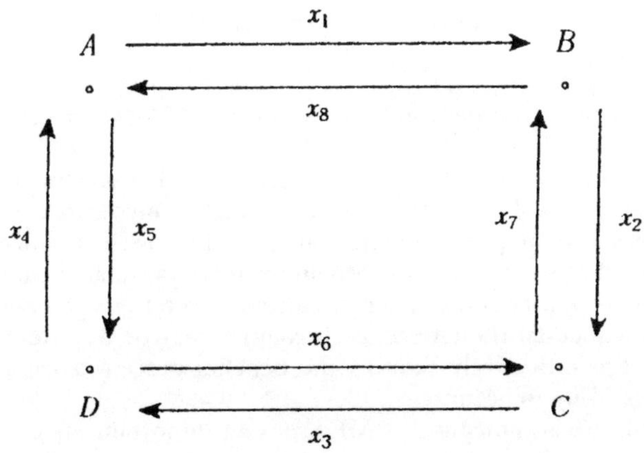

FIGURE 1

Each bargain is resolved at the Nash bargaining solution. The solution is simplified by noting that the payoff in any bilateral bargain is independent of the outcome of other bargains: this follows from the separability in the utility function. Hence to compute the outcome of the bargain between A and B in the absence of MFN, we need only vary the t_1 and t_8 arguments in the utility function. Note also that the disagreement point between A and B involves reversion to the non-cooperative tariff level of T. Hence,

$$U^A(t_1, t_8) - \bar{U}^A(T,T) = -(t_1^2 + (t_8 - T)^2) + T^2 = 2t_8T - t_1^2 - t_8^2 \tag{26}$$
$$U^B(t_1, t_8) - \bar{U}^B(T,T) = -(t_8^2 + (t_1 - T)^2) + T^2 = 2t_1T - t_1^2 - t_8^2$$

The Nash bargaining solution solves,

$$\max_{t_1,\, t_8, \geq 0} (2t_8T - t_1^2 - t_8^2)(2t_1T - t_1^2 - t_8^2). \tag{27}$$

Manipulation of the first order conditions gives the solution $t_1 = t_8 = T/2$, so that bilateral Nash bargains yield the symmetric welfare optimum. This is not surprising in light of the simple pattern of trade in the model.

With MFN, a country sacrifices more than a tariff reduction without gaining more from its partner's willingness to cut tariffs. Concretely, A and B bargain over (t^A, t^B) with utility functions,

$$U^A(t^A, t^B) = -[t_B^2 + 2(t_A - T)^2] \text{ and} \tag{28}$$
$$U^B(t^A, t^B) = -[t_A^2 + 2(t_B - T)^2].$$

As before, the threat point is (T, T), with reference utility level $\bar{U}^A = \bar{U}^T = -T^2$. Hence the Nash bargaining solution solves,

$$\max_{t_A,\, t_B \geq 0} \{T^2 - [t_B + 2(t_A - T)^2]\} \{T^2 - [t_A^2 + 2(t_B - T)^2]\}. \tag{29}$$

Examination of the first order conditions yields $t = 2T/3$, so that the introduction of MFN raises tariffs and lowers welfare.

In general, there seem to be three reasons why MFN treatment may impede bilateral negotiations. First, MFN treatment makes any tariff concession more costly since it has to be given to more countries. This is the essence of the point we have detailed above. Second, the benefits of receiving a tariff cut on its exports are smaller to a country since the tariff cuts are given to its competitors as well. Finally, in a sequential framework, each country may be free riding on another negotiation. This effectively reduces the benefits perceived from negotiation, making it less likely to occur.

Against this are arguments that MFN has an important effect in preventing future bargains which unravel existing agreements. To examine these possibilities, we must introduce dynamic considerations.

VI. MFN AND BARGAINING: SOME DYNAMIC ASPECTS

In this section we present an extremely stylized model of non-cooperative bargaining, based on the work of Rubinstein (1982). The model shows that an important aspect of the MFNC may be its effect on the distribution of gains between countries. We believe that other important aspects of MFNC will be best understood in dynamic bargaining models, and view this as a promising avenue of research.

A Stylized Model of the MFNC

In a non-cooperative setting, the possibility of free riding on other negotiations alters the balance of power.[8] How it might do so is the focus of this section.

There is assumed to be a "trade pie" which can be obtained if countries can only agree to its division. The "trade pie" is of a fixed size. There are assumed to be three countries, labeled 1, 2 and 3. The simplest possible pattern of offers is specified. Country 1 makes offers to Country 2 or 3, who can only accept or reject Country 1's offers. Only bilateral negotiations are allowed, and Country 1 is assumed to negotiate with 2 and 3 in sequence. The structure of the bargaining game is illustrated in Figure 2. At $t = 0$, Country 1 makes an offer to Country 2 of x. An offer of x is a proposal that Country 1 get a payoff of x. While Countries 2 and 3 also benefit, Country 2 does less well than Country 3 who free rides, via MFN, on the negotiations between 1 and 2. It is assumed that while both Countries 2 and 3 share $1-x$ equally, country 2 also incurs a negotiation cost of $ø$. Thus, Country 2 gets $\frac{1-x}{2} - ø$ and Country 3 gets $\frac{1-x}{2}$, as shown in Figure 2.

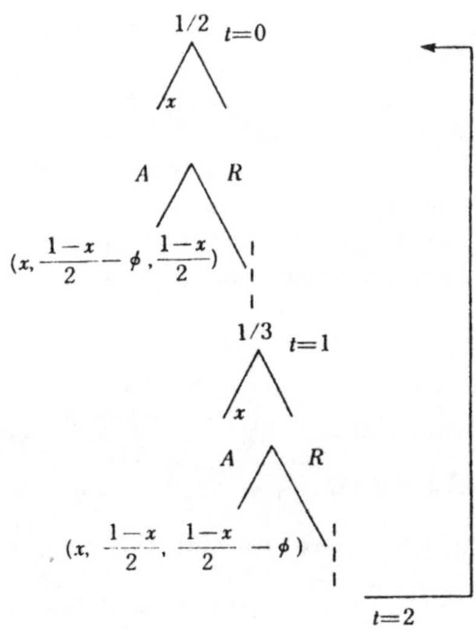

FIGURE 2

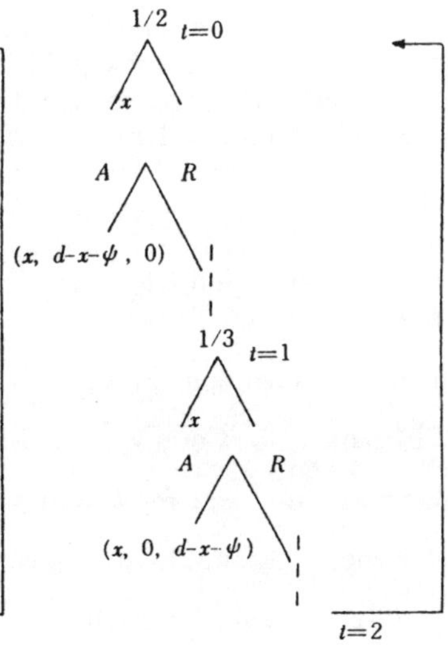

FIGURE 3

If Country 2 refuses 1's offer, then we move into the next period, $t = 1$, when Country 1 makes an offer to Country 3 of x. If Country 3 accepts the offer, then it must pay the negotiation costs and Country 2 free rides since the payoffs are now $(x, \frac{1-x}{2}, \frac{1-x}{2} - ø)$.

If Country 3 refuses, then we move into the next period and Country 1 makes an offer to Country 2 – so that we are back in the same position as at $t = 0$. As usual, a crucial driving force of the model is impatience, and this is captured by the discount for $\delta < 1$.

Before analyzing the equilibria of this game, consider its analogue in the absence of MFN, when there is no free rider problem. In this case all benefits can be internalized between the bargaining parties. Thus, if Countries 1 and 2 bargain and come to an arrangement, there are no benefits for Country 3. As before, Country 2 incurs some cost of negotiating denoted by φ. The game, in the absence of an MFN, is represented in Figure 3. An agreement between Countries 1 and 2 leaves Country 3 with zero, while one between Countries 1 and 3 leaves Country 2 with nothing. The total size of the pie to be split between Countries 1 and 2 or 1 and 3 is given to be $d > \varphi$.

We show that the inability to free ride on bargains curtails the ability of Countries 2 and 3 to *credibly* threaten to refuse offers of Country 1 which give them a low share of the trade pie. The result of this lack of credibility is that in the unique perfect equilibrium Country 1 is able to obtain a payoff of $d - \varphi$ so that 2 and 3 are left with a payoff of zero in equilibrium. As usual, agreement is reached immediately in equilibrium.

To confirm that this is a perfect equilibrium outcome, consider the following strategies which form a Nash equilibrium in every subgame. Countries 2 and 3 accept any offer which gives them at least zero in net payoff and reject any offer which does not. Country 1 cannot do better than always offering $x = d - \varphi$. It would not do better by offering a lower x, since $d - \varphi$ is accepted. It will not offer more than $d - \varphi$ at any time since its offer would be rejected. Countries 2 and 3 can do no better by rejecting such offers of $d - \varphi$ in any subgame, so that accepting is a best response for them. The uniqueness of the equilibrium is shown in Proposition 1 of the Appendix.

Similarly, for small enough ø, i.e. $\frac{1-\delta}{2} \geq ø$. the unique perfect outcome of the MFN game is for Country 1 to obtain a share, x, of $1 - \frac{2ø}{1-\delta}$, for Country 2 to obtain $\frac{\delta ø}{1-\delta}$, and for Country 3 to obtain $\frac{ø}{1-\delta}$. Agreement is again reached immediately and the strategies which support this outcome are as follows. 1 always offers a share for itself of $x^* = 1 - \frac{2ø}{1-\delta}$ to both 2 and 3. 2 and 3 accept any offer x weakly below x^* and reject any x above x^*. These strategies constitute a Nash equilibrium in every subgame. x^* is the largest acceptable offer and so 1 can do no better than to offer it, given the strategies of 2 and 3. Similarly, 2 would obtain $\frac{\delta ø}{1-\delta}$ by rejecting an offer so that the best response is to accept any offer that gives more than $\frac{\delta ø}{1-\delta}$ i.e. any x such that $\frac{1-x}{2} - ø > \frac{\delta ø}{1-\delta}$. Rearranging terms shows that this means accepting any x weakly below x^*. Similarly, 2 would be best off rejecting any offer x above x^*. The same arguments apply for 3, so that these strategies do support a sub-game perfect equilibrium. Uniqueness of this equilibrium is established in Propositions 2 of the Appendix.

Thus, in the absence of MFN Country 1 can exclude the country it is bargaining with, 2 or 3, by bargaining with its opponent. This allows it to appropriate all the surplus in the transaction. However, MFN prevents such exclusion, giving more bargaining power to countries 2 and 3, and prevents 1 from appropriating all the surplus.

VII. CONCLUSIONS

We have outlined some new approaches to assessing the economic impact of the Most-Favored-Nation Clause. Preliminary analysis suggests that the Clause may not have the powerful liberalizing effects suggested by proponents. Further empirical and theoretical analysis is required before more definitive statements can be made. Such work may also suggest more appealing alternatives to MFN in tariff agreements. The topic is made urgent by the current round of trade negotiations which continue to place MFN in a central position.

APPENDIX

Proposition 1

In the game depicted in Figure 3, it is a dominated strategy for 2 (or 3) to accept any offer by 1 of $x > d - \varphi$ and to reject any offer $x \leq d - \varphi$. Also, it is a dominated strategy for 1 to offer any x other than $x = d - \varphi$.

Proof: It is a dominated strategy for 2 (or 3) to accept a share for 1 exceeding $d - \varphi$ since this gives 2 (or 3) a negative payoff. By refusing all offers 2 can attain his security level of zero.

It is also a dominated strategy for 2 (or 3) to reject any offer by 1 of $x < d - ø$. The proof consists of the iterated removal of dominated strategies. To begin with, 2 will never refuse an offer by 1 or $x = 0$ which gives him a payoff of $d - \varphi$. This is therefore the most 2 can get after two periods. Thus, any offer today which gave 2 more than $\delta^2[d - \varphi]$ could not be rejected by 2. Therefore, any x such that $d-x-\varphi>\delta^2[d - \varphi]$ could not be rejected, i.e, any $x<[1-\delta^2][d - \varphi]$ could not be rejected by 2 in two periods. Thus, I would at most offer an $x=[1-\delta^2][d - \varphi]$ so that at best 2 could hope for $d - \varphi - [1-\delta^2][d - \varphi] = \delta^2[d - \varphi]$ in two periods. Thus, 2 could not reject any x which gave him more than $\delta^4(d - \varphi)$ today – i.e. any x such that $d - x - \varphi > \delta^4(d - \varphi)$ or $x < (1-\delta^4)(d - \varphi)$. Continuing the iteration shows that at the Nth step, any $x < (1-\delta^{2N})(d - \varphi)$ could not be rejected. As $N \to \infty$ this shows that no $x < d - \varphi$ can be rejected by 2 in a perfect equilibrium. The same arguments also show that 3 cannot reject any $x < d - \varphi$. This leaves only the strategy accept any $x < d - \varphi$ and reject any $x > d - \varphi$ for 2 and 3. This rules out any strategies for 1 which do not involve offering $x = d - \varphi$. Offering $x < d - \varphi$ is dominated by offering a slightly higher x which is also accepted. Offering an $x > d - \varphi$ is dominated by offering $d - \varphi$ since the former is rejected and the latter accepted, so that the most 1 can get is $\delta[d - \varphi]$ by offering $x < d - \varphi$, which is less than $d - \varphi$. It is then iteratively weakly dominated for 2 (or 3) to reject $x = d - \varphi$.

Proposition 2

If $ø < (1 - \delta)/2$, the unique perfect equilibrium outcome consists of 1 obtaining $1 - \dfrac{2ø}{1-\delta}$, 2 obtaining $\dfrac{\delta ø}{1-\delta}$, and 3 obtaining $\dfrac{ø}{1-\delta}$.

Proof: As above, it can be shown by iterated removal of dominated strategies that the equilibrium strategies are unique and correspond to 1 offering $x^* = 1 - \dfrac{2ø}{1-\delta}$ and 2 and 3 accepting any x weakly below x^* and rejecting any x above x^*.

It is worth noticing that if $ø \geq 1/2$, there are no gains from agreement possible for the person being bargained with and so no agreement can be reached. If

$1/2 > ø \geq \frac{1-\delta}{2}$, no stationary equilibrium exists. However, two non-stationary equilibria exist. One involves 1 always offering $x^*=1-2ø$ and 2 accepting any $x \leq x^*$ and rejecting any $x > x^*$ while 3 only accepts x which gives 3 at least $\delta ø$. The other has the roles of 2 and 3 reversed. The first equilibrium involves immediate agreement, while the second involves a one-period delay.

NOTES

1 See David (1942), which is the basis for much of this early history.
2 GATT allows a number of exceptions to the application of the MFNC. The three most important are the structure of imperial preferences, the possibility of having customs unions and the exceptions contained in Article XVI of GATT. [Seoul Journal of Economics 1988, Vol. 1, No. 3]
3 This was apparently the effect of the discriminatory reduction of duties on Hawaiian goods in 1875 – Hawaiian sugar exports to the U.S. rose but the U.S. price was unaffected.
4 This mirrors to some extent a finding by Finger that LDC's which took an active part in the Kennedy Round (rather than merely sitting back and demanding special treatment) did far better in that round in terms of concessions received. See Finger (1979, p. 435).
5 See Brander and Spencer (1982), and Eaton and Grossman (1986) on these issues.
6 See, for example, Pasvolsky (1936, p. 77), Curzon (1965, p. 68) and Gruenspecht (1985, pp. 2 and 4).
7 See, for example, "The New Multilateralism: Can the World Trading System Be Saved?" by Camps and Diebold (1986).
8 There are many unrealistic aspects of the game as specified. The payoffs are not based on a model of tariff setting, but rather are meant to capture one effect of the MFNC – that of free riding being possible. The timing of moves is exogenously specified rather than being endogenous, and the cost, o/, incurred by the party being negotiated with is thought of as being independent of x.

REFERENCES

Baldwin, R., and Murray, T. "MFN Tariff Reductions and Developing Country Trade Benefits under the GSP." *Economic Journal* (March 1977): 30–46.

Brander, J., and Spencer, B. "Triff Protection and International Competition." in H. Kierzkowski (ed.), *Monopolistic Competition and International Trade*. Oxford, UK: Oxford University Press, 1984.

Camps, M., and Diebold, W., Jr. *The New Multilateralism*. Council on Foreign Relations, 1986.

Corden, Max. Chapter 2 in R. Jones and P. Kenen (eds), *Handbook of International Economics*. North Holland, 1984.

Curzon, G. *Multilateral Commercial Diplomacy*. London: Michael Joseph, 1965.

Davis, H. *America's Trade Equality Policy*. Washington, DC: American Council on Public Affairs, 1942.

Eaton, J., and Grossman, G. "Optimal Trade and Industrial Policy under Oligopoly." *Quarterly Journal of Economics* (May 1986): 383–406.

Finger, J. "Trade Liberalization: A Public Choice Perspective." In R. Amacher, G. Haberler, and T. Willet (eds), *Challenges to a Liberal International Economic Order*. Washington, DC: American Enterprise Institute, 1979.

Fries, T. "A Theory of the Most-Favored-Nation Principle and Preferential Trade." Mimeo, 1987.

Gruensprecht, H. "MFN: An Economic Analysis of the Most-Favored-Nation Clause." Mimeo, 1985.

Johnson, H. "An Economic Theory of Protectionism, Tariff Bargaining, and the Formation of Customs Unions." *Journal of Political Economy* (June 1965): 256–83. Reprinted in *Aspects of the Theory of Tariffs*. Cambridge, MA: Harvard University Press, 1971.

Pasvolsky, L. "Comments on the Improvement of Commercial Relations between Nations." in *The Improvement of Commercial Relations between Nations and the Problem of Monetary Stabilization*. Paris: Carnegie Endowment International Chamber of Commerce Joint Committee, 1936.

Rubinstein, A. "Perfect Equilibrium in a Bargaining Model." *Econometrica* 50 (1982): 97–109.

Viner, J. "The Most-Favored-Nation Clause in American Commercial Treaties." *Journal of Political Economy* (February 1924). Reprinted as Chapter 1 of *International Economics*. Glencoe, IL: The Free Press, 1951.

——. "The Most-Favored-Nation Clause." *Index, Svenska Handelsbanken, Stockholm* (January 1931). Reprinted as Chapter 5 of *International Economics*. Glencoe, IL: The Free Press, 1951.

——. "Comments on the Improvement of Commercial Relations between Nations." In *The Improvement of Commercial Relations between Nations and the Problem of Monetary Stabilization*. Paris: Carnegie Endowment – International Chamber of Commerce Joint Committee, 1936.

4. Managing International Trade Conflicts: Explanations and Prescription

H. A. C. Conybeare

International trade conflicts have been occurring at least since the times of classical Greece.[1] During the past twenty years, trade issues have become part of the realm of "high politics," the subject of major inter-state threats, negotiations, and occasionally even trade wars. In the current age of "interdependence," trade issues are thought to have a major impact on national welfare, and are therefore too important to be left to lower levels of bureaucracies. Trade policy, some have argued, will determine whether or not we may avoid a global recession of the magnitude of the 1930s, and may have major implications for world political alignments.

Such claims are undoubtedly exaggerated. A major trade war would cost the United States little more than 2 percent of its national income.[2] Unless a country is small and highly trade-dependent, the effect of trade policy is small, compared to other types of policy. It is also highly unlikely that U.S. trade policy alone could effect any major change in international political relationships. Yet trade policy is still a worthy object of study, since a relatively small part of national income may be a large absolute value, and trade policy does have a propensity to spill over into political affairs, irritating otherwise friendly relations. Domestically, trade policy may be of great legislative importance, if it affects concentrated groups of strategically placed actors, even though the absolute and relative value of the trade may be small.

This paper will set out a basis for classifying, explaining and prescribing solutions for international trade conflicts. Most trade bargaining issues may be explicated in terms of size: relatively equal-size countries generally reach cooperative solutions, and larger countries usually impose asymmetric solutions on smaller countries. In the latter case, there is little evidence that large countries provide "free" benefits for small countries, as is argued by proponents of "hegemonic stability" theory.[3] There are other factors that may distort the simple size criterion for assessing trade conflicts; I deal with these under the rubric of the length of time of the conflict, numbers of bargainers, linkage to non-trade issues, and transaction costs.

A FRAMEWORK OF ANALYSIS

There are three basic varieties of trade bargaining relationships. The first is where peaceful trade relations produce high individual and joint gains for both parties, and where disruption of trade would produce high individual and joint losses. Such a situation is likely when there are two simple economies that are highly specialized in producing vital raw materials. There is little incentive to engage in trade-disrupting activities that can only hurt both parties.

A second category of trade relationship is that which may prevail between two large countries. Each country has a strong incentive to impose optimal tariffs as a way of taxing the other and shifting the maximum possible amount of income to itself by changing the prices at which goods are traded (i.e., the terms of trade). Each can gain by imposing unreciprocated taxes on the other's trade, but both lose (relative to free trade), when mutual trade barriers are imposed. This situation is analogous to that faced by two supermarkets engaging in a price war: both would be jointly better off if they colluded and kept prices high, but each would be better off individually if it undercut the other's prices. When both engage in price cutting, both experience mutual losses. The problem is often referred to as the Prisoners' Dilemma game, the dilemma being that each has an incentive to implement a predatory policy (trade taxes or cutting prices), regardless of what it thinks the other will do. If the other does not take similar measures, the initial predator will be much better off; if the other also imposes restrictions, the predator will still be better off than if it had allowed itself to be exploited.

The dynamic prognosis for such conflicts is not quite so dismal. If the interaction is one that persists for a reasonable amount of time, the two parties may actually end up in a highly cooperative pattern of behavior. If each adopts the tactic of "tit-for-tat," punishing the other for predatory practices, they may reach an equilibrium in which they cooperate because mutual cooperation is preferable to mutual conflict. The equilibrium is fragile, however, since the incentive to cheat is ever present. Furthermore, in situations where there are a large number of major negotiating powers, the threat of retaliation may be insufficient to induce cooperation, for reasons that I will discuss below.

A third variation on the structure of trade negotiations is that which may prevail when a large power faces a small power. The smaller power will only hurt itself by imposing trade restrictions against the larger power, either unilaterally or in retaliation. The large power may gain by imposing predatory trade taxes on the small power, even if the small power retaliates. When the structural asymmetries in the bargaining situation are of this magnitude (technically speaking, when the small country cannot change the prices at which it trades with the large country), the outcome is likely to be one where the small country suffers the large country's tariffs, and makes large concessions in order to try to alleviate the degree of predation.

There is ample historical evidence for all three conjectural variations. The examples cited below are anecdotal and too few in number to be considered valid tests of the above hypotheses. Their function here is simply to illustrate both the essential aspects of the above typology, to introduce some of the many intervening variables that may distort or offset the effects of relative size, and to emphasize the need for sensitivity to the historical uniqueness of individual trade conflicts.

THE ANCIENT AND MEDIEVAL WORLDS

There are few international trade taxing conflicts prior to the late medieval period. A principal reason is that the period fits the characteristics of the first type of trade negotiating framework cited above. In classical Greece, for example, trade patterns were highly complementary exchanges of raw materials that were vitally needed by each party to the transaction (or, as an economist would say, they were low elasticity of demand items). When all parties to a transaction are extremely vulnerable to its disruption, the incentive to engage in trade-disrupting disputes over prices or taxes will be very low. Athens, for example, exported wine and olives, and imported grain. Trade disputes that did occur were likely to be quickly settled through violence, so that negotiations over trade issues per se were rare. During the Dark Ages, from the fall of the Roman Empire to the fourteenth century, trade conflicts were unusual because the value of trade was too low (relative to the value of labor and land) for such issues to be worth a major investment of rulers' resources.

LARGE POWER TRADE CONFLICTS

There have been numerous trade conflicts between large countries able to inflict mutual harm on each other. England and the Hanseatic League of northern German cities fought a trade war over control of the Baltic trade routes, from the middle of the fourteenth to the middle of the seventeenth centuries. England and France virtually closed off trade between each other from the 1650s until 1860, largely as a result of the French desire to protect its "infant" textile industries from English competition, and because of the belief held by both sides that trade war might weaken the ability of the other to seek its global political and military objectives. More recently, the United States and the European Community (EC) have been involved in chronic disputes over sectoral trade in industries such as steel and farm products. The simple theory applicable to such disputes would predict the evolution of a pattern of cooperation through the exercise of strategies of contingent retaliation such as tit-for-tat. Yet such cooperation has often not occurred, or has taken many years to do so.

There are numerous reasons why cooperation may not result from such conflicts. The conflict may not be one of the Prisoners' Dilemma variety. Countries may have incentives to keep the conflict going. In the 1960s "Chicken War" between the United States and the EC, when the EC refused to remove restrictions on U.S. poultry exports, cooperation may not have evolved because the EC's internal political need to satisfy its own farm sector outweighed the costs of U.S. retaliation.

Cooperation may also be prevented in trade disputes between large countries if one or both parties believe that if the other is punished long enough it will give up the stakes. In the case of the two supermarkets cited above, their price war may lead them to cooperate and fix prices, but it may also lead them to think that by prolonging the price war, the other firm will go out of business. This is especially true if there is some asymmetry of strength between the parties.

This produces a phenomenon known to economists as the "chain store paradox," following the parable of a chain store that eschews the benefits of collusion with smaller rivals and seeks the larger benefits of putting them out of business, albeit at some cost.[4]

In some cases lack of cooperation may be a result of very high transaction costs to bargaining. This is particularly true of the pre-modern period. During the Anglo–Hanseatic wars, negotiations were hampered by domestic disunity on both sides, long delays in sending emissaries to the other side, and the high cost of diplomacy in an era when most rulers lived from hand to mouth. One of the reasons for the English establishment of regulated trading companies (from the fourteenth century) was to force the private sector to bear some of these onerous transaction costs, which will at best delay negotiations and at worst remove the gains from any negotiation at all.

Most large power trade disputes arise during periods of sectoral or macro-economic depression. Economic hardship will (if states have declining marginal utility for income) raise the incentive to indulge in predatory income transfers, even in the face of retaliation.[5] The Anglo-Hanse trade wars began during a major European recession, coinciding with the plague. Recent U.S.–EC trade conflicts over steel have occurred at a time when the steel sector of the industrial countries has been suffering a slow and painful decline. Several European tariff wars occurred during the agricultural recession of the last thirty years of the nineteenth century, when larger European countries shut out their smaller suppliers.

Finally, trade conflicts between major powers may not evolve into cooperation when there are problems in accurately directing sanctions. The Anglo–Hanse wars provide one example of this: the Hanseatic League suffered from attacks on its shipping by English privateers and, being unable to retaliate against the privateers, compensated its merchants by seizing the goods of English merchants, who would in turn obtain a "letter of reprisal" from the English authorities to do the same, leading to ever-escalating rounds of retaliation.

In the modern period there is a similar problem: the Most-Favored-Nation (MFN) rule, which requires tariff concessions negotiated between two parties to be extended to third countries. The result is a "public good" problem, in which countries have an incentive to refuse to negotiate because they cannot deny the benefits of the negotiations to other countries. When countries A and B agree on a tariff reduction on commodity i, country C, which also exports commodity t, will derive free benefits. If this problem of "free riding" becomes too great, the trade negotiating system will break down, as did occur during the Smoot-Hawley tariff wars of the 1930s.

ASYMMETRIC TRADE CONFLICTS

Cases of small countries involved in trade disputes with large countries exhibit much less variation, mainly because small countries realize their vulnerability and either take care not to provoke larger powers or give in quickly when disputes do arise. A few deviant cases exist. During the late nineteenth century, tariff wars occurred between France and Switzerland, France and Italy, and between

Germany and Russia. In each case the wars were largely provoked by the smaller power, which was then severely punished and forced to make large concessions in order to return the trading relationship to a semblance of cooperation.

Several general factors may induce a small country to initiate a trade war that may not otherwise appear to be in its interest. The Swiss objected to the high rates of the Meline Tariff of 1890, and hoped (mistakenly) that a provocative demonstration of resolve might induce France to give them special concessions. In two cases, Germany's tariff war with Russia from 1893 to 1894, and France's tariff war with Italy from 1886 to 1898, the smaller powers appear to have misperceived the stakes, thinking that the larger power needed their agricultural exports and would be critically hurt without them. This was also a time of major agricultural recession in Europe, and agricultural exporters, like Italy and Russia, were desperately trying to avoid being shut out of their traditional markets, which may have made them more belligerent than would normally be prudent for smaller powers.

In addition, there were domestic interests in the small countries that stood to gain from the tariff wars even though the country as a whole might lose. These included nascent manufacturing interests that sought protection from the exports of Germany and France, and cared little about French or German retaliation. This is another public good problem: domestic interests may benefit from trade conflict and cannot be denied its benefits (at least not through foreign retaliation).

These asymmetric tariff wars were also exacerbated by the incentives facing the larger powers. France, for example, needed to punish Italy in order to set an example for the many other small powers with which it had MFN treaty relationships (and might be encouraged to make similar demands), and because any concessions granted to Italy would have to be extended to all other countries with which France had trade treaty relationships. The dispute with Italy also became linked to Italy's membership in the Triple Alliance with Germany (renewed in 1887), and France prolonged the tariff war by demanding that Italy leave the alliance as a precondition for ending the tariff dispute. Both France and Germany also had agrarian interest groups that actively promoted these tariff wars with smaller agricultural suppliers.

In recent times, small countries have been more cautious in their dealings with larger powers. During the Smoot-Hawley period, most small countries were careful not to retaliate directly against large countries, preferring to seek the protection of a regional hegemon or to attempt to band together with other small powers. This is also true of contemporary trade politics. The small countries hurt by, for example, U.S. textile and steel quotas, have not retaliated.

ASYMMETRY AND HEGEMONIC STABILITY

I have suggested that asymmetric trade bargaining solutions will result in skewed outcomes in which the smaller country will be forced to suffer higher tariffs at the hands of the larger country, while at the same time lowering its own tariffs. There is a major body of literature in international political economy that directly contradicts this proposition: the theories of "hegemonic stability." These theories propose that when large countries dominate a trading environment they will actually behave in a benevolent fashion, providing a lower (not higher) level of trade barriers. Hegemonic stability theorists make this argument on the grounds that freer trade is a public good (i.e., a benefit to the world from which no trading country can be excluded), and that hegemonic countries benefit enough from unhindered trade that they will provide an open trading system "free" to the rest of the world. In this view, it is the small countries that exploit the hegemon, not the other way around.

The theory of hegemonic stability appears, however, to be both theoretically and historically flawed. Free trade is not a public good, since countries can easily be excluded from its benefits. The only true publicness in the system would be if countries adhered to the MFN rule and allowed others to free-ride on the negotiation system, in the manner noted above. Such free-riding can easily be constrained, and has historically been constrained, as I will suggest below in discussing the Smoot-Hawley period. Furthermore, even if the MFN rule is left unconstrained (i.e., there is a genuine public good in the system), the economic benefit of large countries is better served by preying on smaller powers, not by being benevolent. The first best economic policy for a hegemon should always be predation.

The theory also seems inconsistent with the historical record. Large countries throughout history have generally used their power to restrict trade for their own benefit, not to provide free trade. When the Athenians controlled the Bosphorus, they taxed trade heavily. The Romans imposed much higher trade taxes on trade that moved over the frontier of the Empire than on intra-empire trade. Late medieval England, possessing a monopoly on the supply of the wool to Europe, similarly imposed heavy taxes on trade. Both England and France raised their import duties to high levels as they became global world trading powers from the sixteenth to the nineteenth centuries. The United States imposed high trade taxes until after World War II, long after it had become the major world trading power.

Hegemonic stability theorists cite two periods of history in which they see hegemons providing free trade as a public good to the rest of the world: nineteenth-century Britain and the United States after World War II. Britain's turn to free trade in the 1840s was, however, less likely to have been due to any national interest of Britain as a hegemon than to domestic interest-group factors. Free trade benefited a powerful lobbying force at the time, the cotton textile manufacturers, who both imported raw materials and produced more than 50 percent of the value of British exports.[6] They hoped that free trade in Britain would lead foreign countries to adopt similar policies and so expand their export markets. In pursuit of this goal, the cotton textile producers provided much of the financing for the Anti-Corn Law League, the primary parliamentary lobbying force for free trade.

The U.S. policy of promoting free trade after World War II is also suspect as evidence for theories of hegemonic free trade. In the first place, the United States has used strict "principal supplier" rules in trade negotiations, giving concessions only on commodities exported to the United States by one or a few countries that can offer equivalent concessions of goods exported by the United States, hence there has been little in the way of free public goods offered to the rest of the world. During the GATT Kennedy Round from 1964 to 1967, usually cited as the crowning achievement of the U.S. drive for free trade, 94 percent of concessions granted by the United States were on imports originating in other participating countries, and 78 percent were on imports from only ten countries (i.e., those large enough to give equivalent concessions).[7] Insofar as the United States ought to be given some credit for promoting postwar tariff reductions, it is more likely that we will also find the reason in domestic interest-group factors (the demands of U.S. exporters of manufacturers), than in any hegemonic goal of free trade.[8]

SANCTIONING AND ASYMMETRY

Trade politics in the interwar period brings together several of the bargaining problems cited above, namely, the problem of accurately directing sanctions in the presence of MFN rules and the issue of predicting the trade policy of a hegemonic power. The Smoot-Hawley tariff wars began in the early 1920s, when international tariff negotiations started to break down, and illustrate the crippling effect on the international trading system, when both hegemonic predation and public good problems are present.

The system had not broken down prior to this period because there were only two major trading powers in the negotiation game, France and Germany. Both had two-tier tariff systems that could effectively mete out geographically discriminatory sanctions (a low tariff for cooperative countries and a high one for others). Furthermore, most trade treaties were for long periods of time (ten to twenty years), locking in the aggregate global benefits of tariff treaties, and set to expire all at once, so that multiple public good or free-riding problems could be dealt with easily and simultaneously. After World War 1, there were many more trading powers in the negotiating system, including new European states, countries that had hitherto been clients of a larger state (e.g., Canada, Australia), and countries that had been peripheral to the system (e.g., Japan, Brazil). The result was a major sanctioning problem, if MFN rules were to be sustained. Treaties were also much shorter and staggered, leading to cycles of recontracting as countries sought to change the terms of treaties when new treaties created free-riding problems.

The period immediately after World War 1 also presented another problem: the emergence of a major trading power, the United States, that behaved in a manner consistent with the asymmetric model presented above. With the passage of the Fordney-McCumber tariff of 1922, the United States declared that its tariff were not negotiatable, but demanded the benefits of all other countries' negotiations, under threat of retaliation. The United States attempted both to free-ride on the MFN system and to exercise its power as an emerging hegemon. This tactic had some success in the 1920s but finally broke down with the wave of global retaliation against the Smoot-Hawley tariff of 1930.

Trade retaliation in this period took two forms: a general rise in trade barriers and the construction of geographically discriminatory barriers in order to overcome the public good problem inherent in the MFN rule to which most countries still adhered. Geographic discrimination was achieved by the use of quotas, exchange controls and regional free trade arrangements. Their purpose was to enable trade negotations to resume after a period in which the MFN rule, combined with the large numbers of actors in the system, and the free-riding, predatory behavior of the United States, had caused the negotiating system to grind to a halt.

The next two decades of U.S. trade policy were taken up by the effort to extract the United States from this predicament in a way that both preserved the benefits of being a predatory hegemon imposing high tariffs on smaller countries, and brought the United States rather undeserved credit for leading the world back to freer trade. U.S. policy took the form of the Reciprocal Trade Agreements Amendment of 1934, which empowered the President to negotiate tariff reductions. However, contrary to the mythology of free trade embedded in the hegemonic stability view of the world, this was a change in tactics rather than strategy.

First, the United States limited the commodity coverage of negotiations, so that most concessions were limited to goods for which there was little import-competing production in the United States. Second, the trade agreements were based on the principal supplier technique of negotiating only with countries that were the major suppliers of particular commodities to the United States. This enabled the United States to adhere to the MFN rule while offering geographically discriminatory tariff concessions that were sufficient to induce individual countries to negotiate in a bilateral environment in which the superior bargaining strength of the United States could be brought to bear.

Third, most of the trade agreements concluded prior to 1948 were with small, weak countries exporting raw materials to the United States, so that in addition to the bargaining asymmetry, the effective rate of protection fell much less than the nominal rate of protection.[9] Since two thirds of U.S. tariff concessions prior to 1948 were on raw materials, the resulting fall in tariffs was much greater for raw materials than for manufactures, and it is safe to assume that the effective rate of protection fell by much less than the nominal rate (the latter fell from around 55 percent in 1930 to about 40 percent by 1940).[10]

STRATEGIC INDUSTRY CONFLICTS

The discussion so far has implicitly assumed that trade conflicts arise with regard to the overall national level of tariff protection. However, it appears to be increasingly the case that trade conflicts are industry specific. The United States and the EC, for example, may have a major conflict over trade in steel, but otherwise have a peaceful commercial relationship. Industry-specific trade conflicts are likely when the market for internationally traded goods is oligopolistic, resulting in the existence of "pools" of supernormal profits that would not be present in a more competitive market. The state may set in place taxes (such as tariffs) or subsidies that will force foreign firms to reduce production, allowing domestic oligopolists to secure a larger share of this profit pool, at the expense of foreign firms.

I will leave aside some of the more difficult problems of the strategic industry approach to trade policy (i.e., how do we judge the foreign firm's production response to our tariffs? How do we know, in a world of internationally diversified portfolios, what firms are "foreign" and what firms are "domestic"). The relevant question here is whether strategic industry trade conflicts set up different types of trade conflict scenarios from the ones previously suggested above.

An obvious problem with strategic industry policy, as with optimal tariffs, is that other states can do the same, and the result may be mutual losses. One may infer that size should again be a good initial predictor of outcomes. Two large countries, each subsidizing or protecting their firms, should be in a Prisoners' Dilemma situation from which both will eventually extract themselves. In the early 1980s, the United States, the EC and Japan reached such a cooperative state by dividing up their steel markets, after pursuing the strategic industry policies of protection and subsidization for about fifteen years. In the international air passenger market, similar market-sharing agreements are reached (e.g., the Bermuda Two agreement between Britain and the United States in 1977), again after the United States has helped its airlines by restricting foreign carriers' access to U.S. gateway cities, and foreign governments have subsidized their carriers. The current U.S.–EC agricultural export subsidy wars should lead to similar restraints. A newly emerging issue with the same type of payoff structure is the conflict between the United States and the EC over the market for wide-bodied passenger aircraft, and particularly over the EC subsidies for the Airbus.

The case of an asymmetric strategic industry conflict will be slightly different from the asymetric optimal tariff case, since a small country should gain from an unreciprocated subsidy of its own oligopolist (unlike the optimal tariff case described above, where the small country hurts itself with an unreciprocal tariff). In a mutual subsidy war, the smaller country will have a higher opportunity cost per dollar of subsidy funds, and it will run out of subsidy funds sooner, than the larger country. If the large country can always "out-subsidize" the smaller country, the latter is better off giving up and allowing the large country to take its larger share of the market (i.e., it is better off being exploited than retaliating). I do not know of any subsidy wars between big and small countries, which is not surprising, since the theory predicts that such wars should not occur.

If each is trying to subsidize its oligopolists indirectly, through protecting domestic markets, the outcomes will be different again. The small country can gain from unreciprocated protection of its domestic market, but may lose (relative to free trade) if it protects its oligopolist's domestic market at the expense of being excluded from the market of the large country. Nevertheless, it is better off under mutual protection than allowing the large country to protect its market without retaliating, since retaliation will at least allow its home firm to keep its small domestic market. The large country should be better off with mutual protection than with free trade, since its oligopolist will prefer all of its domestic market to half of its domestic market and half the market of the smaller country. The game is constant sum (the sum of the two domestic markets), with little basis for cooperation.

The airline industry again may be an example. Australia would be better off if its carriers had half the Australian domestic market and half the U.S. domestic market, assuming that Australian carriers could compete in the U.S. market. Given that the United States protects its domestic market against foreign carriers, Australia is better off doing the same. U.S. carriers are better off with mutual protection, preferring all the U.S. market than half of both. The current policy of shutting out developing country steel producers from U.S. markets may be similarly explained. Since the United States is the largest steel market in the world, U.S. producers are better off with all of their domestic market than with any international market competition. This interest was fulfilled by the 1984 decision of the Reagan Administration to reduce foreign steel imports to 20 percent of the U.S. market, through shutting out developing country suppliers.

A SYNTHESIS

A theory of international economic conflict based on relative size would predict that such conflicts should rarely escalate into sustained trade wars (i.e., periods of repeated, prolonged and high-intensity mutual retaliation). This should be true because of the ease of conveying threats that are both credible and effective – either because strategies of contingent retaliation will quickly remove the gains from predatory policies between large countries, or else because asymmetry will be quickly manifested in a manner that will usually (the one exception being the last-mentioned strategic industry market share case) induce the weaker party to back down and accept the best deal it can get. This generalization is historically well supported: trade conflicts rarely do escalate to the point of trade war. Yet it is also true that the size-based prediction of cooperative conflict resolution is not always consistent with outcomes. Credible threats do not always work, and in order to explain why trade conflict may escalate into war, one may need to introduce other variables that affect outcomes.

The examples cited above suggest several reasons why trade conflicts may escalate in spite of the existence of asymmetries or tit-for-tat punishment, both of which ought to shorten such disputes. These are time, numbers of actors, linkage to non-trade issues, and transaction costs.

The introduction of a time dimension may help dampen trade conflicts, as it provides the opportunity for the making and implementing of credible threats of retaliation. However, there are at least two ways in which time may also promote more lasting conflicts. First, a dynamic conflict may inspire one or both sides to prolong the battle in order to exhaust the other party and force them to withdraw (the chain store problem). Many trade wars have undoubtedly been prolonged by such incentives. Long trade wars between Venice and Genoa in the thirteenth century, England and the Hanse from the fourteenth to the seventeenth century, and between England and Holland in the seventeenth century, ended with one side simply giving up. The same incentive exists in asymmetric disputes: a large country may feel the need to prolong a trade dispute with a small country in order to deter future challenges to its position. The case of France and Italy in the late nineteenth century, cited above, may be an example.

Second, time may discourage settlement of trade conflicts if one of the parties believes that the situation will become more unfavorable over time. One reason that Russia provoked a tariff war with Germany in the 1890s was that Germany had been diversifying its sources of agricultural supplies away from Russia, so that the latter, feeling that a tariff war was inevitable, was better off having the war sooner rather than later, while it still had some leverage in German markets.

A second problem occurs when trade conflicts involve large numbers of actors. This raises sanctioning issues of the kind I have discussed above. The problem exists at both the domestic and the international levels. At the international level, the major issue is adherence to MFN rules, which encourage non-participation in the tariff reduction process, and free-riding behavior of the kind pursued by the United States in the 1920s. The primary solution is to constrain the operation of the MFN rule. The sanctioning issue also operates at the level of domestic interest groups. The privateering problem cited above is one example, but the problem is still present today. It is in the interests of the U.S. steel industry to lobby for protection, even if it knows the EC will retaliate, since the EC can only retaliate against other U.S. industries. Here the solution is simply to have stronger central control of trade policy in order to internalize these effects.

Third, the linkage of trade issues to other political matters may inhibit the solution of the former. Linkage is usually introduced as a means of making it costly for the other party to refuse cooperation. In the early 1980s, for example, Brazil threatened not to pay its bank debt if the United States restricted imports of steel from Brazil. Such linkages rarely work, because they tax the cognitive capacity of decision-makers, create risks, set dangerous precedents, or may not even be taken seriously. An example of the latter would be the U.S. threat in the 1960s to link troop levels in Europe to the latter's cooperativeness in reducing agricultural tariffs. Only when linkage creates large and asymmetric changes in the structure of the interaction is it likely to facilitate resolution of the conflict. In the Russo-German tariff war of the 1890s, for example, Germany was encouraged to end the war when Russia entered a military alliance with France. A more recent example would be the success of France in retrieving its Rainbow Warrior bombers from New Zealand, by restricting the latter's access to EC markets.

Finally, transaction costs can be a brake on any negotiations, particularly in the pre-modern period. In negotiations dependent on contingent retaliation (e.g., tit-for-tat) in order to evolve into cooperation, high transaction costs increase the problem of "noise." This may lead to unstable patterns of cooperation, as trading partners exchange not only intended actions, but random noise. Even in the modern period, high transaction costs may arise simply through the presence of large numbers of negotiating parties. In the extreme case, transaction costs may be high enough to prevent any negotiation at all. One of the reasons why MFN-based negotiations broke down in the 1920s was because of the large numbers of actors in the system.

INSTITUTIONAL MANAGEMENT

The problems discussed above are not insurmountable, but clearly require some careful institutional innovation. The type of trade negotiating system required (assuming that our goal is the global good) is one that will make transaction costs low, encourage countries to believe that they will be punished for uncooperative behavior, proscribe hegemonic predation and discourage tactics of linkage to wider political issues. The GATT certainly scores high on several of these criteria: it provides a forum for negotiation that lowers transaction costs; it tries to isolate trade from other more contentious issues; and it provides universal rules for retaliation. However, it has one major fault. GATT's MFN rule introduces the public good sanctioning problem, and the incentive for countries to hold back from negotiations.

So far, this has been constrained by two practices. One is the principal supplier method of negotiation discussed above. Most GATT negotiations have been based on this technique, with the result that the bulk of trade concessions are exchanged between a small group of large countries. The other is the tendency to remove trade negotiations from GATT altogether. The major trade barriers today consist of bilaterally negotiated quotas. Neither of these solutions is conducive to global welfare gains.

The policy equation is, then, how to retain GATT's central role of reducing transaction costs, legitimating sanctions and spreading the benefits of negotiation globally, while avoiding the tendency for an MFN-based system to break down due to free-riding problems. Allowing negotiations to continue to drift away from GATT will result in the loss of GATT's obvious benefits. Negotiation purely on a principal supplier basis will restrict negotiations to a small group of countries. Some have proposed to give GATT stronger powers, but this is more likely to simply drive its members further away.

The first objective would be to recapture the diversification of trade barriers away from tariffs into non-tariff barriers, such as quotas. Since such measures are too well entrenched to be proscribed, the best we could do would be to devise a common method of measuring them, so that each country's level of protection across industries could be comparable to a common numeraire. Since non-tariff barriers can be measured in terms of their tariff equivalents, this is merely a data collection problem, albeit a massive one.

Once this has been done, the problem would be to devise a GATT-based bargaining system that would encourage globally beneficial negotiations. One possible solution would be to devise a global "points" system. Once all trade barriers were converted to a common index, their negative effect on global welfare[11] could be calculated and countries could be assigned a base level of points, representing the total amount of global welfare reducing protection allowed to them. These points could then be traded across countries. This would allow countries that have a high demand for protection in certain industries (perhaps for domestic political reasons) to buy protection points from other countries, either with financial payment or by trading points.

The scheme might combine the ease of bilateral negotiation (avoiding the MFN problem of free-riding), with avoidance of the negative consequences of the principal supplier solution to the MFN problem (the tendency for negotations to be restricted to small groups of large countries). Under the old principal supplier method, a large country has no incentive to negotiate a tariff reduction that would benefit a number of small countries, since once it had negotiated the reduction with one of the small countries (for a small return concession), all of the small countries would get the concession for free. However, if the "points" are valued according to world welfare losses, a country could get "credit" for tariff reductions that would not occur in a principal supplier framework. If the United States, for example, wished to add protection to a politically important industry, it would need to "buy" some protection points, which it might do by reducing protection on a good (or goods) exported by a larger number of small countries. The scheme would be analogous to the Environmental Protection Agency's system for controlling pollution: firms are given pollution allowances and allowed to trade them.

Such a system might save the United States considerable embarrassment. At the present time the U.S. attempts to takes the high ground in GATT negotiations, arguing for general free trade, while at the same time massively violating the principles it is recommending to the international community. The United States claims not to have quotas; it has "voluntary export restraints." The EC is constantly criticized for its agricultural protection, yet the United States restricts agricultural imports with quotas on, for example, sugar and beef. The developing countries are castigated for restricting the export of U.S. services (e.g., banking, data processing), at the same time as the United States imposes "voluntary" quotas on their exports of steel and textiles. A "points" system may help move it away from such unproductive and pseudo-moralistic posturing, recognizing that domestic politics will always require some deviations from free trade, but allowing these deviations to be measured and traded in an efficient and equitable manner.

CONCLUSION

The factors that produce and prolong trade disputes are many and complex. I have attempted to outline some of the basic variables involved. These are relative size, numbers of bargainers, linkage to non-trade issues and transaction costs. It is unlikely that any negotiation forum can simultaneously ameliorate all of these problems. Yet it may be that with a bit of imaginative institutional innovation, GATT could do a better job of bringing back within its purview much of what it has lost, as trade negotiations have steadily moved off into bilateral talks outside of its formal rule structure.

NOTES

1 This paper draws heavily from my *Trade Wars* (New York: Columbia University Press, 1987).

2 John Whalley, *Trade Liberalization Among the World Trading Areas* (Cambridge, MA: MIT Press, 1985), p. 248

3 C. P. Kindelberger's *World in Depression* (Berkeley, CA: University of California Press, 1973) was the work that inspired this school of thought.

4 Reinhard Selton, "The Chain Store Paradox," *Theory and Decision* 9 (April 1978) 127, 159.

5 Put more simply, if an extra dollar is worth more to you as your income declines, you are more likely to engage in predatory income redistributions as you get poorer.

6 See G. Anderson and R. Tollison, "Ideology, Interest Groups and the Repeal of the Corn Laws," *Journal of Institutional and Theoretical Economics* 141 (June 1985) 197–212.

7 J. Finger, "Trade Liberalization," in R. Amacher, G. Haberler and T. Willett, eds, *Challenges to a Liberal International Economic Order* (Washington, DC: American Enterprise Institute), pp. 421–453.

8 This is, of course, the marxist explanation for U.S. free trade policy; see Fred Block, *Origins of International Economic Order* (Berkeley, CA: University of California Press, 1977).

9 The effective rate of protection is the tariff on an industry's output, adjusted downward to reflect the penalty imposed on the industry by tariffs on its imported inputs. Hence if the United States simply lowers tariffs on raw material inputs, the effective rate of protection for U.S. manufacturers will actually rise. A list of RTAA treaties may be found in Conybeare, *Trade Wars*, table 10.2, p. 254.

10 See U.S. Tariff Commission, *Operation of the Trade Agreements Program* (Washington, DC: U.S. Government Printing Office, 1948), vol. 3, p. 66; vol. 4, pp. 26, 27.

11 This could be measured either as the global deadweight loss resulting from the higher prices of protected commodities, or as the deadweight loss plus the income redistribution effected by the trade restriction (on the grounds that much of this redistribution is wasted in the process of acquiring and administering trade barriers).

5. GATT Tariff Concessions and the Exports of Developing Countries – United States Concessions at the Dillon Round[1]

J. M. Finger

I. INTRODUCTION

At the 1960–61 GATT tariff conference (the Dillon Round) the United States negotiated with the European Economic Community and 11 other developed countries (DC) as well as with six less developed countries (LDC) (Cambodia, Haiti, India, Israel, Pakistan and Peru) and agreed to reduce its duties on products covering some $2 billion of imports in 1960. While this 20% reduction of tariffs on some 20% of dutiable imports was small compared with the 35% cut on almost 55% of dutiable imports achieved in the more recent Kennedy Round, they were more extensive, both in terms of the magnitude of the reductions and extent of import coverage, than the reductions achieved in any of the previous five GATT rounds except the first in Geneva in 1947.

II. PURPOSE AND METHOD

In this paper I present estimates of the effects of these concessions on United States imports, with separate figures for imports from developed countries and from the less developed countries.

Method

An extension of the "Reduced Group, Non-Reduced Group" method of analysis introduced by Krause and also used by Kreinin to investigate the effects of United States concessions at earlier GATT rounds has been employed here. The method involves the selection of a sample of products on which tariff cuts were made (the reduced group), and a corresponding sample of similar products with approximately equal values of imports on which tariffs were not changed (the non-reduced group). The reduced and non-reduced groups are then interpreted as samples from the population of products on which tariffs were reduced and from a population of products similar in every respect except that they were not subject to tariff cuts. The import statistics for 1960 and 1965 are then compared, so as to obtain the percentage movement in value, quantity and unit value for each group, and the difference between the two percentages for each of these is taken as an estimate of the effect of the tariff cuts. Standard z and t tests were used to see whether or not the observed differences between the groups were statistically significant.

Data

A complete revision of United States tariff nomenclature which went into effect in mid-1963 made the collection of "before" (1960) and "after" (1965) data extremely difficult.[2] Though considerable effort was expended in collecting data, the sample included only 9% of the trade on the concessions list (see line 1, Table 1).[3]

Quantity and value of imports data were taken from the United States Census Bureau publications cited in the references, and tariff rates from the State Department report. Changes in value, quantity and unit value for each item were expressed as percentages of the average of their 1960 and 1965 levels, and average changes for the reduced and non-reduced groups were then computed using 1960 plus 1965 value of imports as weights.[4]

III. EXTENT OF THE CONCESSIONS

Not only were the concessions concentrated on manufactures, where the LDCs are relatively small suppliers, but within both the materials and manufactured goods categories the cuts were concentrated on products imported from DCs. Indeed, the cuts affected 11% of United States imports of materials from DCs but only 2% of materials imports from LDCs. For manufactures, comparable figures at 28% and 21%.

As United States bargaining at the Dillon Round was on a bilateral, item by item basis, it is not surprising that more than 70% of United States imports of concession items originated in the country with whom the concession was negotiated. However, "spillover" (imports of concession items from other countries) accounted for 93% of concessions on imports from LDCs – indicating that the major part of benefits to the LDCs resulting from these GATT concessions accrued to them as bystanders rather than as participants.

While this spillover was large relative to concessions granted directly to the LDCs it amounted to only 3% of United States imports from them not directly affected by concessions. In contrast, spillover accruing to DCs amounted to almost 8% of United States imports from these countries which were not directly affected by concessions, reflecting again the understandable fact that the cuts, which were in the main negotiated *with* DCs, were concentrated on products imported for the most part *from* DCs.

IV. EFFECTS OF THE CONCESSIONS ON TOTAL IMPORTS

As was the case with the GATT concessions implemented in the mid-50s and examined by Kreinin (1961), the Dillon Round concessions had a significant effect on United States imports. Lines 3 and 4 of Table 1 show a much bigger

TABLE I *Effects of United States Dillon Round Concessions, 1960–1965*

(Changes in per cent)

	Materials (SITC 0–4 plus 67, 68)			Manufactures (SITC 5–8 less 67, 68)		
	From all countries	From developed countries	From developing countries	From all countries	From developed countries	From developing countries
1. Value of Imports, 1960 ($ millions)						
(a) Concession list	550	432	118	1,446	1,350	96
(b) Included in sample	28	18	10	145	116	29
2. Change of value of total imports	22.6	42.4	4.7	50.0	47.6	72.1
3. Average change of value for sampled items						
(a) Reduced group	118.3	132.9	69.2	47.5	40.0	71.5
	(49)	(45)	(25)	(140)	(140)	(64)
(b) Non-reduced group	43.9	38.5	48.7	28.1	21.7	74.2
	(46)	(42)	(27)	(140)	(140)	(69)
(c) Difference	74.4*	94.4*	20.5	19.4*	18.2*	–2.7
4. Average change of quantity for sampled items						
(a) Reduced group	117.2	134.2	46.0	33.5	24.1	57.3
	(49)	(45)	(25)	(140)	(140)	(64)
(b) Non-reduced group	39.6	51.4	26.7	14.6	7.4	52.6
	(46)	(42)	(27)	(140)	(140)	(69)
(c) Difference	77.6*	82.8*	19.3	18.9*	16.7*	4.7
5. Change of tariff (as % of foreign price)	–2.1	–1.4	–4.1	–2.5–	–2.5	–2.3
6. Average change of unit value (foreign price)						
(a) Reduced group	3.2	–1.2	39.2	14.9	16.6	16.6
	(49)	(43)	(22)	(140)	(139)	(36)
(b) Non-reduced group	2.8	–17.7	22.9	14.1	15.3	27.0
	(46)	(42)	(22)	(140)	(139)	(33)
(c) Difference	0.4	16.5	16.3	0.8	1.3	–10.4
7. Implicit change of domestic price	–1.4	15.1	12.5	–1.5	–1.0	–12.5

Numbers in parentheses are numbers of observations included in each calculation.
*Indicates that the difference between the means is significant at the 99% confidence level

percentage rise for imports of the reduced group than for the control group, whether the calculation is done in terms of value or quantity. In contrast, Krause, in his examination of the effects of the earlier Torquay and Annecy Rounds found that only the few cuts in excess of 30% of the existing tariff levels had a significant impact on imports.

By the mid-50s and especially by the time of the implementation of the Dillon Round cuts, the erosion of specific and compound duties by price inflation as well as the concessions granted at earlier GATT rounds seemed to have taken almost all of the excess protection out of the United States tariff. And by the early 60s Europe and Japan had become competitive with the United States on a wide range of industrial goods, both in terms of comparative costs and in terms of capacity to supply exports on the scale of the United States market. This interpretation is borne out by the significant effects of the concessions on imports of both materials and of manufactures, and also by the small proportion of the tariff cuts which accrued to exporters in the form of higher f.o.b. prices. Calculations in this field are inevitably precarious, but line 6 of Table 1 shows that unit values rose on average by a rather bigger percentage for the reduced group than for the control group, and the small difference provides a rough estimate of the effects of the concessions on the price charged by the foreign exporter. Comparison of this with the cut in the tariff, expressed as a percentage of the foreign price (line 5) suggests that the f.o.b. price of manufactures rose, because of the tariff cuts, by about one-third of the magnitude of the cuts, while about one-fifth of the 2.1 percentage points reductions in the price of materials went to the foreign suppliers. By contrast, Kreinin (1961, p. 317) found a proportion of about half for the mid-50s concessions. In addition, while the 1955–59 cuts examined by Kreinin were of roughly equal magnitude with the Dillon Round cuts, they caused increases of quantity of imports of 12%, while the Dillon Round cuts produced increases of nearly 80% for materials and of nearly 20% for manufactures.

V. DEVELOPED *VS.* LESS-DEVELOPED COUNTRIES

Materials

In value terms, imports of materials from the LDCs lagged behind imports of materials from DCs in to respects. First, disregarding the effects of the tariff cuts, imports from LDCs did not increase as rapidly as imports from DCs, either in total (line 2 of Table 1), or on the sort of products on the concession list (lines 3(*a*) and (*b*)). Second, the effects of the tariff concessions (lines 3(*c*), 4(*c*)) were less on imports from LDCs than on imports from DCs in terms of import value and of import quantity. This, and the observation that the unit value of imports from the LDCs rose more than the unit value of imports from DCs suggest that the elasticity of supply of materials exports is lower in the LDCs than in the DCs.

This lower elasticity of supply could be explained by two factors: (1) specialisation by LDCs in products for which the elasticity of supply is low, wherever they are produced, or (2) less responsiveness on the part of LDC exporters to expanding markets and/or relative price changes.

Additional calculations,[5] some of which are reported in Table 11[6] suggest that the first of these factors is much more important than the second. When the average change of unit value of imports from all countries was recalculated, using imports from LDCs and from DCs as weights, we found that the average change of unit value when weighted by imports from LDCs is much larger than when weighted by imports from DCs, both for the reduced and for the non-reduced group. That is, regardless of their origin, unit value rose more on the sort of products in which the exports of the LDCs are concentrated. Also (Table II, lines 2, 4) calculations of average changes of quantity of imports of materials from each of the country groups indicate that the quantity increase for both groups was less for the products in which developing countries' exports are concentrated. Finally, LDC exports of materials responded to the tariff cuts more strongly than did DC exports for both the LDC and DC baskets. This suggests no lack of supply response on the part of LDC exports.

Viewed another way, comparing rows 1 and 2 with rows 3 and 4 of Table II we see that imports of products in the developed country basket were more responsive to the Dillon Round cuts than imports of products in the developing country basket of exports to the United States. But column *vs.* column we see that basket by basket the supply response of the developing countries to the concessions was at least as strong as the developed countries'.

Manufactures

In contrast with imports of materials, line 1 of Table 1 shows that United States imports of manufacturers from LDCs increased more rapidly than total imports of manufactures.[7] For manufactures of the type on the concession list, lines 3 and 4 show that imports from LDCs grew more rapidly, both in value and in quantity. But the tariff cuts seem to have had a significant impact only on imports from DCs. Imports from the LDCs of products in the reduced and in the non-reduced groups increased by roughly equal percentages.

Cause of Rapid Growth of Imports from LDCs. A detailed look at the results presented in Table II allows us to be confident that the relative increase of United States imports from LDCs resulted from supply increasing more rapidly there than in the DCs, rather than from a disproportionate increase in United States import demand for products in which the LDCs specialise. When the export performances of the two country groups are compared over the same basket of goods – whether the DC or the LDC basket – we see that exports of the LDCs to the United States increased more than exports of the DCs. Also, we note that United States imports of the DC basket from all countries increased in parallel with United States imports of the LDC basket from all countries – ruling out the hypothesis of relative increase of import demand for the LDC basket.

In addition, we note that LDC exporters did much better competing with the strength of DC exporters (the DC basket) than did DC exporters competing with the strength of LDC exporters. Comparing the figures in rows 1 and 2, column F – LDC exports of the DC basket – with those in rows 3 and 4, column E – DC exports of the LDC basket – confirms this. In fact, not only did LDC

TABLE II *Average Changes of Value and Quantity of United States Imports, 1960–1965, Weighted by Imports from Developed Countries and by Imports from Developing Countries*

(Per cent)

	Materials			Manufactures		
	From all countries (A)	From developed countries (B)	From developing countries (C)	From all countries (D)	From developed countries (E)	From developing countries (F)
Adopted country basket †						
Average change of value						
(a) Reduced group	131.8	132.9	151.1	48.4	40.0	92.3
(b) Non-reduced group	40.0	38.5	18.9	27.2	21.8	78.5
(c) Difference	91.8*	94.4*	132.2*	21.2*	18.2*	13.8**
Average change of quantity						
(a) Reduced group	133.8	134.2	149.4	34.0	24.1	84.8
(b) Non-reduced group	53.9	51.4	35.0	13.5	7.4	44.7
(c) Difference	79.9*	82.8*	114.4*	20.5*	16.7*	40.1*
Developing country basket ‡						
Average change of value						
(a) Reduced group	73.2	–7.8	69.2	44.9	14.3	71.5
(b) Non-reduced group	47.4	150.0	48.7	35.1	–28.9	74.2
(c) Difference	25.8*	–157.8	20.5	9.8**	43.2*	–2.7
Average change of quantity						
(a) Reduced group	61.3	–19.1	46.0	32.0	1.3	57.3
(b) Non-reduced group	26.9	133.0	26.7	22.9	–48.2	52.6
(c) Difference	34.4*	–152.1	19.3	9.1	49.5*	4.7

* Denotes significance at the 99% confidence level.
** Denotes significance at the 95% confidence level.
† Averages computed using imports, by product, from developed countries as weights, *i.e.* the averages are $\bar{X}_{2i}$.
‡ Averages computed using imports, by product, from developing countries as weights, *i.e.* $\bar{X}_{3i}$.

exports of the LDC basket expand more rapidly than DC exports of that basket of goods, but LDC exports to the United States expanded even more rapidly for the DC basket than for the LDC basket.

Effects of the Tariff Reductions. As to the effects of the tariff reductions, DC exports to the United States of products on the concession list were significantly affected by the tariff concessions: the average increase of imports from the DC of the reduced group is significantly larger than the average increase for the non-reduced group, for both baskets of goods.

The effect of the concessions on manufactured exports from LDCs seems to be a little more complicated. We see that while LDC exports of the LDC basket of goods to the United States were not significantly influenced by the tariff concessions, their exports of the other basket did respond in a significant fashion. This is consistent with the supposition that LDC exports to the United States are concentrated on products in which the cost difference between the United States and the LDC supplier is so large that a tariff concession equivalent to 2.5% of f.o.b. price is not a significant *additional* export incentive.[8] The large increases of supply of exports from LDCs which account for the increase of exports both of the reduced and non-reduced groups are perhaps responses to the existence of this cost differential rather than to marginal changes of one or more exogenous factors.

But on products which might be called atypical LDC exports (the DC basket) we observe not only a significant increase of supply from the LDC, but also a significant response (especially in terms of quantity) to the marginal incentive of the tariff reductions. This could be explained in several ways. It is possible that production of these products for export from the LDCs is dominated by multi-national firms, who switch their global pattern of production in response to marginal signals such as that provided by the Dillon Round tariff concessions. Or it is possible that the cost difference between the United States and the LDCs on these products is not as large as on the others, so that an opportunity of the magnitude offered by the tariff concessions is not swamped by other incentives to export.

VI. APART FROM THE EFFECTS OF THE CONCESSIONS

With the advantage of hindsight, it is interesting to speculate on the constellation of political forces and objectives which determined the make-up of the United States concessions list. The supposition that the pre-concession screening process had as an objective the minimisation of the effect of each concession on United States imports appears to be too simple a view.

Apart from the effects of the concessions, we find that the sorts of materials on which concessions were made were products of which United States imports were increasing *more rapidly* than total imports of materials. For materials, the mean increase of import value from 1960 to 1965 of both the reduced and non-reduced groups was significantly larger (at the 99% confidence level) than the increase of the total of United States imports.

Again, apart from the effects of the concessions, the opposite pattern seems to apply to imports of manufactures – the hypothesis that the products on which concessions were offered were not those experiencing strong import competition seems to be valid. Imports of products in the non-reduced group (*i.e.* the products similar to those on which concessions were made, but on which themselves no concessions were made) increased significantly less than total imports.

Thus it is possible that the concessions on materials, at least to some extent, were on materials falling into relatively short supply in the United States, and that in reducing duties on these materials the United States was reducing the cost squeeze on the manufacturing sectors which use them as inputs.

The net increase of imports, or increase attributable to the concession (value and quantity), was considerably larger for materials (75–80%) than for manufactures (20%). This again is consistent with the proposition that concessions on imported materials were granted on products the domestic supplies of which were becoming bottlenecks to more advanced stages of domestic manufacturing. The opportunity for a small cost saving seems to have caused a number of users to switch away from domestic sources of supply.

VII. SUMMARY

If we apply the median estimates of the percentage effect of the tariff cuts (Table I, line 3*c*) to the volume of trade affected, we estimate that in 1965 imports were about $700 million higher than they would have been had the United States Dillon Round concessions not been made. Although over 70% of the imports affected by the concessions were manufactured products, 65% of the imports which resulted from these concessions were imports of materials: the explanation is that the percentage effect of the cuts was larger on materials imports than on manufactures.

Almost all of the "additional" imports came from DCs. Using the median percentage figures[9] we estimate that United States imports in 1965 from LDCs were only about $24 million larger than they would have been without the concessions – this amount being about 3% of the increase of imports 1960–65 from developing countries, or less than one half of 1% of the level of United States imports from these countries in 1965.[10]

There seem to be three reasons for the small impact of the United States Dillon Round concessions on LDC exports:

First, these concessions were negotiated primarily with other industrial countries on goods traded primarily among industrial countries.

Second, there is evidence to suggest that the sort of materials on which concessions were made to LDCs are products with relatively inelastic supplies in the short run both in the LDCs and in DCs (*e.g.* bauxite, wooden timber and various unprocessed minerals such as talc, graphite and kaolin).

Third, although LDC exports of some manufactured goods included in the concessions have been expanding rapidly, this expansion seems to be based on cost differences between the LDCs and the United States which are so large that a tariff concession equivalent to a 2 $^{1}/_{2}$% increase of f.o.b. priced no significant *additional* export incentive.

Finally, the results reported here indicate that in those instances in which concessions did apply to them, LDC suppliers responded at least as strongly as their DC competitors, and thus that further concessions negotiated with the LDCs would contribute significantly to the expansion of exports.

NOTES

1 An earlier version was presented at the Econometric Society Meetings, New York, 28 December 1973. I am grateful for helpful comments from R. E. Baldwin, W. B. Reddaway, and an anonymous referee. They are not responsible for any remaining shortcomings.

2 Details of such problems are given in a longer version available from the author.

3 Automobiles and five other large items which could not be traced across the changes in data nomenclature accounted for over half of imports on which concessions were granted. Because the results in Tables I and II which are statistically significant are significant at very high confidence levels and those which are not significant would not have been significant even if the sample size were several times larger (assuming that the values of the test statistics would be the same), the possibility that my conclusions are based on sampling error rather than on fact does not seem abnormally high.

4 While there was a total of 189 products in the reduced group, for a number of these there were no imports from LDCs and for a few others none from DCs. But as changes of unit value could be calculated only for observations for which both 1960 and 1965 imports were non-zero (so that unit value could be determined each year), the number of observations usable for calculating changes of this variable was considerably reduced, especially for imports from LDCs. While the numbers of observations thus excluded from the reduced and non-reduced groups were roughly equal in most cases, elimination of a product from one group was not usually accompanied by elimination of its "partner" from the other group, and as a result the reduced and non-reduced groups used to calculate changes of unit value for the country subgroups were not as closely matched as to composition as the complete groups.

5 Let subscript i (= 1, 2, 3) represent the country groups, *i.e.* all countries, DC, LDC, respectively, and the subscript j represent individual products. The weight W_{ij} is equal to the share of product j in total value of imports from country group i. X represents any one of the three variables' change of value of imports, change of quantity of imports, or change of unit value of imports. The averages in Table II were computed from the formula $\bar{X}_{0i} = \sum_j W_{ij}X_{ij}$. In these calculations, the average change of a variable for a country group is weighted by own imports, *i.e.* imports from that country group. Additional calculations were made using the formulae

$$\bar{X}_{1i} = \sum_j W_{1j}X_{ij}\ (i = 1, 3),\quad X_{2i} = \sum_j W_{2j}X_{ij}\ (i = 1, 3),\quad \bar{X}_{3i} = \sum_j W_{3j}X_{ij}\ (i = 1, 3).$$

Of course $\bar{X}_{ki} = \bar{X}_{0j}$ when $k = i$. The $\bar{X}_{2i} = \bar{X}_{3i}$ for value and quantity are reported in Table II and the other calculations are available on request.

6 Row *vs.* row, Table II compares a country group's performance on one basket with that group's performance on the other basket. Column *vs.* column, Table II compares the relative supply responses of the country groups on the same basket of goods.

7 This trend has continued through 1972. See GATT, *International Trade* 1972, Appendix Table A.

8 A study by the United States Tariff Commission revealed that unit labour cost in the LDC in the assembly of many products imported by the United States averaged about 32% of unit labour costs in the United States in the production of wearing apparel; about 14% of United States unit labour costs in the assembly of such articles as radios,

phonographs, television receivers and related sub-assemblies; and about 27% in the assembly of various manufactures, ranging from baseballs (7%) to scientific instruments (46%).

9 Because the estimate of the percentage effect on imports of manufactures from LDCs is negative, that median volume estimate was taken to be zero.

10 If 95% confidence interval estimates of the percentage effects are used, the value estimate for 1965 from all countries is $400 million. The estimate of the percentage effect and hence the value estimate for LDC exports is not significantly greater than zero at the 95% confidence level.

REFERENCES

Hunsberger, W. S. (1959). "Discussions of Krause," *American Economic Review Papers and Protocol*. May, Vol. 49, pp. 555–8.

Krause, L. B. (1959). "United States Imports and the Tariff," *American Economic Review Paper Proceedings*, May, Vol. 49, pp. 542–51.

Kremin, M. E. (1961). "Effect of Tariff Changes on the Prices and Volumes of Imports," *American Economic Review*, June, Vol. 51, pp. 310–24.

United States Bureau of the Census (1961). *United States Imports of Merchandise for Consumption*, Calendar Year 1960 (Report No. FT 110), Washington.

——, (1966). *US Imports, TSUSA Commodity by Country*, 1965 Annual (FT 246), Washington.

United States Tariff Commission (1972). *Economic Factors Affecting the Use of Items 807.00 and 806.30 of the Tariff Schedule of the United States* (T.C. Pub. No. 339), Washington.

6. Trade Liberalization as Politically Optimal Exchange of Market Access

A. L. Hillman and P. Moser

I. INTRODUCTION

A. Perspectives on Trade Liberalization

THE FORMAL MODELS OF THE theory of international trade provide the analytical framework for two accounts of the phenomenon of trade liberalization, one unilateral and other bilateral. In both accounts, the reason for trade liberalization is related to efficiency gains. In the unilateral framework, governments liberalize to realize gains from trade; the counterpart in practice is the observation that governments with a new-found appreciation of the advantages of freer trade, and in recognition of the adverse outcomes of past protectionist policies, unilaterally dismantle trade barriers.[1] In the bilateral portrayal found in the literature, trade liberalization occurs when countries, that can influence their terms of trade and have levied optimal tariffs on one another, return to a regime of mutually beneficial free trade; efficiency is enhanced as both countries' consumption equilibria are moved onto or closer to the contract curve.[2]

A third account of trade liberalization, that is less formal and more institutionally oriented, describes how liberalization occurs in practice as the outcome of negotiations in which governments seek to secure improved conditions of market access for exporters in foreign markets.[3] In the course of negotiations that are bilateral or are conducted in the multilateral forum of the GATT,[4] governments make reciprocal "concessions" regarding market access in return for like "concessions" from foreign governments. Adherence to reciprocal liberalization agreements is enforced by the prospect of retaliatory denial of access to foreign markets.

This reciprocal market access explanation for liberal trade policies is set within a property rights conception of markets. Property rights are reflected in the presumption that domestic firms, as providers of domestic employment and income, have preeminent rights to sell in their own home markets. Sales by foreigners constitute an intrusion on these rights. Strict adherence to these property rights, however, disadvantages the individuals whose employment and income are tied to a country's export sector, since via reciprocity the restriction of competitive imports is at the expense of the opportunity of sale abroad. Governments are therefore prepared to compromise the rights of some domestic producers to advantage others by agreeing to an exchange of market access, and are prepared to defend free trade when subsequent protectionist pressures arise.

B. Policy Motives

In cases where liberalization is indeed the unilateral corrective response to past protectionist policies, or where governments do indeed announce mutual elimination of optimum tariffs, efficiency as proposed in the standard models can be imputed as the policy motive of government. Efficiency has, on the other hand, a more subsidiary role, if governments are viewed as optimizing agents conducting trade policy in accord with political-support objectives. Income-distribution consequences of trade policy decisions then become prominent, and trade policy is determined with reference to political benefits and costs of acceding to industries' requests for different types of government intervention. This political-economy perspective explains protectionist policies as arising in a system of representative democracy, because the issue of protection for any one industry is not substantive for voters, who have reason to be rationally ignorant regarding policies proposed and adopted, and who in general in any event will not have had the opportunity to separate one issue from other issues in choosing among candidates. The prospects for protectionist outcomes are enhanced because the significance of the issue of protection for an industry is diminished for any particular voter by the dispersion of the costs of protection of an industry over society at large, whereas the benefits of protection are on the other hand more concentrated, in accruing to residual claimants to industry rents. The more diffused coalition of losers from protection and the higher stakes of the beneficiaries combine to make protection a politically optimal response, hence the observed Pareto-inefficient protectionist policies.[5]

Yet trade liberalization is nonetheless observed to occur, raising the question: if the political-economy explanation for the determination of international trade policy is appropriate, why do governments liberalize trade? The observation that reciprocal trade liberalization takes the form of exchange of market access provides the basis for an answer; since exchange of market access is predicated less on national aggregate welfare or Pareto-efficiency concerns than on implications for sectoral or industry incomes and employment.[6] The benefits to a country's export sectors underlie governments' quests to secure foreign market access, and it is, conversely, adverse affects on domestic import-competing sectors that underlie the reluctance to grant market access. Such calculation of trade-offs among beneficiaries and losers from different policies is characteristic of governments choosing trade policy to maximize political support.[7] That is, trade liberalization via exchange of market access emerges not as the consequence of pursuit of efficiency objectives, but via the implications for domestic political support from individuals who, by association with different industries, gain or lose from market access.[8]

In this political-economy framework, consumers gain from trade liberalization, but nonetheless have a limited role in influencing the determination of liberal trade policies that are to their advantage.[9] Property rights to markets concern industry interests. The property rights of import-competing industries to domestic markets are respected in consideration of political support from individuals whose incomes and asset values are sustained by protection, and these same property rights are comprised in consideration of political support from individuals who gain when export industries are granted, via reciprocity, foreign market access. The politically optimal trade policy trades off this satisfaction and dissatisfaction of domestic producers with the "concessions" made to foreign producers. Gains to consumers from the liberalizing consequences of exchange of market access for producers are incidental.[10]

C. Mutual Political Gain from Trade Liberalization

In this paper we show, against the background of a specific-factors or Ricardo-Viner model that captures industry interests and income-distribution effects of trade policy, how the incentive for exchange of market access derives from mutual political gains to liberalizing governments. A foundation for explaining trade liberalization is thus offered that differs from the descriptions of liberal trade policies as emerging from the pursuit of efficiency or social-welfare maximizing objectives by apolitical governments. The political-economy explanation for *trade liberalization* that we develop complements the political-support maximizing explanation for *protectionist* policies.

Two aspects of the model that we formulate merit consideration.

(i) Small and large countries: The countries that we consider are not "small", in the sense of the trade literature of confronting given world prices at which producers can sell any quantities they wish in "world" markets; quite evidently, in the typical circumstances of the "small country" model of international trade, issues of foreign market access do not arise.[11] Terms of trade consequences of trade restrictions are thus present; however, we view governments as not primarily concerned with the implications for national welfare of terms of trade changes, but rather predicating policies on how terms of trade changes affect political support via effects on incomes in import-competing and export industries.

(ii) Tariff revenue and political benefits: In addition to confining our attention to countries that are not "small", we also confine ourselves to democracies with developed fiscal and tax systems wherein (1) tariff proceeds are not significant sources of government revenue and (2) government officials or bureaucrats have no direct claims to revenues accruing to the Treasury. The disposition of revenue from trade restrictions imposed on a particular industry then has no particular consequences for the political support that the politicians composing the incumbent government can secure; political support associated with the exercise of discretion over trade policy requires benefitting either import-competing or export industry interests, and in these circumstances tariff revenue cannot be designated for this purpose.[12] The revenue accrues to the Treasury where it is unidentifiably lost in terms of perspective benefit from political allocation. Revenue associated with a trade policy decision is, however, a source of political gain if it can be transformed to a form that allows political designation of the beneficiaries.

We shall demonstrate under these conditions that (1) beginning from initial circumstances where governments have independently chosen political-support maximizing protectionist policies,[13] exchange of market access always permits the realization of mutual gains in domestic political support for liberalizing governments, but (2) although there are mutual political gains from negotiated trade liberalization, a change in policy preferences that leads a government to favor more liberal trade evokes increased protection in foreign markets. Hence a very fundamental distinction emerges between outcomes that arise as the consequence of negotiated reciprocal liberalization, and outcomes when one country's government liberalizes and then proposes to another country's government that it do likewise. In the first case, the foreign government's political self-interest leads it to reciprocate the liberalization; in the second case, political self-interest leads the foreign government to respond to liberalization with *increased* protection, which is then a source of potential conflict between trading partners.

We shall also show how political-support motives of governments constrain and define trade liberalization possibilities, and we shall distinguish and compare incentives to participate in predetermined as opposed to bilaterally negotiated liberalization arrangements.

We begin with the vantage for one government whose policies are interdependent with market access offered to exporters abroad, and then proceed to consider political motives underlying incentives to exchange market access.

II. THE VANTAGE FOR ONE GOVERNMENT

A. The Economy

For purposes of exposition, we adopt a two-good specific-factors framework[14] that associates industry interests with claims to the returns to industry-specific capital, physical and human. In the export sector, owners of specific capital earn a real return Γ that is increasing in the domestic relative price $P^d(\equiv P^d_X/P^d_M)$ of that sector's output; in the import-competing sector the real return π is decreasing in P^d.[15] A change in the relative price P_d leads competitive markets to reallocate mobile factors between the export and import-competing sectors, and with constant-returns-to scale neo-classical technologies, marginal products of specific capital respectively increase and decrease in the sectors which mobile factors enter and exit, hence establishing the following relationship between relative output prices and real incomes of undiversified claimants to industry-specific capital:

$$\Gamma = \Gamma\,(P^d) \quad \Gamma' > 0 \tag{1}$$

$$\pi = \pi\,(P^d) \quad \pi' < 0. \tag{2}$$

Consequently, when a tariff t is imposed on imports, residual claimants in the import-competing and export sectors respectively gain and lose, as expressed in

$$\Gamma = \Gamma\,(t) \quad \Gamma' < 0 \tag{1'}$$

$$\pi = \pi\,(t) \quad \pi' > 0. \tag{2'}$$

The tariff, if not non-prohibitive and non-zero, is a source of government revenue. The revenue is distributed in a neutral manner over the population.

Neutral distribution implies that the revenue is not directed to losers from protection, nor to any other specified group.

B. Effects of the Trading Partner's Policy

The trade policy of the foreign country affects real income of specific factors in the domestic economy if we are not dealing with a "small" country that confronts given relative prices in the international market. As we have observed, such a country confronts no problems of market access for exports. We wish, however, to consider an economy for which market access abroad is constrained by protectionist barriers.

A tariff T imposed by a foreign government is an export tax from the perspective of exporters. Or alternatively the foreign tariff is a price of foreign market access. Under competitive conditions, the relative prices received by exporters from domestic and foreign sales are equal. Hence via arbitrage,

$$P^d = P^f(1 - T) \tag{3}$$

with the relative price in the foreign country denoted as $P^f (\equiv P^f_X / P^f_M)$. An increase in foreign protection, from T to T', deteriorates the terms of trade of the domestic economy;[16] as depicted in Figure 1, the price received for exports falls from P^d to $P^{d\prime}$ $(= P^{f\prime}(1 - T'))$.

Increased foreign protection also has domestic income distribution consequences. Demand for the export sector's output falls due to the increased foreign tariff, and imports are reduced since imports become relatively more expensive. Domestic mobile factors will respond by moving into the import-competing sector. The deteriorated conditions of foreign market access for exporters therefore benefit residual claimants to return to factors specific to the domestic import-competing sector, while claimants to capital specific to the export sector lose.

C. The Symmetry between Domestic and Foreign Protection

An increase in a protective domestic tariff improves the terms of trade. As demonstrated in Figure 2, an increase in the tariff from t to t' increases the relative domestic price of imports from $1/P^d$ to $1/P^{d\prime}$ while the relative foreign supply price of imports declines from $1/P^t$ to $1/P^{t\prime}$. The increased price for imports increases domestic import-competing output, and the improved terms of trade reduces the demand for domestic exports. Hence, an increase in the domestic tariff benefits residual claimants in the domestic import-competing sector and disadvantages residual claimants in the export sector. As indicated in Figure 3, via competitive arbitrage, the domestic relative price of imports $\left(\frac{P^d_M}{P^d_X} = \frac{1}{P^d}\right)$ is equal to the relative foreign supply price $\left(\frac{P^f_M}{P^f_X} = \frac{1}{P^f}\right)$ with the levy of the tariff added,

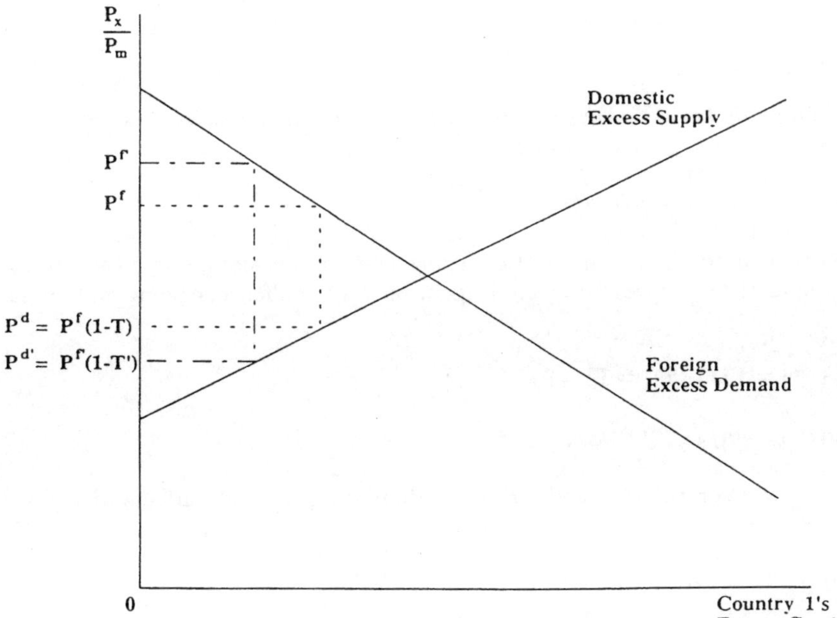

FIGURE 1

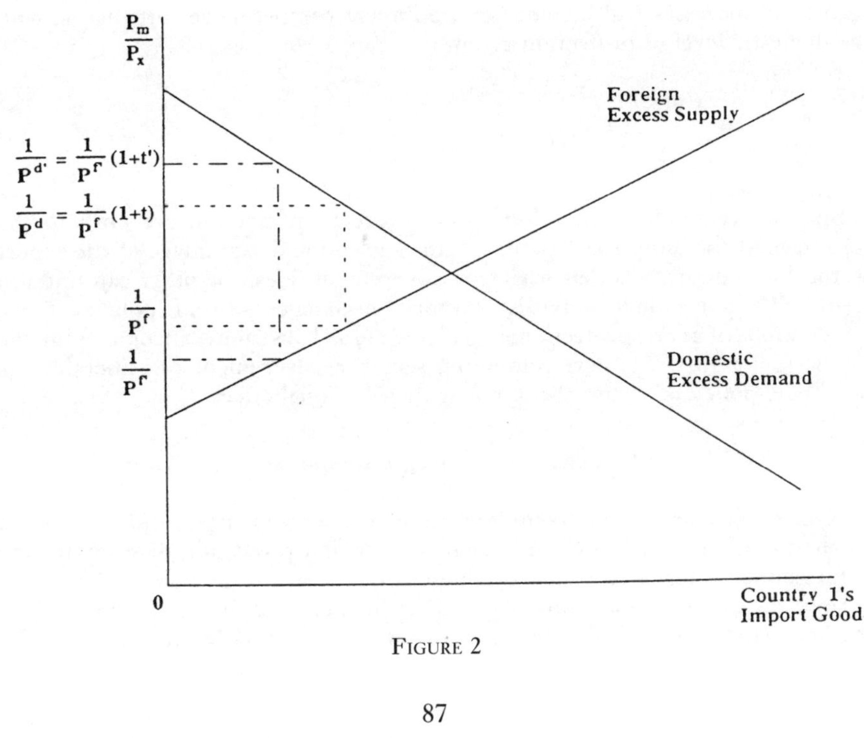

FIGURE 2

$$\frac{1}{P^d} = \frac{1}{P^f}(1 + t) \tag{4}$$

Combining (3) and (4) establishes the domestic relative price as a function of the protectionist policies adopted by the home and foreign governments,

$$P^d = P^f \frac{(1-T)}{(1 + t)} = f(t, T). \tag{5}$$

Real incomes in the domestic export and import-competing sectors can consequently be expressed as contingent on trade policies at home and abroad via

$$\Gamma(P^d) = \Gamma[f(t,T)] = \Gamma(t, T) \tag{6}$$

$$\pi(P^d) = \pi[f(t,T)] = \pi(t, T). \tag{7}$$

For any given value $\bar{T}$, an increase in domestic protection affects incomes in accord with

$$\frac{\partial\Gamma(t,\bar{T})}{dt} < 0, \frac{\partial\pi(t,\bar{T})}{\partial t} > 0. \tag{8}$$

An increase in foreign protectionism also reduces real incomes in the export sector and increases real incomes in the import-competing sector; that is, with the domestic level of protection given,

$$\frac{\partial\Gamma(\bar{t},T)}{\partial T} < 0, \frac{\partial\pi(\bar{t},T)}{\partial T} > 0. \tag{9}$$

Since increases in either domestic or foreign protection are both to the advantage of the import-competing sector and to the disadvantage of the export sector, the indication is that what one government does, the other can undo in terms of the domestic income-distribution consequences of trade policies. Thus, for example, if more protectionist policies abroad distribute income from the export sector to the import-competing sector, a government can liberalize its own trade policy to secure the opposite distributional effect.

D. Terms of Trade Effects and Strategic Responses

A home government cannot completely undo the consequences of protectionism by the foreign government, since increased foreign protection deteriorates the home country's terms of trade. By liberalizing its own trade policy to counterbalance the distributional consequences of the increased foreign protectionism, the home government is deteriorating its own terms of trade further.

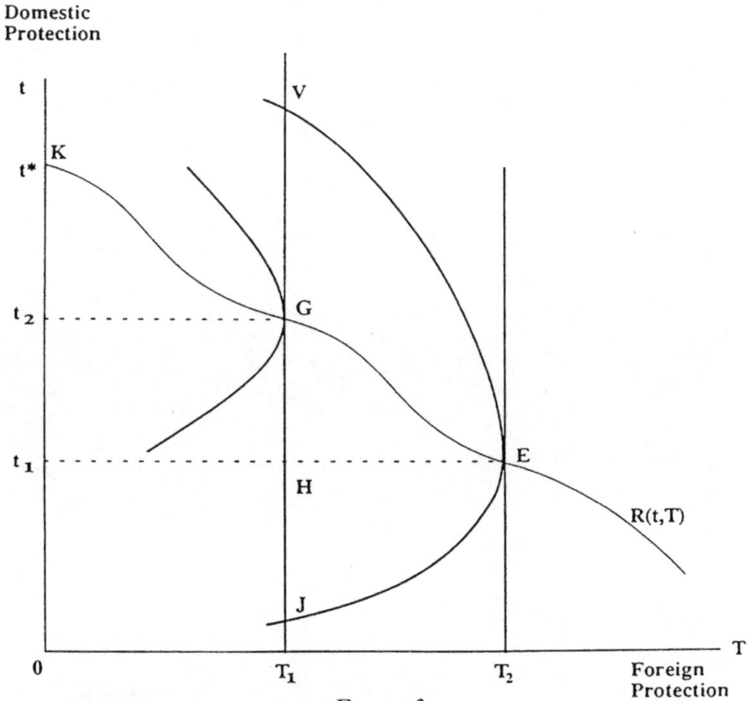

FIGURE 3

Strategically, via this response, the home government would also be granting improved conditions of market access to foreign producers, in return for the deterioration of conditions of market access for its own exporters.

E. Politically Optimal Response: The Reaction Function

The government maximizes political support

$$M[t, T] = M[\Gamma(t,T), \pi(t,T)] \tag{10}$$

(where $M_i > 0$, $M_{ii} < 0$, $i = \Gamma$, π, *and* $M_{\pi\Gamma} > 0$) subject to the effects of protection on real incomes as given by (6) and (7) by choosing t in accord with

$$\frac{\partial M(t,T)}{\partial t} = M_{\Gamma}\frac{\partial \Gamma(t,T)}{\partial t} + M_{\pi}\frac{\partial \pi(t,T)}{\partial t} = 0. \tag{11}$$

How a government responds to increased foreign protection is determined by what is politically optimal, as reflected in the properties of the home government's reaction function indicating how home trade policy changes in response to foreign trade policy. This reaction function is depicted in Figure 3.

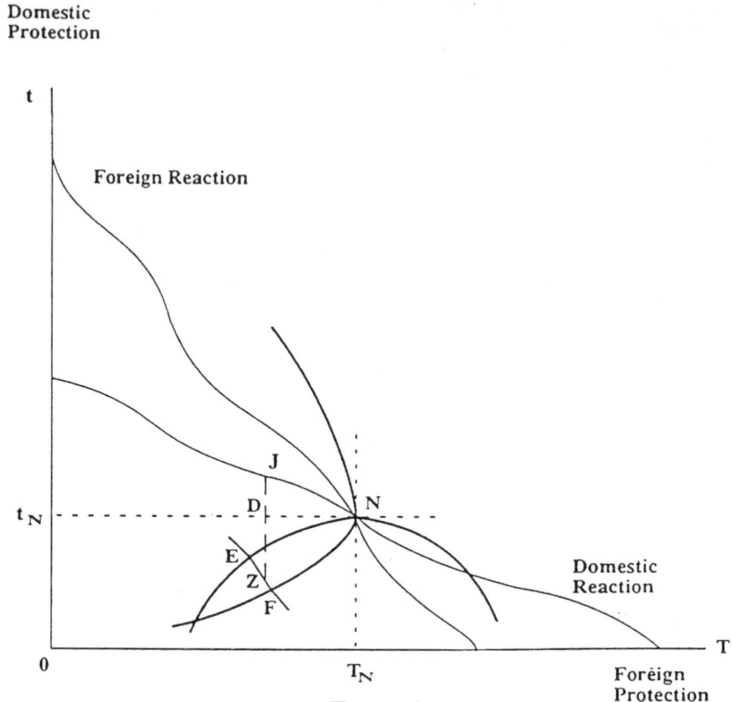

FIGURE 4

When the foreign government adopts a free trade policy, the home government maximizes political support by choosing t^* such that political support is equal at the margin. However, consider the politically optimal response to an increase in foreign protection from T_1 to T_2. The slope of the reaction function described by (11) is

$$\frac{dt}{dT} = -\frac{M_{tT}}{M_{tt}}. \tag{12}$$

Since the government is choosing t to maximize political support

$$M_{tt} < 0 \tag{13}$$

and from (11)[17]

$$M_{tT} = \Gamma_t[M_{\Gamma\pi}\pi_T + M_{\Gamma T}\Gamma_T] + \Gamma_{tT}M_\Gamma + \pi_t[M_{\pi\pi}\pi_T + M_{\pi\Gamma}\Gamma_T] + \pi_{tT}M_\pi < 0. \tag{14}$$

It follows from (13) and (14) that (12) is negative and that the reaction function, $R(t,T)$ has the negative slope depicted in Figure 4.

This negative slope reflects the general principle of politically optimal redistribution, of redistributing the burden of exogenously imposed gains and losses from the group of individuals on whom the initial impact fell to others. Thus, in Figure 4 consider the home government's response to a foreign level of protection T_2. The home government chooses the politically optimal level of protection t_1, reflected in the tangency of an iso-political support contour at the point E on the reaction curve. Now let the foreign government unilaterally liberalize trade by reducing protection to T_1. This unilateral liberalization moves the government off its reaction curve, to H. The move from E to H benefits individuals who are residual claimants in the domestic export sector by offering improved conditions of foreign market access, and disadvantages individuals who are residual claimants in domestic import competing sector. Also, the terms of trade have been improved by the unilateral foreign liberalization. To restore political equilibrium, the government increases the level of domestic protection to t_2, yielding the new political equilibrium on the reaction curve at the point G, so compensating the import-competing sector but also thereby sharing the benefits that accrued to the export sector as a consequence of the improved terms of trade reflected in improved conditions of foreign market access.

From the point G on the reaction curve, the government could return to the lower level of political support at E, either by increasing protection to V to disadvantage the export sector by more than the import-competing sector gains; or by liberalizing to J, to disadvantage the import-competing sector by more than the export sector gains. Political support has therefore increased to G relative to E. Real incomes of residual claimants in both sectors can potentially be increased, due to the terms of trade improvement. Movements along the reaction function towards K yield greater political support. Maximal political support is attained at K when there are no barriers to foreign market access, and when also protection for the domestic import-competing sector is maximal along the reaction curve.

III. EXCHANGE OF MARKET ACCESS

A. The Nash Equilibrium

The Nash equilibrium (t_N, T_N) when each of the two governments independently chooses trade policy to maximize political support subject to the trade policy adopted by the other is depicted at the point N in Figure 4.[18]

B. Mutual Political Gains from Trade Liberalization

There exists a set of mutually politically superior, and more liberal, trade policies than the Nash equilibrium. In Figure 4, such policies lie along EF, the end points of which characterize the range of conflict in negotiations between the governments to determine reciprocal trade liberalization.

Figure 4a depicts a case where mutually politically superior policies include mutual free trade, and hence where a free trade agreement is a politically feasible outcome.

This establishes that (i) governments choosing trade policy to maximize political support can always improve on their political optimization by cooperation to provide mutual exchange of market access for each others' exporters, and (ii) the politically superior outcomes attainable by mutual exchange of market access may or may not include free trade.

C. Why the Mutual Political Gain from Trade Liberalization?

Evidently, a Nash equilibrium with positive levels of protection t and T reflects the political influence of residual claimants in domestic import-competing sectors in each economy in securing policy responses that depart from free trade. A movement away from the Nash equilibrium via mutual liberalization disadvantages the residual claimants in the import-competing sectors in both countries, to the benefit of export sectors. While trade liberalization yields mutual gains from trade and is Pareto-superior to the more protectionist Nash equilibrium, this is not a matter of consequence for a government that chooses discretion over trade policy to maximize political support. The Pareto-inefficiency of the protectionism of the Nash equilibrium clearly reflects this. Political support is predicated on income-distribution consequences of the conduct of trade policy, and in the move from the Nash equilibrium at N to mutually more liberal trade policies, the import-competing sector in each country has unambiguously lost and the export sector has gained, *with no compensation for the losers*. This raises the question, why has there necessarily been a mutual increase in political support as a consequence of mutual trade liberalization?

D. The Prisoners' Dilemma and the Resolution

To address this question, we first specify the nature of the Prisoners' Dilemma that arises here and the manner of the resolution. Consider a unilateral liberalization by the foreign government from the Nash equilibrium, as reflected in a move from N to the point D in Figure 4. As we have seen, the home government's politically optimal response to such unilateral foreign liberalization is to *increase* protection, to the point J on its reaction function; that is, the government shares the benefit of the unilateral foreign liberalization between the export sector (whom the initial change advantaged) and the import-competing sector (whom the initial change disadvantaged).

However, an agreement of reciprocal liberalization makes increased protection in response to foreign liberalization non-feasible; that is, the home government cannot move from D to J, but is obliged, from D, to liberalize, or move "downward" to a point on EF. If the home government were to defect from the agreement and move "upward", we can presume a return to the mutually politically inferior Nash equilibrium. This is avoided if both governments commit themselves to a liberalizing response to the other's liberalization.

E. Identifying the Source of Mutual Political Gain

Suppose that Z in Figure 4 is the cooperative liberalization equilibrium. In moving from the Nash equilibrium N to the mutually politically superior equilibrium Z, each government has transferred income to each others' exporters. This is the internalization via cooperation that is the source of the mutual political benefit from trade liberalization.

If the governments have seen fit to move from N to Z, the political cost of benefitting exporters in each country must have fallen; since, in the Nash equilibrium at N, each government was at the margin precisely trading off the political support of the domestic import-competing sector against political support of the export sector. That is, marginal political support form both sectors in each country was equalized in the Nash equilibrium.

The political gains from liberalization derive not only from the traditional efficiency gains that occur to the foreign exporters but, more importantly, from the transformation of revenue, which in the Nash equilibrium had been received from the tariff, to rents for foreign exporters. The tariff revenue by this transformation is politically directed and allocated to designated beneficiaries. The rent transfer to foreign exporters takes place in exchange for a reciprocal transfer from the foreign government. Mutual politically beneficial rent transfers are thereby made by exchange of market access.

F. The Scope for Mutual Political Gains

To depart via mutual liberalization from the Nash equilibrium at N, a government must be politically prepared to disadvantage its import-competing sector. Relative political weights and the magnitude of the redistributional effects determine a government's incentive to do this.

In the example of Figure 4b, both governments' political incentives to disadvantage their respective domestic import-competing sectors are minimal, and there is little that can be achieved politically by rent transfers to export sectors via mutual liberalization. Formally, at the Nash equilibrium, the slope of the home government's iso-political support contour is

$$\frac{dt}{dT}\Big|_{\bar{M}} = -\frac{[M_\pi \pi_T + M_\Gamma \Gamma_T]}{[M_\pi \pi_t + M_\Gamma \Gamma_t]} = -\frac{M_T}{M_t} = \infty.$$

Liberalization along this iso-political support contour entails a move into the range where $M_t < 0$, and the incentive to do this depends upon what the government has to gain in terms of M_T. That is, how much increased political support is there to be secured by benefitting exporters by exchanging market access? As least for a marginal decrease in Γ, there is mutual political benefit from trade liberalization, since a source of rent transfer to exporters is not utilized at N – that is, the transfer of part of the foreign government's tariff revenue to the domestic export sector.

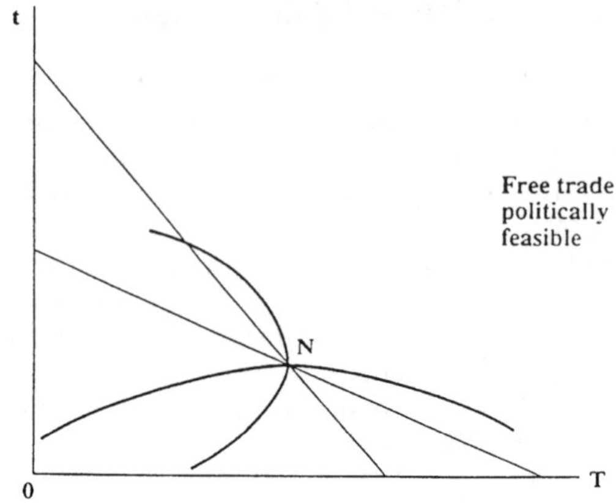

FIGURE 4A

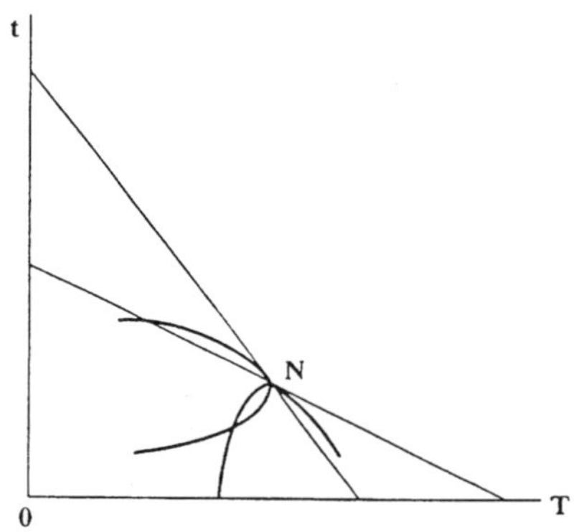

FIGURE 4B

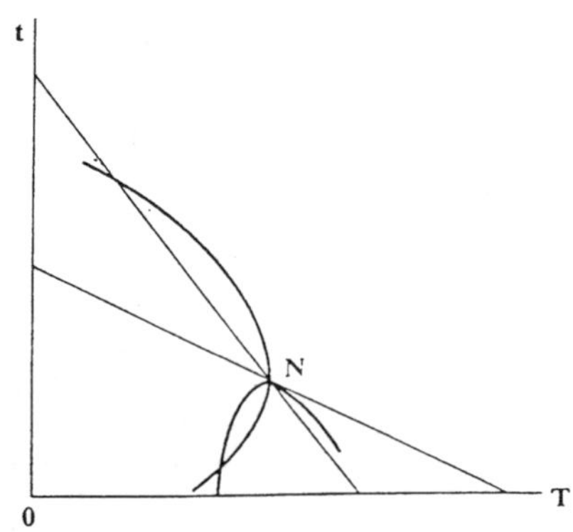

FIGURE 4C

In Figure 4b the iso-political contours reflect circumstances where there is overall minimal political gain to either government from transformation of foreign tariff revenues into domestic exporters' rents, because the transformation can only be facilitated by income distribution that disadvantages the domestic import-competing sector, which is relatively prominent in the government's political support function (M_{π} is high, M_{Γ} is low). The interaction of two such political support functions then yields the limited possibilities for exchange of market access depicted.

G. Asymmetric Political Gains

In Figure 4c the import-competing and export sectors exhibit different political prominence in the governments' political support functions. The home government is more prepared than is the "foreign" government to compromise the interests of its import-competing sector in order to advantage the export sector. Consequently, the range EF of mutually politically superior policies exhibits an asymmetry relative to the Nash equilibrium outcomes. Because of the respective political sectoral weights, the home government is here obliged to provide substantial market access for limited reciprocity by the foreign government.

H. Credibility of Political Sensitivity to Liberalization

The move from the Nash equilibrium at N to a point on EF takes place via negotiations. It is evident that in these negotiations governments have an incentive to exaggerate the political sensitivity of disadvantaging their import-competing sectors. Suppose that the political sensitivities of the foreign government are in fact as portrayed in Figure 4. A claim that political sensitivities are of the manner of Figure 4c moves the range of perceived politically feasible exchange of market access so as to advantage the foreign government. The range of the terms of trade outcomes – or how much market access one government is obliged to provide in order to secure improved market access abroad - is improved for the foreign government.

IV. UNILATERAL POLICY CHANGES

A. Exogenous Change in Policy Preferences

Suppose that the home government were unilaterally to reevaluate its political support function, and were to decrease the political weight attached to the interest of the domestic import-competing sector. Figure 5 depicts such a reevaluation, reflected in a downward shift of the home government's reaction function over the range of trade policies abroad.

B. Policy Outcomes

Since the home government now provides a lower level of protection for any level of foreign protection, the Nash equilibrium moves from N to N′, where the home government has adopted a more liberal trade policy and the foreign government a more protectionist policy. The range of outcomes consistent with politically mutually beneficial exchange of market access is also asymmetrically biased toward greater foreign protectionism (as indicated by the relative locations of the line segments EF and E′F′).

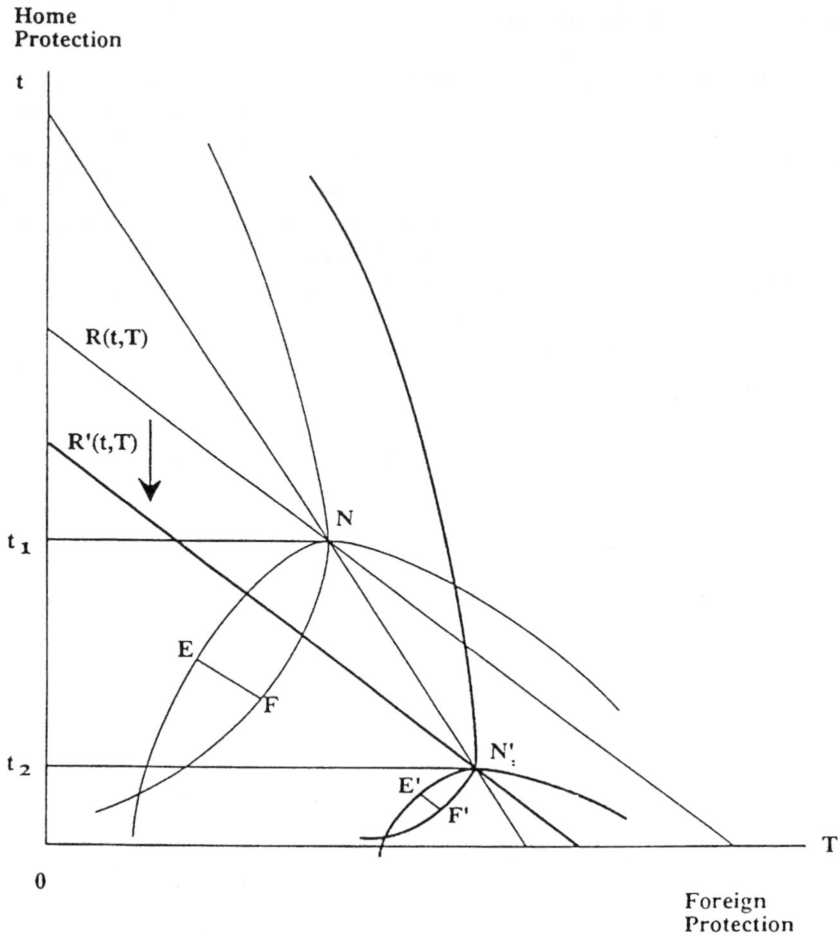

FIGURE 5

C. Policy Conflicts

When the liberalizing economy's government has unilaterally changed its position on the desirability of free trade, political-support maximization is thus inconsistent with a reciprocal liberalizing response to the plea, "we liberalized, why don't you?" It is thus of importance to distinguish between unilaterally granting market access to foreign producers accompanied by an invitation to reciprocate, and a binding credible agreement to undertake an exchange of market access. The distinction is summarized in the following proposition:

> A liberalizing change in the trade preferences of a politically optimizing government will not evoke a reciprocal liberalizing response by an optimizing government in a trading partner, but on the contrary will be met with a protectionist response.

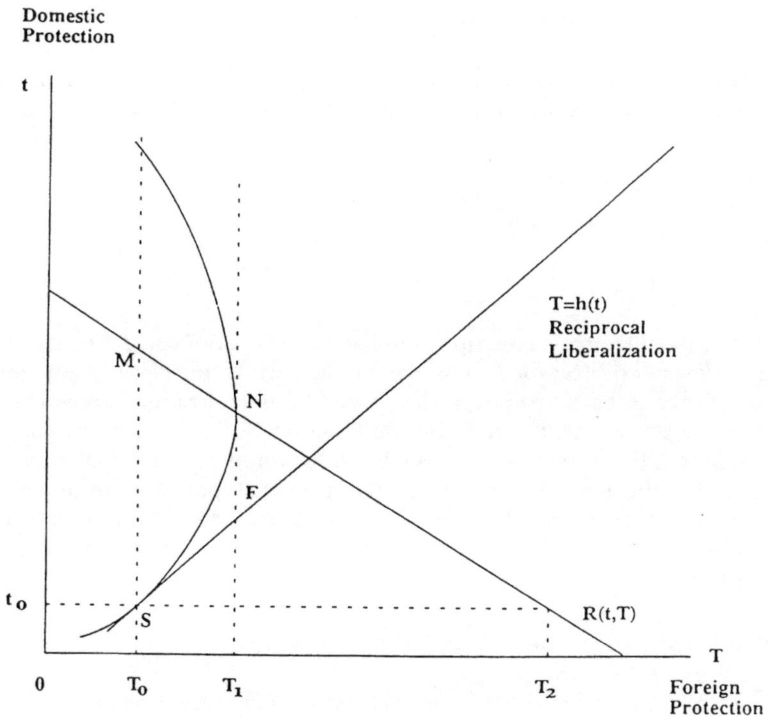

FIGURE 6

V. PREDETERMINED RECIPROCAL AGREEMENT

A. A Given Liberalization Rule

In the previous sections, we considered bilateral incentives to agree to reciprocal granting of market access. Under most-favored-nation clauses, bilateralism becomes multilateralism, since countries are precluded from discriminating in the trade "concessions" that they offer trading partners.

Consider now a political-support maximizing government confronted with the option of participating in an already negotiated multilateral agreement that specifies given conditions of reciprocal market access, in accord with the relationship between trade policies

$$T = h(t) \tag{15}$$

as depicted in Figure 6. That is, the more liberal the government's trade policy, the more liberal are foreign governments in reciprocally granting access to their domestic markets.

B. The Decision to Participate

Whether a government has an interest in agreeing to enter into such a multilateral agreement depends on political-support outcomes that can be achieved. Maximization of political support subject to (17) yields the Stackelberg equilibrium at S in Figure 6 where

$$h'(t) = -\frac{[M_\pi \pi_t + M_\Gamma \Gamma_t]}{[M_\pi \pi_T + M_\Gamma \Gamma_T]} \tag{16}$$

Whether this outcome is superior to unilateral protectionism evidently depends upon the level of protection T in foreign markets which the government confronts in the absence of participation in the reciprocal liberalization agreement. Since points along the segment of the reaction function MN are politically superior to points along SF on $h(t)$, for default levels of foreign protection in the range $T \in [T_0, T_1]$, the government's politically optimal response is not to participate in a multilateral reciprocal liberalization agreement. However, a level of foreign protection in excess of T_1 provides an inducement to move to the Stackelberg equilibrium S.

C. The Implications of Unilateral Concessions

The lack of incentive is thereby demonstrated to engage in reciprocal exchange of market access when reciprocal commitments are not expected, as from the less-developed countries in the GATT, or when unilateral concessionary trading arrangements are available, as via the Generalized System of Preferences (GSP). If the GSP offers an outcome in the range of MN of the reaction function, politically optimizing governments will refrain from participating in broader multilateral liberalization programs based on reciprocity. A more liberal international trade regime could be established by unilaterally increasing the level of protection that the GSP beneficiary confronts in foreign export markets. Graduation from GSP status then results in reciprocal improvement of market access and a consequently more liberal trade regime, since political-support maximization leads the government in the graduating economy to liberalize in order to secure improved conditions of foreign market access.[19]

VI. CONCLUSIONS

Traditional approaches to explaining trade liberalization impute efficiency motives to governments and employ aggregate conceptions of social welfare to demonstrate (i) how a country gains from unilateral liberalization if it is unable to influence its terms of trade, and (ii) how countries that are able to influence their terms of trade gain by eliminating monopsonistic "optimum" tariffs they have imposed upon one another. These explanations of trade liberalization abstract from the income-distribution consequences of trade policies, and do not include in their accounts related political-support considerations that evidence indicates to influence international trade policy.[20] The models that assign efficiency motives to governments are also inconsistent with the institutional framework for negotiated mutual trade liberalization, where the focus has been on attainment of reciprocal market access for producers, rather than maximization of conceptions of aggregate consumer welfare.

In this paper we have presented a positive theory of the determination of trade policy that gives rise to predictions of reciprocal market access predicated on mutual gains to political-support maximizing governments. We have shown how exchange of market access influences incomes of individuals with claims to capital specific to economies' export and import-competing industries, and how governments confront a political incentive to respond to the relation between individuals' incomes and market access in the conduct of international trade policy. The source of mutual political benefit from international exchange of market access has been identified in the transformation of tariff revenue to export industry rents. We have also shown how different configurations of industry political prominence influence governments' opportunities for mutual political gain from international exchange of market access.

Sources of conflict in international trade negotiations have been identified, in the range of mutually politically beneficial reciprocal market access equilibria; in the credibility of claims regarding political sensitivities to the interests of export and import-competing industries; and in the foreign protectionist response to unilateral liberalization that is evoked by a liberalizing change in a government's preferences. The Stackelberg case has been associated with the option to participate in a predetermined reciprocal multilateral liberalization agreement; a government choosing trade policy to maximize political support then need not have an incentive to participate in reciprocal liberalization, and unilateral concessions such as the GSP are disincentives for participation.

The revenue transfer considerations also have implications for the scope of reciprocal trade liberalization possibilities. In countries where tariff receipts are important components of government revenues, the political costs of transferring tariff revenues into rents for foreign exporters is high and therefore reciprocal trade liberalization possibilities are encumbered relative to countries where revenue primarily derives from other tax bases. The greater political value of tariff revenue in many developing countries thus at least partially underlies the observed disinterest in reciprocal trade negotiations and the pressures from these countries' governments for preferential trade agreements that open the markets of developed countries without reciprocal liberalization requirements.

Reciprocal liberalization possibilities are also indicated to be constrained if foreign exporters confront import quotas but acquire the quota rents via voluntary export restraints. The rents from trade restrictions in that case have already been transferred to foreign producers, and it is not evident that foreign producers' rents will increase if trade is liberalized to expand market access. On the contrary, expanded market access may well reduce foreign exporters' profits.[21] Hence, the implication is that in industries which are dominated by voluntary export restraints, intra-industry reciprocal trade liberalization is politically more difficult than in industries protected by tariffs.[22]

NOTES

1 See Rodrik (1992) for a compendium of recent instances of unilateral trade liberalization in developing countries. As Rodrik notes, liberalization may also be a less than completely voluntary component of conditionality requirements of World Bank lending and technical assistance. Unilateral trade liberalization is also a component of the transition from socialism; see Hillman, Hinds, Milanovic and Ursprung (1992). A case of unilateral liberalization that has been extensively studied is that of the repeal of the English corn laws: see for example Schonhardt-Bailey (1991) and the references cited therein.

2 See in particular Mayer (1981) and the exposition and survey by Vousden (1990).

3 See, for example, Baldwin (1980), Hauser (1986), Winters (1987), Moser (1990), and Finger (1988, 1991).

4 The GATT agreements are subject to the most-favored-nation rule that requires market access offered to one country to be offered to all. See Moser (1990).

5 For a survey of this literature, see Hillman (1989).

6 See Marvel and Ray (1983) and Baldwin (1985) on political considerations in the Kennedy and Tokyo Rounds of the GATT, and also Hauser (1986), Moser (1990), Finger (1991).

7 See Hillman (1982).

8 On the incentives that accordingly arise for industry interests to lobby to influence trade policy decisions, see Mayer (1984a).

9 Under direct democracy, matters are different. The principal-agent problem between voter and representative of representative democracy is absent, since individuals can vote on an issue such as the level of protection to be provided to any particular industry, and the policy outcome of majority voting or the median voter rule then displaces the politician as an intermediating agent between the voter and the executive. On the determination of trade policy under direct democracy in accord with a median-voter rule, see Mayer (1984b) and Weck-Hannemann (1990).

10 On the secondary role of consumer gains in influencing trade policy in a representative democracy, see Magee et al. (1989).

11 Although, because of analytical convenience we would presume, the "small-country" model predominates in the international trade literature, it is not at all evident who is in fact "small" enough to have no market access concerns. We conjecture that the number of countries wherein market access concerns are absent is small: Israel and Switzerland are for example as small as one might wish to identify in categorization of the archetypical small country of international trade models, yet exporters in these countries nonetheless express concerns about impediments to foreign market access, and seek to have their governments enter into agreements to provide such access, which by reciprocity is to the disadvantage of import-competing industries.

12 The distribution of revenue is thus formally distributionally neutral (see also Mayer 1984b and Long and Vousden 1991).

13 That is, Nash equilibria in the choice of trade policies.

14 Two goods are of course an abstraction from the many different import-competing and export industries that exist in practice and whose particular concerns governments are obliged to consider. For each of such many industries, one expects distinct outcomes in terms of the liberalization to which an industry is exposed if import-competing or the foreign market access which it secures if an exporter. For consistent evidence of industry-specific responses reflected in deviations for U.S. industries from reciprocal liberalization rules in GATT negotiations, see Marvel and Ray (1983) and Baldwin (1985).

15 Again for exposition, we represent these real returns as uniformally accruing from specific-factor ownership. Our analysis and results are unaffected by real returns in practice differing among individuals because of differences in factor specifity (see Mussa (1982) and Grossman (1983)) and because of different quantitative holdings of factors (see Mayer, 1984b). In keeping with the characteristics of the expository model, everybody is employed; in practice, rents decline in conjunction with unemployment (see Hillman (1989), chapter 1).

16 In considering terms of trade effects, we abstract from the possibility that the terms of trade of the tariff-imposing country improve to such an extent that the domestic relative price of imports declines.

17 The signs in (11) follow from (i) the relation between policies t and T and industry incomes, (ii) the properties of the political support function, and (iii) an additional requirement that t and T remain marginally effective as means of influencing Γ and π which is sufficient for Γ_{tT} and $\pi_{tT} < 0$.

18 There is a unique and stable Nash equilibrium if $(\frac{dt}{dT})^d < (\frac{dt}{dT})^f$. This condition is always satisfied if both governments adjust their tariff rates less than proportional to a change of the other tariff size.

19 See Ray (1987) for evidence of the relation between political influence of import-competing industries and liberalization under the GSP.

20 See the review of empirical studies that focus on the U.S. in Hillman (1989), chapter 11, and with respect to the European Community, see Schuknecht (1992).

21 On the role of revenue transfers in political optimization in the case of voluntary export restraints, see Hillman and Ursprung (1988).

22 This is, for example, consistent with the continuing extension of the quota system in textiles sector since the first agreement in 1961. U.S.-Japan automobile trade is also subject to VERs, with implications for the outcome of visits of U.S. presidents and accompanying heads of U.S. automobile manufacturers to Japan.

REFERENCES

Baldwin, Robert E., 1980. "The economics of the GATT," in Peter Oppenheimer (ed.), *Issues in International Economics*, Oriel Press, London, 82–93.

Baldwin, Robert E., 1985. *The Political Economy of Postwar U.S. Trade Policy*, MIT Press, Cambridge, Mass.

Hauser, Heinz, 1986. "Domestic policy foundation and domestic policy function of international trade rules," *Aussenwirtschaft*, 41, 171–184.

Hillman, Arye L., 1982. "Declining industries and political-support protectionist motives," *American Economic Review*, 72, 1180–1187.

Hillman, Arye L., 1989. *The Political Economy of Protection*, Harwood Academic Publishers, Chur.

Hillman, Arye L. and Heinrich Ursprung, 1988. "Domestic politics, foreign interests, and international trade policy," *American Economic Review*, 78, 729–745.

Hillman, Arye L., Manuel Hinds, Branko Milanovic, and Heinrich Urspung, 1992. *International trade liberalization in a privatizing economy*, EMENA Discussion Paper, The World Bank, Washington D.C.

Finger, J. Michael, 1988. "Protectionist rules and internationalist discretion in the making of national trade policy," in Nahs-Jürgen Vosgerau (ed.), *New Institutional Arrangements for the World Economy*, Springer-Verlag, Heidelberg, 310–323.

Finger, J. Michael, 1991. "The GATT as an international discipline over trade restrictions," in Roland Vaubel and Thomas D. Willett, (eds), *The Political Economy of International Organizations*, Westview Press, Boulder, 125–141.

Grossman, Gene M., 1983. "Partially mobile capital: A general approach to two-sector trade theory," *Journal of International Economics*, 15, 1–17.

Long, Ngo Van and Neil Vousden, 1991. "Protectionist responses and declining industries," *Journal of International Economics*, 30, 87–103.

Magee, Stephen P., William A. Brock, and Leslie Young, 1989. *Black Hole Tariffs and Endogenous Policy Theory: Political Economy in General Equilibrium*, Cambridge University Press.

Marvel, Howard P. and Edward Ray, 1983. "The Kennedy Round: Evidence on the regulation of international trade in the United States," *American Economic Review*, 95, 190–197.

Mayer, Wolfgang, 1981. "Theoretical considerations on negotiated tariff adjustments," *Oxford Economic Paper*, 33, 135–153.

Mayer, Wolfgang, 1984. "The political economy of tariff agreements," *Schriften des Vereins für Socialpolitik*, 148, 423–437.

Mayer, Wolfgang, 1984. "Endogenous tariff formation," *American Economic Review*, 74, 970–985.

Mussa, Michael, 1982. "Imperfect factor mobility and the distribution of income," *Journal of International Economics*, 12, 125–141.

Moser, Peter, 1990. *The Political Economy of the GATT*, Verlag Rüegger, Grüsch.

Ray, Edward, 1987. "The impact of special interests on preferential trade concessions by the U.S.," *Review of Economics and Statistics*, 69, 187–195.

Rodrik, Dani, 1992. "The limits of trade policy reform in developing countries," *Journal of Economic Perspectives*, 6, 87–105.

Schondhardt-Bailey, Cheryl, 1991. "Specific factors, capital markets, portfolio diversification, and free trade: Domestic determinants of repeal of corn laws," *World Politics*, 43, 545–569.

Schuknecht, Ludger, 1992. *Trade Protection in the European Community*, Harwood Academic Publishers, Chur.

Vousden, Neil, 1990. *The Economics of Trade Protection*, Cambridge University Press, Cambridge.

Weck-Hannemann, Hannelore, 1990. "Protectionism in direct democracy," *Journal of Institutional and Theoretical Economics*, 146, 389–418.

Winters, L. Alan, 1987, "Reciprocity," in J. Michael Finger and Andrzej Olechowski, editors, *The Uruguay Round: A Handbook on the Multilateral Trade Negotiations*, The World Bank, Washington, D.C., 45–51.

7. Designing and Implementing Effective Dispute Settlement Procedures: WTO Dispute Settlement, Appraisal and Prospects

J. H. Jackson

5.1 INTRODUCTION AND REVIEW OF THE POLICIES OF TRADE DISPUTE SETTLEMENT PROCEDURES

5.1.1 The Success of the Uruguay Round

On 1 January 1995 a new organization, the World Trade Organization (WTO), came into being for the purposes of assisting governments in the world to better manage problems of international economic interdependence. This event occurred fifty years after the establishment of the Bretton Woods system (with the World Bank and International Monetary Fund charters), and almost fifty years after the 1947 establishment of the General Agreement on Tariffs and Trade (GATT) and the later failure of the International Trade Organization (ITO) Charter, which would have been the institution to complete the Bretton Woods system.[1]

The WTO was one of the major results of the extended Uruguay Round negotiations on trade, under the auspices of the GATT. The Uruguay Round was the eighth major trade negotiating round of the GATT, and had been under way since September 1986. This massive undertaking resulted in a final act signed at Marrakesh, Morocco, on 15 April 1994, consisting of 26,000 pages (undoubtedly a record for a treaty length).[2] The length of time for the negotiation as well as the number of pages indicate the enormous complexity of the endeavor that had been undertaken. Although most of these pages are detailed schedules of tariff and service obligations, nevertheless about 1,000 pages of carefully negotiated treaty text covers subjects such as tariffs, financial services, intellectual property, antidumping measures, escape clause and safeguard measures, textile trade, agricultural trade, and many more crucial questions of international economics. But perhaps the most significant measure included in the Marrakesh Final Act was the new "charter" for a "World Trade Organization," which would now replace the GATT as the central institution for international trade cooperation in the world.

5.1.2 The Institutional Problems of the WTO

The launch of the WTO is now obviously quite successful. After coming into force on 1 January 1995, the WTO after twenty months has 122 members, and the numbers are climbing (there are about 30 more nations in the process of negotiating for membership). It is also remarkable that, although the WTO and the Uruguay Round evolved from almost fifty years of GATT history, nevertheless this new WTO institutional framework, arguably a relatively minimal change, does have some profound implications.[3] It embraces the so-called single-package idea, which requires every nation to accept the entire package (or at least 95 percent of it). This is in contrast to results under prior rounds, such as the Tokyo Round, whereby nations could pick and choose among a series of protocol agreements (a process called "GATT à la carte").

One of the central features of the new WTO institution (indeed, some are calling it *the* central feature), is the new dispute settlement process. This paper focuses on these new procedures. In particular, section 5.3 discusses several significant and central issues concerning international dispute settlement procedures in the context of the WTO. Almost all of these issues relate to a broader question of "sovereignty" (whatever that means today). A number of the diplomats to the WTO have begun to realize the significance of the new procedures, and in some cases are worried or a bit fearful of them. The key attribute of the new procedures, as we will see below, is 'automaticity." No longer will it be feasible for a nation to block the results of a dispute settlement procedure. In addition, during the U.S. Congressional hearings on the implementing act for the Uruguay Round results, there was a considerable amount of debate about whether the intrusion on U.S. sovereignty by the WTO, and its dispute settlement process, was too great. I have testified on that subject (see appendix A). In my opinion, there are adequate checks and safeguards in the WTO against inappropriate incursions on "sovereignty," but it must be recognized that, even for the United States, the new procedures will effectively require some alternation in traditional thinking about diplomacy connected with international economic relations. Already there have been some effects (for example in the U.S.–Japan dispute concerning automobile exports to the United States.)[4]

At the outset, it should be noted that there are some strong policy underpinnings for an effective dispute settlement process, which are often overlooked, or at least not often mentioned explicitly. Basically the goal is what has been termed a "rule-oriented system" (Jackson 1989, chap. 4), a system that gives guidance in the way of predictable and generally stable rules to millions of entrepreneurs around the world. Such guidance is very necessary for investment decisions, market opening decisions, technological decisions, and so forth. In economists' terms, this is a system that will reduce the so-called risk premium for some of those decisions.

5.2 THE GATT, ITS BIRTH DEFECTS, AND THE NEW WTO PROCEDURES

5.2.1 The GATT and the Uruguay Round

It is common knowledge that the GATT itself was never intended to be an organization. Rather, after the other Bretton Woods institutions were established (in 1945), world government leaders determined that it would be necessary to add another institution, one devoted to trade – the ITO. The GATT was merely designed to be a multilateral trade and tariff agreement that would depend on the ITO for its institutional infrastructure. When the ITO did not come into force because parliaments, particularly the U.S. Congress, would not approve it in the late 1940s, the GATT gradually became the central focus of coordinating activity among nations regarding trade.

Despite this inauspicious beginning, the GATT has been remarkably successful during its nearly five decades. Partly this is because of ingenious and pragmatic leadership, particularly in its early years. Nevertheless, because of this unfortunate history, the GATT endured a number of "birth defects" that proved increasingly troublesome in recent years as world economic affairs became more complex and harder to manage. These defects included

* provisional application and grandfather rights exceptions embraced by the Protocol of Provisional Application;
* ambiguity about the powers of the contracting parties to make certain decisions;
* ambiguity regarding the waiver authority and risks of misuse;
* murky legal status leading to misunderstanding by the public; media, and even government officials;
* certain defects in the dispute settlement procedures; and
* lack of institutional provisions generally, leading to constant improvisation.

The Uruguay Round, negotiated from 1986 to 1994, resulted in a new treaty text on dispute settlement, the "dispute settlement understanding" (DSU).[5] For the first time, therefore, we have substantial binding treaty text with respect to dispute settlement in the GATT/WTO system. The GATT clauses were very brief; three paragraphs essentially, embellished at the end of the Tokyo Round in 1979 by a so-called understanding. The DSU contains about forty pages. Beyond that, there are a number of specific provisions in various other texts of the Uruguay Round. The major change is the elimination of "blocking" of a final panel report. Blocking was a major defect of the previous system (Jackson 1990), which is no longer permitted. Thus the DSU provides "automaticity," whereby reports of a dispute settlement panel and the appellate panel (the final result of these processes) will almost always become binding in some sense, discussed below.

Some may ask what is the true relevance of "binding treaty texts." Skeptics may say that treaties are difficult to enforce and can often be evaded anyway, so that nonbinding treaty clauses, "hortatory" or "policy guidance," would be just as substantial. However, there is extensive commentary by both scholars and persons with considerable experience in international affairs that a binding treaty obligation under international law principles does have some important additional effects (Henkin 1994). In addition to the diplomatic advantages of being on the "right side" of international law, there are a number of potential domestic legal consequences of binding international law obligations compared to "soft law," which is not binding. For example, in some legal systems a binding treaty may have domestic law "statutelike" effect (Jackson 1992, 310; 1987, 141–70). Even in jurisdictions where such direct effect does not occur, a binding treaty can have various other legal effects in a domestic law system, such as influencing interpretation of statutes or other laws in such system.

In addition to the considerations above, the dispute settlement procedure resulting from the Uruguay Round is also a *unified* procedure. The previous system was fragmented, with eight or ten different dispute settlement processes. This change has very great implications, particularly for enhancing public understanding, including high government officials' understanding of the system.

The prior history of the GATT (see Jackson 1990, 1989, 1969, 1995a, 1995b) is related to the WTO by a very important clause in the WTO Charter, sometimes called the "guidance clause." Article XVI:1 of the WTO Charter explicitly says that the new organization and all of its component parts shall be "guided by" the practice and decisions, and so forth, of the GATT. That is a very significant clause that carries over what legal scholars would call the "jurisprudence" of the GATT as part of the underpinnings of a more stable and predictable system for the future in the WTO.

5.2.2 The WTO Dispute Settlement Procedures: Statistics and the "State of Play"

The new dispute settlement system has faced certain hurdles in its first years. The first hurdle was of course the U.S.–Japan controversy over automobiles, which was fortunately settled. The second was the selection of the appellate body itself, which was a very interesting process that turned out to take a half year longer than expected, but in the end worked out very well, with the establishment and swearing in of that body in December 1995. The third was the first case that went all the way through appellate body, the case against the United States on gasoline regulations (which now seems to be headed for a satisfactory resolution).[6] The fourth problem is the question of resource allocation needed for the dispute settlement process. As to the fourth point, there has been quite an encouraging amount of resources allocated to the dispute settlement process and to the appellate body within a secretariat that otherwise is very short of resources. But projections for the near future suggest the possibility of cases outstripping those resources.

As of 25 February 1997, there was a total of sixty-eight complaints initiated under the new dispute settlement process (WTO 1997a; see also Williams 1997; *WTO Focus*). That's two or three times the normal rate of application for dispute settlements, as witnessed and experienced in the later years of the GATT. Perhaps this is a tribute to the new process. These sixty-eight complaints involved forty-five discrete cases (because many complaints now have multiple complainants). Already, seventeen cases seem settled, which is a very encouraging aspect of the new process. Indeed, the tendency toward settlement is partly influenced by the "automaticity" of the system mentioned earlier.

Recently there were fourteen active cases with thirteen panels operating, and there are as many as thirty cases in operation, which will push the limits of resources for that activity. Three appeals were completed by the end of February 1997. The few appeals completed in 1997 is a relatively light load, and certainly in the future there may be many more. On the other hand, the first year of the appellate body has given its seven members a chance to study the processes and develop rules of procedure. Some of the members were not particularly expert yet in the GATT/WTO law and jurisprudence, so this has worked out reasonably well.

There are consultations going in the other disputes. By February 1997, the United States had brought twenty-five disputes – a really remarkable reliance on this new procedure, and it could represent confidence by the U.S. government in the new system (House 1996). The United States on the other hand is defending in eleven cases. Of all the cases brought by the United States, there already are settlements in five, and indications from the U.S. government that settlements in others are expected. The European Community (EC) has brought nine and is defending in thirteen, while Japan has brought four (one of which has been settled) and is defending in nine. But one of the most remarkable phenomena in this area is the fact that developing countries are using this process among themselves, namely, developing countries have complained against other developing countries. This was extraordinarily rare in GATT history.

5.2.3 The Procedures: GATT and WTO

A few words of explanation of the WTO dispute settlement procedures, with some comparisons to those of the GATT, might be useful (see, generally, Jackson 1989, chap. 4). Appendix B reproduces a WTO document that outlines the new procedures.

Under the old GATT, as indicated, the treaty clauses were spare and the GATT developed through practice a relatively sophisticated set of procedures for dispute settlement. This practice was largely embodied in a 1979 understanding resulting from the Tokyo Round (GATT 1979). The practice under the GATT that led to these procedures included a shift in the late 1950s from the use of a "working party" to consider disputes, to that of a "panel of experts." This signaled a shift to a more juridical, rather than negotiating, procedure. The experts on a dispute panel were acting in their own right, and not as representatives of other governments. They had an obligation to be impartial and to apply careful reasoning to the cases brought before them.

In addition, the GATT language of dispute settlement focused on something called "nullification or impairment," in the language of article XXIII. This language did not necessarily require a breach of the international law obligations under the treaty, but merely a defeat of reasonable expectations for enhanced exports and trade, and a looser concept laid out in earlier documents. In a 1962 case brought by Uruguay, the panel introduced a revolutionary concept of "prima facie nullification or impairment." Under this panel's concept, a breach of the GATT would be "prima facie" nullification or impairment, and this would, if established, require the responding nation to carry the burden of proof for showing that there was no nullification or impairment. If it failed to fulfil this burden of proof, the responding nation would be required by the recommendations and findings of the panel report to change its law or practice to bring it into conformity with the treaty obligations.

As time went on, the GATT panels consistently cited the 1962 Uruguay case, and relied upon it for this principle. The principle was also embodied in the 1979 understanding resulting from the Tokyo Round. In the 1980s, as the procedures became more legally precise and juridical in nature, there developed the idea that there were two types of cases in the GATT: the violation cases (based on the prima facie concept), and certain "nonviolation cases," which did not involve a violation, but nevertheless alleged "nullification or impairment." In fact, the nonviolation cases have been relatively rare. One group of scholars has indicated that there are only from three to eight of this type of cases in the history of the GATT (Jackson, Davey, and Sykes 1995a, 362). Nevertheless, some of these nonviolation cases have been quite important (GATT 1990; Jackson, Davey, and Sykes 1995a, 357).

The procedure under GATT was for the panel to make its report and deliver it to the Council, which as a standing body met regularly and disposed of most of the business of the GATT. (This body was also not provided in the GATT text, but arose through practice.) The practice then became firmly established that, if the Council approved the report by consensus, it became "binding." If the Council did not approve, then the report would not have a binding status. The problem was "consensus." In effect, the nation that "lost" in the panel and might otherwise be obligated to follow the panel obligations, could 'block" the Council action by refusing to participate in the consensus. Thus, the losing party to the dispute had a technique of avoiding the consequences of its loss. This was deemed to be the most significant defect in the GATT process.

Thus we see in the results of the Uruguay Round and as embodied in the WTO DSU (appendix B), that several important reforms have been established. For one, blocking is no longer possible. A panel report will be deemed adopted unless there is a consensus *against* it. As a sort of quid pro quo for this automaticity, however, a new appeal process was established so that a party to the dispute that was not satisfied with the basic panel report could appeal to an appellate panel of three persons, drawn from a relatively permanent roster of seven persons. The result of this appeal then is also a report made to the Council (technically to the Dispute Settlement Body, which is the Council acting as the DSB). Again, however, the report is deemed adopted unless there is a consensus *against* it. Therefore in the end, after either one step or two steps, depending on whether an appeal was taken, it will be virtually automatic that the parties are by treaty law obligated to carry out the recommendations.

There are a series of new clauses in the 1994 DSU regarding the case where a nation does not adequately fulfil its obligations after a dispute settlement process. The treaty text provides for "compensatory measures," which some would describe as retaliations. There are limits on these, however. They must be tailored to amount to approximately the same trade effect as that caused by the treaty violation, and only the country harmed can take the measures (this point is in contrast to the looser language in the GATT).

In addition, the DSU has a separate set of procedures for "nonviolation" cases. This is the first time that there has been this treaty-text separation between "violation" and "nonviolation" cases. Interestingly enough under the DSU, the end result of a nonviolation case is not to impose an obligation on the "losing party" to perform. This is logical, since they have not breached any obligation to do anything. However, they do have an obligation in good faith to negotiate some kind of compensatory measures. Thus, compensation becomes the prime remedy under nonviolation cases, but only a fallback remedy under the violation cases.

5.3 SEVERAL SIGNIFICANT AND CENTRAL ISSUES ABOUT THE WTO DISPUTE SETTLEMENT

We now turn to seven very significant issues about the dispute settlement process. These are not all of the issues that are important, by any means, but they do stand very high in any sort of inventory ranking of important issues. To some extent, most of these issues are central to problems of any legal system, including national government systems and the relationship of the courts to legislatures, and so forth. In addition, these issues were significant issues under the GATT, as well as now under the WTO. The key question, of course, is whether the WTO has improved some of the problems that lurk in these issues. It may have exacerbated others.

These problems include the question of incursions upon "sovereignty," and the questions of the appropriate allocation of power (both in the vertical and horizontal sense, that is, at what level of government – international, national, subnational – should power be allocated; and between what kinds of institutions on the same level – judicial, legislative, administrative). For some of these issues, we now have some important clues in the first few appellate panel reports under the WTO procedures, and these will be indicated.

5.3.1 Rule Orientation of the WTO Procedures

From the beginning of the GATT there was a certain bifurcation in the thinking about what the dispute settlement process was (Jackson 1989). Was it designed to be merely a procedure to assist parties to settle their disputes, and thus really to engage in diplomatic maneuvering with what is sometimes called a power-oriented approach? Or was it a system that was designed to be more rule-oriented in the sense of arriving at just results, in terms of the real obligation undertaken by parties through the negotiated treaty texts?

At the beginning of the GATT this was quite murky. To the very end of the GATT's history (at the end of 1995) there were differing attitudes about which was the true goal of these procedures. Even now in the WTO there is some dispute on that. However, the history of the GATT demonstrates a steady evolution toward a more rule-oriented approach. This was manifest even in the 1950s when the venue of disputes was shifted from "working parties" to "panels," then in the 1960s when the general concept of "prima facie nullification or impairment" was developed to apply to all violations of treaty obligations. In the 1970s the DSU developed in the Tokyo Round continued this development, and in the 1980s the GATT moved strongly toward a rule-oriented approach in the actual practice of the dispute panels.

With the new DSU text, the question is, what approach does it take? There are classes that arguably go both ways, but if you read the DSU through carefully, and inventory the clauses that relate to this issue, you can easily come to the conclusion that the DSU opts for the rule-oriented procedure.[7] After several years of appeals, to an appellate body that obviously seems to lean toward that direction very strongly, this will likely be even more definitive.

The first appellate body report (see note 6) is extraordinarily interesting, even apart from the substance of what it was addressing (the environmental protection matters of U.S. regulation and how they related to at least three different clauses in the GATT, most particularly article XX). The flavor of that report is significant. Among other things, the report definitely says that this process, and the GATT and the WTO generally, are a part of "international law" as such. (There has been some dispute as to whether it was a "separate regime," sort of sealed off from normal concepts of international law, but the appellate body explicitly states that the WTO is part of international law, and it goes on to engage international law principles of treaty interpretation very deeply, referring to the Vienna Convention on the Law of Treaties.)[8] The appellate body report seems thus to embrace an even stronger endorsement of the rule-oriented concept.

5.3.2 The Legal Effect of a Dispute Panel Report: Obligation to Perform?

Second, what is the legal effect of a report? There are also contrary opinions on this (Jackson 1994a). Indeed, some statements by government officials on both sides of the Atlantic and elsewhere in the world have been misleading.

The alternatives are the following: At the end of a procedure, after the first-level panel report, or the appellate panel report, do the findings of the report mean that the nation that has lost the case, the nation to which the panel addresses a series of recommendations (usually recommending that the country concerned bring its practice into consistency with its international obligations under the Uruguay Round texts), has an international law obligation to conform its law practice to the recommendations? Or does it mean that such nation has a choice either to perform or to compensate? In other words, can you compensate and "get off"? (The word "compensation," incidentally, has some ambiguities in it also.)[9]

Government officials, including some in the United States who testified before Congress during 1994, have said that all a report requires is for a nation to "compensate," that it does not create a legal obligation of any kind to *perform*. There are strong arguments that this is wrong. Unfortunately, the negotiators for the DSU did not quite nail that down explicitly. However, at least one of the negotiators that participated in that negotiation said they thought they had it nailed – that they discussed it for hours – and it was clearly meant that there was a legal obligation to perform. It turns out not to be quite that clear.

The DSU has at least twelve clauses that are relevant,[10] and all these add up to quite a strong propensity toward the legal obligation, including, and perhaps most interesting, a clause that says that, even if there is compensation, the matter remains on the agenda of the DSB until compliance occurs (DSU article 22.8). The idea is that compensation is only a temporary measure or a fallback measure as implied by the context of the other clauses, including the distinct preference expressed for bringing measures into consistency, and an interesting clause in a separate procedure that is now designed for "nonviolation cases."

In the nonviolation cases, there is no obligation to perform (DSU article 26), which is perfectly logical, as explained above. But expressing it there suggests that, in the violation cases, there *is* an obligation to perform.

Does this matter? Is compensation and/or retaliation the real underpinning of this system? I would suggest that the compensation retaliation measures are not what is really at the center of dispute settlement, and have not been so in the GATT historically. It is really the *credibility* of the judgment that is rendered that raises a series of diplomatic hurdles to a country that tries to ignore them. Even the most powerful trading entities in the world find it difficult diplomatically to ignore the results of the dispute settlement process, although in some sense they could get away with it.[11]

5.3.3 The Standard of Review

The third issue to discuss here is the standard of review. This paper does not address the standard of review of the appellate body when it reviews the first-level report. Instead it addresses the degree to which the WTO dispute settlement process as a whole, both panel levels, should second-guess national government administrative decisions that relate to treaty clauses in the Uruguay Round.

National governments will inevitably be interpreting some of these broad clauses themselves; they will have to, because of the ambiguity mentioned earlier. So to what degree should the international dispute settlement bodies give deference to those national decisions on interpretation? This is the "standard-of-review" question. I and my colleague have recently published an article (Jackson and Croley 1996) about this very question, discussing in particular some of the efforts by certain negotiators, mostly those of the United States, who tried to achieve a very restricted standard-of-review treaty obligation in the Uruguay Round, especially in the context of the antidumping measures. The U.S. negotiators did not succeed entirely in their endeavour. They were trying to translate the domestic U.S. jurisprudence of the Chevron case into the international obligation in the treaties, but they did not succeed in doing that. There is, however, some very curious language in the antidumping text about the degree of deference that a panel should give to national governments.[12] Basically it says that if an analysis, according to normal interpretation procedures under international law, results in ambiguity and if a government has chosen one among "permissible options" for interpretation, the international panel should allow the government to continue with that option. There are numerous other problems with that approach, but without going into these it can be noted that the particular language of article 17.6 of the antidumping text applies only to antidumping decisions. It does not apply to the rest of the dispute settlement process, and regardless of what it means, therefore, in the other areas perhaps a different approach can be expected.

The DSU text, other provisions in the Uruguay Round text, and resolutions of the Marrakesh meeting provide for several possibilities that the antidumping standard-of-review text will apply more broadly than to antidumping decisions. For one thing, a Marrakesh decision notes, but does not require, the possibility that countervailing-duty decisions should be consistent and similar to antidumping decisions. In addition, a Marrakesh resolution provides for a review of this antidumping article 17.6 language at the end of five years.[13]

Nevertheless, this issue is an important one. It seems clear there should be *some* measure of deference to national government decisions at the international level in the dispute settlement process. There is support for that in other areas of international law, particularly in the European Convention of Human Rights (Macdonald 1993). At the very end of the 1996 first appellate body report, on the U.S. gasoline case, the panel includes this language: "WTO members have a large measure of autonomy to determine their own policies on the environment, including its relationship with trade" (WTO 1996b, 30).

This appears to be a declaration of intention by the first appellate report to give some measure of latitude to national governments in this respect. That raises a host of other issues. For example, how far should this go? What issues are more appropriately decided at the national level instead of the international level? Europeans sometimes call this the "subsidiarity" issue.

5.3.4 The Question of Panel "Judicial Restraint" Compared to "Activism"

The next "fundamental principle of WTO jurisprudence" discussed in this paper is the question of how much "judicial activism," or "judicial restraint" should be exercised by the international panel system. This question obviously relates to the standard of review, but there are other concepts and ideas that are involved, including how far an international body should "push the envelope" of interpreting ambiguous clauses to suit certain policy preferences, possibly preferences of the panel alone, or possibly policy preferences that the panel detects that the negotiators, or currently the governments, have. Again the DSU has some interesting clauses on this. Article 3:2 says: "The dispute settlement system of the WTO is a central element in providing security and predictability to the multilateral trading system. The Members recognize that it serves to preserve the rights and obligations of Members under the covered agreements, and to clarify the existing provisions of those agreements in accordance with customary rules of interpretation of public international law. Recommendations and rulings of the DSB cannot add to or diminish the rights and obligations provided in the covered agreements." What does that mean? Arguably it resonates in the direction of a caution to the panels to use "judicial restraint," and not to be too activist. Of course the U.S. Congress feels quite strongly about that, and in the Dole Commission proposal, the language "rights or obligations" is picked up again.[14] It is also included, incidentally, in the WTO Charter. So this notion of restraining changes in the rights and obligations of the nation states is quite prevalent in the system.

The United States arguably would be one of the most jealous about that, yet it seems that the United States wants to push the envelope in some of the disputes it is bringing. For example, with reference to the so-called nonviolation cases, almost uniquely in the GATT/WTO system, there is an opportunity to bring a case that does not involve any violation of treaty obligations. Instead, a case may involve what is called "nullification of impairment," which is a very ambiguous phrase. These are termed "nonviolation" cases, as they have developed in the jurisprudence of the GATT. The DSU for the first time has an explicit procedure designed for those cases, as mentioned before.

When the United States or another country brings a case that does not involve a violation, but targets something like competition policy, or the Japanese Keiretsu, or something else that is not included within the current treaty texts, it is likely to be asking a panel to change the "rights and obligations." In other words it is saying to a panel, "we want you to interpret nullification or impairment to embrace some of these results that for policy reasons we would like to see in this case." That is risky – it is almost doing with one hand what the other hand was trying to prevent. Obviously this has longer-term fundamental implications.

5.3.5 Resources and Their Implications

An important issue for any institution, particularly a new one, is the allocation and adequacy of resources. The "judicialization" of the WTO procedures does not necessarily come cheap. Already, there is a considerably enhanced budget for dispute settlement compared to the GATT. Under the GATT, however, dispute settlement was almost always a "part-time affair," with virtually no specific allocated resources, except some secretariat lawyers to assist panels. Now there is an appellate body with significant staff and other resources, including retainers and per diems, as well as travel and support funds for staying in Geneva. There is a new legal staff devoted to the appellant body, consisting of a director and three staff lawyers, as well as some nonprofessional staff. Considerable and, one must say, very admirable space has been allocated for this effort in the secretariat building of the WTO on the shore of Lake Geneva. The regular legal staff continues from its former embodiment but is finding its work greatly increased, partly resulting from the large number of disputes that have been initiated.

So far, the resource allocation has been quite good. However, if disputes continue at the current rate, and there are not a larger number of settlements, we will shortly see some important strains on the resource possibilities. In addition, the issues that will need to be addressed by the dispute settlement system may incur special resource requirements. For example, some of the issues may be very technical (such as some of the financial services issues, or the intellectual property issues) and may require special expertise (some of which is allowed for in the DSU; see article 13). In addition, some issues may call upon a more serious examination of "facts" than the system has been able to provide in prior cases. This could be particularly true if "competition policy" type issues begin to flow into the WTO system.

5.3.6 Fact Examination

By and large the GATT dispute settlement process was not able and did not try to explore facts to any degree. Indeed, it was generally assumed that the facts would be brought to the attention of the international panel by written and oral arguments of the representatives of the disputing nations.

In the WTO procedure, this may also continue. Indeed, in the antidumping text on "standard of review," section 17.6, it is largely contemplated that the facts will be determined at the national level. However, this text applies only to the antidumping cases (so far), and may be difficult to sustain. Certain kinds of issues, such as environmental issues or financial services and other service issues, as well as intellectual property, may require some greater attention to facts. It has been noted that competition policy decision in national legal systems tend to be very fact-oriented, with massive hearings and massive records to contend with. Indeed, in the potential dispute between the United States and Japan concerning film (Kodak and Fuji), the two private firms that are perhaps the major contenders in the dispute have produced very extensive fact accounts (most of which can be found on the Internet). A serious and prolonged fact-type hearing could easily bankrupt the resources allocated to the WTO dispute settlement system. (For example, one party told me of a hearing on environmental matters in Canada that lasted about 120 days! This would exceed all the hearing dates of all the procedures in a typical GATT dispute settlement year, and would probably involve budgetary allocation exceeding all the normal procedures for a year.)

Clearly some care will have to be taken about where the dividing line should be drawn between an essential examination of facts in order to determine how the law applies, and more extensive fact records.

5.3.7 Nonviolation Cases of "Nullification or Impairment"

One of the potentially very troublesome issues is involved in the unique attention given to "nonviolation" cases. Under the GATT, this attention developed through practice by the language in the GATT text, including the phrase "nullification or impairment" (as discussed above). This language has been carried into the WTO, and for the first time, a special separate procedure under the DSU has been designed, as the route to take when a nonviolation case is pursued. As indicated above, the problem with nonviolation cases is the generality of the language "nullification or impairment," which creates great ambiguity about what would be an appropriate way to analyze these cases and to determine when one nation had some sort of right of relief from another nation. It is interesting that, in the rules for nonviolation cases, there are no similar clauses to those in the violation cases that would suggest that there is an obligation to actually perform recommendations, that is, to bring one's law into consistency with the international rule. The relief allowed under the DSU is merely "negotiation for appropriate compensation." This makes sense, since the basis of a nonviolation case is *not* the alleged inconsistency of national laws or practices with an international rule.

One must hope that nations and the responding WTO institutions will be very cautious about entertaining nonviolation cases for new types of issue for which there are not adequate or adequately precise rules contained in the Uruguay Round treaty texts. This is an issue that has been discussed in connection with so-called competition policy. Competition policy is not centrally or explicitly taken up in the Uruguay Round and GATT treaty texts. Indeed, the fact that such policy was contained in the 1948 ITO Charter, which failed to come into force, has led the GATT itself to be very cautious about taking up these policy issues. On the other hand, there are a number of clauses in the new treaty texts for services and intellectual property, and so forth, which do relate to competition policy. If a country were to bring a nonviolation case that essentially would be based on competition policy considerations, it would seem that such an approach would be truly law-making rather than law-applying. In essence the WTO panel would be asked to establish the rules of conduct concerning competition policy, so as to apply them in the particular case that was brought. This could be considered inconsistent with the clause in the DSU that is supposed to restrain panels from "changing the rights or obligations of parties."

5.4 IMPLICATIONS AND CONCLUSIONS

Dispute settlement has now moved to the center stage of international economic diplomacy, as it is embodied in the Uruguay Round and WTO texts. In many ways this is a welcome step toward a more rule-oriented system that will hopefully allow better adjustment of frictions between nation-states, as well as greater predictability and reliability for entrepreneurs. It should to some measure reduce the "risk premium" of international trade and other economic transactions, such as investment. However, there are a number of problems lurking just under the surface of those waves. These shoals and boulders could, if not evaded carefully, cause considerable distress to the trading system. In the worst case, they could cause a general backlash by governments and public citizens, particularly international traders, against the WTO and bring it into disrespect. One will hope that the diplomats and statesmen involved in the international trade system will have the capability and perception to avoid these consequences.

Apart from these grave consequences, it is nevertheless clear that the new dispute settlement system is already having its effects on international economic diplomacy. The way negotiators negotiate has been considerably altered by the existence of the process as a fallback for a failed negotiation. In many of the press reports of disputes now, we see on one side or the other "threatening to bring a case in the WTO." And it still seems the case that governments are very uneasy about being hauled before the International Trade Court of Justice as well as being very eager to avoid their nation from being "branded" as a rule breaker. All of this appears to bode well for this new development of international dispute settlement. It is likely to be seen in the future as one of the most important, and perhaps even watershed, developments of international economic relations in the twentieth century.

APPENDIX A

Excerpts from Testimony Prepared for the U.S. Senate Committee on Foreign Relations 14 June 1994 Hearing on the World Trade Organization and U.S. Sovereignty

A careful examination of the WTO Charter leads me to conclude that the WTO has no more real power than that which existed for the GATT under the previous agreements. This may seem surprising, but in fact the GATT treaty text contained language that was quite ambiguous, and could have been misused (but fortunately was not) to provide rather extensive powers. For example, in Article XXV of the GATT the Contracting Parties acting by majority vote were given the authority to take joint action "with a view to facilitating the operation and furthering the objectives of this agreement." This is very broad and ambiguous language. Under the WTO Charter, considerably more attention has been given to the question of decision making in a number of different contexts, and certain restraints have been added, such as increasing the voting requirements for certain actions (to three-fourths of the members for many waivers and for formal interpretations), and a provision in the amending clauses that a country will not be bound by an amendment which it opposes if the amendment would "alter the rights and obligations of the members." Likewise, the waiver authority is more constrained and will be harder to abuse. Furthermore, formal "interpretations" shall not be used in the manner that would undermine the amendment provisions." Thus there are more legal grounds to challenge overreaching of the power of the WTO institutions.

Regarding the practice of "consensus", as established for several decades in the GATT, several characteristics are worth noting. In the GATT, there is no explicit indication of a "consensus practice," and the word "consensus" is not used. The reason that the consensus practice developed was partly the uneasiness of governments about the loose wording of GATT decision-making powers, particularly that in GATT Article XXV. Partly because of this uneasiness, the practice developed of avoiding strict voting. Instead, the Contracting Parties have for several decades taken virtually all of their decisions by "consensus." Even when a formal vote was required (such as for a waiver), there would generally be a negotiation for a consensus draft text before such text was submitted to capitals for the formal vote.

In the practice of GATT, however, the word "consensus" was not defined. In the legal sense, if some sort of "consensus" could not be achieved, the fallback was the loose voting authority of the GATT. In the WTO Charter, however, consensus is defined (at least for some purposes) as the situation when a decision occurs and "no member, present at the meeting when the decision is taken, formally objects to the proposed decision." It should be noted that this is not the same as unanimity, since consensus is defeated only by a formal objection by a member present at the meeting. Thus, those absent do not prevent a consensus, nor does an abstention prevent a consensus. Furthermore, the practice in GATT and surely also in WTO is that some countries who have difficulty with a particular decision, will nevertheless remain silent out of deference to countries with a substantially higher stake in the pragmatic economic consequences of a decision. Thus the consensus practice itself involves some deference to economic power. This has certainly been the practice in the GATT, and the WTO Charter provides that the WOT shall be guided by such "customary practices."

The WTO is considerably more explicit about the situation where consensus fails. In a few instances, a decision must be by consensus and there is no fall-back to a majority vote. (For example, adding plurilateral agreements to Annex 4, Article X:9: and amendments to the dispute settlement procedures in Annex 2.) In many other situations, when consensus fails there is an explicit fallback vote, such as three-fourths of the membership. It is considered quite difficult to achieve such a heavy fallback vote as three-fourths of the membership (not three-fourths of those voting), since often 25 percent of the membership is not involved in a particular decision and may not show up at the meeting.

Thus the protections of national sovereignty built into the WTO Charter rules on decision making are substantially enhanced over that of the GATT.

The amending authority (Article X) is itself quite intricate and ingenious. It obviously has been carefully tailored to the needs of the participating nations related to each of the different major multilateral agreements (GATT, GATS (Services), and intellectual property). Amendments for some parts of these require unanimity. Other parts require two-thirds (after procedures in the Ministerial Conference and Councils seeking consensus for amendment proposals). In most all cases, as mentioned above, when an amendment would "alter the rights and obligations," a member which refuses to accept the amendment, is not bound by it. In such a case, however, there is an ingenious procedure (partly following the model in GATT) whereby the Ministerial Conference can by three-fourths vote of the members require all to accept the amendment, or withdraw from the agreement, or remain a member with explicit consent of the Ministerial Conference. Quite frankly, it is therefore very hard to conceive of the amending provisions being used in any way to force a major trading country such as the United States to accept altered rights or obligations. As stated above the spirit and practice of GATT has always been to try to accommodate through consensus negotiation procedures, the views of as many countries as possible, but certainly to give weight to views of countries who have great weight in the trading system. This will not change.

APPENDIX B

The Uruguay Round and GATT/WTO Dispute Settlement Procedures[15]

One of the many achievements of the GATT, despite its "birth defects," has been the development of a reasonably sophisticated dispute settlement process. The original GATT treaty contained very little on this, although it did specifically provide (in Article 22 and 23) for consultation, and then submittal of issues to the GATT Contracting Parties. As time went on, however, the practice began to evolve more towards a "rule-oriented" system. For example, in the late 1950s the practice introduced a "panel" of individuals to make determinations and findings and recommend them to the Contracting Parties. Before that, disputes had been considered in much broader working parties comprised of representatives of governments.

In the Uruguay Round 1994 text, there is a major new text concerning dispute settlement procedures, the "Understanding on Rules and Procedures Governing the Settlement of Disputes."

The new text solves many of the issues that plagued the GATT dispute settlement system, although not all of them. It accomplishes the following:

1. It establishes a unified dispute settlement system for all parts of the GATT/WTO system, including the new subjects of services and intellectual property. Thus, controversies over which procedure to use will not occur.

2. It reaffirms the right of a complaining government to have a panel process initiated, preventing blocking at that stage.

3. It ingeniously establishes a new appellate procedure which will substitute for some of the Council approval process of a panel report, and overcome blocking. Thus, a panel report will automatically be deemed adopted by the Council, unless it is appealed by one of the parties to the dispute. If appealed, the dispute will go to an appellant panel. After the appellate body has ruled, its report will go to the Council, but in this case it will be deemed adopted unless there is a consensus *against* adoption, and presumably that negative consensus can be defeated by any major objector. Thus the presumption is reversed, compared to the previous procedures, with the ultimate result of the procedure that the appellate report will in virtually every case come into force as a matter of international law.

It should, however, be understood that the international legal system does not embrace the common law jurisprudence that prevails in the United States which calls for courts to operate under a stricter "precedent" or "stare decisis" rule. Most nations in the world do not have stare decisis as part of their legal systems, and the international law also does not. This means that technically a GATT panel report is not strict precedent, although there is certainly some tendency for subsequent GATT panels to allow what they deem to be the "wisdom" of prior panel reports. Nevertheless, a GATT panel has the option not to follow a previous panel report, as has occurred in several cases. In addition, although an adopted panel report will generally provide an international law obligation for the participants in the dispute to follow the report, the GATT Contracting Parties acting in a Council or the Ministerial Conference, can make interpretive rulings or other resolutions which would depart from that GATT panel ruling, or even establish a waiver to relieve a particular obligation.

It is clear both that no system will be perfect, and that not all cases will be decided in the most appropriate way. There will be mistakes. There will be situations where the United States or other countries will lose cases which they should lose; but also there will be cases where the U.S. and others will lose cases they did not deserve to lose. This is not different from domestic legal processes. Nevertheless, in the broader context there is a great deal of utility in a creditable and efficient rule-oriented dispute settlement system that has integrity, and the U.S. is an important beneficiary of such system.

It is quite interesting how significant dispute settlement systems have become in major international trade agreements in the last decades. For example, they are a very intricate part of the European Union with its Court of Justice sitting in Luxembourg. They are also an important and enhanced part of the U.S.-Canada Free Trade Agreement, the NAFTA (North American Free Trade Agreement), and in other similar regional arrangements that are currently evolving.

NOTES

1 The interested reader may also wish to see the following: Jackson 1990, 1989, 1969; Jackson, Davey, and Sykes 1995a.
2 WTO 1994, 1140. See also US House 1994.
3 WTO 1994, 1140. See primarily the part devoted to dispute settlement, entitled "Dispute Settlement Understanding" (DSU), *see also* US House 1994; Jackson 1995b, 11–31.
4 Both sides threatened to use the dispute settlement procedure, and the settlement was importantly influenced by the possibilities of the results of this procedure (GATT 1994).
5 DSU article 26. See Understanding on Rules and Procedures Governing the Settlement of Disputes, annex 2 to WTO agreement.
6 Appellate body reports include *United States Standards for Reformulated and Conventional Gasoline* (WTO 1996b). See also WTO 1996a, 1997b.
7 See, for example, DUS article 3: 2, which in part reads "3.2 The dispute settlement system of the WTO is a central element in providing security and predictability to the multilateral trading system." Also see the speech of King Hassan II for the host government of the April 1994 Marrakesh ministerial meeting to conclude the Uruguay Round, where he said, "By bringing into being the World Trade Organization today, we are enshrining the rule of law in international economic and trade relations, thus setting universal rules and disciplines over the temptation of unilateralism and the law of the jungle" (*GATT Focus*, no. 107 (May 1994): 4).
8 Vienna Convention on the Law of Treaties (1969), entered into force 1980, article 31: 3(b). The Vienna Convention is deemed to express the general rules of international customary law, even for many nations who have not technically accepted the Vienna Convention itself. The convention clearly notes the obligation of "pacta sunt servanda," namely, the treaties will be fulfilled. It also sets up a series of principles for interpreting treaties (article 31), most notably the question of "preparatory work," in a way that is often different than such treatment in national legal systems. In the case of all these principles, the appellate body's statement that GATT/WTO law is part of international law means that these general principles of international law apply to its work and that of the WTO generally. This could have the most significance with respect to principles of interpretation of treaties.
9 The word appears particularly in the DSU at article 22. Under GATT practice, compensation always meant trade measures and not any sort of liquid monetary compensation. It probably will be similarly interpreted under the WTO DSU also, although there is some ambiguity about that.
10 SEe DSU articles and paragraphs 3.2, 3.7, 7.1, 11, 15.2, 15.3, 17.13, 21.1, 21.3, 22.1, 22.2, 26.1(b).
11 The United States, for example, has complied with most of the cases under the GATT that found the United States in noncompliance.
12 Jackson, Davey, and O. Sykes 1995b, 195. "17.6 In examining the matter referred to in paragraph 5: (i) in its assessment of the facts of the matter, the panel shall determine

whether the authorities' establishment of the facts was proper and whether their evaluation of those facts was unbiased and objective. If the establishment of the facts was proper and the evaluation was unbiased and objective, even though the panel might have reached a different conclusion, the evaluation shall not be overturned; (ii) the panel shall interpret the relevant provisions of the Agreement in accordance with customary rules of interpretation of public international law. Where the panel finds that a relevant provision of the Agreement admits of more than one permissible interpretation, the panel shall find the authorities' measure to be in conformity with the Agreement if it rests upon one of those permissible interpretations."

13 Decisions at Marrakesh: Decision on Review of Article 17.6 of the Agreement on Implementation of Article VI of the General Agreement on Tariffs and Trade 1994 (antidumping text); Declaration on Dispute Settlement Pursuant to the Agreement on Implementation of Article VI of the General Agreement on Tariffs and Trade, 1994, or Part V of the Agreement on Subsidies and Countervailing Measures (subsidies text). See Jackson, Davey, & Sykes 1995b, 435.

14 This proposal was part of a compromise agreement between Senator Dole and President Clinton, just before the Senate vote on 1 December 1994. The agreement and the later bill introduced by Senator Dole (but not yet passed as of this writing) called for a special commission of U.S. federal judges to review the panel report of every WTO dispute settlement proceeding affecting the United States. The commission would give its advice to the Congress on the appropriateness of such report, in the light of four specified criteria in the Dole proposal. A description of the proposal is contained in Senate 1995.

15 Based partly on the DSU (Jackson 1994b).

REFERENCES

General Agreement on Tariffs and Trade. 1979. *Understanding Regarding Notification, Consultation, Dispute Settlement, and Surveillance*. Geneva: GATT Document.

——, 1990. *EEC: Payments and Subsidies Paid to Processors and Producers of Oilseeds and Related Animal-Feed Proteins*. Geneva: GATT Document.

——, 1994. *Panel Report: U.S. Taxes on Automobiles*. DS31/R. Geneva: GATT Document.

Henkin, Louis, 1994. *How Nations Behave: Law and Foreign Policy*. New York: Columbia University Press.

Jackson, John H. 1969. *World Trade and the Law of GATT*. Indianapolis: Bobby-Merrill.

——, 1987. United States of America. In *The Effect of Treaties in Domestic Law*, ed. Francis G. Jacobs and Shelley Roberts, 141–70. London: Sweet and Maxwell.

——, 1989. *The World Trading System: Law and Policy of International Economic Relations*. Cambridge: MIT Press.

——, 1990. *Restructuring the GATT System*. London: Royal Institute for International Affairs.

——, 1992. States of Treaties in Domestic Legal Systems: A Policy Analysis. *American Journal of International Law* 86: 310–40.

——, 1994a. The Legal Meaning of a GATT Dispute Settlement Report: Some Reflections. In *Towards More Effective Supervision by International Organizations: Essays in Honour of Henry G. Schermers*, ed. Niels Blokker and Sam Muller, 149–64. Deventer, The Netherlands: Kluwer Academic.

——, 1994b. Testimony Prepared for the U.S. Senate Committee on Foreign Relations, June 14, 1994. In *Hearing on the World Trade Organization and U.S. Sovereignty*. Washington, DC: Government Printing Office.

——, 1995a. The Uruguay Round, World Trade Organization, and the Problem of Regulating International Economic Behaviour. In *Policy Debates/Debats Politiques*, 1–33. Ottawa: Centre for Trade Policy and Law.

——, 1995b. The World Trade Organization: Watershed Innovation or Cautious Small Step Forward? *World Economy* 11—31.

Jackson, John H, and Steven P. Croley. 1996. WTO Dispute Procedures, Standard of Review, and Deference to National Government. *American Journal of International law* 90:193–213.

Jackson, John H., William J. Davey, and Alan O. Sykes. 1995a. *Legal Problems of International Economic Relations*. 3d edition. Minneapolis: West.

——, 1995b. *1995 Documents Supplement to Legal Problems of International Economic Law*. 3d edition. Minneapolis: West.

Macdonald, R. St. J. 1993. The Margin of Appreciation. In *The European System for the Protection of Human Rights*, ed. R. St. J. Macdonald, F. Matscher, and H. Petzold, chap. 6. The Hague: Martinus Nijhoff.

U.S. House, 1994. *Uruguay Round Agreements, Texts of Agreements, Implementing Bill, Statement of Administrative Action and REquired Supporting Statements, Message from the President of the United States Transmitting These Matters to the Congress*. H. R. Doc. 316. 103d Cong., 2d sess.

——, 1996. *Testimony before the House Ways and Means Trade Subcommittee by Ambassador Michael Kantor, March 13, 1996*. Washington, DC: Government Printing Office.

U.S. Senate, 1995. *To Establish a Commission to Review the Dispute Settlement Reports of the World Trade Organization and for Other Purposes*. S. 1438, 104th Cong., 1st sess.

Williams, Frances. 1997. WTO: Sets Up Panel to Probe U.S. Shrimp Now. *Financial Times*, 26 February.

World Trade Organization. 1994. Final Act Embodying the Results of the Uruguay Round of Multilateral Trade Negotiations. Marrakesh. *International Legal Materials* 33:1140–67.

——, 1996a. *Japan: Taxes on Alcoholic Beverages*. Appellate Body Report and Panel Report. WT/DS8, 10, 11/AB/R. Geneva: WTO Document.

——, 1996b. *United States: Standards for Reformulated and Conventional Gasoline*. Appellate Body Report and Panel Report. WT/DS2/9. Geneva: WTO Document.

——, 1997a. Overview of the State-of-Play of WTO Disputes, [updated 25 February 1997]. From Web site <http://www.wto.org/wto/dispute/bulletin.htm>.

——, 1997b. *United States: Restrictions on Imports of Cotton and Man-Made Fibre Underwear, Complaint by Costa Rica*. Appellate Body Report and Panel Report. WT/DS24. Geneva: WTO Document.

8. GATT, Dispute Settlement and Cooperation

D. Kovenock and M. Thursby

1. INTRODUCTION

Post-WWII tariff history is characterized not only by trade liberalization under the General Agreement on Tariffs and Trade (GATT), but also protectionist episodes in which countries suspended tariff concessions (or appeared to violate GATT rules in other ways). In some instances, protectionist episodes have been resolved without resort to GATT legal proceedings, but in over two hundred cases, countries have initiated GATT dispute settlement procedures (DSP) under Articles XXII or XXIII. In this paper we examine a theoretical trade model which incorporates both the trade liberalization and DSP aspects of GATT. We focus on how tariff cooperation is affected by the existence of a legal agreement such as GATT and by the structure of its dispute settlement procedures. Economic models often abstract from these issues, but legal experts make frequent reference to the importance of GATT as a legal obligation. Moreover, governments perceive weaknesses in DSP as the key to enforcement problems in GATT.

Existing studies take several approaches to modeling trade liberalization. In one approach, tariff determination is modeled as a cooperative game in which binding agreements can be made and enforced. This approach is taken by Mayer (1981), Riezman (1982), and Chan (1988) and has the appealing interpretation that reduced tariffs come out of negotiations. The problem with this approach is that although GATT represents a legal obligation, its rules are not directly enforceable in most of its member countries (Hudec (1986, 1990a, 1990c), Jackson (1979, 1989)).[1] Because of this, Dixit (1987), Bagwell and Staiger (1990), and Riezman (1991) adopt noncooperative approaches to explaining tariffs. These studies examine when cooperation can be sustained in infinitely repeated tariff games where tariffs are determined noncooperatively (i.e. with zero or low tariffs are the result of implicit cooperation).[2] Low tariff levels are supported along the equilibrium path by the threat of punishing any "cheating" by reverting to "retaliatory" subgame (equilibrium) paths with lower payoffs. Dixit's focus is on free trade as a noncooperative equilibrium, but periods of both high and low tariffs can occur in equilibrium in Bagwell and Staiger (1990) and Riezman (1991). Equilibria in all three games are self-enforcing, so that there is no role for an independent enforcement mechanism or explicit international agreement. Thus they give no insight into the role of GATT as an explicit agreement or the role of GATT DSP.

Only a few tariff models incorporate DSP. Ludema (1990) incorporates the notion of DSP by restricting the equilibria in an infinitely repeated tariff game to be renegotiation-proof. In this game, if a country deviates from the cooperative tariff, any retaliation must be approved by both the deviating and retaliating country. Modeled in this way, DSP has the effect of making potential retaliation less severe than otherwise, so that within any given class of feasible punishments, the lowest supportable equilibrium tariffs are higher than without DSP. Hungerford (1990) incorporates DSP in a model of tariff and nontariff barriers. In his model, countries can punish cheating only by initiating a costly investigation of foreign actions. Because potential punishment is less severe, the equilibria involve higher levels of nontariff barriers than without DSP. Thus DSP has detrimental effects in both studies.

What are the implications of this work for the Uruguay Round? It is clearly unrealistic to think of countries setting up anything like an independent enforcement agency, hence any intuition must come from noncooperative models. These models (in particular, those of Ludema and Hungerford) suggest that more cooperation would be forthcoming in GATT if DSP were simply eliminated. This is difficult to believe given the importance negotiators attach to its reform. In both the Tokyo and Uruguay Rounds, most governments claimed that successful negotiations would be contingent on DSP reform.[3] A more likely scenario is that the existing models are too abstract to be useful in evaluating current negotiations.

This paper bridges the gap between the cooperative and noncooperative approaches to trade liberalization. In cooperative models agreements are binding, and hence infinitely costly to violate. One often thinks of these agreements as being explicit, detailed contracts. In noncooperative models, agreements are not binding (and hence may be costlessly violated), but are enforced through the future actions of the involved agents. Often, these agreements are taken to be implicit and noncontractual.

In the pages to follow, we construct a supergame model of international trade featuring both explicit and implicit agreements. Our "marriage"[4] of the cooperative and noncooperative approaches assumes that an explicit agreement, such as GATT, may be violated at some finite, but positive, cost; this cost is incurred in addition to any change in future actions that might be induced by such a violation. We interpret this cost as arising from "international obligation", a concept familiar to scholars of international law, but to our knowledge, not widely analyzed by economists. International obligation acts as a cost imposed upon any country violating an explicit international agreement. The cost is incurred regardless of whether such violations are detected or punished.

In section 2 we explain in more detail what is meant by international obligation. In subsequent sections we explore the implications of incorporating international obligation in our noncooperative tariff model. We focus on how international obligation affects two "real world" aspects of GATT-DSP: unilateral retaliation as well as use of the DSP and the effect of inordinate delays in the operation of DSP.

2. INTERNATIONAL OBLIGATION, GATT-DSP AND RETALIATION

Although GATT rules are not directly enforceable in domestic courts, they do represent legally binding obligations. To the extent that governments try to settle disputes through GATT-DSP (rather than unilaterally retaliating), it is clear they take this international obligation seriously. As noted above, governments have initiated GATT legal proceedings in over two hundred disputes. Legal experts refer to international obligation as a crucial element in enforcement of GATT rules. For example, Hudec (1990c, pp. 12 and 14) notes:

> True, like the Pope, international law has no army. But the Pope still makes a pretty good living without one. And so does international legal obligation. Governments do respond, not invariably but more than just occasionally. The greater a government's own reliance on the system of international rules in question, the more influence such obligations will have over its conduct . . . Governments are assuming that enforcement of GATT legal rulings will continue to rely on the twin engines of international obligation and retaliation.

Similarly, Jackson (1989, p. 83) notes

> It is important for the policy advisor, the statesman, or the practitioner to accurately evaluate the real impact of the international rules recognizing that some of those rules do have considerable effect and influence on real government and business decisions. For example, despite cynical statements by members of the U.S. Congress that GATT rules are "irrelevant," there are a number of proven instances when congressional committees and their staff members have taken considerable trouble to tailor legislative proposals so as to minimize the risk of a complaint to GATT.

Although international obligation tends to be ignored in economic models, it provides an interesting interpretation for several computational studies. Brown and Whalley (1980) used a general equilibrium model to calculate welfare effects of Tokyo Round tariff cuts. One of their most striking results was that countries gained more from tariff-cutting proposals other than their own. For example, the United States gained more from the Japanese proposal than its own. The EC gained more from any proposal other than its own. Baldwin and Clarke (1987) found similar results in their study of Tokyo Round tariff-cutting proposals. One interpretation of these results is that standard welfare measures don't adequately capture government objectives in setting trade policy. As noted by McMillan (1988), tariff-cutting formulae may have been motivated by employment or industry objectives, rather than aggregate country welfare. Alternatively, if countries take international obligation seriously, they may formulate negotiating proposals with that in mind.

If international obligation plays a role in enforcing GATT rules, it must do so by affecting not only the incentives for countries to violate rules, but also retaliation to apparent violations. The GATT-DSP is clearly intended to provide alternatives to retaliation as an enforcement mechanism. Article XXII allows for consultation among disputing countries, and Article XXIII provides for panels to investigated and rule on alleged violations. Although retaliation can be recommended under Article XXIII procedures, this has occurred only once in GATT history. When disputes are settled through working parties, countries are often encouraged to negotiate settlements. In this case, the disputing parties may agree on some form of retaliation (as in the Japanese leather dispute listed in Table 1 below). In many cases, however, countries simply agree to terminate the policies in question, or they agree on suitable compensation. This presumably is why previous attempts to model DSP have done so in ways that limit retaliation.

Nonetheless, there is nothing in GATT to prevent retaliation. It is easy to find cases in GATT history where countries retaliate without filing disputes, as well as cases where they file disputes but eventually retaliate because of extraordinary delays in the legal process. Table 1 presents ten cases of U.S. retaliatory actions between 1974 and 1989. All of these cases involved retaliation under U.S. Section 301 law. In half of the cases, the United States retaliated without filing a GATT dispute. In two of these, disputes were filed eventually against the United States for its retaliatory actions. In the Japanese semiconductor case, the United States had increased tariffs on $300 million of imports from Japan in response to alleged Japanese violation of a bilateral semiconductor agreement. In the other case, Brazil filed a dispute in response to U.S. tariff retaliation to alleged inadequate patent protection in pharmaceuticals. In the rest of the cases listed, retaliation occurred after the United States had filed a dispute. In the Japanese leather case, this retaliation was GATT-legal in the sense that it occurred after the panel report and was mutually agreeable to both parties. However, the other cases involved unilateral retaliation before successful completion of the legal process. In the case of wheat flour, a retaliatory subsidy was instituted two months before the panel ruling. In the other cases, the United States retaliated after panel reports were blocked by the European Community.

Notice the contrast between this dispute history and the way DSP has been modeled. Neither Ludema (1990) nor Hungerford (1990) incorporate the type of delay in retaliation that occurs when countries follow GATT-DSP. Moreover, their models do not capture the variety of options countries have taken in settling disputes. In reality, countries have followed GATT-DSP in some cases, while in others they retaliated quickly to apparent violations, or retaliated when the GATT legal process stalled (either due to delays or blocked reports). These features should be incorporated in any model of DSP since much of the dissatisfaction with GATT-DSP concerns either delays or unilateral retaliation. We shall consider both aspects of DSP in Section 4B.

3. IMPLICIT COOPERATION IN A GATT-LESS WORLD

A. The Model

We examine implicit tariff cooperation in an infinitely repeated game. The constituent game is one in which two countries, 1 and 2, choose tariff levels $\tau_i \in [0, \infty)$ to maximize a one-period utility function, $U_i(\tau_i,\tau_j)=E_{\underset{\sim}{\theta}} u_i(\tau_i,\tau_j,\underset{\sim}{\theta})$, where $\underset{\sim}{\theta} = (\theta_1,\theta_2)$ is an unobserved random variable in $\mathbb{R}^2_+$. We abstract from whether this function is an index of aggregate utility (as in Dixit (1987)) or the indirect utility of interest groups that influence tariff policy. We make standard trade-theoretic assumptions on the derivatives of u_i with respect to own and foreign tariffs,[5] and on the random variable $\underset{\sim}{\theta}$ in order to ensure the existence of a static

TABLE 1 *Examples of Retaliation U.S. 301 Cases*

Original Action or Complaint	Country	GATT DSP	U.S. Retaliation	Timing
Export subsidy on wheat flour	EC	Yes	Export subsidy on wheat flour	Before panel report
Preferences on citrus imports	EC	Yes	Tariff on pasta	After EC block of citrus panel report
Export subsidy	EC	Yes		
Nontariff measure*	Canada	No	Symmetric nontariff barrier	Not applicable
Failure to abide by bilateral agreement	Argentina	No	Termination of agreed tariff concessions	Not applicable
Quantitative restrictions on leather	Japan	Yes	U.S. tariff and Japanese tariff concession	Agreement of U.S. & Japan after panel report
Failure to abide by semiconductor agreement	Japan	Yes (Complaint filed by Japan on U.S. tariff retaliation)	Tariff	Not applicable – no ruling
EC tariffs on imports of Spain	EC	No	Tariff	Not applicable
Inadequate patent protection	Brazil	Yes (Filed by Brazil)	Tariff	Before panel
Import ban on treated beef	EC	Yes	Tariff	Panel appointment blocked

*Canadian government denied tax deductions to Canadian businesses that advertised on U.S. border stations.

Sources: Hudec (1990b) and Hamilton and Whalley (1991).

best response function $\tau_i(\tau_j)$ that is well-behaved in the sense that the best response functions generate a unique non-autarkic Nash equilibrium in tariffs. Let $U_i^R(\tau_j)=U_i(\tau_i(\tau_j),\tau_j)$ denote country i's static best-response payoff, and let τ_i^N and U_i^N denote the one shot Nash equilibrium tariffs and payoffs for $i = 1, 2$, respectively.

The tariff game is infinitely repeated with per period payoffs denoted by $U_{it}(\tau_{it},\tau_{jt})\equiv E_{\underset{\sim}{\theta}} u_i(\tau_{it},\tau_{jt},\underset{\sim}{\theta}_t)$ where $\underset{\sim}{\theta}_t=(\theta_{1t},\theta_{2t})$ are iid across periods. Taking the other country's supergame strategy as given, each country chooses its strategy to maximize its discounted expected utility,

$$E\left[\sum_{t=0}^{\infty} \beta^t u_{it}(\tau_{it},\tau_{jt},\underset{\sim}{\theta}_t)\right] \tag{1}$$

where $\beta < 1$ is the common discount factor.

We define a contingent strategy to be an infinite sequence $s_i=(s_{i0}, s_{i1}, \ldots)$, such that $s_{i0}=\tau_{i0}$ and for $t > 0$, s_{it}: $\mathbb{R}_+^{2t}\times\mathbb{R}_+^{2t}\rightarrow\mathbb{R}_+$. Let S be an arbitrary subset of the set of such contingent strategies, S. s_{it} determines country i's tariff level at time t as a function of the history of tariffs levied by both countries in periods $0,\ldots,t-1$ and past realizations of a pair of summary statistics $\omega_{is}(\tau_{1s},\tau_{2s},\theta_{1s},\theta_{2s})$, $s=0,\ldots t-1$, $i=1,2$. Call the history of past tariffs and summary statistic realizations up to time t, H_t.

One example of such a strategy arises in Reizman (1991) where tariff levels are assumed to be unobservable. In this country i's period t action is not directly dependent on past tariff levels, but depends only on the observed sequence of country 2 imports, where period t imports are a function of τ_{1t},τ_{2t}, and $\underset{\sim}{\theta}_t$. Hence the contingent strategies in Riezman are restricted to a set S of strategies that are independent of past tariffs. Another example would arise in a model in which tariffs are observable but the per period utility function arises from a random political process which dictates the weights of various interest groups in determining trade policy. In this case, allowing period t tariffs to be contingent upon $\omega_{is}(\tau_{1s},\tau_{2s},\theta_{1s},\theta_{2s})$, $s=0,\ldots t-1$, $i=1,2$, could represent the dependence of the governments' policies on a random process of political influence.[6]

A continent strategy pair (s_1^*, s_2^*), determines a stochastic process of summary statistics and tariffs. Denote the expectation of this process by Es_1^*,s_2^*. A Nash equilibrium in S is a pair of contingent strategies (s_1^*, s_2^*), $s_i^* \in S$ satisfying.

$$Es_1^*,s_2^*\left[\sum_{t=0}^{\infty} \beta^t u_{it}(s_{1t}^*,(H_t),\ s_{2t}^*(H_t),\underset{\sim}{\theta}_t)\right]$$

$$\geq Es_i,s_j^*\left[\sum_{t=0}^{\infty} \beta^t u_{it}(s_{it},(H_t),\ s_{jt}^*(H_t),\underset{\sim}{\theta}_t)\right] \qquad \forall s_i \in S \quad i = 1,2\ j\neq i. \tag{2}$$

As do Green and Porter (1984) and Riezman (1990), we focus on contingent strategies that involve reverting to the one shot Nash equilibrium for $T - 1$

periods, starting at time $t + 1$ if the observed summary statistic at time t is in a certain set.[7] Specifically let $\underset{\sim}{\omega}_t=(\omega_{1t}(\tau_{1t},\tau_{2t},\theta_{1t},\theta_{2t}),\ \omega_{2t}(\tau_{1t},\tau_{2t},\theta_{1t},\theta_{2t})) \in \Omega \supset \mathbb{R}^2_+$ trigger such a reversion. We are interested in determining when a profile of low "cooperative" tariffs (τ_1,τ_2) can be supported as an equilibrium choice in "normal" periods by the threat of $T - 1$ period reversion. Define period t to be normal if one of the following holds: (a) $t = 0$, or (b) $t - 1$ was normal and $\underset{\sim}{\omega}_{t-1} \notin \Omega$, or (c) $t - T$ was normal $\underset{\sim}{\omega}_{t-T} \in \Omega$. Otherwise t is reversionary.

A pair of tariffs (τ_1,τ_2) that are lower than the one-shot equilibrium tariff levels can be supported in a subgame perfect equilibrium by such a "trigger" strategy if the one-period gain from deviating to a higher tariff does not outweigh the potential loss from increasing the probability of triggering reversion.[8] Let $F(\tau_1,\tau_2)$ be the probability that $\underset{\sim}{\omega}_t(\tau_1,\tau_2,\theta_{1t},\theta_{2t}) \notin \Omega$. Since $\underset{\sim}{\theta}_t=(\theta_{1t},\theta_{2t})$ are iid across periods. F depends only upon the tariff levels set, and is not time dependent. $1 - F(\tau_1,\tau_2)$ is the probability that the "punishment" of reverting to the one-shot Nash equilibrium for $T - 1$ periods is imposed. We assume that Ω is chosen in such a way that F is decreasing in τ_i, so that the probability of punishment is increasing in τ_i.

Given this probabilistic punishment, the value to country i from setting a level of protection τ_i given that country j has set τ_j is

$$V_i(\tau_i,\tau_j) = U_i(\tau_i,\tau_j) + (1 - F(\tau_i,\tau_j))\left\{\sum_{t=1}^{T-1} \beta^t U_i^N + \beta^T V_i(\tau_i,\tau_j)\right\} + \beta F(\tau_i,\tau_j) V_i(\tau_i,\tau_j) \quad (3)$$
$$i = 1,2, j \neq i$$

which, after rearrangement, gives

$$V_i(\tau_i,\tau_j) = \frac{U_i^N}{1-\beta} + \frac{U_i(\tau_i,\tau_j) - U_i^N}{1 - \beta^T + F(\tau_i,\tau_j)(\beta^T - \beta)}. \quad (4)$$

An implicitly cooperative agreement (τ_i^c,τ_j^c) is supported as a noncooperative equilibrium by this $T - 1$ period trigger if

$$V_i(\tau_i^c,\tau_j^c) \geq V_i(\tau_i,\tau_j^c) \qquad \forall \tau_i \quad i = 1,2\ j \neq i. \quad (5)$$

By imposing conditions on the function $F(\tau_i,\tau_j)$ and U_i, we can represent a noncooperative equilibrium as a solution to the pair of first order conditions,

$\dfrac{\partial V_i}{\partial \tau_i}(\tau_i^c,\tau_j^c) = 0$, $i = 1,2\ j \neq i$, which can be written as

$$\frac{\partial U_i(\tau_i^c,\tau_j^c)}{\partial \tau_i}[1 - \beta^T + F(\tau_i^c,\tau_j^c)(\beta^T - \beta)] + (\beta - \beta^T)[U_i(\tau_i^c,\tau_j^c) - U_i^N]\frac{\partial F(\tau_i^c,\tau_j^c)}{\partial \tau_i} = 0 \quad (6)$$
$$i = 1,2\ j \neq i.$$

If the punishment and trigger probabilities support an equilibrium more cooperative than the one-shot Nash equilibrium, the first term is positive because of the static incentive to increase the tariff above τ_i. The second term is negative since F is decreasing in τ_i.[9]

B. Special Cases

(i) $T = \infty$

Suppose that the reversionary periods are grim trigger strategies ($T = \infty$). Then

$$V_i(\tau_i, \tau_j) = \frac{U_i^N}{1 - \beta} + \frac{U_i(\tau_i, \tau_j) - U_i^N}{1 - \beta F(\tau_i, \tau_j)}. \tag{7}$$

and the equilibrium conditions are adjusted accordingly.

(ii) Complete Information or Certain Punishment

Suppose $\omega_{it}(\tau_{1t}, \tau_{2t}, \theta_{1t}, \theta_{2t}) = \tau_{it}$, $i = 1,2$, and that the trigger set Ω is the set $\{(\tau_1, \tau_2)$: $\tau_1 > \tau_1^c$ or $\tau_2 > \tau_2^c\}$. Then the model outlined reduces to the complete information trigger strategy model with $T - 1$ period reversion.

(iii) Demons

In the model outlined so far, in equilibrium countries know the tariffs that are set. Whether or not tariffs are observable, countries can deduce tariff levels in equilibrium. If a punishment path is initiated, it is initiated despite the fact that no deviation from the implicitly cooperative tariff occurs. Reversionary periods are triggered by bad realizations of the random variable rather than "cheating" on cooperative tariffs.

In a GATT-less world, such a motivation for reversionary periods is not unduly restrictive. However, many GATT disputes involve panel investigations of whether deviations from tariff bindings are legitimate (for example, in escape clauses actions) or whether they are true deviations from the agreement. In order to analyze the role of DSP in such determinations, the basic model must allow for deviations from cooperative tariffs in equilibrium. One way to do this is to extend the model to allow reversionary periods to be triggered by a random deviation by one country from the implicitly cooperative tariff level. In this way, the decision to punish by reverting to the one-shot Nash equilibrium may be the result of a deviation from the implicitly cooperative tariff level (i.e. "cheating") or it may not.

We model these random deviations by borrowing from Segerstrom (1988) the notion of a "demon." We assume that, in each period, with probability $1 - \alpha$ country 1 plays a static best response to country 2's equilibrium action for that period. When this happens, country 1 is "possessed (temporarily) by a demon."

Of course, when the countries are in a period of reversion to the static Nash equilibrium, the possessed and unpossessed are indistinguishable. We will generally take $1 - \alpha$ to be small, representing a small amount of irrationality.

Suppose τ_2^c is the proposed implicitly cooperative tariff level of country 2. Country 1's discounted expected utility as a function of its own tariff level, τ_1, becomes

$$V_1(\tau_1,\tau_2^c) = \alpha U_1(\tau_1,\tau_2^c) + (1-\alpha)U_1^R(\tau_2^c) +$$

$$\alpha[(1 - F(\tau_1,\tau_2^c))\left\{\sum_{t=1}^{T-1} \beta^t U_1^N + \beta^T V_1(\tau_1,\tau_2^c)\right\} + \beta F(\tau_1,\tau_2^c)V_1(\tau_1,\tau_2^c)] \tag{8}$$

$$+(1-\alpha)[(1 - F(\tau_1,(\tau_2^c)\tau_2^c))\left\{\sum_{t=1}^{T-1} \beta^t U_1^N + \beta^T V_1(\tau_1,\tau_2^c)\right\} + \beta F(\tau_1,(\tau_2^c)\tau_2^c)V_1(\tau_1,\tau_2^c)].$$

Define

$$\mathcal{V}_1(\tau_1) \equiv V_1(\tau_1,\tau_2^c),\ \mathcal{U}_1(\tau_1) \equiv \alpha U_1(\tau_1,\tau_2^c) + (1-\alpha)U_1^R(\tau_2^c),\ \bar{F}(\tau_1) \equiv F(\tau_1,\tau_2^c)$$

and

$$\bar{F} \equiv F(\tau_1,(\tau_2^c),\tau_2^c).$$

Then

$$\mathcal{V}_1(\tau_1) = \frac{U_1^N}{1-\beta} + \frac{\mathcal{U}_1(\tau_1) - U_1^N}{1 - \beta^T + (\beta^T - \beta)[\bar{F}(\tau_1)\alpha + (1-\alpha)]} \tag{9}$$

Country 2 is never possessed with a demon and, hence, for any proposed cooperative tariff pari (τ_1^c,τ_2^c), τ_2^c must maximize.

$$V_2(\tau_1^c,\tau_2), = \alpha U_2(\tau_1^c,\tau_2) + (1-\alpha)U_2(\tau_1,(\tau_2^c),\tau_2)$$

$$+\ \alpha[(1 - F(\tau_1^c,\tau_2))\left\{\sum_{t=1}^{T-1} \beta^t U_2^N + \beta^T V_2(\tau_1^c,\tau_2)\right\} + \beta F(\tau_1^c,\tau_2)V_2(\tau_1^c,\tau_2)] \tag{10}$$

$$+(1-\alpha)[(1 - F(\tau_1,(\tau_2^c)\tau_2))\left\{\sum_{t=1}^{T-1} \beta^t U_2^N + \beta^T V_2(\tau_1^c,\tau_2)\right\}$$

$$+\ \beta F(\tau_1,(\tau_2^c),\tau_2)V_2(\tau_1^c,\tau_2)].$$

Collecting terms, an expression analogous to (9) may be obtained.

4. THE WORLD ACCORDING TO GATT

A. International Obligation

We model international obligation by assuming that countries bear a cost when they deviate from the GATT-determined cooperative tariff levels, (τ_1^g,τ_2^g), in cooperative periods or from GATT specified strategies in reversionary periods. In the political economy interpretation of this model, we can think of this disutility as a loss of goodwill in the international arena or the political embarrassment that comes from being suspected of violations, regardless of whether retaliation is actually triggered. In the imperfect monitoring interpretation of the model, the disutility could be viewed as a domestic political cost or loss of goodwill within an internal circle of policymakers.[10] Finally, as in other human endeavors, this cost could be interpreted simply as the disutility of a "guilty conscience" arising from the violation of an agreement (and incurred even if the violation is undetected).

We examine three possible forms that this disutility might take: (i) A fixed cost c incurred by a country the first time it deviates (with future deviations generating no disutility); (ii) A fixed cost that is incurred after the initial deviation and upon the first deviation after any reversionary period;[11] and (iii) A cost c incurred by a country in every period in which it deviates from GÄ*f*T-determined tariff levels. Note that if the punishment period is $T = \infty$, alternatives (i) and (ii) coincide. If punishments are certain,[12] then (ii) and (iii) coincide. In the version of the model with a demon, we shall assume that being a demon means not incurring a cost; that is, demons feel no international obligation.

First we examine a fixed cost, as in case (i), for the basic model without demons. In this case, equation (4) remains as before for $\tau_i = \tau_i^g$, where τ_i^g denotes the GATT-determined cooperative tariff. But for $\tau_i \neq \tau_i^g$,

$$V_i^0(\tau_i, \tau_j) = -c + \frac{U_i^N}{1-\beta} + \frac{U_i(\tau_i, \tau_j) - U_i^N}{1-\beta^T + F(\tau_i, \tau_j)(\beta^T - \beta)}. \quad (11)$$

Hence, the cost incurred in violating GATT rules simply shifts down the function $V_i(\tau_i, \tau_j)$ for $\tau_i \neq \tau_i^g$, generating a discontinuity in the function at τ_i^g. If the fixed cost is incurred in every period of deviation, as in case (iii), equation (4) remains as before for $\tau_i = \tau_i^g$, but for $\tau_i \neq \tau_i^g$,

$$V_i^0(\tau_i, \tau_j) = \frac{U_i^N}{1-\beta} + \frac{U_i(\tau_i, \tau_j) - c - U_i^N}{1-\beta^T + F(\tau_i, \tau_j)(\beta^T - \beta)}. \quad (12)$$

Hence, a discontinuity remains at $\tau_i = \tau_i^g$, but the effect on $V_i(\tau_i, \tau_j)$ for $\tau_i \neq \tau_i^g$ is no longer a constant shift down.

These two cost formulations allow us to illustrate an important principle governing the role of GATT-determined tariffs in a world with implicit cooperation. If these tariffs are set too low, international obligation may be ineffective in achieving lower cooperative tariffs. To illustrate this, suppose that the implicitly cooperative tariff levels in a GATT-less world, (τ_1^c, τ_2^c), are greater than zero. This implies that $V_i(0,0) < V_i(\tau_i, 0)$ for some $\tau_i > 0$, as shown in Figure 1. Suppose the GATT-determined tariff level is zero (i.e. $\tau_1^g = \tau_2^g = 0$). In this case, the international obligation induced by GATT may or may not be sufficient to enforce free trade as an implicitly cooperative outcome. Figure 1a depicts a situation where $V_i(0,0) < V_i^0(\tau_i,0)\ \forall\tau_i$, so that free trade can be enforced. In other situations international obligation may not sufficiently reduce the gain from deviating from free trade, and the relevant value functions could be depicted by Figure 1b. In the latter case, there will generally be some tariff level $(\hat{\tau}_1, \hat{\tau}_2)$ lower than the GATT-less implicitly collusive level, (τ_1^c, τ_2^c), which, if specified as the GATT-determined cooperative tariff level, would be immune to deviation. This is depicted in Figure 1c. Hence, a properly chosen GATT tariff can lead to greater cooperation, but attempts to reduce tariff levels too much may lead to cooperative tariff levels no lower than in a GATT-less world.

Indeed, the danger from GATT-determined tariffs being too low is ever more striking if international obligation imposes costs in each period (as in case (iii)). In that case, when GATT-determined tariffs are not enforceable, then the existence of GATT-determined obligation may cause the most collusive (implicitly cooperative) tariff levels to increase. For any given tariff of country j.

$$\operatorname{sgn}\left\{\frac{dV_i^0(\tau_i,\tau_j)}{d\tau_i}\right. = \tag{13}$$

$$\operatorname{sgn}\left\{\frac{\partial U_i(\tau_i,\tau_j)}{\partial\tau_i}[1-\beta^T+F(\tau_i,\tau_j)(\beta^T-\beta)]\right.$$

$$\left.-[U_i(\tau_i,\tau_j)-c-U_i^N]\frac{\partial F(\tau_i,\tau_j)}{\partial\tau_i}(\beta^T-\beta)\right\}.$$

Hence, for any cooperative tariff level, τ_j, if country i's best response satisfies the first order condition, $\frac{dV_i^0(\tau_i,\tau_j)}{d\tau_i} = 0$, totally differentiating this equation yields

$$\operatorname{sgn}\left(\frac{d\tau_i}{dc}\right) = \operatorname{sgn}\left(\frac{\partial F(\tau_i,\tau_j)}{\partial\tau_i}(\beta^T-\beta)\right) > 0. \tag{14}$$

An increase in c will cause country i's optimal tariff response to a tariff τ_j to increase. Intuitively, the dynamic optimal response $\tau_i^D(\tau_j)$ balances the marginal one-period gain to deviating from the cooperative tariff in a normal period with the expected loss due to the increased probability of triggering a reversionary period. For a given probability of reversion, this loss is reduced (due to the decrease in the payoff from deviating) from $U_i(\tau_i,\tau_j)$ to $U_i(\tau_i,\tau_j) - c$. Hence the marginal gain from increasing τ_i must be reduced to maintain equality. This is done by setting τ_i at a higher level.

A similar effect occurs in the presence of demons, in which case equation (9) becomes

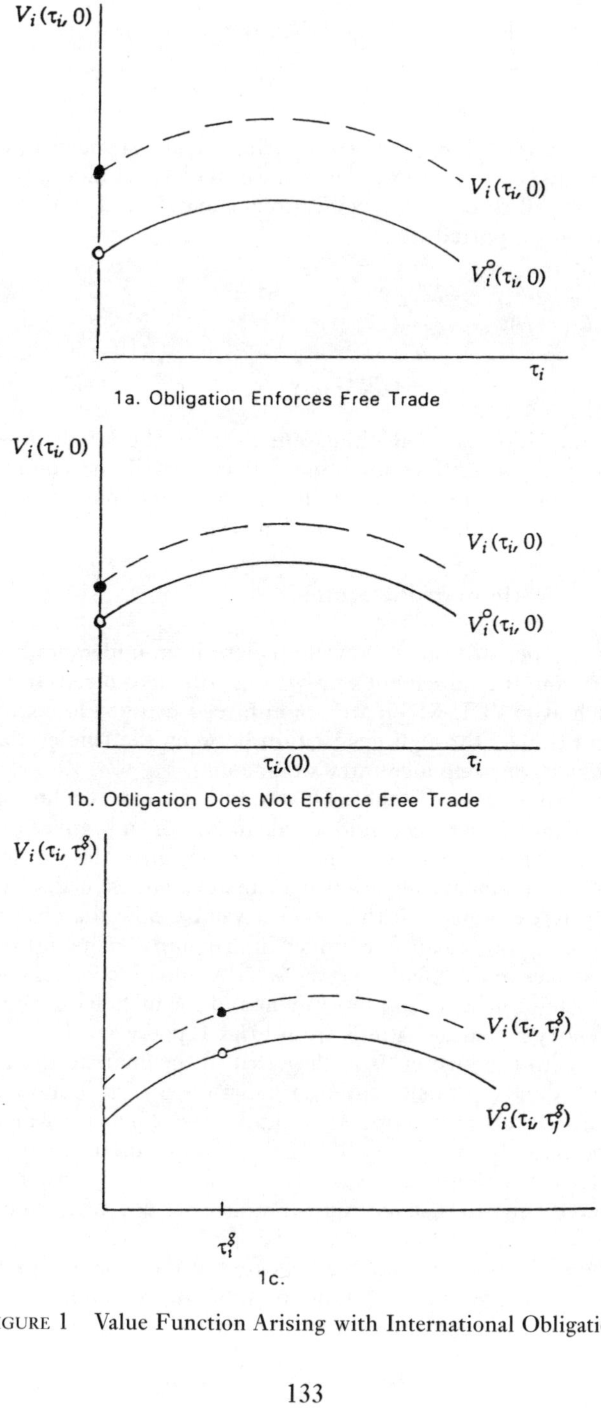

FIGURE 1 Value Function Arising with International Obligation.

$$\mathcal{V}_1(\tau_1) = \frac{U_1^N}{1-\beta} + \frac{\mathcal{U}_1(\tau_1) - \alpha c - U_1^N}{1 - \beta^T + (\beta^T - \beta)[\bar{F}(\tau_1)\alpha + \bar{F}(1-\alpha)]}, \tag{15}$$

where again the cost is as in case (iii). The interpretation of this effect remains the same.

Finally, in the case of infinite horizon grim trigger strategies ($T = \infty$) and certain punishments, the representation of the cost of violating international obligation is simplest. All three cost specifications coincide and GATT-determined tariff levels can be supported if

$$U_i^R(\tau_i^g) - c - U_i(\tau_i^g, \tau_j^g) \leq \frac{\beta}{1-\beta}(U_i(\tau_i^g, \tau_j^g) - U_i^N). \tag{16}$$
$$i = 1,2,\ j \neq i$$

To the extent that international obligation reduces the left-hand side of the inequality, it facilitates tariff cooperation. Of course, if the cooperative tariff pari, (τ_1^g, τ_2^g), is so low that the inequality in (16) does not hold (for given β), then the international obligation of GATT has no effect.

B. The Dispute Settlement Procedure

Essential to the proper working of any agreement is an understanding as to how disputes arising from the agreement's provisions will be resolved. In international agreements such as GATT, which are not enforced by outside institutions, disputes are often resolved through negotiation between the parties and threats of unilateral actions to back up a country's demands.

It seems reasonable to justify the inclusion of a dispute resolution procedure in GATT by claiming that it would be difficult for any government to feel international obligation if there were no such procedure. Having demonstrated the benefits of international obligation it seems evident then that the existence of a DSP is easily explained. In this section we ask how the characteristics of such a procedure might enhance or hinder international cooperation. Given the observed deficiencies in the DSP, it seems worthwhile to focus on two particular issues: the problem of delay until punishment and the inability of the mechanism to properly identify actual deviations from GATT policy.

We deal first with the former. It is clear that in the context of our model any mechanism that delays punishment or retaliation makes it more difficult to support low tariff levels in a cooperative outcome.[13] This is because, in equilibrium, the one-period gain from cheating on cooperation is balanced by the potential loss from triggering reversion. If reversion occurs with delay, not only is its cost lowered (due to discounting), but also the deviating country may be able to benefit from its deviation for a longer period.

To assess the effect of this delay, we look first at the model with grim trigger strategies ($T = \infty$) and certain punishments. In modeling a delay in punishment within the GATT system, it is not clear what tariffs should be assumed to be in place between the time that a reversionary period is triggered and the punishment starts. In a sense the "status quo" should be maintained, but it is not clear whether this could be equilibrium behavior. In the case of certain punishment the optimal deviation from a GATT tariff is to play a one-period best response $\tau_i = \tau_i(\tau_j^g)$. That is, if a deviation is desirable, the dynamic best response $\tau_i = \tau_i^D(\tau_j^g)$ is also the static best response $\tau_i(\tau_j^g)$. When this is true, as long as a punishing country does not punish outside of the GATT system, a deviating country has no incentive to alter its strategy in the period between the identification of cheating and the initiation of punishment. At this point, we assume that all punishment is within the framework of GATT. We will later remove this assumption, to determine whether adhering to GATT-DSP is Nash equilibrium behavior when countries have the option of punishing outside of the system.

Suppose punishment is delayed s^* periods and the cost structure of international obligation is (i) or (ii). Then a cooperative tariff pair (τ_1^g, τ_2^g) can be sustained in equilibrium if and only if

$$U_i(\tau_i(\tau_j^g), \tau_j^g) - c - U_i(\tau_1^g, \tau_2^g) \leq \sum_{s=1}^{s^*} (U_i(\tau_1^g, \tau_2^g) - U_i(\tau_i(\tau_j^g), \tau_j^g))\beta^s. \tag{17}$$

$$+ \sum_{s=s^*+1}^{\infty} (U_i(\tau_1^g, \tau_2^g) - U_i^N)\beta^s$$

or

$$-c + \left(\frac{1-\beta^{s^*+1}}{1-\beta}\right)(U_i(\tau_i(\tau_j^g), \tau_j^g) - U_i(\tau_1^g, \tau_2^g)) \leq \frac{\beta^{s^*+1}}{1-\beta}(U_i(\tau_1^g, \tau_2^g) - U_i^N). \tag{18}$$

Clearly, an increase in s^* reduces the right-hand side of this inequality and increases the left-hand side, making cooperation more difficult. The above formulation also easily accommodates stochastic delay until punishment, in which case $E(\beta^{s^*+1})$ replaces β^{s^*+1}. For instance, s^* could be generated by a geometric or negative binomial random variable. In the former case

$$E(\beta^{s^*}) = \sum_{t=1}^{\infty} \beta^t p(1-p)^{t-1} = \frac{\beta p}{1-\beta(1-p)} \tag{19}$$

where $\text{Prob}(s^* = t) = p(1-p)^{t-1}$, $0<p<1$.

When international obligation imposes a cost as in (iii), the inequality in (18) is altered, but the same qualitative result goes through. This is also true when punishment is finite and uncertain or when demons are incorporated. Generally, increasing s^* increases the value of τ_i that maximizes $V_i(\tau_i, \tau_j^g)$. However, in these cases the specification of the countries' strategies in the interim period between the identification of cheating and the onset of punishment is more complicated. Static and dynamic best responses do not coincide and there is a non-trivial decision whether to adhere to a GATT-determined policy during the period.

The issues of international obligation and delay until punishment interact in affecting the choice to pursue remedies within the GATT system or outside of the system. Due to international obligation, a decision to punish a deviating country outside the DSP guidelines imposes a cost on the country initiating the punishment. This cost must be weighed against the losses that might occur due to delay in punishment within the system, or possibly even a finding of no violation.[14]

Again, we illustrate these considerations in the special case of certain punishment and grim trigger strategies. Suppose that s^*, which may be deterministic or random, is the period of time before punishment may be pursued within the DSP. If the cost to a punishing country from deviating from the DSP is a one-time cost as in (i), the country will punish outside of the DSP if

$$U_j^N - c - U_j(\tau_j^g, \tau_i(\tau_j^g)) + E\left(\sum_{s=2}^{s^*} \beta^{s-1}(U_i^N - U_j(\tau_j^g, \tau_i(\tau_j^g))) \right) \geq 0 \tag{20}$$

or

$$-c + \frac{1 - E(\beta^{s^*})}{1-\beta}(U_j^N - U_j(\tau_j^g, \tau_i(\tau_j^g))) \geq 0. \tag{21}$$

For instance, when s^* is distributed according to a geometric distribution with parameter p, $E(\beta^{s^*}) = (\beta p)/[1 - \beta(1 - p)]$, and the above inequality becomes

$$-c + \frac{1}{1 - \beta(1 - p)}(U_j^N - U_j(\tau_j^g, \tau_i(\tau_j^g))) \geq 0. \tag{22}$$

The inequality in (21) can be used to assess the benefit from punishing outside of the DSP at any point in the DSP itself. Suppose a country has pursued a grievance in the DSP up to some time t and let s^* represent the number of periods beyond t that the country must wait until the DSP allows punishment. Then the inequality in (21) determines whether it is worthwhile to punish outside of the procedure at t. If the distribution of the punishment time exhibits a decreasing hazard rate then it is possible that a country might pursue a grievance within the DSP and decide to punish outside of the framework if the procedure has not specified a punishment by the time t is reached.[15] Hence, our formulation of the interaction of delay and international obligation is consistent with the pursuit of punishment within the DSP, punishment outside of the DSP, and a combination of both.

If the cost to a country punishing outside of the DSP is a per period cost as in (iii) then the decision whether to punish within or outside of the mechanism is independent of the anticipated delay until punishment. The payoff per period obtained while waiting to be able to punish within the mechanism is $U_j(\tau_j^g, \tau_i(\tau_j^g))$. The payoff from punishing outside of the mechanism is $U_j^N - c$. Of course, once the mechanism itself specifies a punishment, it is best for a country to punish within the mechanism. This formulation of cost is then consistent with a policy of punishing outside of the DSP while pursuing a grievance within the procedure.

The above discussion of the decision to punish within or outside the DSP must, of course, be taken into account when determining the gain to a country from cheating on the GATT tariffs. The ability to punish outside of the DSP enhances the ability to reach low cooperative tariff levels. Of course, under both specifications of the cost of violating international obligation, a DSP that reached a verdict rapidly in the event of a violation could possibly support even lower tariffs.

C. Identifying Violations

A feasible role for DSP, and one which it arguably was created to perform, is as a monitoring device that distinguishes between true deviations from a cooperative agreement and mistaken perceptions or claims that such a deviation has occurred. These claims may be due to the imperfect observability of cheating or simply to opportunistic behavior. In modeling a monitoring role for the DSP it seems important to construct an analytical framework in which, in equilibrium, the procedure may be justifiably triggered, due to deviations from an implicitly cooperative agreement, and triggered when no actual deviation occurs. This creates a nontrivial inference problem in resolving the dispute.

The extension of our basic model involving demons provides such a framework. In an implicitly cooperative agreement in the demon model, reversionary periods may be triggered following periods in which both countries adhere to the agreement or they may be triggered due to the existence of a demon. For simplicity, suppose that the implicitly cooperative tariff levels are the GATT levels, $(\tau_1^c,\tau_2^c)=(\tau_1^g,\tau_2^g)$, there is no delay until punishment if a violation is detected, and the DSP detects violations instantaneously if a complaint is initiated. If the countries set tariffs at (τ_1,τ_2), complaints will be initiated with probability $1 - F(\tau_1,\tau_2)$. If a complaint is initiated and no violation takes place ($\tau_i=\tau_i^g$, $i=1,2$) then no punishment occurs, and the countries continue in a normal period (setting τ_i^g). Hence, allowing instantaneous and perfect determination of a violation if a complaint is brought forward allows us to set $F(\tau_1^g,\tau_2^g) \equiv F(\tau_1^g) = 1$ in equation (15) while maintaining $F(\tau_1) < 1$ for other values. This raises the payoff to behaving cooperatively, while allowing a non-zero probability of a violation (due to a demon) and the resulting reversion that would occur.

Of course, the DSP is not instantaneous, nor does it perfectly separate violations from compliance. To the extent that these imperfections exist, the monitoring benefit of the procedure would be muted and perhaps even reversed when erratic decisions and international obligation prevent countries from punishing actual violators.

5. CONCLUSION

Previous theoretical treatments of GATT (see Ludema (1990) and Hungerford (1990)) have provided a skeptical view of the role of GATT in facilitating trade liberalization. We believe strongly that this view results directly from the ease in fitting the deficiencies of GATT and DSP into formal mathematical models and the difficulty in formally modeling GATT benefits. Since countries clearly believe that GATT is important, it is hard to concur with the conclusion of these papers that GATT restricts the ability to maintain low tariffs.

To model the benefits of GATT, we focus on the role of international obligation. Roughly, international obligation is a perceived cost that is incurred if a country deviates from an international agreement. In vague terms, it might be viewed as the political equivalent of "living with one's conscience." By including international obligation in a repeated game model of implicitly cooperative trade agreements, we provide a parametric class of models spanning the range between the standard noncooperative supergame models of implicit collusion, where obligation is zero, and the cooperative game models of collusion, where obligation is infinite (agreements are binding).[16] While we are aware of the limitations of such brute force modeling, we think, as do legal experts who have written on the topic, that it is international obligation that makes GATT and a DSP desirable, as long as the DSP doesn't make identification and punishment of violators too difficult.

Taking the institution as given, our analysis shows that the GATT-specified tariff levels are an important determinant of the degree to which the institution facilitates international cooperation. If these tariff levels are unrealistically low relative to the implicitly cooperative levels in the absence of GATT, the institution will not aid in lowering tariffs (and, conceivably, could raise them). The DSP may hinder the ability to cooperate by delaying punishment or making it more costly. When this is true, punishment outside of GATT may work well as a second-best mechanism to facilitate cooperation. By explicitly modeling these forces, we have attempted to capture the essence of the "twin engines of international obligation and retaliation" (Hudec, 1990c, p. 14), which are emphasized in the legal literature.

Of course, institutions as complicated as the GATT and DSP are reflections of and are influenced by a vast array of factors not captured by these simple models. Foremost among these factors is the fact that GATT itself is a nexus of contracts that is incomplete in its coverage of future contingencies. This is, of course, a principal reason why the DSP may be viewed as a major component of GATT; it is the mechanism by which incomplete provisions of GATT are completed. Given this role, it is quite possible that the original agreement would not have been signed without the DSP.

We have also ignored other aspects of GATT that beg analysis. We have chosen tariffs as the strategic choice of countries, although our analysis could be carried out for a variety of instruments. Our analysis also focuses on bilateral, rather than multilateral, conflict and cooperation. In a multilateral treatment, a reputational justification for international obligation might be possible. This would address the current weakness of our reduced-form treatment of international obligation. This, however, appears to be a formidable task.

NOTES

This paper was prepared for the Conference of Analytical and Negotiating Issues in the Global Trading System, October 31–November 1, 1991, Ann Arbor, Michigan.

We thank Robert Hudec and John Walley for providing access to unpublished materials on GATT legal disputes. Jack Barron, John Cross, John Jackson, Manu Kalwani, Rodney Ludema, Bob Plante, Jerry Thursby, Gordon Wright, and participants of the conference are thanked for useful comments.

1 Although GATT rules are legally binding, they are directly enforceable in domestic courts only when they have been incorporated into domestic law. None of the Articles of GAA provide for disputes to be taken to the World Court. See Jackson (1989) on how this relates to the origins of GATT and unsuccessful attempts to set up the International Trade Organization (ITO).

2 Baldwin and Clark (1987) examine both cooperative and noncooperative equilibria. Jensen and Thursby (1984) examine implicit cooperation in a finitely-repeated context. Stahl and Turunen-Red (1990) examine cooperation when government policy changes randomly.

3 We have modeled the inclusion or omission of DSP as an exogenous decision, although it could be thought of as a decision made at a pre-supergame stage. The motivation for this approach is that GATT negotiations are conducted in distinct negotiating rounds so that GATT rules adjust slowly to world market conditions; much more slowly than the rapid-paced change in the nature and frequency of trade disputes. Rod Ludema, in suggesting that perhaps decisions regarding the DSP should be viewed as arising endogenously, has pointed out that abolishing DSP would be a time inconsistent policy. However, when explaining the endogenous determination of institutions within this framework, it is not clear to us what time inconsistency means. If the decision to agree upon institutions can itself be subject to trigger-type punishments, then it appears as if the endogenous determination of institutions may become a problem of infinite regress in the endogenous determination of the rules of the game.

4 We thank Rod Ludema for suggesting this term.

5 That is, each country's utility is increasing in its own tariff given a zero foreign tariff, and each country's utility is decreasing in the foreign tariff.

6 This is in the spirit of Feenstra and Lewis (1987) where governments face varying degrees of protectionist political pressure at home, or Jensen and Thursby (1990) where a random political process influences which interest group's preferences to follow when levying tariffs.

7 There is nothing sacred about Nash reversion. Most, if not all of our qualitative insights would apply to a wide range of reversionary strategies. However, non-Nash reversion does make the treatment of demons in Section 3Biii considerably more complicated.

8 We have ignored here the issue of renegotiation proofness analyzed elsewhere (see Ludema (1990)). One implication of incorporating renegotiation is that the ability to credibly punish may be severely restricted, because of the ability to renegotiate away from undesirable subgame perfect equilibria, thereby making initial cooperation more difficult. While this concept is rather elegant mathematically, we are not sure as to the importance of this phenomenon. Our feeling is that other factors such as revenge, which is more difficult to model mathematically, may tend to bias outcomes in the other direction, allowing punishments not only worse than standard negotiation proof equilibria, but also subgame perfect equilibria in general. A more thorough treatment of revenge would have to await a more thorough theory of games in which preferences over outcomes depend on the complete game tree itself, as well as the strategies and path followed. In the context of this paper it might suffice to say that a country (or policymaker) may actually derive utility from punishing a "cheater" and hence may have preferences over, say, per period trade flows that are not history independent.

9 When first order conditions are not sufficient, the condition (5) reduces to

$$[U_i(\tau_i^c, \tau_j^c) - U_i(\tau_i, \tau_j^c)](1 - \beta^T) - (\beta - \beta^T)\{[U_i(\tau_i^c, \tau_j^c) - U_i^N]F(\tau_i, \tau_j^c) - [U_i(\tau_i, \tau_j^c) - U_i^N]F(\tau_i^c, \tau_j^c)\} \geq 0 \quad \forall \tau_i \; i = 1,2 \; j \neq i.$$

10 This latter interpretation, while perhaps less appealing than the political economy interpretation, does not require that other countries observe the violation.

11 In the event of probabilistic retaliation, deviations that occur after an unpunished deviation incur no cost.

12 In the imperfect monitoring interpretation of the game, this means information is complete.

13 See Abreu, Milgrom and Pearce (1991) for an example of a model in which this may not hold.

14 Domestic laws such as U.S. Section 301 might be viewed as an attempt to lower this cost by supplanting international obligation by domestic obligation.

15 As mentioned earlier, domestic legislation such as U.S. 301 may serve to precommit governments to discount international obligation by requiring punishment after a certain time period. In this case, a country might pursue a grievance in the DSP but retaliate in a GATT-illegal fashion even without a decreasing hazard rate.

16 An anonymous referee has suggested that our formulation of the cost imposed by international obligation is reminiscent of Crawford's (1982) treatment of the cost of backing down from a precommitted bargaining stance in the process of negotiation.

REFERENCES

Abreu, D., P. Milgrom and D. Pearce, 1991, Information and timing in repeated partnerships, *Econometrica* 59, 1713–1733.

Bagwell, K. and R. Staiger, 1990. A theory of managed trade, *American Economic Review* 80, 779–795.

Baldwin, R. E. and R. N. Clark, 1987, Game-modeling multilateral trade negotiations, *Journal of Policy Modeling* 9, 257–284.

Brown, F. and J. Whalley, December 1980, General equilibrium evaluations of tariff-cutting proposals in the Tokyo Round and comparisons with more extensive liberalization of world trade, *The Economic Journal*, 90, 838–866.

Chan, K., November 1988, Trade negotiations in a Nash bargaining model, *Journal of International Economics*, 25, 353–364.

Crawford, V., 1982, A theory of disagreement in bargaining, *Econometrica*, 50, 607–637.

Dixit, A., 1987, Strategic aspects of trade policy, in T. Bewley, ed., *Advances in Economics Theory: Fifth World Congress*, New York: Cambridge University Press.

Feenstra, R. and T. Lewis, September 1987, Negotiated trade restrictions with private political pressure, NBER Working Paper #2374.

Green, E. and R. Porter, January 1984, Noncooperative collusion under imperfect price information, *Econometrica*, 52, 87–100.

Hamilton, C. and J. Whalley, 1991, *What kind of future for the world trading system?*, Washington: Institute for International Economics, mimeo.

Hudec, R. E., 1990a, Dispute Settlement, in J. Schott, ed., *Completing the Uruguay Round*, Washington, D.C.: Institute for International Economics.

——, 1975, *The GATT Legal System and World Trade Diplomacy*, 2nd ed., Salem, NH: Butterworth.

——, September 1990b, GATT legal complaints, Appendix to *Enforcing International Trade Law: Gatt Dispute Settlement in the 1980s*, mimeo.
——, November 1990c, The judicialization of GATT dispute settlement, mimeo, University of Minnesota.
——, The legal status of GATT in the domestic law of the United States, 1986, in *The European Community and GATT*, Studies in Transnational Economic Law, Volume 4, Deventer, The Netherlands: Kluwer.
Hungerford, T., 1990, GATT: A cooperative equilibrium in a noncooperative trading regime?, mimeo.
Jackson, J., 1989, *The World Trading System: Law and Policy of International Economic Relations*, Cambridge, Massachusetts: MIT Press.
——, 1979, Governmental disputes in international trade relations: a proposal in the context of GATT, *Journal of World Trade Law*, 13, 1–21.
Jensen, R. and M. Thursby, 1984. Free trade: two non-cooperative equilibrium approaches, Ohio State University Working Paper #58.
——, 1990, Tariffs with private information and reputation, *Journal of International Economics*, 29, 43–67.
Ludema, R., 1990, Optimal international trade agreements and dispute settlement procedures, University of Western Ontario Working Paper.
McMillan, J., 1988, A game theoretic view of international trade negotiations: implications for the developing countries, in *Rules, Power, and Credibility*, ed. by J. Whalley, London, Ontario: Centre for the Study of International Economic Relations.
Mayer, W., 1981, Theoretical consideration on negotiated staff adjustments, *Oxford Economic Papers*, 33, 135–153.
Riezman, R., 1991, Dynamic tariffs with asymmetric information, *Journal of International Economics*, 30, 267–283.
——, 1982, Tariff retaliation from a strategic viewpoint, *Southern Economic Journal*, 48, 583–593.
Segerstrom, P., 1988, Demons and Repentance, *Journal of Economic Theory*, 45, 32–52.
Stahl, D. and Turunen-Red, A., 1990, Tariff games: sustainability of free trade with variation in policy regimes, Center for Economic Research, Working Paper 90–3.
Whalley, J. (ed), 1988, *Rules, Power and Credibility*, London, Ontario: Centre for the Study of International Economic Relations.
——, 1989, *The Uruguay Round and Beyond*, London, U.K.: MacMillan Press.

9. The WTO's Trade Policy Review Mechanism – From Through the Looking Glass

S. Laird

1. INTRODUCTION

The Trade Policy Review Mechanism (TPRM), established during the Uruguay Round of multilateral negotiations, is the main transparency mechanism of the World Trade Organisation, the looking glass through which Members examine each other's trade policies and practices. Unlike many WTO activities which focus on the conformity of Members' actions with specific aspects of WTO rules, the reviews look at the full range of the trade policies of individual Members. They are to be seen as an exercise in transparency, founded in the public choice literature, rather than assessments of how well individual Members are adhering to particular WTO rules. As such, the TPRM has been beneficial to WTO Members by throwing light on the policies of countries that have a major impact on world trade and the trading system. It has also been of benefit to smaller countries in the pursuit of trade policies which promote their own economic welfare.

The paper argues that the mechanism faces a number of challenges in carrying out the mandate set by Members, mainly arising from resource constraints. In particular, it is not clear how to carry out the full programme of reviews, especially in the light of the increasing membership of the organisation. The paper looks at some of the hard choices facing WTO Members in this regard.

The organisation of the paper is as follows: Section 2 covers the origins and objectives of the TPRM, Section 3 discusses: the TPR process (the cycle of reviews, the stages of a review, the Secretariat and Government reports and procedural changes), Section 4 provides an evaluation of the mechanism, Section 5 draws together some lessons from the reviews conducted over the last ten years, and Section 6 discusses some of the challenges facing the mechanism.

2. ORIGINS AND OBJECTIVES OF THE MECHANISM

The purpose of the TPRM is to

> contribute to improved adherence by all Members to rules, disciplines and commitments made under the Multilateral Trade Agreements and, where applicable, the Plurilateral Trade Agreements, and hence to the smoother functioning of the

multilateral trading system, by achieving greater transparency, and understanding of, the trade policies and practices of Members (Annex 3 of the Marrakesh Agreement, WTO, 1995).

There has been some debate in the literature concerning the objectives of the Trade Policy Review Mechanism, with Qureshi (1990, 1992 and 1995), in particular, emphasising the importance of the mechanism as part of the enforcement of GATT/WTO legal obligations, while Blackhurst (1988) and others have emphasised the transparency as a key to the adoption of good economic policies.

The legal interpretation seems to have been formulated on the basis of certain aspects of the legal texts, in particular, the phrase 'improved adherence . . . to rules, disciplines and commitments'. Thus, Qureshi (1990 and 1992) essentially argues that the mechanism is intended to ensure compliance with GATT obligations. There is some support for that among statements made by some GATT contracting parties in the Uruguay Round Group on the Functioning of the GATT System (FOGS), reported in GATT (1988). Thus, India, in particular, suggested that the surveillance should contribute to improved adherence to GATT disciplines and obligations. In this respect it is useful to recall that the widespread use of 'grey areas measures', such as voluntary export restraints, and subsidy wars in the area of agriculture, had been seen as undermining the GATT system, to the point that Lester Thurow was to declare 'GATT is dead".

However, it is important in looking at the legal text also to take account of objectives expressed in the phrases 'understanding of the trade policies and practices' or 'collective appreciation and evaluation . . . of the full range of . . . trade policies and practices and their impact on the functioning of the multilateral trading system'. Moreover, the Marrakesh text is quite explicit that the mechanism 'is not intended to serve as a basis for the enforcement of specific obligations under the [WTO] Agreements or for dispute settlement purposes, or to impose new policy commitments on Members'.

Such a broader indication of the original intention of the mechanism may also be obtained from Blackhurst (1988), then Director of the GATT's Economic Research and Analysis Unit. Blackhurst traces the concept of a transparency mechanism at the national and international levels to the economic literature on public choice. The basic line of argument in this literature is that elected officials and civil servants may become influenced by vested interests ('rent seekers') to make decisions which help such groups and run counter to the promotion of general public welfare. Transparency is said to lead to better decision-making by alerting the public at home to the potential costs and benefits of policies as well as signalling potentially harmful changes to trading partners. For these reasons, there is 'a very strong case for surrounding all facets of economic policy making with a high degree of transparency and surveillance'. In the same vein, Curzon Price (1991) argues that TPRM surveillance will apply peer group pressure to help overcome the natural tendency of countries to want to be free-riders, encouraging them to co-operate for enhanced international welfare.

The views of some delegations in the FOGS group echo this economic interpretation. Thus, the United States noted that the Trade Policy Review process is broader than a limited review of GATT obligations:

> Its aim is to improve understanding of the total context of trade policies and make contracting parties reflect on their economic policies (GATT, 1988).

A number of developing countries, including China (which was party to the negotiations although not a GATT contracting party), emphasised the importance of looking at policies in a development context. The United States said it was important to put trade policies into the context of other economic policies. Switzerland said the reviews should include the impact of fiscal, financial and monetary policies on the trading system. However, there was also disagreement about the extent to which the wide context of policies should be taken into account.

It is also clear from the earlier discussion as well as repeated statements by a wide range of Members that at no time was there any view held that the mechanism would be part of the formal dispute settlement system. The main EU spokesman on TPRM in 1993, Roderick Abbott, roundly criticised Qureshi for having missed this point in his second article which mainly concerned the review of the EU (Abbott, 1993). Indeed, one of the strengths of the TPRM is its role as a forum where policies can be explained on a non-confrontational and non-legalistic basis. However, one can understand how a jurist might take a narrower, enforcement interpretation, while economists with a background in the public policy debate would focus on the economic issues, seeing no fundamental dichotomy between good domestic policies and good international citizenship.

It may be noted that, in a later article, Qureshi (1995) places greater emphasis on the transparency aspect, while arguing that reviews should take fuller account of GATT/WTO provisions for developing countries in reviews of those countries (Qureshi, 1995). Mavroidis (1992), also a jurist, recognises the importance of the transparency element, but is disappointed by the reluctance of the Secretariat to express more forceful views on the GATT-consistency of measures.

Another element in the background to the objectives of the TPRM is the weight placed on the need for surveillance by Leutwiler et al. (1985), the so-called GATT 'Wise Men's Report'. The surveillance element subsequently filtered into the Punta del Este Declaration in the areas of standstill and rollback as well as the functioning of the GATT system. While there were, and remain, many other elements of surveillance in the GATT/WTO system, many felt that this was not sufficiently systematic and needed to be strengthened.

Several authors have focused on the benefits of the TPRM for improved domestic policies and only indirectly about the effects on other countries or for the trading system (Spriggs, 1991; Laird and Messerlin, 1990; and Banks, 1992). They see the TPRM as the multilateral complement to national transparency mechanisms, which they maintain can help improve domestic policy-making and the allocation of resources in the domestic economy. In meeting these domestic goals, such a mechanism would also produce domestic policies which are compatible with the goals of the multilateral trading system: freer trade, domestic deregulation, etc.

A number of writers have drawn out the parallels in the surveillance mechanisms of the OECD, in particular, as well as the IMF (Blackhurst, 1988; Robertson, 1992; and Mavroidis, 1992). Mavroidis notes that, in all cases, 'undergoing the review and becoming stronger in the process is consistent with the growing interdependence in international relations'. Robertson noted that the reviews had already become more analytical by 1991, when the Secretariat's success in identifying gaps between policies and practices on the one hand with stated objectives on the other aroused a hostile reaction in Brussels. He also noted that:

> the GATT review process provides a valuable flow of information for businessmen and academics, and government agencies should be able to use the information to pursue more liberal trade policies.

3. THE TPR PROCESS

a. Cycle of Reviews

Trade Policy Reviews are conducted by the Trade Policy Review Body (TPRB), which is equivalent in status to the General Council and the Dispute Settlement Body, the principal organs of the WTO. The TPRB undertakes the regular collective appreciation of the trade policies and practices of all individual Members. By the end of 1998, the TPRB had conducted 109 reviews, or 102 if grouped reviews of certain Members are counted as one (Table 1). Allowing for repeat reviews, 67 Members' policies have been reviewed, counting the European Union as a single trading entry. Overall, there has now been extensive coverage of all regions and countries at different levels of development.

There is a predetermined rhythm of reviews under which Canada, the European Union (as a single entity), Japan and the United States (the 'Quad') are reviewed every two years, the next 16 trading entities in terms of the share of world trade in goods and services are reviewed every four years and the remainder of the Membership is reviewed every six years. Once a country is included in the process, its next review takes place according to this cycle, except that a leeway of six months may be allowed. The essential idea behind the differential cycles is that traders with the greatest impact on world trade and the multilateral system should be reviewed more frequently; acceptance of this principle by the larger traders was also seen as important in drawing developing countries into the review process.

There has been some discussion in the TPRB on possible changes to the cycle of reviews. Proposals include a modification to provide for a three-year cycle for Members currently on a two-year review pattern (i.e., the Quad), but there was no support from other Members for such a change. However, it was agreed that, in the case of two-year reviews, every second review might have an 'interim' character, although this was not to detract from the comprehensive nature of reviews of such Members. The allowance of six months leeway for all Members may be seen as a compromise on the proposal for changes in the cycle.

There has been a progressive build-up of the review programme from 1990, when only four reviews were held, to 1998, when 15 reviews were conducted covering 20 Members (WTO, 1998a). However, the number of reviews still falls

TABLE 1 *Trade Policy Reviews: WTO Members Reviewed Under GATT 1947 and WTO Provisions, 1989–1998*

Europe/Middle East	Asia/Pacific	Africa	America
Austria[1a]	Australia (3)[c]	Benin[b, d]	Argentina[c]
Czech Republic[b]	Bangladesh[a, d]	Botswana[b]	Bolivia[a]
Cyprus[b]	Fiji[b]	Burkina Faso[b, d]	Brazil (2)[c]
European Union (4)[c]	Hong Kong, China (3)[c]	Cameroon[a]	Canada (5)[c]
Finland[1a]	India (2)[c]	Côte d'Ivoitre[b]	Chile (2)[c]
Hungary (2)[c]	Indonesia (3)[c]	Egypt[a]	Colombia(2)[c]
Iceland[a]	Japan (4)[c]	Ghana[a]	Costa Rica[b]
Israel[a]	Korea (2)[c]	Kenya[a]	Dominican Republic[b]
Norway (2)[c]	Macau[a]	Lesotho[b, d]	El Salvador[b]
Poland[a]	Malaysia (2)[c]	Mali[b,d]	Jamaica[b]
Romania[a]	New Zealand (2)[c]	Mauritius[b]	Mexico (2)[c]
Slovakia[b]	Pakistan[a]	Morocco (2)[c]	Paraguay[b]
Sweden[1] (2)[a]	Philippines[a]	Namibia[b]	Peru[a]
Switzerland (2)[c]	Singapore (2)[c]	Nigeria (2)[c]	Trinidad and Tobago[b]
Turkey (2)[c]	Solomon Islands[b, d]	Senegal[a]	United States (4)[c]
	Sri Lanka[b]	South Africa (2)[c]	Uruguay (2)[c]
	Thailand (2)[c]	Swaziland[b]	Venezuela[b]
		Tunisia[a]	
		Uganda[b, d]	
		Zambia[b, d]	
		Zimbabwe[a]	
15	17	21	17

Notes:
()Figures in brackets show the number of reviews where this is greater than 1.
[1] Included in EU from 1995.
[a] Reviewed under GATT 1947.
[b] Reviewed under the WTO.
[c] Reviewed under GATT 1947 and the WTO.
[d] Least developed country.

Number of reviewed conducted at end-1998	= 109
Number of WTO Members reviewed	= 81 out of 132 (counting EU as 15)
	= 61 per cent of WTO Members (of which, 26 in Europe, 17 in Asia/Pacific, 21 in Africa and 17 in America)
Number of WTO Members reviewed	= 67 out of 118 (counting EU as 1)
Number of least-developed WTO Members (*)	= 8
Share of world trade of WTO Members reviewed (excluding significant double counting and EU intra-industry trade)	= 84 per cent

Source: WTO (1998a).

short of the total required annually to meet the full programme. Thus, two Members of the Quad must be reviewed each year plus four Members of the group of 16 on a four-year cycle. In addition, there are some 132 WTO Members (December 1998), of whom 15 are Members of the European Union and are not reviewed separately. Thus, 117 Members need to be covered on the six-year cycle, or just under 20 each year. This gives a total of 25–26 reviews. In addition, the WTO membership is likely to increase to some 150 Members in the next few years, increasing the number of reviews by five each year to a total of 31 annually.

In fact, there is some latitude for reviewing least-developed countries on a longer cycle,[1] but the number of reviews must still increase if the current cycle and comprehensive coverage are to be met. However, while there is a tendency for repeat reviews now to dominate the calendar, during 1998 nine countries were reviewed for the first time, including four least-developed countries.[2] The inclusion of least-developed countries arises from a perception that the reviews can be of benefit to the countries under review in taking stock of and planning their trade policies, as discussed later.

The ranking of Members and, hence, their review cycles can change in several ways. For example, in the past, the enlargement of the European Union caused several countries to drop out of the group of 16 countries on the four-year cycle and others to move into the group. In addition, variations in trade in goods and services flows may affect the rankings, for example, as a result of changes in commodity prices, although in practice this has not been very important. However, the accession of new Members to the WTO, particularly China and Russia, could affect the position of existing Members in all the three review cycles.

b. Stages of Review

The reviews by the TPRB are conducted on the basis of a report prepared by the WTO Secretariat and a 'policy statement' by the Member under review. An overview of the process is given in Table 2.

The scheduling is agreed between the Secretariat and the country under review. Today, first reviews are mostly done by countries volunteering to be reviewed. In the case of second reviews, the date of the review meeting should normally take place within the fixed cycle, plus the grace period of six months if requested by the country under review. Another factor is the availability of staff resources. Normally, reviews of the Quad require two economists, because of the volume of material to be taken into account. In other countries, the work is normally carried out by one economist, but two may be used to help make adjustments in the scheduling. This has the advantage of providing a back-up in case of staff movements, but it has been found in practice that the use of two staff Members does not lead to a halving of the time for the preparation of the Secretariat report. The date for the review meeting determines the timing of other steps, given the time required to complete various tasks and the rules of procedure agreed by WTO Members. For example, documents must be available in the three working languages of the WTO four weeks prior to the meeting, and the editing, assembly and translation of the completed Secretariat report takes about six weeks (four weeks for translation alone).

In some cases, the routine shown in Table 2 is varied. Thus, the Secretariat has sometimes tried to work largely from published sources, including official reports. In such cases, there is a request for data and publications, while the draft Secretariat report includes questions on policy or to seek further details on operational aspects of policy measures. This draft is then discussed with the authorities on the mission to the capital. This approach can reduce the overall time for the preparation of a review by about 1–2 months, but it shifts a substantial burden of research to the Secretariat and can only work effectively where there are adequate published sources. Otherwise, it is essential to prepare detailed questionnaires and an early mission to the capital for fact-finding purposes, and this is the most common approach. In such cases, comments by the authorities on the draft Secretariat report are handled in writing, with clarifications being made through the Geneva missions of the country or directly by telephone and fax, as appropriate.

During the mission to the capital, the Secretariat team often consults with private enterprise (Chambers of Manufacturers, Commerce, etc.) and research institutes. Private sector meetings are often useful to identify constraints on the operations of firms, for example, deficiencies in infrastructure, excessive red tape, shortcomings of the financial system, etc. Academic economists have often made studies of aspects of the trade regimes in their home countries, and are able to provide additional research material.

At the meeting of the TPRB, the Government whose policies are under review makes an introductory statement, followed by comments from two discussants, chosen from the Membership to act on their own responsibility (and not as representatives of their Governments) to stimulate the debate in the TPRB.

The majority of the Members being reviewed have been represented at Ministerial or Deputy Ministerial level; in most other cases, they have been represented by senior officials from the capital. However, in its report to the Singapore Ministerial Meeting in December 1996, the TPRB noted that the level of representation had not always been matched by the participation – either in numbers or level – by other Members of the TPRB (WTO, 1996). Thus, the TPRB suggested that if the role of the TPRM were to be preserved and strengthened, it was important both that there be a substantial number of delegations present in Trade Policy Reviews and that these delegations be represented at appropriate level. Since that report the level of representation from the capital has, if anything, increased, while the attendance at meetings continues to be related to the number of trading partners with close ties. Nevertheless, even when attendance has been limited, the quality of debate itself has improved. Questions are more pointed and detailed answers are provided, sometimes in writing after the meeting when the subject is highly technical.

Two discussants are chosen to represent a balance between developed and developing countries as well as regional interests. One week before the meeting, the discussants distribute an outline of the main points they intend to raise. Subsequent to the discussants' statements, other Members make statements and raise questions. Written questions may be submitted prior to the meeting and countries which do so are given priority in being called to make their statements. At the end of the first morning, the Chairperson, the Government delegation,

TABLE 2 *Stages in Preparing a Trade Policy Review*

Stage	Time Required	Comments
Secretariat starts initial research and prepares a country questionnaire	1–3 weeks	Country is consulted on programme for review.
National authorities prepare and provide replies (including Government publications and other official documents on core issues).	3–4 weeks	A focal point in the Ministry of Trade normally allocates questions to other ministries and agencies, and co-ordinates the replies.
Based on the replies received, the Secretariat starts the initial drafting process. A second questionnaire is sent to capital 4 weeks before the mission to the capital.	ca. 8 weeks	Second questionnaire provides basis for discussions on policies during mission.
Mission to capital.	5–10 days	Replies to second questionnaire are made available on arrival of the team (normally 2–3 persons). Replies are discussed with ministers and officials.
Secretariat prepares its draft report; national authorities prepare a policy statement (the 'Government Report')	12–13 weeks	Draft chapters of the Secretariat report are sent to national authorities for factual verification and comment; replies are required within 2–3 weeks.
Completion of the Secretariat report, arrival of Government report.	ca. 2 weeks	
Editing of Secretariat report, translation of Secretariat and Government reports in other official languages, reproduction and circulation of the reports.	5 weeks	The two reports from the basis for discussions at the TPRB meeting. Under the mandate, the reports must be made available to other delegations at least 4 weeks before the meeting.
TPRB meeting. The meeting starts with a policy statement by the country official (15 minutes) and statements by two discussants.	2 days (mornings only)	The formal review process ends with the Chairperson's Concluding Remarks.
Secretariat prepares minutes of the meeting and the final publication of the documents.	ca. 2 weeks	

the two discussants and the Secretariat agree on a series of headings for the presentation of responses the following day. When the replies are given, there is an informal debate and follow-up questions. Answers are expected immediately, but sometimes written technical answers are provided later.

At the end of the meeting, the Chairperson then presents his or her Concluding Remarks, which are meant to represent his or her assessment of the collective views of the meeting. This is not a negotiated text, but is delivered on the Chairperson's own authority, drafted with the assistance of the Secretariat. There are no formal recommendations on actions to be taken by the Member under review.

Inter-governmental organisations (e.g., IMF, World Bank, OECD, UNCTAD) are allowed to attend the meetings as observers.

Subsequent to the meeting, the Chairperson gives a press conference and the documentation is immediately declassified. The summary observations in the Secretariat report and the Chairperson's concluding remarks are published on the Internet immediately following the meeting. (The documentation is made available to press beforehand, subject to an embargo till the completion of the meeting.) The Secretariat then prepares the minutes, which, together with the reports, the Chairperson's concluding remarks and any written responses to questions raised at the meeting are published, usually within a few months of the meeting.

c. Secretariat Report

The Secretariat report provides the bulk of the information for consideration by the TPRB on the trade policies of the WTO Member under review. The main sources of information for the Secretariat report are published information from national and international sources, such as the IMF and the World Bank. The WTO Secretariat's document data base, also on the Internet, is another key source, which has become even more important given the increased notification requirements decided in the Uruguay Round. Tariff information may also be available from the WTO's Integrated Data Base and schedules of tariff concessions, but up-to-date information on applied tariffs, which are sometimes different from the rates bound in past multilateral negotiations, is usually obtained from the Government. Articles in newspapers, periodicals and professional journals are useful sources, but have to be checked. The Internet has become an important source of information, including of official material in an increasing number of countries.[3]

The most critical source of information is the set of responses to questionnaires completed by the Government whose policies are under review. The questionnaires for first reviews of a country are largely standardised, and adjusted to the situation of the country on the basis of the initial research carried out in Geneva. Questionnaires for subsequent reviews focus on changes since the previous review. The tailoring of the questionnaires to particular cases is the main reason why the Secretariat does not make them available publicly, but Governments may do so if they choose. However, the structure of the questionnaires follows the general structure of the Secretariat report (see below).

In some cases, there have been delays in the agreed timetables as a result of late responses to questionnaires by the authorities. In this respect, the TPRB in its report to the Singapore Ministerial Meeting in December 1996 stressed that Members owed it to the health of the system to observe strictly the deadlines laid down for answering questionnaires and delivering documentation (WTO, 1996). Delays in the completion of reviews also have knock-on effects on other reviews and can lead to rewriting by the Secretariat, wasting already scarce resources.

The Secretariat progressively submits its draft report to the Government whose policies are under review for verification of the factual content. The national authorities have two to four weeks to verify and furnish comments on the Secretariat drafts, depending on the amount of information to be checked. The Secretariat then revises its text in the light of the Government's comments and evaluation, the summary observations are not subject to the same checking process, but are provided as a courtesy to the Government some 24 hours before the release of the report to the WTO membership.

The structure of Secretariat reports has evolved over time on the basis of some experimentation, but today the reports normally contain a 'Summary Observations' and four chapters. Chapter I covers the major features of the economy, recent economic developments, trade patterns in goods and services, evolution of foreign investment, and trade-related aspects of the foreign exchange régime. Chapter II covers institutional aspects of trade and investment policy-making, including through participation in multilateral and regional agreements, and trade disputes and consultations. Chapters III and IV cover trade policies and practices; Chapter III deals with measures directly affecting imports, exports and production, while Chapter IV looks at measures by sector (agriculture/forestry/fisheries, mining, industry and services). This standardised format helps to ensure consistency of treatment, and delegates value being able to find topics in the expected place across reports.

On the whole, the Secretariat reports have been welcomed by the WTO membership, although, as might be expected, countries under review tend to focus on the more critical aspects, indicating their disagreement with the Secretariat's assessment. In some instances, they have also questioned the evaluation of policies and their implementation by the Secretariat, rather than mere factual reporting of the existence of measures. The TPRB noted the concern of Members to ensure that, as an exercise in transparency, the progress made by Members in implementing the WTO Agreements be clearly reflected (WTO, 1996). The Secretariat was therefore encouraged to continue providing, in its reports, systematic information on measures taken by Members under review in the context of the Agreements, the mechanisms by which these are implemented, and notifications made. While notifications of measures are the main source of such reporting, the extended scope of notification requirements under the WTO has proven to be a burden, especially for smaller countries, and technical assistance is offered to assist them in this process. The TPR process has identified a number of lacunae in such reporting which has improved as a result.

The Secretariat reports also appear to have been well appreciated by academics and other international organisations. Early criticism that they were insufficiently analytical was based largely on the factual nature of the first reports, when the mechanism was provisional, while in the last 3–4 years there has been an increase in analysis and criticism, albeit sometimes in cautious language. While there is detailed quantitative information on tariffs and trade, much of the analysis is qualitative, based on generally accepted economic principles. Given the resource constraints, it is in practice impossible for econometric or modelling work to be undertaken, and it is likely to be welcomed by WTO Members. Criticism by delegates of over-emphasis on macro-economic issues has led to more succinct treatment on the economic environment, more focused to the linkages with trade policy.

The reports have been the subject of considerable scrutiny, not the least in the annual, special issues of *The World Economy* by experts from countries reviewed. Drawing on this material and his own reading, Keesing (1998), in what is the most comprehensive analysis of the mechanism by an outsider, notes that the reports have evolved from:

> largely descriptive catalogues of countries' protectionist measures into more thorough, incisive and analytical surveys of the trade policies and practices.

However, he goes on to describe what he what he regards as a number of weaknesses. For example, he believes that each report should be complete in itself, rather than providing an update from the previous review. He argues that the reports have sometimes been over-optimistic, and should comment more forthrightly on their credibility and sustainability, although he acknowledges that the cautious tone relates to the diplomatic environment of the WTO. On the other hand, careful scrutiny shows that there is a tendency for Secretariat reports for second and subsequent reviews to provide a more thorough treatment of critical issues in national trade policies and to be more explicit about the welfare effects of policies. This is also reflected in greater caution by the authorities and sometimes longer delays in the provision of material for these reviews. Increasingly, the Secretariat is confronted with questions, such as 'Why do you need this information?' or 'What has this to do with the WTO?'

Keesing argues that reports need to pay more attention to the 'bottom line', attempting to summarise total taxes on imports and calculate the total costs of protection. This would be an ideal, but may not be feasible in practice, given the difficulties in computing the effects of non-tariff measures in goods and services. Moreover, such computations are complex and resource-intensive, which should strictly be carried out in the context of an inter-industry assessment, perhaps in a CGE framework; this would require a different level of resource input from that which is available to the TPRD.

Keesing also identifies a number of areas which he believes need more comprehensive and critical treatment in Secretariat reports. In this regard, he singles out anti-dumping, regional agreements and export promotion schemes as well as bribery and corruption as obstacles to trade, investment and government procurement. He also believes more attention should be called to the:

> glacially slow reduction of protective measures in textiles, clothing and agriculture, as well as the threat to the Uruguay Round agreement on trade-related investment measures posed by the imminent glut in automobile productive capacity world-wide.

Of course, most of these issues are covered in the reports, but the point is well taken about the need to draw out more fully the implications of the detailed descriptive material, and this has been an ongoing concern of the senior staff of the TPRD. Given the staff turnover (see later), it is perhaps inevitable that there be some variation in treatment, but, by and large, the working procedures are designed to minimise such variability. Of course, not everyone can be an expert on all facets of policy, and it is often difficult for staff to evaluate the practical importance of certain measures, e.g. where implementation rather than basic legislation is what counts; interviews with the private sector and the academic community in the country under review help to a degree to remedy this weakness of the system.

d. Government Report

Reports by Members under review have also evolved and nowadays take the form of policy statements, outlining the objectives and direction of trade policies. They often contain a short presentation of recent trends and problems, including those encountered in foreign markets. They are usually much shorter than the Secretariat reports, mostly between 10 and 30 pages. However, the actual form and length are in the final instance determined by the Member under review.

Preparation for and participation in a trade policy review can be onerous for small developing countries, and the WTO Secretariat has, on request, assisted such countries at different stages of the process. This is relatively rare, perhaps simply because countries are unaware that such help was available. Where requested, such assistance has been provided both by the Trade Policies Review Division as well as Technical Cooperation and Training Division of the WTO.

c. Procedural Changes

There has been a fairly continuous process of self-examination within the TPRB over the years, leading to a number of improvements in procedures. The procedural issues addressed include preparatory documentation (e.g., structure and content of reports), choice of discussants, level of representation at meetings, the Chairperson's concluding remarks, and the follow-up to meetings. As noted earlier, there has already been a trend towards higher level of representation by the country concerned, and the documents have evolved in structure and content. The question of selection of discussants from outside the Geneva delegations, for example, by drawing on government officials from capitals or academics, has been discussed, but there has been no agreement to go outside the Geneva delegations. (In one case an official who had been posted back to his capital came to Geneva to act as a discussant, but this was an exception.) There has also been a concerned attempt to ensure that questions asked at meetings receive replies in writing and that these are included in the final publication.

4. EVALUATION OF THE TPRM

By and large, the WTO Members seem to be reasonably happy with the operation of the TPRM. Thus, the TPRB report to the Singapore Ministerial Meeting noted:

> There is a clear value for WTO Members in having a forum where they can openly discuss each other's trade and trade-related policies, elicit information and register concerns. The benefits for the country under review are also significant: the TPRM can provide a valuable input into national policy making, serving as an independent, objective assessment of trade and economic policies; Members have also commented on the extent to which the experience of review has helped to strengthen inter-agency discussion and co-operation in their own countries. The trading system as a whole benefits in that the process can sometimes assist Governments in pursuing desirable trade policy reforms; it also frequently illuminates areas of WTO obligations which may have received insufficient attention to date and thus helps to ensure that these are addressed (WTO, 1996).

This assessment illustrates the public choice rationale behind the TPRM, mentioned earlier. Certainly, the presentation of the trade policies of the larger Members provides ample opportunity for the examination of their effects on trading partners and the system as a whole. Much of that information is already in the public domain but the TPR process brings together the information in a balanced manner and the review meeting gives the authorities an opportunity to explain the development of their trade policies. Indications from the authorities in a number of countries are that the process has also helped them take stock of their policies on the basis of an independent analysis, contributing to the internal debate on policy development. The review process has strengthened the hands of domestic agencies promoting liberalisation, supporting trade reforms and, thus, helping individual Members become better integrated into the multilateral system and the global economy. Members engaged in an active process of trade policy reform have also used the opportunity of the review to present their achievements to a world audience. The dual aspects of self-analysis and external audit underpin the effectiveness of the TPRM exercise for all Members (WTO, 1996).

The benefits to developing countries from their involvement in the TPRM were examined in some detail in a Note of 12 July, 1996, circulated to all WTO Members, from the Chair of the TPRM to the Chair of the Committee on Trade in Development. The summary conclusion in that Note was:

> Involvement in the TPRM is an important way for developing countries, particularly least developed countries, to develop confidence and experience with the WTO. This needs to be borne in mind in (a) planning the TPRM timetable and (b) ensuring that technical assistance is available to those LDCs who would otherwise have difficulty in preparing for and undergoing review. With increased participation of developing countries in the TPRM, it will be particularly important to ensure that lessons learned from these reviews are channelled into the WTO machinery.

The report to the Singapore Ministerial Meeting also noted that the TPRM occupied a unique place within the WTO in promoting non-confrontational discussion of key trade policy issues. 'Its specific de-linkage from dispute settlement procedures is an essential feature which must be safeguarded'. However, it is also noted that further opportunities might be sought for encouraging greater cross-fertilisation between TPRB discussions and those undertaken in other WTO bodies.

Another benefit of the TPRM is that it has led the way in increasing the transparency in the trade policies and practices of WTO Members, and in some degree paved the way for much greater transparency in the WTO as a whole. In doing so, albeit outside the framework of specific legal commitments, the process has often highlighted weaknesses in the fulfilment of WTO obligations, including notifications, and thus helped to ensure that these are addressed. The Mechanism's spotlight has effectively focused on all the main players in the WTO trading system and has illuminated the most significant trends in trade policy, as discussed in the next section.

One aspect of the reviews has been a learning process about trade reforms and the linkages between trade and other policies. Thus, the lessons of trade reforms are being passed on to other countries within the WTO system. As noted in the next section, dealing with lessons from the TPRM, one particularly important feature has been the linkage between macro-economic policies and performance and trade policies and performance. Largely under IMF or World Bank programmes, many developing countries have started to put the emphasis on macro-economic policy to redress savings-investment imbalances as the source of current account deficits; as a result, there is much less frequent use of import restricts to attempt to resolve balance of payments difficulties. The TPR reviews have helped to pass on this lesson.

One criticism by delegates is that the preparation for a review is highly demanding on Government authorities, particularly at a time when many are making public sector cutbacks. In this respect, it is important to note the relative importance of questionnaires in the research stage of preparing a review, compared with other organisations where much greater emphasis is placed on repeated missions to capitals by staff to collect information. The WTO process is designed to keep down the costs of the Secretariat, but this inevitably places a greater burden on the specific countries under review. Moreover, the use of repeated missions by other agencies tends to dissipate rather than reduce the overall effort by national authorities. However, there is also little doubt that the preparation of a review requires more detailed documentation of the legal basis of policies and practices than is evident in the reports of other organisations, reflecting the different character of the WTO as a core of legal texts governing almost all aspects of international economic relations. Moreover, the reviews touch on many aspects of policy and require inputs from a wide range of government ministries and agencies. On the other hand, the Secretariat also draws heavily on the world of other organisations, such as the IMF, the World Bank, regional development banks, regional commissions of the United Nations, and, where appropriate, the OECD. Indeed, the efficiency of the TPR process owes much to the availability of such material, but this does not obviate the need for cross-checking in capitals. It may also be noted that the amount of work has expanded considerably under the WTO, because of the need to include material on services and intellectual property which were not covered by the GATT.

A related criticism has been that the process can focus too much on detail, at the cost of giving insufficient attention to policy direction. However, the TPRM is not just intended to give an idea of the broad sweep of policies but also to cover the practices of Members, that is, the implementation of policy. Often the broad policy thrust is unexceptionable, but this can be undermined at the level of implementation by lower level officials: the Devil is in the detail. This is why shortening reports would not necessarily save time or resources: it is still necessary to explore the detailed implementation of policy to allow an assessment to be phrased accurately albeit in fewer words.

As indicated, the use of resources is also a matter of some concern to WTO Members. The TPR has an annual staff budget of just under six per cent of the total for the organisation. With a staff complement of 27 (17 professionals) it accounts for around 10 per cent of the professional staff of the organisation, excluding translators, interpreters and administration (WTO, 1996).

However, the TPRM must also be seen as a relatively cost-effective process, and good value for money compared with reports by other international agencies. Keesing (1998) comments that:

> the TPRD [the WTO Division with responsibility for the TPR process] has demonstrated itself to be a highly efficient research operation . . . despite limited resources,

and he shows that it compares favourably with other international organisations. He also commends the versatility required of TPRD staff, who must be conversant with all the multiple topics covered in a review. However, he also notes that the heavy volume of highly demanding work has taken its toll in a high staff turnover. Indeed, there is now no professional member of staff who has been in the TPRD since its inception in 1989. This must be a matter of concern through the loss of institutional memory and makes it harder to ensure consistency across reports.

5. LESSONS FROM THE TPR PROCESS

One benefit from the TPR process has been the development of an extensive source of material on trade policies. This has been of value to the WTO itself in the preparation of the Annual Overview of Developments in the International Trading System, provided for in Section G of the Agreement on the TPRM, the annual reports of the WTO itself, and to other organisations and independent researchers on specific countries. The reviews also provide for all countries an independent source of learning experiences with trade policy at all levels of development.

Over the past few years, the over-riding common theme that has emerged is the rapid pace of change, with a sustained shift to more market-oriented and outward-looking trade and investment régimes, deriving in part from autonomous liberalization policies and in part from the stimulus provided by the Uruguay Round. Of course, many of the national experiences reviewed under the TPRM are comparable to information to be found in the studies of other international agencies, particularly the World Bank, which has extensive experience of structural adjustment lending often covering trade policies (see, for example, Papageorgiou, Michaely and Choksi, 1991; and Thomas and Nash, 1991). Thus, a broad overview of the lessons from the first eight years of operation of the TPRM, provided in Chapter III of the First Annual Report of the WTO in 1997, highlights the importance of protectionist policies, including industrial targeting. The report also stressed the importance for durable trade reforms of a transparent and stable long-term policy framework, avoiding slippages through exemptions for particular sectors of the economy with political leverage or through the abuse of contingency measures such as anti-dumping.

It has not been explicitly addressed in the TPR examinations how far and how fast a country can move in the transition from import substitution to outward orientation, or whether it is necessary or desirable to pass through an export orientation phase. Certainly, there is an impression that countries such as Argentina and Chile, which have moved more quickly, have also been able to reap an earlier harvest of benefits, but this sometimes leads to more acute structural adjustment pains. However, the most recent review of Chile (1997) drew attention to the strong growth performance in the 1990s alongside a strong programme to address social disequilibria.

The reports have highlighted the switch to tariffs, as price-based import measures which maintain a linkage with world price movements. However, they have also drawn attention to the persistence of tariff peaks to protect sensitive sectors, tariff escalation to foster domestic value-added, the use of specific tariffs to counter the variability of world prices for many agricultural products and the existence of a range of other charges on trade. Moreover, while quantitative restrictions, reference price systems and variable levies have been phased out, the Trade Policy Reviews were among the first to highlight the increasing use of anti-dumping mechanism by developing countries. The spotlight has also turned to other non-border measures, subsidies, state aids and tax concessions, applied in support of industrial and regional development policies, designed to foster growth in certain sectors or regions which are believed to be the key to long-term growth and employment, including through the fostering of new technologies. Such support is also often granted to small and medium-sized industries in order to help these develop and provide jobs for the future. The major constraint is often seen as access to investment finance, and to meet this need, some Governments direct state-owned banks to lend for specific purposes. In essence, this means that, high as lending rates often are in developing countries, they may not be as high as market rates, given the perceived risks.

Since the formation of the WTO in 1995, TPR reports have included sections on services and intellectual property. Up till now, the sections of the reports dealing with these topics have been largely descriptive, in much the way early reports were on goods trade. However, these new reports are throwing up a wealth of material on these new areas. In particular, they draw attention to the importance of financial services, transport and telecommunications in the development process and as inputs in the production and marketing of goods on international markets. Potentially such information could be useful in the development of an improved GATS framework when new services negotiations begin in the year

2000, compared to the situation at the start of the Uruguay Round where few negotiators (or economists!) knew much about services trade or interventions in the sector. The reports also show that, while many countries have adopted modern legislative frameworks in the area of intellectual property, there are serious deficiencies in implementation, indicating a need for training of officials and technical assistance in this area.

On the export side, the TPR reports have clearly demonstrated the emphasis being given by developing countries to the removal of the anti-export bias of earlier import-substitution industrialisation régimes. While this might best be achieved under free trade, tariffs remain an important source of revenue for developing country Governments, so that many have turned towards exemption schemes or rebates on domestic and import taxes on inputs to compensate exporters for the costs of protection and other tax burdens. Secretariat reports for TPR examinations have highlighted the shift under acute domestic budgetary pressures from direct subsidies to other forms of support which are also less likely to attract countervailing measures in foreign markets. Although export processing zones (EPZs) have often been identified as providing successful bases for export drives, the reports point out that they also tend to be features of a dual economy and are best seen as transition devices, serving to demonstrate the long-term advantages of investing in the host economy. One-stop windows have been particularly helpful in cutting back on red tape for exports. On the other hand, there are often constraints imposed by physical infrastructure and finance. The reports have also drawn attention to the continued use of export restrictions or taxes on agricultural products to capture 'monopoly rents', to ensure low cost supplies of raw materials for domestic processing industries, or to keep down domestic prices of foodstuffs.

Whereas reports by other organisations focus on policy development within individual countries, the TPR process has also highlighted inter-linkages between trade and internal economic reform, that outward-orientation is facilitated by an open multilateral system, and that open trade policies can support macroeconomic policy, for example, by helping to control inflation through the injection of world prices onto domestic markets. As mentioned earlier, it has also been observed in various reviews that membership of the multilateral system has thrown the burden of correcting imbalances in external accounts and domestic imbalances onto macro-economic policies, whereas previously there had often been resort to trade restrictions. The Mexican financial crisis was a case in point, and the lesson also seems to be being applied generally in the wake of the Asian crisis, as noted in the WTO Annual Report for 1998, based in part on experiences of several trade policy reviews, including Indonesia.

The TPR reviews were also among the first to draw attention to the importance of domestic deregulation to ensure that the benefits of trade reforms were not lost through the anti-competitive practices of domestic firms. This is particularly important in the wake of the large-scale privatisations of state-owned enterprises in Latin America as well as in transition economies (although the latter are less well represented as yet in the WTO).

The TPR process has also examined experiences in a number of regional agreements outside the scope of the legal examinations in the WTO Committee on

Regional Agreements, which has been largely deadlocked by disagreement on a number of systemic issues. TPR examination of countries which are members of regional agreements shows a synergy among autonomous, regional and multilateral liberalisation; thus, against the backdrop of unilateral reforms and multilateral liberalisation, regional agreements of the late 1980s and 1990s are less likely to be trade diverting than the inward-looking agreements of some 20 years early. In some cases, they have been used to help lock in autonomous reforms where achieving equivalence in the exchange of concessions in multilateral negotiations would have been more difficult, e.g., Mexico in the NAFTA. However, the WTO (1997) stressed that domestic and regional level efforts are best served by a strong external framework; at the same time, they can also help to support and promote the multilateral process: thus, 'parallelism on all three fronts serves individual Members and the system'. A particular worry among the overlapping agreements, often with differential rules of origin, is the reduced transparency of the trade regime. It has also become clear from tensions in certain agreements that it is important to have a certain degree of co-ordination of macro-economic policies as well as convergence on tax policies and technical barriers to trade between partners. The absence of such co-ordination can lead to disruptive shifts in trade flows, stemming from movements in real exchange rates and capital flows to take advantage of more kindly régimes. This has recently been identified in MERCOSUR, as well as being part of the debate about European integration.

The trade policy reviews of Australia and New Zealand also focused on the role of independent agencies in monitoring and reporting on trade and industrial policy developments in those countries. This is in line with the public choice concept, mentioned earlier, under which a transparency mechanism at the national level helps to offset pressures on elected officials and civil servants from vested interests ('rent seekers') to make decisions which help such groups, counter to the promotion of general public welfare. In the Australian case in particular, transparency appears to have led to better decision-making, and hence to trade liberalisation, by educating domestic audiences to the potential costs and benefits of policies.

6. CHALLENGES FOR THE TPRM

On the whole WTO Members and the Secretariat can take a good deal of satisfaction from the operation of the Trade Policy Review Mechanism over the last 10 years. The operation of this looking glass on trade policies has generally drawn favourable comments from within the academic community and from other organisations. For example, World Bank/IMF (1992) noted that:

> the TPRM has contributed to increased transparency of trade regimes and – through the publication of the reviews – to better awareness of the issues among wider audiences.

A frequent comment is that information is easy to find and consistently recorded in most reports. Others emphasise the value of the reports as reference material and value the fact that the reports are public.

As noted in Section 4, WTO Members too have recently indicated the usefulness of the mechanism as a forum for the open discussion of developments in their trade policies and the value of the TPR as an independent and objective analysis of trade policies. The TPR has not only contributed to the fulfilment of commitments in the multilateral trading system but has also contributed to the development of national policies. However, Members have criticised the amount of work required to prepare for a review and have also expressed some concern about the resource requirements.

Of the challenges faced by the TPRM, the most acute concerns how to meet existing programme requirements for an expansion of the number of reviews so that all countries are covered as scheduled in the agreed cycle of reviews. This preoccupation has intensified with the increased workload, under the enlarged mandate of the WTO. In addition, there have been an increasing number of adjustments to the programme of reviews, mostly derived from delays in the authorities in providing material for the preparation of the Secretariat report. The delays may again be linked to the increased burden of preparation under the WTO or perhaps even to a 'resistance factor' related to the more analytical quality of the reports and more in-depth treatment in second and subsequent reviews. In either case, WTO Members may want to take action to safeguard the mechanism by finding ways to ensure that the programme is kept on schedule and that the independence of the Secretariat reports is maintained.

To meet the challenge of the programme requirements, there are various options: (i) modifying the cycle of reviews, (ii) increasing the resources available to carry out the work along existing lines, or (iii) radically changing the method of working. These are examined in turn.

Modifying the frequency with which the Quad is reviewed (every two years) would make very little difference to the overall programme: major changes can only come from reducing the frequency of review of countries in the four- and six-year cycles. However, this would also have the advantage of reduced monitoring of developments in trade policies and practices, unless this could be taken up in some other way. Another possibility would be to introduce a selective monitoring of countries where trade policies are felt to be a problem, but who would make such a decision? Also, a focus on what is problematic internationally would weaken the usefulness of the mechanism for domestic policy purposes. It is perhaps conceivable that Members would agree not to have periodic reviews of 'dormant Members', often small countries with no representation in Geneva.

One possibility, which could improve the chances of extending the periodicity of the reviews across the board or adopting a more selective approach, would be to develop the regular monitoring aspect of the mechanism, Provision is made for such reporting in the TPRM, but this has been more honoured in the breach than the observance. However, one lesson from the TPRM has been the rapid rate of change in trade policies and their implementation in recent years. In this respect, the gap between reviews for a large number of WTO Members makes it difficult to keep track of developments on a global basis. Thus, improving the operation of the regular reporting requirements could be an effective way of tracking changes in countries on the current four- and six-year cycles, while opening the way for adjusting the cycles or being more selective.

The second possibility is that of increasing resources to carry out the reviews. This mainly affects the preparation of the Secretariat report, including economists, support staff, translation and document reproduction. As Keesing (198) puts it:

> the question is not whether these resources will be provided, but when and how. Not to provide them would lead to a collapse of the TPRM's ability to fulfil the task set for it in the Marrakesh Agreement.

However, Members have already highlighted the extent of resources used in the TPRM, and the impression is that that they would be reluctant to see any substantial increase in staff to carry out their work programme. A partial solution was found in 1998, when only 13 of the 20 Secretariat reports were entirely prepared by WTO staff, while seven were prepared with the collaboration of consultants. Funding for these consultancies was provided on a project or trust fund basis by Australia, Denmark, and the United Kingdom. This does not lead to a complete shift of the burden from the Secretariat which has a responsibility to ensure quality and consistency, which is more difficult with outside consultants. There is an increased burden on supervisors and the work of technical support, translation and document production increases in proportion to the number of reports, even if the economist is an outside consultant.

The third option is to find a quite different way of working by reducing sharply the size of the Secretariat reports, whose preparation is the major time and cost factor. This is a risk since, as noted, the quality of the reports has been appreciated, and an effort has been made in recent years to try to ensure readability and to sharpen the focus. Moreover, the point has often been made that the level of detail is one of the distinguishing features of WTO Secretariat reports. However, in times of resource constraints, it needs to be explored whether there is a way of producing reports in six months instead of nearly a year. This would imply shorter, more focused reports, concentrating on the main trade policy issues (currently in Chapter III of the Secretariat report) as well as providing some statistical annexes on economic performance, production and trade flows.

Another challenge rises from the need to reduce the burden on delegations imposed by the increased meetings. An option for this might be to have fewer review meetings, covering a number of countries each session, similar to Board meetings of the IMF and the World Bank. Statements could have a broader policy sweep, maintaining interest, while detailed questions and answers might be handled in writing for later dissemination to all Members. Such meetings might also serve a managerial function for reviews, helping to maintain deadlines.

Finally, there is a challenge for the TPRM to fulfil a technical assistance role, particularly for smaller, developing countries. For this to be developed, the TPRM would need to become more explicitly prescriptive than at present about trade policy programmes. To some extent this has become necessary to fill a gap in trade policy at the global level: the World Bank, which fulfilled such a role in the past, has been progressively withdrawing from trade policy work and putting greater emphasis on social programmes. To take on such a mantle would be a marked change in the WTO where the emphasis has tended to be on setting limits beyond which bad policies may not be pursued, in keeping with the WTO role as providing the main legal framework for international economic relations. However, beyond this framework, the GATT and the WTO have had little to say on the nature of 'good' trade policies. To take up this challenge of providing guidance of the nature of good trade policies – good for the Member itself and good for its trading partners – would mark an important stage in the maturity of the multilateral system.

NOTES

The views expressed in this paper are those of the author and do not necessarily represent the views of the World Trade Organisation or its Member States. Helpful comments were received from Clem Boonekamp and Peter Tulloch.

1 Annex 3 of the Marrakesh Agreement Paragraph C (ii) provides that a 'longer period' (than six years between reviews) may be fixed for least-developed country Members. In additional, Paragraph D contains provision for 'particular account [to] be taken of difficulties presented to least-developed country Members in compiling their reports'.

2 Countries reviewed for the first time were Botswana, Burkina Faso, Jamaica, Lesotho, Mali, Namibia, Solomon Islands, Swaziland, and Trinidad and Tobago.

3 Dated hard copies of Internet sources are made for file, as it has been found that these can disappear or be modified in the course of a review.

REFERENCES

Abbott, R. (1993), 'GATT and the Trade Policy Review Mechanism: Further Reflections on Earlier Reflections', *Journal of World Trade*, **27**, 3, 117–19.

Banks, G. (1992), 'The Industry Commission: Australia's Domestic Transparency Institution', Introductory Remarks to a special session of the UNCTAD Trade and Development Board on domestic transparency procedures (Geneva, 1–2 October).

Blackhurst, R. (1988), 'Strengthening GATT Surveillance of Trade-related Policies,' in M. Hilf and E. U. Petersman (eds), *The New GATT Round of Multilateral Trade Negotiations: Legal and Economic Aspects* (Kluwer Law and Taxation Publishers, Deventer, The Netherlands).

Curzon Price, V. (1991), 'GATT's New Trade Policy Review Mechanism', *The World Economy*, **14**, 2, 227–38.

GATT (1988), 'Trade Policy Review Mechanism', Compendium of comments made in discussion of Chairman's discussion paper (second revision) in formal and informal discussions in March 1988 (27 April).

GATT (1989), 'Mid-term Meeting' (MTN.TNC/11, 29 April).

Keesing, D. B. (1998), *Improving Trade Policy Reviews in the World Trade Organization*, Policy Analyses in International Economics, 52 (Washington DC, Institute for International Economics).

Laird, S. and P. Messerlin (1990), 'Institutional Reform for Trade Liberalisation', *The World Economy*, **13**, 2, 230–49.

Leutwiler, F. et al. (1985), *Trade Policies for a Better Future* (GATT, Geneva).

Mavroidis, P. (1992), 'Surveillance Schemes: The GATT's New Trade Policy Review Mechanism', *Michigan Journal of Law*, **13**, 2, 374–414.

Papageorgiou, D., M. Michaely and A. Choksi (eds) (1991), *Liberalizing Foreign Trade* (Basil Blackwell, Oxford and Cambridge, Mass.).

Qureshi, A. H. (1990), 'The New GATT Trade Policy Review Mechanism: An Exercise in Transparency or "Enforcement"?, *Journal of World Trade*, 24, 3, 142–60.
Qureshi, A. H. (1992), 'Some Reflections on the GATT TPRM, in the Light of the Trade Policy Review of the European Communities – A Legal Perspective', *Journal of World Trade*, **26**, 6, 103–20.
Qureshi, A. H. (1995), 'Some Lessons from Developing Countries' Trade Policy Reviews in the GATT Framework: An Enforcement Perspective', *The World Economy*, **18**, 3, 489–503.
Robertson, D. (1992), 'GATT's New Trade Policy Review Mechanism', mimeo (Australian National University).
Spriggs, J. (1991), 'Towards an International Transparency Institution: Australian Style', *The World Economy*, **14**, 2, 165–80.
Thomas, V. and J. Nash with others (1991), *Best Practices in Trade Policy Reform* (published for the World Bank by Oxford University Press).
World Bank/IMF Staffs (1992), 'Progress Report on Trade Policy Developments' (prepared for the Development Committee Meeting, 21 September).
WTO (1995), *The Results of the Uruguay Round of Multilateral Trade Negotiations – The Legal Texts* (Geneva).
WTO (1996), *Trade Policy Review Mechanism – Report to the Singapore Ministerial Conference* (WTO document WT/TPR/27, 22 October).
WTO (1997), *Annual Report – 1997* (Geneva).
WTO (1998a), Report of the Trade Policy Review Body for 1998 (WTO document WT/TPR/59, 15 November).
WTO (1998b), *Annual Report – 1998* (Geneva).

10. International Trade Bargaining and the Most-Favored-Nation Clause

R. D. Ludema

I. INTRODUCTION

IN DETERMINING TO PURSUE "reciprocal and mutually advantageous arrangements directed to the substantial reduction of tariffs and other barriers to trade and to the elimination of discriminatory treatment in international commerce,"[1] the signatory countries of the General Agreement on Tariffs and Trade (GATT) began an enduring debate over whether nondiscrimination is consistent with the other elements of this objective. For while a series of GATT negotiating rounds and a general adherence to the most-favored-nation (MFN) clause,[2] have produced substantial tariff reductions since 1947, many exceptions to MFN have been defended on the grounds that trade liberalization could not proceed without discrimination.[3] Recent challenges to MFN in the Uruguay Round and a proliferation of bilateral free-trade areas have magnified this issue, with much of the debate centering around the effect of MFN on the formation of international trade agreements. This paper examines the role of the MFN clause in the formation of trade agreements within a model of multilateral trade negotiations.

The most frequently cited criticism of the MFN rule is that it creates a "free-rider" problem: since any GATT member not party to a given agreement receives the benefit of reductions in protection abroad without being required to make cuts of its own, countries will wish to avoid entering agreements [e.g. Baldwin (1987)]. On the other hand, one of the chief arguments in favor of MFN is that were MFN dropped, exclusive coalitions of countries would form for the purpose of lowering trade barriers internal to the coalition, while maintaining high trade barriers against countries outside [e.g. Jackson (1987)]. The problem of theoretically evaluating the merits of the MFN clause, in view of these conflicting presumptions, awaits resolution.

In general, the nature of agreements reached in trade negotiations will depend on the negotiating procedures followed. Of critical importance to the MFN question is whether negotiations are assumed to proceed on a bilateral or multilateral basis. A bilateral trade negotiation is one in which two countries met to jointly determine reductions in their trade barriers. To the extent a GATT country not party to particular bilateral negotiation would receive a windfall from the resulting trade policy changes, it is a free-rider, not by choice but by the structure of negotiations. In multilateral negotiations, all countries meet and participate in determining world-wide reductions in trade barriers. Since no country is excluded from the bargaining table, all countries must choose whether or not to enter an agreement. It is in this case that MFN becomes interesting, and it is this case that is most relevant to GATT negotiations of the last three decades.

Caplin and Krishna (1988) have studied two models of bilateral negotiations. In their model of simultaneous bilateral bargaining, each pair of countries applies the Nash bargaining solution to determine its bilateral tariff reductions, taking as given the tariffs of all other countries. The result is that countries reduce tariffs less with MFN than without it.[4] In their model of sequential (or dynamic) bilateral bargaining, there are three countries, and one country alternates between making a tariff-cutting proposal to the second and to the third, until one of them agrees (then the game ends). In this model, the absence of MFN results in all tariff reduction gains being captured by the proposing country, while in the presence of MFN, gains are distributed more evenly, as MFN ensures that all countries have at least some bargaining power.

The present analysis presents a model of multilateral trade negotiations as a three-player, noncooperative, dynamic bargaining game (like the two-player, noncooperative game due to Rubinstein (1982), in which the choice between bilateral agreement (in which only two countries make tariff reductions) and multilateral agreement (all countries make tariff reductions) is endogenous. This enables us to address both the free-rider problem (in the presence of MFN) and the discriminatory coalition problem (in the absence of MFN) within a unified framework. The central result is that bargaining in the presence of MFN results in multilateral trade agreements which are mutually advantageous and, in a restricted sense, Pareto efficient. Further, under a symmetry condition, reciprocity (equal gain) is approached in the limit.

The free-rider problem commonly attributed to the presence of MFN does not arise. This result has an intuitive explanation: when bargaining over time, countries are always faced with a trade-off between concluding and continuing negotiations. It is shown that a rational proposal makes each country receiving the proposal indifferent between concluding and continuing. If in the presence of such a proposal a country attempts to free-ride, then rather than conclude the other countries will choose to continue negotiating. Hence the existence of the MFN externality results in no advantage for free-riders.

In the absence of MFN, many of these properties may not hold. Examples are given in which at most two of the three countries benefit from agreement, and hence the criteria of reciprocity and mutual advantage are not met. In one case, a single country exploits the other two, while in another case, two countries band together in a preferential agreement, excluding the third. These results suggest that many of the criticisms levied against the MFN clause are misplaced; moreover, attempts to replace of unconditional MFN with conditional MFN[5] may sacrifice several important GATT objectives.

II. THE MODEL

The approach taken here is write down two games that differ only in that in one the players (countries) are required to observe the MFN rule and in the other they are not. The equilibria of these games are evaluated against such criteria as Pareto efficiency, mutual advantage and reciprocity, i.e., "first-difference" reciprocity [Bhagwati (1988)] or "equal gains" in bargaining parlance. The premise for this approach is that GATT institutions can be represented by a game form, or a set of "rules" of a game. The problem of designing good institutions to achieve GATT objectives is related to the problem of implementation in game theory [e.g., Maskin (1985)].[6]

A. Bargaining with MFN

We take a situation where there are three countries, $N=[1,2,3]$, involved in international trade negotiations for the reduction of protectionist measures. For concreteness, we will call these protectionist measures tariffs.[7] So that MFN is an issue for each country, we assume that no country imports any good exclusively from one source. This way, when considering its tariff schedule, a government must confront the question of whether or not to apply different rates to goods that differ only by origin. MFN is simply the requirement that governments apply *uniform* tariff rates to such goods, while in the absence of MFN, governments would be able to apply *preferential* (or discriminatory) rates on the basis of origin. For now, we consider only uniform tariffs.

Let x_i denote the tariff the government of country i maintains against imports from the other two countries. The world tariff schedule is a vector of such tariffs $x = (x_1, x_2, x_3)$. Let $x^0 >> 0$ be the world tariff schedule in place when negotiations begin, and let $X \in R^3$ denote the set of all feasible tariff reductions, i.e. $x \leqq x^0$.

Each country sends a delegation to the bargaining table equipped with a continuous utility function $X \rightarrow R$, where $u_i(x^0)$ is normalized to zero. We assume for all $i, j \in N$, $i \neq j$, and $x \in X$:

$$u_i \text{ is monotonically increasing in } x_i \tag{1}$$
$$u_i \text{ is monotonically decreasing in } x_j. \tag{2}$$

Assumptions (1) and (2) assert that the interests of the negotiating parties are opposed. Without that negotiations would be unnecessary. As an empirical matter, it is well-documented that governments involved in trade negotiations typically regard their own trade barriers as valuable,[8] while viewing foreign trade barriers as harmful. Even the language of GATT reflects this: tariff reductions are referred to as "concessions" which are usually granted by a country only when concessions are forthcoming from other countries. For a summary of some political and economic models supporting these preferences, see Baldwin and Clarke (1987) and McMillan (1987).

Although world tariff schedules must be feasible, they need not be Pareto efficient nor better for any player than x^0; however, it will be useful to distinguish those that are. Denote the set of individually rational uniform tariff schedules $X^+=\{x \in X \mid u_i(x) \geq 0 \text{ for all } i\}$ and the strictly individually rational set $X^{++}=\{x \in X \mid u_i(x) > 0 \text{ for all } i\}$. We assume $X^{++} \neq \emptyset$.

The set of schedules that are Puerto efficient on the set X is denoted $X^*=\{x \in X \mid$ there is no $x' \in X$ such that $u_i(x') \geq u_i(x)$ for all i and $u_i(x') > u_i(x)$ for some $i\}$. There are several features of this set worth noting. First, since X is a restricted set (i.e. it excludes preferential tariff schedules), this is a restricted Pareto efficiency. Second, this is Pareto efficiency with respect to the utility functions $u_i(x)$, rather than the individual consumer utility functions used in traditional welfare economics. Though there need to be no difference, no assumptions made so far rule out an underlying political structure in which the objectives of the government differ from those of consumers. Finally, this is Pareto efficiency defined over tariff schedules rather than global resource allocations. In most international trade models, the only tariff schedule corresponding to an efficient resource allocation is free trade. By concentrating on tariff (or other trade policy) schedules, we are implicitly assuming the absence of international lump-sum transfers of income and utility. Although this assumption can be relaxed without altering the result (as will be demonstrated in section II.B), it is important to bear in mind when interpreting them.

Since the Kennedy Round (1962–1967), negotiations for the reduction of tariffs have employed the so-called multilateral or formula approach. In it, proposals for tariff reduction take the form of a single tariff-cutting formula applying to all dutiable manufactured goods "across-the-board". We will abstract from the particulars of the formulas proposed and, without loss of generality, adopt the convention that a proposal for tariff reduction take the form of an $x \in X$, which we assume to originate from a negotiator (rather than from a mediator).

For a proposal to be adopted, some country must accept it. A combination of a proposal and an acceptance by another player will be called an agreement, and agreements are binding. In keeping with the conventions of the GATT and the purpose of this paper, we do not require that all countries be party to an agreement. For example, a substantial group of developing countries neither agreed to nor implemented the formula agreed to by most of the countries in the Tokyo Round (1974–1979) [Winham (1986)], even though they participated in the negotiations. For our purposes, we will suppose that if only one country accepts a proposal the agreement is called bilateral, if both accept, it is multilateral. Let $B = \{N, (1,2), (1,3), (2,3), \emptyset\}$ be the set of groups that could possibly reach an agreement. Either all agree, a pair of countries agrees, or no one agrees. We will use $v_i{:}X \times B \rightarrow R$ to denote country i's valuation of an agreement reached by an element of B. It follows by definition,

$$v_i(x, N) = u_i(x) \tag{3}$$
$$v_i(x, \emptyset) = 0. \tag{4}$$

If two countries reach a bilateral agreement over a proposal x, the two countries implement the elements of the proposal over which they have control, while the country not party to the agreement does nothing. With MFN, a bilateral agreement between, say, 1 and 2 over a proposal $x \in X$ gives rise to the actual schedule (x_1, x_2, x_3^0). In this case, the utility of the agreeing countries is lower (by condition (2)) and the utility of the third country higher (by condition (1)) than in the corresponding multilateral agreement. Put differently, for all $i, j, k \in N$, $i \neq j \neq k$ and all $x \in X$, NFN treatment and conditions (1) and (2) imply,

$$v_i(x; i, j) \leq v_i(x, N) \tag{5}$$
$$v_k(x; i, j) \geq v_k(x, N) \tag{6}$$
$$v_k(x; i, j) \geq 0. \tag{7}$$

If $x^0 >> x$, then the above inequalities are strict. Note that condition (7) implies that a country can always do at least as well as zero by not participating in an agreement.

The sequence of moves in a bargaining game is typically of considerable importance, and indeed it is here also. There are few specific rules in the GATT as to the sequence of moves in negotiations of the formula type. In the Tokyo Round, the US made the first proposal (March 1976), which was not widely accepted. The EC, in particular, disliked the US formula and countered with a proposal of its own (July 1976). After the US rejected this formula, the Swiss proposed a formula (October 1976), which was agreeable to nearly all the developed countries, although many developing countries rejected it. In the end, the Swiss formula was implemented by all that agreed to it.[9] Present in these negotiations, as throughout the entire history of GATT, was the rule that acceptance of tariff reductions is never final until all parties are heard from. Usually a country will accept a proposal on an *ad referendum* basis, finalizing the acceptance only after other countries have done the same. Thus finding itself in a position where it has accepted a proposal that another country has rejected, a country can withdraw its acceptance instead of signing the agreement.

We now formalize these concepts in a bargaining game. At each time period $t (t=1, 2, \ldots.)$, prior to which no agreement has been reached, each country i is selected with probability $p_i(t) \in [0,1]$ $(\sum_{i \in N} p_i(t) = 1)$ to propose a reduction to the other two countries, i.e., to select a reduction $x^i \in X$. The two countries then simultaneously return an answer to country i either accepting (a) or rejecting (r) the proposal. If both countries accept the proposal, the game is ended in a multilateral agreement, with each country receiving $v_j(x^i, N)$. If one country accepts but the other rejects, the accepting country is given an opportunity to accept or reject again with the understanding that accepting will result in a bilateral agreement. Thus the initial acceptance is an *ad referendum* agreement. If both countries reject a proposal, then no agreement is reached in period t, the game moves on to period $t + 1$ and country i is selected with probability $p_i(t + 1)$ to make a new proposal in period $t + 1$. For simplicity, we will assume that $p_i(t) = 1$ for $t = i, i + 3, i + 6, \ldots.$; in other words, country 1 proposes in periods 1, 4, 7, . . ., country 2 in periods 2, 5, 8, . . ., and country 3 in periods 3, 6, 9, . . . Figure 1 describes the game in extensive form.

Either because of impatience or because of a constant probability of termination without agreement, the present value of agreements not immediately reached is discounted by the factor $\delta \in (0,1)$. Therefore an agreement reached in period t gives present value payoff $\delta^t v_i(. , .)$. It is worth noting that δ is, in part, a measure of the pace of negotiations. If the amount of time elapsing between discrete periods is long, the discount factor will be low. If this time is short, it means that proposals rapidly follow one another and δ approaches unity.

In period t the action of the proposer i is $x^t \in X$. However, countries j and k must make two decisions: (1) whether to accept or reject a proposal (*ad*

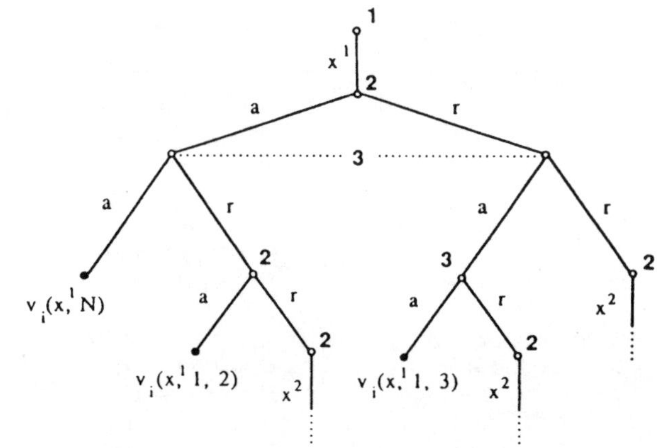

FIGURE 1

referendum); and (2) whether to accept or reject after learning that the other country has rejected. These decisions result in an action $\alpha\beta$ drawn from the set S = {aa, ar, ra, rr}. If a country has rejected a proposal, then whether it accepts or rejects after learning of the other country's rejection is entirely irrelevant. We only distinguish between ra and rr for notational completeness.

A strategy in an infinite sequence of functions $\{s^i(t)\}_{t=1}^{\infty}$, where each s^i prescribes an action for player i as a function of all previous actions of all players. More formally we can write: $s^i(t)$: $X^{t-1}\times S^{t-1}\rightarrow X$ for $t=i$, i + 3, i + 6, . . ., and $s^i(t)$: $X^t\times S^{t-1}\rightarrow S$, for all other t. One particular class of strategies is called *stationary*. A stationary strategy conditions current actions on previous actions only to the extent that they affect the current state of the game. Formally, denote a stationary strategy $\sigma^i=\{s^i(t)\}_{t=1}^{\infty}$; where $s^i(t)$: $\{0\}\rightarrow X$ for $t = i, i + 3, i + 6, \ldots$; $s^i(t)$: $X\rightarrow S$, for all other t. Let $\sigma=(\sigma^1,\sigma^2,\sigma^3)$ denote a combination of statutory strategies, one for each country.

The most useful solution concept for N-player noncooperative bargaining models is that of stationary perfect equilibrium. A subgame perfect equilibrium is a combination of strategies such that, after every possible sequence of previous actions, no player can do better than to follow her strategy given the strategies of the other players. A stationary perfect equilibrium is a subgame perfect equilibrium in which players use stationary strategies. Herrero (1985) and Binmore (1987) have argued that stationary perfect equilibrium is the only reasonable solution for a 3-player bargaining game similar to this one. Since a sequence of previous proposals and rejection affects the future of the game only in that it forces contained negotiation, what changes from period to period is only the identity of the country with initiative and (for the other countries) that country's proposed tariff reduction. In a stationary perfect equilibrium no country would respond differently at different times to the same proposed reduction from the same player. Stationarity also requires, and indeed it follows from dynamic

TABLE 1 *Summary of First Period Stage Game Equilibria Induced by* x^1

Payoffs given x^1	Subgame Perfect Equilibria
$v_2(x^1; 1, 2) \geq \delta w_2$, $v_3(x^1; 1, 3) \geq \delta w_3$	s^{*2}=aa, s^{*3}= ra; s^{*2}=ra, s^{*3}= aa (s^{*2}=ra, s^{*3}= ra)†
$v_2(x^1; 1, 2) < \delta w_2$, $v_3(x^1; 1, 3) \geq \delta w_3$	s^{*2}=rr, s^{*3}= aa (s^{*2}=rr, s^{*3}= ra)
$v_2(x^1; 1, 2) \geq \delta w_2$, $v_3(x^1; 1, 3) < \delta w_3$	s^{*2}=aa, s^{*3}= rr (s^{*2}=ra, s^{*3}= rr)
$v_2(x^1; N) \geq \delta w_2 > v_2(x^1; 1, 2)$, $v_3(x^1; N) \geq \delta w_3 > v_3(x^1; 1, 3)$	s^{*2}=ar, s^{*3}= ar; s^{*2}=rr, s^{*3}= rr (s^{*2}=ar, s^{*3}= rr; s^{*2}=rr, s^{*3}= ar)

† Strategy combinations in parentheses are subgame perfect equilibria which arise when the weak inequalities hold with equality.

programming, that a country will propose the same reduction each time it has the initiative.

We begin by solving the first period "stage" game, using the continuation payoff vector $w = (w_1, w_2, w_3) \geq 0$, which is a vector of payoffs expected to result from a subgame beginning in period 2. Now suppose country 1 has proposed $x^1 \in X^+$.[10] We can solve for the perfect equilibria of the subgame induced by country 1's proposal using backwards induction. First, notice that for any i, if x^1 is such that $v_i(x^1; 1, i) \geq \delta w_i$, then country i would be willing to accept x^1 after rejection by the other player, i.e. β = a. Whereas if $v_i(x^1; 1, i) < \delta w_i$, country i would reject after rejection by the other country i.e. β = r. Thus if one player rejects the proposal initially, the other player is assured the payoff max $[v_i(x^1; 1, i), \delta w_i]$. This gives rise to four possible cases, whose equilibria are easily found. Following any x^1, the equilibrium pure strategy pair $s^{*2}(x^1)$, $s^{*3}(x^1)$ for countries 2 and 3 can be summarized as follows:[11]

Although all of these equilibria are subgame perfect, not all of them are very sensible. Of particular interest is the case where $v_i(x^1; 1, i) < \delta w_i$ for both 2 and 3. In this case, although s^{*2} = ar, s^{*3} = ar and s^{*2} = rr, s^{*3} = rr are both equilibria, it would appear that (ar) is a better choice than (rr) for both countries. To see this consider this game in normal form as in Figure 2.

Since $v_i(x^1;1, i) < \delta w_i$, the strategy (aa) is dominated, and so each country knows the other will not play (aa). Considering then the game with only (ar), (ra), and (rr) left, the strategy (ar) dominates both (ra) and (rr), so long as $v_i(x^1; N) > \delta w_i$, for 2 and 3. Hence, s^{*2} = ar, s^{*3} = ar would appear to be the most sensible equilibrium. Although Nash equilibrium refinements in normal form games do not generally apply to extensive form games, here the logic of iterated dominance appears sufficiently compelling to rule out the (rr, rr) as an

		Country 3 aa	ar	ra	rr
Country 2	aa	$v_i(x;\,N)$	$v_i(x;\,N)$	$v_i(x;1,2)$	$v_i(x;1,2)$
	ar	$v_i(x;\,N)$	$v_i(x;\,N)$	δw_i	δw_i
	ra	$v_i(x;1,3)$	δw_i	δw_i	δw_i
	rr	$v_i(x;1,3)$	δw_i	δw_i	δw_i

FIGURE 2

equilibrium. Therefore, we treat s^{*2} = ar, s^{*3} = ar as the unique equilibrium when $v_i(x^1;\,N)>\delta w_i\, v_i(x^1;\,1,\,i)$ for 2 and 3.

Next we must consider the proposer's problem. Since it knows the subgame and corresponding equilibria following each of its proposals, country 1 will choose a proposal which induces the most favorable outcome for itself. Table 1 shows that the fate of a proposal x^1 depends on the utility it promises 2 and 3. If a proposal of x^1 is to result in a multilateral agreement in period 1, the conditions,

$$v_2(x^1;\,N)\geq\delta w_2>v_2(x^1;\,1{,}2) \qquad (8)$$
$$v_3(x^1;\,N)\geq\delta w_3>v_3(x^1;\,1{,}3)$$

must hold. If not, the proposal will either fail or result in a bilateral agreement. Condition (8) will hold at an interior solution[12] to the problem: maximize $v_1(x^1;\,N)$ subject to $v_2(x^1;\,N)\geq\delta w_2$ and $v_3(x^1;\,N)\geq\delta w_3$. The properties of such a tariff vector $x^{*1}(< <x^0)$ are established in Proposition 1:

Proposition 1: *If $x^{*1}\in X$ maximizes $v_1(x^l;\,N)$ subject to $v_2(x^{*1};\,N)\geq\delta w_2$ and $v_3(x^l;\,N)\geq\delta w_3$, then*

(i) $v_1(x^{*1};\,N)\geq w_1$ and $v_{1},(x^{*1};\,N)>0$
(ii) $v_2(x^{*1};\,N)\geq\delta w_2$
(iii) $v_3(x^{*1};\,N)\geq\delta w_3$
(iv) x^{*1} is Pareto efficient

Proof: Begin with property (ii). As long as $v_2(x^{*1};\,N)>\delta w_i$, condition (1) and the continuity of u_i imply that it is possible to lower 2's utility continuously by lowering 2's tariffs (raising 2's concession). By (2) such an operation raises the utility of 1 without violating the constraint on 3, but this contradicts the definition of x^{*1}. An analogous argument establishes (iii). Given (ii) and (iii), x^{*1} is Pareto efficient. That w is a feasible payoff vector and $w_i>\delta w_i$) except when w_i=0) implies $v_1(x^{*1};\,N)\geq w_1$; further, $v_1(x^{*1};\,N) = w_1$ only when w_i= 0 for both 2 and 3. Thus $X^{++}\neq\emptyset$ implies $v_1(x^{*1};\,N)>0$.

Q.E.D.

By definition, $v_1(x^{*1};\,N)$ is the best payoff country 1 can obtain in any equilibrium resulting in a multilateral agreement. The payoff $v_1(x^{*1};\,N)$ is also greater than 1's payoff in the no agreement outcome (by property (i)). Further, it can be shown that $v_1(x^{*1}; N)$ is greater than 1's payoff from any proposal that induces a bilateral agreement (see the proof of this result along with some necessary qualifications in the appendix). Therefore, if countries 2 and 3 choose (ar, ar) in response, x^{*1} is the best proposal 1 can make. What remains to be shown in that x^{*1} always induces (ar, ar).

Proposition 2: *Given the continuation payoff* w, *the combination* $s^{*1}=x^{*1}$, $s^{*2}=ar$, $s^{*3}=ar$ *is an equilibrium in period 1; further, if* x^{*1} *is unique, then this equilibrium is unique.*

Proof: Since $s^{*2}=ar$, $s^{*3}=ar$ is an equilibrium in the subgame following x^{*1}, and $v_1(x^{*1}; N)$ is the maximum payoff country 1 can obtain in any subgame equilibrium it can induce, $s^{*1} = x^{*1}$, $s^{*2} =$ ar, $s^{*3} =$ ar is a subgame perfect equilibrium. For uniqueness consider that since (x^{*1}, ar, ar) is the only equilibrium which can deliver as much as $v_1(x^{*1}; N)$ to country 1, if there exists another equilibrium, country 1 can do better by proposing $x'^{1}=(x_1^{*1}-\epsilon, x_2^{*1}, x_3^{*1})$ for $\epsilon>0$, which forces countries 2 and 3 to play (ar, ar)

Q.E.D.

We have shown that if in period 1 countries expect to receive utility w in period 2, then they will reach a multilateral agreement over $x^{*1} \in X$. Since strategies are stationary, this must be true for t=1, 4, 7, . . . Similarly, by considering w' for periods t=2, 5, 8, . . ., we can find x^{*2}, and by considering w'' for periods t=3, 6, 9, . . ., we can find x^{*3}. Putting these together, we can solve for the stationary perfect equilibrium in a fairly straightforward way. Let ψ^i denote the stationary perfect equilibrium proposal of country i. This solution must simultaneously solve:

$$\begin{aligned}
&\max v_1(x^1; N) \text{ s.t. } v_2(x^1; N) \geq \delta v_2(\psi^2; N),\ v_3(x^1; N) \geq \delta v_3(\psi^2; N)\\
&\max v_2(x^2; N) \text{ s.t. } v_1(x^2; N) \geq \delta v_1(\psi^3; N),\ v_3(x^2; N) \geq \delta v_3(\psi^3; N)\\
&\max v_3(x^3; N) \text{ s.t. } v_1(x^3; N) \geq \delta v_1(\psi^1; N),\ v_2(x^3; N) \geq \delta v_2(\psi^1; N)
\end{aligned} \tag{9}$$

From proposition 2, we get

$$\begin{aligned}
v_1(\psi^2; N) &= \delta v_1(\psi^3; N) = \delta^2 v_1(\psi^1; N)\\
v_2(\psi^3; N) &= \delta v_2(\psi^1; N) = \delta^2 v_2(\psi^2; N)\\
v_3(\psi^1; N) &= \delta v_3(\psi^2; N) = \delta^2 v_3(\psi^3; N).
\end{aligned} \tag{10}$$

These six equations coupled with the fact that $\psi^1, \psi^2, \psi^3 \in X^*$, suffice to give a solution: the equilibrium proposal is ψ^1, and this proposal is accepted by both countries 2 and 3. Thus, the game ends in the first period in an agreement which is Pareto efficient (in the restricted sense described above), multilateral and strictly beneficial for every country.

In this model of tariff bargaining all parties have some power because of their ability to force continued negotiation. We have shown that a rational offer always makes the recipients of the offer indifferent between accepting a multilateral agreement or continuing negotiation. If a country is indifferent between a multilateral agreement and continued bargaining, it will always reject a bilateral agreement once this choice is forced upon it by rejection from the other country. Therefore, no country has the power to force the others to accept a bilateral agreement, and so can neither completely exploit its opponents nor free-ride.

First-difference reciprocity in general does not hold. However, it will be approached as $\delta \rightarrow 1$, if the payoff functions are symmetric, in the sense that $v_1(\psi^1; N) = v_2(\psi^2; N) = v_3(\psi^3; N)$. Nor is symmetry such a ludicrous supposition. Often in GATT practice reciprocity is considered to hold when there is a balance of concessions, where a concession defined as the percentage tariff cut multiplied by the volume of imports to which the tariff applies. If countries believe that a balance of concessions is equivalent to equal gains, then they must be assigning common value to concessions, hence symmetry. McMillan (1987) argues that equating payoffs with concessions is a way of establishing a focal point for bargaining, e.g., if there is asymmetric information about what payoffs actually are, bargainers may choose to use concessions as an arbitrary but known means of keeping score. This model demonstrates that such behavior actually will bring about balanced concessions in the limit.

Bargaining as modeled here always results in a multilateral, mutually advantageous, Pareto-efficient agreement. In fact, this is the same agreement that would be reached in a model in which the *ad valorem* agreements assumption is replaced by a unanimity requirement. Such a model has been studied by Herreto (1985). Further, requiring unanimity and dropping the MFN rule would give an outcome that is Pareto efficient in an unrestricted sense because the tariffs would no longer have to be uniform. Of course, this may be objectionable to those who would treat nondiscrimination as an objective rather than a rule, since bargaining without MFN would in general result in discriminatory tariffs.

Finally, it should be emphasised that, while the present solution is Pareto efficient on the set X, it is not necessarily free trade. In a typical trade model, free trade will be Pareto efficient; however, in the absence of international transfers, i.e., when the only means of distributing utility is through tariffs, the Pareto efficient set will consist of various combinations of tariffs. Redefining the strategy set X to include international transfers would give us a larger Pareto-efficient set (and a linear Pareto frontier) consisting of free trade and various combinations of transfers. Allowing for international transfers reduces the above problem to a divide-the-surplus game, as considered in the next section.

B. The Simplest Case: Divide the Surplus

To illustrate the basic strategic relationships found in the foregoing sections, we consider a divide-the-surplus game. In so doing, we abstract from the tariff vectors underlying the payoffs and consider simply the Pareto frontier, which we assume to be linear. Normalizing the sum of the payoffs to unity along the frontier, a proposal amounts to a suggested division and a country's utility is equated with its share.

Denote country i's proposal $z^i = (z^i_1, z^i_2, z^i_3)$, where z^i_j is the share country i proposes for country j and $\sum_{j \in N} z^i_j = 1$. To illustrate the effect of MFN, we assume that a bilateral agreement reached between i and j over a proposal z^i gives country k utility 1 and countries i and j zero. This satisfies conditions (5) and (6) of Section II.A.[13]

As before consider a continuation payoff vector **w** and some period when country 1 proposes. In the event country 1's proposal is not accepted, the outcome will be δw. The best multilateral agreement country 1 can bring about is $z^{*1} = (1 - \delta w_2 - \delta w_3, \delta w_2, \delta w_3)$. Clearly, no bilateral agreement is better for 1, since it would receive zero. Hence, the equilibrium strategies are (z^{*1} ar, ar) in this period, given **w**. That every country i, when it has the initiative, would propose $z_i^{*i} = 1 - \delta w_j - \delta w_k$, $z_j^{*i} = \delta w_j$ and $z_k^{*i} = \delta w_k$ implies:

$$\begin{aligned} \psi_1^2 &= \delta\psi_1^3 = \delta^2\psi_1^1 \\ \psi_2^3 &= \delta\psi_2^1 = \delta^2\psi_2^2 \\ \psi_3^1 &= \delta\psi_3^2 = \delta^2\psi_3^3. \end{aligned} \tag{11}$$

These six equations, along with the three equations $\sum_{j\in N}\psi_j^i=1$ for all $i\in N$, yield a solution for the equilibrium proposals of each country. Since country 1 is assumed to propose first the outcome is:

$$\psi_1^1 = \frac{1}{(1+\delta+\delta^2)}$$

$$\psi_2^1 = \frac{\delta}{(1+\delta+\delta^2)}$$

$$\psi_3^1 = \frac{\delta^2}{(1+\delta+\delta^2)} \tag{12}$$

Notice as the time between offers becomes very small, i.e. as $\delta \rightarrow X$, this solution converges to (1/3, 1/3, 1/3). The first mover advantage arbitrarily accorded to country 1 evaporates, and the solution converges to equal gains, or reciprocity. This is because each country values an increment in its payoff equally.

It should be pointed out that the reciprocity of the solution to this model is due in part to the symmetry of the model itself. In particular, the fact that each country regularly takes a turn proposing and that those not proposing always get a chance to respond results in each country having roughly equal access to the bargaining process. In an alternative specification, like that of Caplin and Krishna (1988), where one always proposes and the others alternate responding, the result typically does not converge to equal gains. On the other hand, both models share the feature that MFN itself, by raising the specter of free-riding, tends to equalize bargaining power.

C. Bargaining without MFN

The unconditional most-favored-nation rule creates a preference ranking that favors free-riding over entering into a multilateral agreement (even though free-riding is never observed in equilibrium). Specifically, MFN implies (5) and (6) which can be summarized as follows:

$$v_j(x; i,k) \geq v_j(x; N) \geq v_j(x; i,j) \text{ for all } x \in X,\ i, j, k \in N,\ i \neq j \neq k. \quad (13)$$

In the absence of MFN, this ranking may not hold. Without MFN, countries that opt out of multilateral agreements do not necessarily gain. In fact, it is quite possible that they lose. This is because without MFN, this ranking may not hold. Without MFN, countries that opt out of multilateral agreements do not necessarily gain. In fact, it is quite possible that they lose. This is because without MFN, countries are not confined to uniform tariff vectors; instead, countries may maintain high tariffs against free-riders and lower tariffs exclusively between members of agreements.

If we let y_{ij} denote the tariff of country i against imports from country j, we can write a world tariff schedule $y=(y_{12}, y_{13}, y_{21}, y_{23}, y_{31}, y_{32})$. In case of a bilateral agreement between say, 1 and 2 over a tariff vector y, the actual vector implemented is $(y_{12}, y^0_{13}, y_{21}, y^0_{23}, y^0_{31}, y^0_{32})$. Given the assumptions about payoffs made so far, there is very little we can say about this outcome relative to $u_i(y)$ or $u_i(y^0)$ (which again can be normalized to zero). It could be that a multilateral agreement is achieved in this environment. However, given this ambiguity about the preference orderings, it will be most useful to illustrate the absence of MFN by way of example. A particularly interesting case for illustrating the absence of MFN by way of example. A particularly interesting case for illustrating the difference between a world with and world without MFN is where it is possible that a pair of countries does better in a bilateral agreement than some multilateral agreements. For this we can use the divide the surplus game, revising the bilateral agreement payoffs as follows:

$$v_i(z^i; i, j) = \frac{z^i_i}{z^i_i + z^i_j}$$

$$v_j(z^i; i, j) = \frac{z^i_j}{z^i_i + z^i_j}$$

$$v_k(z^i; i, j) = 0. \quad (14)$$

The standard theory of optimal tariffs argues that if a country (or customs union) is sufficiently large relative to the rest of the world, it can gain at the expense of the rest of the world by a positive tariff. Johnson (1954) showed that this can be true even when the rest of the world retaliates. It may be useful to think of the preferences (14) in these terms.

In this example, to consider all of the equilibrium in all the subgames that could be induced by a proposal z^1 with continuation of payoffs w would be an immense undertaking. Fortunately, we can simplify the task by positive payoff.

This follows from three facts which can be easily verified: (1) if $z_i^1 > \delta w_i$, then country i has (aa) as its dominant strategy; (2) If $z_2>0$ and $z_2>0$, then (aa, rr), (aa, ra), (ra, aa) and (rr, aa) cannot be equilibria; (3) if $v_2(z^1; 1, 2)<\delta w_2$ and $v_3(z^1; 1, 3)<\delta w_3$, then z^1 will certainly be rejected [i.e. (ar, rr), (rr, ar), (rr, rr) are the only equilibria]. These three facts enable us to establish the following lemma.

Lemma: There exists $\epsilon>0$ such that either $z' = (1 - \delta w_2 - \epsilon, \delta w_2 + \epsilon, 0)$ or $z'' = (1 - \delta w_3 - \epsilon, 0, \delta w_3 + \epsilon)$ strictly dominates any $z>>0$ for country 1.

Proof: Given fact (1), (aa) is country 2's best response to z' and country 3's best response to z''. Thus z' and z'' would be accepted either bilaterally or multilaterally, and the payoff for country 1 is $1 - \delta w_2 - \epsilon$, or $1 - \delta w_3 - \epsilon$. We can find an ϵ which makes this better than any proposal that would be rejected by both players: there exists $\epsilon>0$ such that $1 - \delta w_2 - \epsilon > \delta w_1$ for $\delta<1$. Fact (2) implies that no bilateral agreements can be reached when $z>>0$. The only alternative is a multilateral agreement in which, by fact (3), at least one country i must have $z_i/(1-z_j)\geq\delta w_i$ for $i, j \neq 1$. This implies $z_i+\delta w_i z_j \geq \delta w_i$ and therefore since $\delta<1$ there exists an $\epsilon>0$ such that $z_i+z_j>\delta w_i + \epsilon$. If $i=2$, then z' dominates z, and if $i=3$ then z'' dominates z.

Q.E.D.

This lemma enables us to restrict our attention to proposals giving at least one player zero. Further, fact (3) implies that the player (possibly) receiving more than zero must receive at least its continuation payoff. However, z' and z'' are not equilibrium proposals either, as country 1 can always replace ϵ with $\epsilon/2$ and do strictly better. It would appear then that the only equilibrium candidate proposals are $(1 - \delta w_2, \delta w_2, 0)$ and $(1 - \delta w_3, 0, \delta w_3)$. The equilibria in subgames following these proposals are plentiful. Following $(1 - \delta w_2, \delta w_2, 0)$ we can say there always is a multilateral agreement equilibrium, a bilateral agreement (between 1 and 2) equilibrium, and a disagreement equilibrium, but there is only a bilateral agreement equilibrium between 1 and 3 if $\delta w_2=0$. Analogous results hold for $(1 - \delta w_3, 0, \delta w_3)$. Thus either $(1 - \delta w_2, \delta w_2, 0)$ or $(1 - \delta w_3, 0, \delta w_3)$, whichever is better for country 1, coupled with a multilateral or bilateral agreement equilibrium in the subgame following that proposal constitutes an equilibrium in period 1 with continuation payoffs δw. Uniqueness does not hold; however, the outcome is the same regardless which type of agreement is reached.

Moving to the statutory perfect equilibria for the repeated game, note that if $\delta w_1=0$ and $\delta w_3=0$, then $(1 - \delta w_2, \delta w_2, 0)$ and $(1 - \delta w_3, 0, \delta w_3)$ are the same proposal. The proof of proposition 3 shows that this is always true in a stationary perfect equilibrium.

Proposition 3: *The utility vector (1, 0, 0) is the stationary perfect equilibrium outcome.*

Proof: Suppose the continuation payoff in period $t>1$ is δw, *where* $\delta w_2 \geq \delta w_3$, and suppose it is country 1's turn to propose. Then an equilibrium proposal in period t will be $(1 - \delta w_3, 0, \delta w_3)$. So the continuation payoff in period t–1 is $(\delta - \delta^2 w_3,$

0, $\delta^2 w_2$. Country 3's t–1 equilibrium proposal will be (0, 0, 1). In period t–2, country 2's equilibrium proposal is (0, 1, 0), as country 1 has a continuation payoff of zero. Extending this logic to the first period, country 1's equilibrium proposal is (1, 0, 0). Clearly this constitutes a stationary perfect equilibrium for the supergame. Notice also that since the outcome in period 2 would be (0, 1, 0), the continuation payoff at any time country 1 proposes is (0, δ, 0) and so $\delta w_2 > \delta w_3$.

To demonstrate the uniqueness of this outcome, suppose instead $\delta w_2 \leq \delta w_3$ is the continuation payoff in period t and country 1 proposes $(1 - \delta w_2, \delta w_2, 0)$. If $\delta w_2 < 1/2$, this cannot be stationary perfect equilibrium in the supergame, since the equilibrium proposal for in period t–1 for country 3 is $(0, \delta^2 w_2, 1 - \delta^2 w_2)$. In period t–2, country 2's equilibrium proposal is (0, 1, 0), as country 1 has a continuation payoff of zero. By the induction argument above the equilibrium proposal for country 1 would be (1, 0, 0), and hence $\delta w_2 \leq \delta w_3$ is contradicted. Indeed, if in any period the continuation payoff is below one half for the country who proposes in the following period, backwards induction gives (1, 0, 0) as the equilibrium for country 1.

Thus the only possibility for an alternative outcome is one in which in *every* period the continuation payoff exceeds one half for the country who proposes in the following period. Let $\gamma^1 = (1 - \delta w_2, \delta w_2, 0)$. In such an equilibrium it must be that, $\gamma^1_1 = 1 - \delta\gamma^2_2$, $\gamma^2_2 = 1 - \delta\gamma^3_3$ and $\gamma^3_3 = 1 - \delta\gamma^1_1$. Solving gives, $\gamma^1_1 = \gamma^2_2 = \gamma^3_3 = \frac{(1 - \delta)}{(1 - \delta^2)}$, which implies that $\delta\gamma^i_i < 1/2$ for all i. Thus the unique equilibrium outcome must be (1, 0, 0).

Q.E.D.

This result is similar to the one obtained in part IV of Caplin and Krishna (1988). The intuition is quite simple: if in every continuation payoff vector at least one country receives zero, then the proposer can always offer that player zero (perhaps plus epsilon) and be assured of an agreement. Thus the result is determined *entirely* by who proposes first.

While the first mover advantage in the presence of MFN disappears as the time between offers becomes very small, this is not so here. The rule of order is of utmost importance to this case. We may think it unreasonable to suppose that each country, when making its proposal, knows exactly which country will propose next. Modifying the above model to include uncertainty does indeed alter the result somewhat, but first mover advantage does not disappear.

To demonstrate, suppose that country 1 proposes first ($p_1(1)=1$), and if country i proposes in t, then $p_i(t+1)=0$, $p_j(t+1)=p_k(t+1) = 1/2$, for all $t>1$. In other words, countries 2 and 3 will propose in the second period with equal probability, and if, say 3 actually proposes in the second period then countries 1 and 2 propose with equal probability in period 3 and so on. At each point in time, the expected continuation payoff for a country j receiving a proposal from country i is $\frac{\delta(z^j_j + z^k_j)}{2}$, i.e. the expected value of the share j would propose for itself plus that which k

would propose for j all discounted one period. Now we can see that unless it proposes zero for itself in the next period, a country always has a continuation payoff greater than zero.

In the first period, country 1 again will choose either $[1 - (\delta/2)(z_3^3+z_3^2), 0, (\delta/2)(z_3^3+z_3^2)]$ or $[1 - (\delta/2)(z_2^2+z_2^3), (\delta/2)(z_2^2+z_2^3), 0]$, whichever gives it a higher payoff. We can show that the following are equilibrium proposals:

$$\begin{aligned}
ø^1 &= \{1 - (\delta/2)(ø_3^3+ø_3^2),\ 0,\ (\delta/2)(ø_3^3+ø_3^2)\} \\
ø^2 &= \{(\delta/2)(ø_1^1-ø_1^3),\ 1 - (\delta/2)(ø_1^1+ø_1^3),\ 0\} \\
ø^3 &= \{0,\ (\delta/2)(ø_2^2+ø_2^1),\ 1 - (\delta/2)(ø_2^2+ø_2^1)\}
\end{aligned} \tag{15}$$

Noting that $ø_3^2=ø_1^3=ø_2^1=0$, we find that

$$\begin{aligned}
ø_1^1 &= 1 - (\delta/2)ø_3^3 \\
ø_2^2 &= 1 - (\delta/2)ø_1^1 \\
ø_3^3 &= 1 - (\delta/2)ø_2^2
\end{aligned} \tag{16}$$

As before this solves to give $ø_1^1=ø_2^2=ø_3^3=\dfrac{(1 - (\delta/2))}{(1 - (\delta^2/4))}$, which converges to 2/3 as $\delta \rightarrow 1$. Given that $ø_2^2=ø_3^3$, $ø_3^2=0$ and $ø_2^3>0$, it follows that $1 - (\delta/2)\,(ø_3^3+ø_3^2)>1 - (\delta/2)(ø_2^2+ø_2^3)$ which implies $ø^1$ is indeed country 1's best proposal given $ø^2$ and $ø^3$. A similar argument establishes that,

$$\begin{aligned}
ø^1 &= \{1 - (\delta/2)(ø_2^2+ø_2^3),\ (\delta/2)(ø_2^2+ø_2^3),\ 0\} \\
ø^2 &= \{0,\ 1 - (\delta/2)(ø_3^3+ø_3^1),\ (\delta/2)(ø_3^3+ø_3^1)\} \\
ø^3 &= \{(\delta/2)(ø_1^1+ø_1^2),\ 0,\ 1 - (\delta/2)(ø_1^1+ø_1^2)\}.
\end{aligned} \tag{17}$$

is also a combination of equilibrium proposals.

From this example we see that complete exploitation of the surplus by the first proposer does not take place; however, the first mover advantage is not completely eliminated either. Instead, country 1 receives the lion's share, another country the remainder, and one country nothing. Although both countries 2 and 3 may agree to this proposal, it is equivalent to a bilateral agreement between country 1 and either 2 or 3. In any case, bargaining with the preferences (14) does not generate reciprocity endogenously; instead, it always leaves at least one country out of the benefits of the tariff reduction process.

III. CONCLUSION

The central conclusion of this paper is that in presence of the MFN clause, countries will reach mutually beneficial, Pareto-efficient, multilateral agreements. The free-rider problem is avoided because countries would rather continue bargaining than be forced to accept a bilateral agreement. Further, MFN and the achievement of reciprocity are compatible. Hence, this model does not support many of the traditional criticisms against the MFN clause.

In contrasting this with the case where MFN is absent, fewer conclusions can be reached emphatically. For example, this analysis does not exclude the possibility that mutually beneficial, multilateral agreements can arise in the absence of MFN. In fact, if such an agreement does arise and it is Pareto efficient, it is quite possibly better than any agreement possible under MFN. This is because X^*, the set of PE uniform tariff schedules, is contained in the set of all PE tariff schedules. What we have shown in this paper is that without MFN it is possible to have agreements which are not mutually beneficial (i.e. lying outside of the set of strictly individually rational tariff schedules) and hence not reciprocal. In the presence of MFN, all agreements lie in both X^* and X^{++}.

A question related to that of this paper is whether or not countries, given a choice of rules, would unanimously choose MFN. Naturally, the answer depends on how well each country could expect to do under a given rule. The outcome of bargaining with MFN does not typically dominate that without MFN for all players; however, if there is *a priori* uncertainty about, say, the order of moves (and hence the payoffs each country will receive in the absence of MFN), then MFN would likely give every player higher expected utility than no MFN at all. As discussed earlier, however, there are other rules, such as unanimity, which will typically dominate MFN.

The fact that nondiscrimination was part of the original GATT suggests that some countries (namely, those that would have benefited from discrimination) either did not know what position they would occupy in the future or were being generous. However, the more frequent use of bilateral free-trade areas (as permitted under Article XXIV) and sentiment among developed countries in the Uruguay Round to dispense with MFN in several key negotiations (e.g. services) suggests that this is no longer true. This trend toward not only the practice but the instutionalization of bi- and pluri-lateralism constitutes a threat to the MFN clause.

Nor are developing countries innocent of undermining the effectiveness of MFN. Article XXXVI of the GATT, an article adopted in 1965 to aid development, reads: "The developed contracting parties do not expect reciprocity for commitments made by them in trade negotiations to reduce or remove tariffs and other barriers to the trade of less-developed contracting parties." Placing it in the context of our model, Article XXXVI amounts to restricting the set of possible tariff schedules to ones requiring no tariff reductions on the part of, say, country 3. Obviously, if we cannot ask country 3 for anything, then country 3 is a free-rider from the very start. Article XXXVI, therefore, has the effect of institutionalizing free-riding for developing countries, thereby lending credibility to a free-rider argument which would otherwise be only a red herring.

This paper has shown that the GATT's original objectives of mutual advantage, reciprocity, trade liberalization and nondiscrimination or introducing alternative objectives may inhibit the ability of negotiators to reach (through self-interest) these original objectives. If these original objectives remain desirable, it seems reasonable to suggest an exchange: developed countries arrest their movement toward bilateralism, while developing countries participate more fully in negotiations, rather than invoking Article XXXVI. This is basically what Baldwin (1987, p. 65) recommends: "the more successful the multilateral approach, the less pressure there will be from DCs for bilateral negotiations. Thus the LDCs will be better off. The world economy as a whole will also be better off under a negotiating approach that emphasizes multilateralism rather than bilateralism." This paper provides a formal basis on which to make this recommendation.

APPENDIX

It will generally be the case that $v_1(x^{*1}; N)$ is strictly greater for country 1 than the payoff to any proposal that could be accepted as a bilateral agreement, and thus bargaining with MFN will result in a multilateral agreement. However, there are two cases in which it may be possible to reach a bilateral agreement as well or instead. We confine this discussion to the appendix because the cases appear unlikely and they do not contribute to the central message of the paper.

Case 1 is where the condition $x^{*1} << x^0$ does not hold. Case 2 is where exists a tariff vector $x' >> x^{*1}$ in which either

$$\text{(A)} \quad \begin{aligned} v_1(x'; 1, 2) &\geq v_1(x^{*1}; N) \\ v_2(x'; 1, 2) &\geq v_2(x^{*1}; N) \\ v_3(x'; 1, 2) &\leq v_3(x^{*1}; N) \end{aligned} \qquad \text{or (B)} \quad \begin{aligned} v_1(x'; 1, 3) &\geq v_1(x^{*1}; N) \\ v_2(x'; 1, 3) &\leq v_2(x^{*1}; N) \\ v_3(x'; 1, 3) &\geq v_3(x^{*1}; N) \end{aligned}$$

holds. We now demonstrate that there are the only two cases:

Lemma 2: Except in cases 1 and 2, $v_1(x^{*1}; N)$ is strictly greater for country 1 than the payoff to any proposal that could be accepted as a bilateral agreement.

Proof: First, it follows from property (iv) of Proposition 1 that any proposal that would be accepted as a bilateral agreement and give country 1 at least $v_1(x^{*1}; N)$ must satisfy either (A) or (B) (both of them cannot hold simultaneously). Next, suppose there exists a proposal x'' satisfying either (A) or (B) whose elements are not strictly greater than those of x^{*1} and $x^{*1} << x^0$. Suppose x'' satisfies (A). In order for country 3 to be no better off as a free-rider on x'' than as a participant in x^{*1}, given that $x^{*1}_3 < x^0_3$, it must be that $x''_1 > x^{*1}_1$ or $x''_2 > x^{*1}_2$ or both. If $x''_1 > x^{*1}_1$ and $x''_2 \leq x^{*1}_2$, then 2 is worse off (violating (A)), and if $x''_1 \leq x^{*1}_1$ and $x''_2 > x^{*1}_2$, then 1 is worse off (violating (A)). If $x''_1 > x^{*1}_1$ and $x''_2 > x^{*1}_2$ then $x'' >> x^{*1}$. Thus either $x'' >> x^{*1}$ or $x^{*1} << x^0$ does not hold. An analogous argument establishes the same result concerning (B)

Q.E.D.

Consider what happens when Case 1 obtains (i.e. $x^{*1} << x^0$ does not hold) but Case 2 does not. Evidently, either $x^{*1}_2 = x^0_2$ or $x^{*1}_3 = x^0_3$, but not both. In the first case $x^{*1}_2 = x^0_2$, $v_2(x^{*1}; N) = v_2(x^{*1}; 1, 3)$ and $v_3(x^{*1}; N) < v_3(x^{*1}; 1, 2)$ and from Proposition 1: $v_2(x^{*1}; N) = \delta w_2 > v_2(x^{*1}; 1, 2)$ and $v_3(x^{*1}; N) = \delta w_3 = v_3(x^{*1}; 1, 3)$. Allowing for this possibility does not affect the existence of a multilateral agreement, but it may bring about multiple equilibria. Suppose $x^{*1} = (x''^1_1, x''^1_2, x^0_3,)$, then country 1 would be willing to make this proposal when under any of three circumstances: s^2 = ar, s^3 = ar; s^2 = aa, s^3 = ar; and s^2 = aa, s^3 = rr. Since each of these is an equilibrium on the subgame induced by x^{*1}, they are all subgame perfect equilibria in period 1. This is truly a degenerate case because country 1 would only allow itself to form a bilateral agreement with, say, country 2, when country 1's best multilateral proposal would require no concessions from country 3 in the first place.

Case 2 though not degenerate appears somewhat implausible. It requires that at x^{*1} there be two countries that can gain and one that loses when every country raises its tariff. Further, the one that loses is the one that raises its tariff up to x^0. Conversely, it says that there is a multilateral reduction (typically welfare improving for the world as a whole) in which one country nets all the gain, and that this is the best multilateral agreement available. Given the assumptions of the paper this cannot be ruled out, and if it were to arise it could bring about a bilateral agreement. However, this is not a free-rider problem, which is a situation where one country forces the others into an (inferior) bilateral agreement. Here two countries would rather reach a bilateral agreement than enter a multilateral agreement with the third country. Moreover, if this were the case even in the presence of MFN, then if MFN were not in place, this would certainly lead to the pathological case described in Section III.3

Both of these cases can be ruled out by additional assumptions on the utility functions. A plausible one is: If $x \in X^*$ and $x \in X^{++}$, then $x << x^0$, i.e. if a proposal is to be Pareto efficient and mutually advantageous it must require some concession from each country. Since x^* is always in both of these sets, Case 1 is ruled out. Further, it may be plausible to assume that if $x >> x'$, then there is at most one i such that $u_i(x) > u_i(x')$. This evidently rules out Case 2.

NOTES

An earlier draft was presented at the Conference on *Political Economy and International Economics*, at Columbia University, February 16, 1990. I think Andrew Caplin, Dan Coates, Avinash Dixit, Susan Elmes, Ronald Findlay and John McMillan for helpful comments, and the Sloan Foundation and Columbia University for financial support. The problem investigated in this paper was suggested by my advisor, Jagdish Bhagwati. The model was pretty nearly defined when Caplin and Krishna (1988) came to our attention. This partly accounts for the major differences between my work and theirs.

1 Preamble to the GATT.

2 Article 1 of the GATT, titled Generalized Most-Favored-Nation Treatment, reads, ". . . any advantage, favour, privilege or immunity granted for any contracting party to any product originating in or destined for any other country shall be accorded immediately and unconditionally to the like product originating in or destined for the territories of all other contracting parties".

3 For example customs unions, free-trade areas, the Generalized System of Preferences (GSP), anti-dumping and countervailing duties, selective safeguards, recent "GATT-Plus" proposals, and the like.

4 Finger (1979) argues, on the basis of evidence from the first six rounds of GATT negotiations (1947–1967), that to avoid making reductions to free-riders countries turned to bargaining over every narrow product classifications.

5 I follow Viner (1936) in treating MFN as unconditional MFN, and conditional MFN as no MFN at all.

6 A planner has in mind a particular social choice rule, mapping each state of the world into an allocation among the agents under its jurisdiction. The state of the world is unknown to the planner but known to the agents. The theory of implementation is concerned with how the planner might write down a mechanism, or game form, which if played by the agents would implement, i.e. give rise to equilibria consistent with, the social choice rule.
7 The model hinges on the preferences of the negotiators not the specifics of trade policy instrument being negotiated.
8 If there is an optimum tariff, it is greater than or equal to x^0_i.
9 For a good brief discussion of these events see Baldwin and Clarke (1987). For a full discussion see Winham (1986).
10 In light of (7), the game is only interesting when $x \in X^+$. This is because rejection is assured in any equilibrium in which $v_1(x^1; N)<0$ for 2 or 3, and country 1 would never propose it if $v_1(x^1; N)<0$.
11 Mixed strategy equilibria do exist. For example, if $v_i(x^1; N)>\delta w_i$, there exists a mixed strategy equilibrium in which player i accepts with probability $v_j(x;1,j)/(v_j(x;1,i) + v_j(x;1,j) - v_j(x;N))$ for i,j=2,3, $i \neq j$. Considerable ink can be saved, however, by restricting attention to pure strategies.
12 Existence of a maximum follows from (1), (2) and the continuity of the utility functions. The assumption that it is interior is sufficient to rule out a degenerate case discussed in the appendix.
13 With international transfers (5) and (6) do not hold generally. To see this consider that, if under a given proposal, one country receives large transfers from the other two, then being a free-rider may be a disadvantage if it entails giving up those transfers. Since we are concerned with cases in which free-riding is advantageous, we will confine our attention to cases in which (5) and (6) hold.

REFERENCES

Baldwin, R. E., 1987, Multilateral Liberalization in J. M. Finger (ed.) *The Uruguay Round: A Handbook on the Multilateral Trade Negotiations, World Bank, Washington D.C.*

—— and R. N. Clarke, 1987, Game-Modeling Multilateral Trade Negotiations, *Journal of Policy Modeling*, 9, 257–284, NBER Reprint No. 1001.

Bhagwati, J. N., 1988, *Protectionism*, MIT Press, Cambridge, Mass.

Binmore, K., 1986, Modeling Rational Players, London School of Economics, STICERD Discussion Paper 86/133.

Caplin, A. and K. Krishna, 1988. Tariffs and the Most-Favored-Nation Clause: A Game Theoretic Approach, *Seoul Journal of Economics*, 1, 267–289.

Finger, J. M., 1979, Trade Liberalization: A Public Choice Perspective, in R. Amacher, G. Haberler and T. Willet, (eds) *Challenges to a Liberal International Economic Order*, American Enterprise Institute, Washington, D.C.

Herrero, M. 1985. *A Strategic Bargaining Approach to Market Institutions*, Ph.D. Thesis, London University.

Jackson, J., 1987, Multilateral and Bilateral Negotiating Approaches for the Conduct of US Trade Policies, in R. M. Stern (ed.) *US Trade Policies in a Changing World Economy*, MIT Press, Cambridge, Mass.

Johnson, H. G., 1954, Optimum Tariffs and Retaliation, *Review of Economic Studies*, 21, 142–153.

Maskin, E., 1985, The Theory of Implementation in Nash Equilibrium: A Survey, in L. Hurwicz, D. Schmeidler, H. Sonnenschein (eds) *Social Goals and Social Organization*, Cambridge University Press, Cambridge.

McMillan, J., 1987, *A Game-Theoretic View of International Trade Negotiations: Implications for the Developing Countries*, University of California, San Diego, IR/PS Research Report 88–11.

Rubinstein, A., 1982, Perfect Equilibrium in a Bargaining Model, *Econometrica*, 50, 97–109.

Viner, J., 1936, Comments on the Improvement of Commercial Relations between Nations, in *The Improvement of Commercial Relations between Nations and the Problem of Monetary Stabilization*, Carnegie Endowment-International Chamber of Commerce Joint Committee, Paris.

Winham, G. R., 1986, *International Trade and the Tokyo Round Negotiations*, Princeton University Press, Princeton, New Jersey.

11. A Game-Theoretic View of International Trade Negotiations: Implications for the Developing Countries[1]

J. McMillan

INTRODUCTION

THE CHAPTERS IN THIS BOOK propose changing the global trading system, to make it work more in the developing countries' interests. What would be the consequences for the developing countries of redesigning the global trading system? Before fixing something, one should understand how it works. This chapter uses game theory to try to throw some light on how the global trading system works.

After developing a game-theoretic interpretation of some of the institutions of world trade, it will be argued that developing countries could gain from adopting an activist role in trade negotiations.

Arbitrariness is an essential feature of any negotiation, whether among nations or among individuals. If a negotiation is potentially fruitful in that there is some overlap of interests among the participants, then usually there will be not one but many possible agreements which will leave all better off than the status quo. In tariff negotiations, for example, there are many different combinations of mutual tariff reductions which would leave each country gaining from the change. This multiplicity of mutually beneficial moves means that there are returns from being actively involved in the process, trying to push the agreement in a favourable direction, since there are many different changes that one's negotiation partner would be willing to agree to.

Since there are many potential agreements that make all participants better off, the fact that the negotiations do not break down is more important to the negotiators than a precise weighing of the gains and losses from the agreement. It follows that there is an advantage to what one might call 'phoney precision' in negotiation. This is illustrated by the rule that has evolved to govern tariff negotiations within GATT. Under the norm of reciprocity, countries in effect barter tariff reductions in such a way as to result in a perceived balance of concessions. The value of a tariff reduction is measured by the percentage tariff cut multiplied by the volume of imports affected. From an economic point of view this measure is meaningless; but, in view of the multiplicity of mutually beneficial agreements, this meaninglessness does not matter. Reciprocity so defined can be simply and unambiguously measured; and it therefore serves as a focal point upon which an agreement can coalesce.

This view of the outcome of the negotiation process as being essentially arbitrary generates qualified optimism about the prospects for success in negotiations over matters more complex than tariff reduction. Consider, for example, a question of concern to both developed and developing nations: how to reduce the subsidies that nations give to their exporting or import-competing industries. The OECD has recently proposed ways of measuring the size of subsidies. Such measures can be criticized for the inevitably arbitrary assumptions upon which they are based. But, once again, phoney precision is useful in negotiations. In order to produce a focal point, it is helpful if there is an accepted way of keeping score in the process of mutual concession-giving. Because there are many potential mutually acceptable agreements, it does not matter that the way of quantifying concessions is itself arbitrary. An agreement on a common definition of the size of subsidies would move the parties a long way toward an agreement to reduce them.

THE TARIFF-SETTING GAME

Game theory analyses situations in which each agent's well-being depends not only on his or her own actions, but also on the actions of others; and all of the agents take these interdependencies into account when deciding their actions. Thus, just as an oligopolist's profit depends on rivals' price decisions, a trading nation's welfare depends on other countries' tariff decisions.

In 1953 Harry Johnson developed an analysis of interdependent tariff-setting that is essentially game-theoretic (although, like the Molière character who did not know he was speaking prose, Johnson was apparently unaware that he was dealing with game theory). Each country is modelled as choosing a tariff rate. To the extent that the country is large enough to be able to influence world prices, one country's tariff affects the other countries' welfare. As is standard in trade theory, each country is assumed to seek to maximize its social utility, which is a function of total domestic consumption of each commodity.

At an equilibrium of this game, each country chooses its best tariff given its rational expectation of the other countries' tariff choices. Johnson shows that this equilibrium tariff is equal to the inverse of the elasticity of demand for the country's exports (Johnson, 1953). It can also be shown that if all countries simultaneously lowered their tariffs below their equilibrium levels, all would gain (McMillan, 1986, pp. 29–31). Thus there is a sense in which the equilibrium, established by the individually rational actions of each country, is collectively irrational. No country can, by its own actions, make itself better off than at the equilibrium: but all countries would gain if some degree of cooperation could somehow be achieved so that coordinated tariff reductions occurred.

Does this model capture the essential features of trade-policy interactions? Two empirical observations suggest that it does not. First, what drives the model is countries setting tariffs so as to improve their terms of trade. Many countries, and in particular most developing countries, are too small to be able to affect world prices. A small country faces an infinitely elastic export demand; thus Johnson's result predicts that small countries will eliminate all barriers to imports. The most casual empiricism contradicts this prediction. Second, in an empirical implementation of Johnson's model, Hamilton and Whalley (1983) estimate equilibrium tariffs for the USA and the EEC to be in excess of 50 per cent: much higher than existing tariffs, but about the level of the tariffs that ruled after the tariff wars of the 1930s. This suggests that since the Second World War the developed countries have succeeded in reducing tariffs far below that which is implied by Johnson's model. Evidently Johnson's analysis omits some mechanism that allows coordinated improvements to be made.

The next section will suggest a resolution of the first objection to the Johnson model: that the countries' aims are not adequately represented by the utility function which is conventionally assumed in the theory of international trade. The next session after that will suggest a resolution of the second objection: that a static model ignores the potential for cooperation inherent in the ongoing nature of international relationships.

PLAYER, PAY-OFFS AND STRATEGIES

In the abstract, a game has three components: the players; a pay-off function for each player; and a set of strategies for each player. Before modelling a real-world situation as a game, we must address the questions of who the players are, what their aims are and what actions are available to them.

For the trade-negotiations game, the obvious answer to the first question is that the players are the nations. This is not, however, the only way of modelling trade negotiations. To answer certain questions requires that the nation's internal decision-making process be considered; for this purpose, the players might be, for example, labour and capital or Congress and the Executive Branch. For still other questions, it might be adequate to represent as players blocs of several nations. Nevertheless, the discussion to follow will presume that the players are nations.

What is the strategy set in the trade-negotiations game? This is essentially a rephrasing of the question 'What is the agenda for negotiation? The answer is not obvious; the strategy set is larger than the traditional GATT agenda, in which strategies are choices of tariff rates. The strategy set might also encompass the various non-tariff barriers to trade and, potentially relevant to developing countries, it might range further beyond the current purview of GATT to include balance-of-payments, international-debt and global-security factors. Whether these other instruments should actually be used by the developing countries depends upon the predicted responses of the other countries.

Finally, what are the countries' aims? The idea underlying the rules of GATT as well as the positions taken by the negotiating countries seems to be that exports are a good thing and imports are a bad thing. The typical economist's view, in contrast, is that the purpose of the economic system is to provide individuals with consumption goods; imports achieve this, and exports are merely a means to this end, needed to pay for the imports. Quantitative evidence on this divergence of views comes from the computations by Brown and Whalley (1980) of the welfare consequences of the various tariff-cutting formulae proposed during the Tokyo Round negotiations. Using standard welfare measures, Brown and Whalley found that each of the USA, the EEC and Japan would have gained more from other countries' proposals being adopted than from their own. This could be explained as a series of mistakes. But more understanding of the process is to be gained if we presume that the countries' negotiators know what they are doing, but that their objectives are not captured by economists' welfare measures.

In order to build a positive or descriptive model, we must investigate the domestic politics of the trading nations. The Stolper-Samuelson theorem implies that changes in trade policy inevitably are redistributional: Some citizens gain, others lose. Thus interest groups lobby for different trade policies. The negotiators' aims can be taken to reflect the workings of this political process. The players in the trade-negotiations game, the nations, can therefore be taken as having utility functions that summarize the outcome of the domestic lobbying. In turn, the political lobbying is itself a game.[2] To analyse the trade-negotiations game it may not be necessary to model explicitly the domestic political game, or to understand in detail how the domestic political process works. It may be enough to know the country's preference ordering that emerges; this can be regarded as a reduced form of the domestic game. In other words, it may be enough for some purposes to regard the country as a black box, provided the objectives the modeler attributes to it are consistent with what actually occurs within the black box. The results of past trade negotiations provide some data on the negotiators' revealed preferences. For instance, econometric studies of the post-Kennedy Round tariff reductions in the USA have indicated that smaller-than-average tariff reductions occurred in industries with higher-than-average labour adjustment costs. Evidently the negotiators sought to protect declining industries and industries with a high proportions of unskilled or elderly workers.[3]

ENFORCING COOPERATION

Two basic distinctions in game theory are between zero-sum and non-zero-sum games, and between cooperative and non-cooperative games. The trade-negotiations game is non-zero-sum; that is, the sum of the players' pay-offs varies depending on their actions. Because the game is non-zero sum, the actions have a common interest in reducing trade barriers; but they have conflicting interests over how the gains from cooperation are to be distributed among them. A cooperative game is defined by the ability of the players to make binding agreements; otherwise, it is non-cooperative.

In a cooperative game the outcome must be Pareto efficient. The argument is simple: from any non-Pareto-efficient point, there is by definition some movement that makes some agents better off and none worse off; since binding agreements can be made, such a movement can be presumed to occur.

The outcome of a non-cooperative game is a Nash equilibrium: each agent does the best he or she can given his or her rational expectation of the other agents' actions. In contrast to cooperative games, a non-cooperative non-zero-sum game, if played only once, typically has an outcome that is not Pareto efficient (Dubey, 1980). This is because no agent has an incentive to take into account the effects of his or her own actions on the other agents' well-being. There is some alternative set of actions that would make all the agents better off; but it is in no agent's interest unilaterally to act differently. The resulting contradiction between what is individually rational and what is collectively rational is exemplified by the prisoner's dilemma, and also by Cournot's oligopolists, who fail to maximize total industry profit. Furthermore, as we have seen, the equilibrium in Johnson's tariff-setting game has this property.

This unfortunate feature may disappear if the game is played repeatedly rather than just once. Provided the agents are sufficiently patient, an efficient outcome can be maintained as a dynamic Nash equilibrium if the agents use strategies which threaten retaliation should anyone deviate from his or her part of the efficient action (Friedman, 1986). Thus cooperative behaviour is enforced by the talion: the law of retaliation in which the punishment resembles the offence committed. In this way, for example, a cartel can maintain itself by having each member threaten to start a price war should any member engage in price cutting.

These caveats must be added. First, the possibility of efficient equilibria requires that the agents do not discount the future too heavily. At any play of the game, an agent faces an immediate temptation to deviate from his or her part of the Pareto-efficient action. Agent A might be deterred by the other agents using 'trigger' strategies: threatening to retaliate in future periods should A defect. Thus the potential deviator faces a trade-off between a short-term gain and a long-term loss; the trigger strategies work as a deterrent only if A does not discount the future too much. We shall throughout assume that this is the case. Second, efficient outcomes are not the only equilibria. Playing the static Nash equilibrium repeatedly is an equilibrium of the dynamic game, as is every outcome that is better in the Pareto sense than the static Nash equilibrium. Also, there are typically many Pareto-efficient outcomes. Thus there are many equilibria and game theory does not predict which equilibrium will be reached. Third, the workability of trigger strategies requires that deviations from the prescribed actions be observable. Uncertainty limits the range of outcomes Pareto-superior to the static Nash equilibrium that can be dynamic equilibria (Porter, 1983).

What is the relevance of these theorems to the international trade game? Because there is no international authority with the coercive power to enforce the terms of contracts, games among nations are necessarily non-cooperative games. From the point of view of the developed nations, at least, GATT has been remarkably successful in reducing tariffs. Given that the international trade game is a non-cooperative game, how has GATT succeeded in generating multilateral tariff reductions? The answer is provided by Dam (1970, p. 79):

> The essence of the GATT system lies not in the abstract legal relationships created by a tariff concession but rather in the enforcement mechanism. Under Article XXIII the principal sanction for the increase of a duty in violation of a binding is the suspension by interested contracting parties of concessions made to the offending contracting party. There is no punitive sanction for nonperformance of the promise implicit in a tariff concession. The consequence of nonperformance is thus merely the re-establishment, at the option of an interested party and subject to the approval of the contracting parties, of the pre-existing situation (although the retaliatory suspension may be on items not originally negotiated with the offending contracting party).

GATT's enforcement mechanism, as described by Dam, resembles the retaliatory strategies in repeated games exposited above; thus the repeated game seems appropriate as a model of the GATT enforcement mechanism.

Incidentally, retaliatory trade restrictions are not a recent innovation. Adam Smith remarked upon their use:

> The case in which it may sometimes be a matter of deliberation how far it is proper to continue the free importation of certain foreign goods is, when some foreign nation restrains by high duties or prohibitions the importation of some of our manufactures into their country. Revenge in this case naturally dictates retaliation, and that we should impose the like duties and prohibitions upon the importation of some or all of their manufactures into ours. Nations, accordingly, seldom fail to retaliate in this manner. (Smith, 1952, p. 199).

It must be stressed that efficient outcomes are not the only equilibria of repeated games. The repeated playing of the equilibrium of the single-play game, with its suboptimal outcome, remains an equilibrium of the dynamic game; as does every outcome between this and any efficient outcomes. Thus there is a surfeit of equilibria. Game theory does not predict an efficient outcome in a repeated game; it only shows that such an outcome is possible. This is sometimes forgotten. For instance, in a historical study of trade wars, Conybeare (1986) suggests that 'The most interesting analytic question is why several hundred years of iterated conflict could produce no lasting cooperation' (p. 156); Conybeare proposes several explanations. But there is no paradox here: non-cooperation is one of the equilibria. Game theory offers no guarantee that, when there are multiple equilibria, a Pareto-efficient equilibrium emerges. The players can be trapped in a low-level equilibrium.

THE NEGOTIATION PROCESS

The Prisoner's Dilemma has become a cliché of game theory. It will be argued here that to model an international confrontation as a prisoner's dilemma is to trivialize it.[4] The Prisoner's Dilemma is a very special game, in that it has only one outcome in which both agents are better off than in the static equilibrium. thus, if the players can somehow ensure that an efficient equilibrium is reached, there is no further source of conflict. Real-world games are much more subtle: they have many efficient outcomes, with the potential for conflicts over how the gains from cooperation are to be shared. To end an analysis of an international situation with the observation that repetition of the game can induce cooperative behaviour is to leave unaddressed what is arguably the most important question: the division of the gains from cooperation.

The theory of cooperative games was designed to address questions about which Pareto-efficient outcome will be reached. A set of supposedly reasonable but essentially arbitrary axioms is proposed, and by applying them a particular efficient outcome is picked out. But this is entirely axiomatic reasoning: no behaviour by rational economic agents is being modelled. Most cooperative-game solution concepts, such as the Nash bargaining solution and the Shapley value, seem to bear little resemblance to the way international negotiations actually proceed. More recently there has been developed a non-cooperative theory of bargaining, in which the costs of delaying agreement, combined with the assumptions that players not only act rationally but also form their expectations about others' actions rationally, yield a unique outcome (Rubinstein, 1987). Although this strategic approach is of great importance for economic theory, the existing analyses seem to be too stylized to be applicable to the international-negotiations game.

We must look, then, to less formally developed ideas in order to understand the negotiating process. Schelling (1960) proposes that focal points can be used to resolve multiple-equilibrium problems in games. A bargaining equilibrium is reached when the bargainers' expectations converge: when they share mutually consistent perceptions about what outcomes the others will agree to. At an equilibrium, 'each expects the other not to expect to be expected to retreat' (Schelling, 1960, p. 70). That there are many equilibria means that there are many outcomes that can be generated by mutually consistent expectations (or, more precisely, there are many subgame-perfect Nash equilibria). A focal point arises if there is some feature of the bargaining situation that serves to focus each agent's attention on a particular equilibrium point, and therefore to coordinate the agents' expectations.

The concept of focal point is not precisely defined. For this reason it must be used with care, lest it degenerate into a question-begging concept: a particular equilibrium occurs because it occurs. This trap can be avoided by listing at the outset the possible determinants of focal points. There are several; a particular outcome might be highlighted by historical precedent; or by some natural mathematical symmetry; or through the intervention of an impartial mediator (Kreps, 1984, Mandel, 195, Roth, 1985, Myerson, 1986).

Laboratory experiments on a simplified bargaining situation conducted by Roth and his co-authors (Roth, 1987) yield some lessons about focal points. The subjects bargained for tokens, which were essentially lottery tickets. Each token was worth four times more to one bargainer than to his rival. When this asymmetry was not public knowledge, most agreements divided the tokens evenly; this is a natural focal point. When the asymmetry was partially or completely known, two focal points typically emerged: each player got either an equal number of the (unequally valued) tokens, or an equal expected value of monetary reward. In repeated plays, the experimenter could manipulate a bargainer's expectations about what his or her opponent would agree to, suggesting that focal points can be established by precedent. Although equal division may be motivated by the bargainers' notions of fairness, there is evidence against this interpretation. When there were two focal points, each bargainer argued for the one that most favoured him or her; also, the frequency of disagreement increased with the distance between focal points, suggesting some kind of strategic behaviour.

One of the main features of the GATT negotiating procedure is the principle of reciprocity: the custom of rewarding another country's concessions by concessions of equal value. Although the preamble of the General Agreement mentions the desirability of 'reciprocal and mutually advantageous arrangements directed to the substantial reduction of tariffs and other barriers to trade' (GATT, 1986a, p. 1), reciprocity is not defined in the General Agreement. Custom has, however, given it a definition: countries in effect trade tariff reductions in such a way as to result in a perceived balance of concessions. The size of a tariff reduction is traditionally measured by the percentage tariff cut multiplied by the value of imports affected.[5] Thus, out of the many possible directions of mutual tariff reduction, a few possible directions are selected for consideration. The reciprocity custom serves to focus the negotiators' attention on a small subset of the possible tariff-reduction combinations: it establishes a Schelling-type focal point.

Reciprocity therefore has the useful effect of reducing the extent of arbitrariness in the negotiating process. As Dam (1970, pp. 88–90) notes, however, the norm of reciprocity is itself arbitrary; Dam describes it as an 'absurd' and 'naive' way of measuring the value of a tariff reduction. The economic effect of a tariff reduction is only loosely related to the volume of trade that it affects; also important are the demand and supply elasticities. Dam suggests that, instead of the volume-of-imports criterion, there should be a criterion based on some estimate, (albeit necessarily inexact) of the change in imports that will result from the tariff change.

If we view the reciprocity norm in focal-point terms, however, its arbitrariness is not a drawback. From a status quo point that is not Pareto efficient there are many mutually advantageous potential agreements. Because of the multiplicity of possible outcomes that would leave all players better off than the status quo, the negotiating process is by its very nature arbitrary. Reciprocity serves to establish a focal point because it is a simple rule cemented by long-standing custom. Its exactness is its virtue. A more economically meaningful but less exact rule, perhaps requiring quantitative estimates of demand and supply elasticities, would leave more scope for disagreement among the bargainers and therefore result in a higher probability of breakdown.

This interpretation of reciprocity is consistent with a lesson that can be extrapolated from the bargaining experiments reported by Roth (1987), summarized above. In these experiments there was a marked tendency for the bargainers to settle for a 50–50 split, despite the fact that units of measurement by which the 50–50 split was defined were arbitrary: the 50–50 split was nominal rather than real. Given the multiplicity of ways of improving upon the status quo, what seems to be needed for a bargaining settlement to be reached is a commonly-agreed way of keeping score in the process of mutual concession-giving; and it does not seem to matter that the units in which the score is kept have no real meaning, or that different but arguably equally valid units of measurement could be devised. In the Roth experiments, the bargainers failed to reach agreement in typically one-sixth to one-quarter of the cases; this is surprisingly frequent given the contrived simplicity of the experimental bargaining situation. We can conclude that, because of the multiplicity of ways of making all parties to a negotiation better off, the exact, true division of the gains from agreement is less important to the negotiators than the fact that the negotiations do not break down. Hence the appearance of equal division may be enough to generate agreement.

In the Tokyo Round negotiations, 'the way reciprocity gets put into practice is through a calculation of balance in the concessions that are being exchanged. This calculation of balance is quantitative, and it produces numerical measures that allow negotiators to evaluate the equivalence of the concessions offered by each side' (Winham, 1986, p. 266). According to one of the participants the final meeting on tariffs ended up being a series of 'long battles fought with hand calculators' (Winham, 1986, p. 266). Moreover, such quid-pro-quo bargaining was not restricted to tariffs. Reciprocity was also applied in the negotiations about NTB codes in the Tokyo Round, with negotiators demanding 'payment' for any actions they took (Winham, 1986, Chapters 6 and 7). For instance, in exchange for an alteration in its method of assessing taxes on distilled spirits, the USA extracted tariff reductions from the EEC and Canada. The US negotiators carefully calculated in dollar terms what they were giving and receiving over this tax issue; although, once again, the measures of the gains and losses made no economic sense.

RECIPROCITY AND THE DEVELOPING COUNTRIES

GATT's relationship with the developing countries has long been based on the principle of non-reciprocal and preferential treatment. This rests, at least on the face of it, on the idea that poor countries' development can be aided by preferential access to developed countries' markets. Recently critics of GATT's treatment of the developing countries have pointed out that practice has not lived up to this ideal. The principle of preferential access has failed to guarantee that the developed countries are open to developing-country exports. This has led to some questioning of the preferential-access and non-reciprocity provisions. Would the developing countries be better off if they were not accorded special status?

GATT rules do not prevent the developing countries from engaging in reciprocal bargaining; but they prevent developed countries from insisting upon it (GATT, 1986b, p. 192). Our analysis of bargaining suggests that, by not requiring that reciprocity be extended to the developing nations, the GATT rules may hinder the developing countries from using a potentially effective bargaining strategy. Developed countries, negotiating among themselves, can offer access to their own markets in exchange for access for their exports. Such offers are credible because the possibility of retaliation provides sanctions against non-performance. For the developing countries, in contrast, the insistence upon preferential status means that they are excluded from the process of finding mutually advantageous reductions in trade restrictions. Non-participants are unlikely to receive much from any agreement that is reached. This common-sense point is confirmed by non-cooperative game theory; if one player makes all the offers, that player gets the better of the bargain (Ausable and Deneckere, 1987).

While a theoretical analysis such as this can identify potential gains from extending reciprocity to the developing countries, it cannot establish its feasibility. It is often argued that reciprocity would not be effective because the developing countries lack the necessary bargaining power. Whether reciprocity for the developing countries would be workable is an open empirical question.

The term 'bargaining power', though often glibly used, is notoriously difficult to define in a precise, measurable and non-tautological way. However, the discussion of reciprocity and retaliation suggests a simple definition that is adequate for our purposes: one's bargaining power is greater the more one has to offer that the other party wants (via reciprocal bargaining) and, conversely, the more the other party would be harmed if one withheld what one has (in retaliation for violation of the agreement).

The aspect of a country's bargaining power in either GATT-based or bilateral trade negotiations that first comes to mind is its ability to offer or withhold access to its domestic market. Does this give significant bargaining power to developing countries, or is it so small as to be useful in negotiations? There is evidence to suggest that market access can in some instances be a viable bargaining tool for developing countries. Some, such as India and Brazil, have domestic markets that are large by any standards. Taiwan's share of world exports now exceeds Switzerland's and Sweden's and is almost one-fifth of the USA's share; while Hong Kong and Korea are not far behind Taiwan (GATT, 1987). Developing countries have a large share of the production and trade in some particular commodities; for instance, Malaysia is a dominant actor in the world markets for palm oil, rubber, copra and tin (Newbery, 1981). In a number of instances, developing countries' threats have achieved their desired ends. The People's Republic of China once threatened to cease grain purchases from the USA if new textile import restrictions were imposed. Malaysia induced Sweden to remove import restrictions on rubber boots by threatening to stop its imports of Swedish trucks. Chile secured access for some of its agricultural exports in Japan by threatening to cease its importation of Japanese cars.[6]

Quantitative evidence on the returns to activist negotiation comes from a study of the consequences of the Kennedy Round by Finger (1979). The nine developing countries that actively participated in the Kennedy Round negotiations induced the USA to lower trade barriers on 33 per cent of its imports from them.[7] This is less than the major developed countries or the other developed countries achieved (70 per cent and 49 per cent, respectively), but markedly more than the inactive developing countries (5 per cent). This perhaps underestimates the returns from active negotiation, for participation in the Kennedy Round by the 'active' developing countries did not necessarily consist of meaningful bargaining. An additional point is that what is under consideration is a set of procedures for trade policy that can be expected to be in place for several years. Thus the current size of developing countries' markets is less relevant than the future size; at current growth rates, the markets of countries like Korea and Brazil can be expected to be increasingly important. The developing countries played a more active and effective role in the negotiations in the Tokyo Round in the 1970s than in the Kennedy Round in the 1960s (Winham, 1986, pp. 272–3), which suggests that their influence is increasing over time.

Furthermore, the developing countries' bargaining options might be broader than just the offering of access to their own markets; trade flows measure only a part of the developing countries' potential bargaining power. The agenda might be expanded to encompass payment regimes, international debt, or global security (Hamilton and Whalley, 1988). Dixit (1987) argues that small countries often have an impact in international relations that is disproportionate to their size. For instance, the Philippines gains strategic leverage in trade negotiations with the USA from the USA's desire to keep its military bases in the Philippines. One interpretation of the history of the GSP is that its very existence is evidence of the bargaining power which the developing countries can extract from security matters. In this account, the GSP was a concession wrung from the Western powers in the 1950s in exchange for the developing countries' participation in the non-Communist bloc rather than the Communist bloc.

Regardless of the effectiveness of a developing country of extended reciprocity in its international interactions, there would be a welfare-improving effect on the political-economy game played within each developing country (sketched in the section on Players, Pay-offs and Strategies above). Admitting the principle of reciprocity strengthens the hand of the free-trade lobby in domestic bargaining, for a reduction in trade restrictions can be sold as the concession needed to ensure market access for the country's exporters. Acceding to the discipline of retaliation has a similar effect: the threat of retaliation from other countries provides an incentive for exporters to engage in lobbying against protection (Abbott, 1985). By making itself subject to GATT-based reciprocity, the government of a developing country would reduce the power of domestic interest groups by reducing its own scope for action. This voluntary relinquishing of power over trade policy would be analogous to the US Congress passing control over trade policy to the Executive Branch, in the Reciprocal Trade Agreements Act of 1934, on the grounds that the Executive Branch would be less responsive to interest groups than Congress itself.

In the focal-point interpretation, GATT's success in reducing tariffs on developed-country trade stems from the simplicity of the reciprocity custom that has evolved: the straightforward focal point is equal volumes of trade. If reciprocity is to be extended to issues of concern to the developing nations, such as agricultural trade and NTBs, equally simple focal points will have to be devised. Similarly, if the agenda is to be expanded to include international-debt and global-security considerations, workable focal points will have to be found. These focal points must be determined by something that is easily observable to all parties, and based on facts about which there is no scope for disagreement. Whether such focal points can be found remains an open question. If they cannot, it may be difficult or impossible for agreements to be reached. Consider for example the vexed question of how to get agreement on reducing the extent to which nations subsidize their industries; agriculture is the prime example. The OECD has recently developed what it calls Producer Subsidy Equivalents and Consumer Subsidy Equivalents, which attempt to measure the trade impacts of subsidies. There are, of course, severe problems of measurement here; some arbitrariness is unavoidable. But, analogous with the arbitrariness inherent in measuring the value of a tariff reduction, it does not much matter how the arbitrariness be resolved. Since there are many mutually advantageous potential agreements, there are many different ways of measuring the economic impact of a subsidy as a way of keeping score in the process of mutual concession-giving. If the focal-point model of the bargaining process is correct, then agreeing on a common definition of the size of subsidies would move the parties a long way toward an agreement on reducing them.

CONCLUSION

It has been suggested that the multiplicity of equilibria caused by the ongoing nature of the trade-negotiations game creates two distinct roles of GATT. One role is to ensure that the nations are not trapped in a low-level equilibrium, as apparently they were in the 1930s. Cooperation is achieved through the retaliation possibilities inherent in the dynamics of the game. The other role is to provide a mechanism for selecting a particular outcome from the set of efficient outcomes and for resolving conflicts over how the gains from cooperation are to be divided. In this, the principle of reciprocity focuses the bargainers' attention on a small set of possible directions of change.

With some oversimplification, one can characterize relations among developed countries as being mediated by their self-interest, via reciprocity and retaliation. In contrast, relations between developing and developed countries are dependent, under the GSP, on the developed countries' goodwill. The developed countries have been remarkably successful in achieving tariff reductions. Evidently, and not surprisingly, self-interest is a powerful force in international relations. Can this force be turned to the developing countries' advantage? Perhaps it can, by using the mechanisms of reciprocity and retaliation which have worked for the developed countries. This might make the developing countries' access to developed countries' markets more secure, for it would be dependent on the developed countries' self-interest rather than, as now, on their goodwill.

NOTES

1 I thank Ashok Desai, Michael Finger, Glenn Harrison, Lawrence Krause, John Whalley, Martin Wolf, and the participants in the Ford Foundation project for comments.
2 For analyses of some aspects of this game, see Hansen and Jaskold-Gabszewicz (1972), Brock and Magee (1978) and Bhagwait (1982).
3 The cited results are due to Cheh (1974) and Bale (1977). For further empirical analysis of the redistributional implications and the domestic political economy of tariff-setting, see Bayard and Orr (1980), Finger, Hall and Nelson (1982), Marvell and Ray (1983), and Ray (1981) on the USA; Caves (1976) and Helleiner (1977) on Canada; and Reidel (1977) on Germany.
4 Open to such criticism are the articles in Oye (1986), analyses of the politics of international security and economic conflicts that take as their basis the prisoner's dilemma game.
5 On the use in the Tokyo Round and the Kennedy Round of this definition of reciprocity, see Evans (1971, pp. 314–15) and Winham (1986, pp. 201, 266). This is what Bhagwati and Irwin (1987) term 'first-difference' reciprocity.
6 The first two of these case are cited by Hudec (1987). The third comes from a World Bank official.
7 The nine active developing countries were Argentina, Brazil, Chile, Dominican Republic, India, Jamaica, South Korea, Peru and Trinidad and Tobago.

REFERENCES

Abbott, K. W. (1985) 'The Trading Nation's Dilemma: The Functions of the Law of International Trade', *Harvard International Law Journal* 26, (Spring), pp. 501–32.

Ausable, L. M., and Deneckere, R. J. (1987) 'A Direct Mechanism Characterization of Sequential Bargaining with One-Sided Incomplete Information', Discussion Paper No. 728, Northwestern University, April, forthcoming in *Journal of Economic Theory*.

Bale, M. D. (1977) 'United States Concessions in the Kennedy Round and Short-Run Labour Adjustment Costs: Further Evidence', *Journal of International Economics*, 7 (May), pp. 145–8.

Bayard, T. and Orr, J. (1980) 'Trade and Employment Effects of Tariff Reductions AGreed to in the MTN', Economic Discussion Paper No. 1, Bureau of International Labor Affairs (Washington, DC: US Department of Labor), April.

Bhagwati, J. H., and Irwin, D. A. (1987) 'The Return of the Reciprocitarians – US Trade Policy Today', *The World Economy*, 10 (June), pp. 109–300.

Brock, W. A., and Magee, S. P. (1978) 'The Economics of Special Interest Politics: The Case of the Tariff'., *American Economic Review: Papers and Proceedings*, 68, pp. 246–50.

Brown, F. and Whalley, J. (1980) 'General Equilibrium Evaluations of Tariff-Cutting Proposals in the Tokyo Round and Comparisons with More Extensive Liberalization of World Trade', *Economic Journal* 90 (December), pp. 838–66.

Caves, R. E. (1976) 'Economic Models of Political Choice: Canada's Tariff Structure', *Canadian Journal of Economics* 9 (May), pp. 278–300.

Cheh, J. H. (1974) 'United States Concessions in the Kennedy Round and Short-Run Labor Adjustment Costs', *Journal of International Economics*, 4 (November), pp. 323–40.

Conybeare, J. (1986) 'Trade Wars: A Comparative Study of Anglo-Hanse, Franco-Italian, and Hawley-Smoot Conflicts', in Oye (1986).

Dam, K. W. (1987) *The GATT: Law and International Economic Organization* (University of Chicago Press).

Dixit, A. (1987) 'Issues of Strategic Trade Policy for Small Countries', *Scandinavian Journal of Economics*, 89, pp. 349–68.

Dubey, P. (1980) 'Nash Equilibria of Market Games: Finiteness and Efficiency', *Journal of Economic Theory*, 22, pp. 363–76.

Evans, J. W. (1971) *The Kennedy Round in American Trade Policy* (Cambridge, Mass.: Harvard University Press).

Finger, J. M. (1979) 'Trade Liberalization: A Public Choice Perspective', in R. C. Amacher, G. Haberler and T. D. Willett (eds) *Challenges to a Liberal International Order* (Washington, DC: American Enterprise Institute).

Finger, J. M., Hall, H. K. and Nelson, D. C. (1982) 'The Political Economy of Administered Protection', *American Economic Review*, 72 (June), pp. 452–66.

Friedman, J. W. (1986) *Game Theory with Applications in Economics*, (Oxford University Press).

GATT (1986a) *Text of the General Agreement on Tariffs and Trade* (Geneva: GATT).

GATT (1986b) *The Texts of the Tokyo Round Agreements* (Geneva: GATT).

GATT (1987) 'International Trade in 1986 and Current Prospects', Press Release, 23 March.

Hamilton, B. and Whalley, J. (1983) 'Optimal Tariff Calculations in Alternative Trade Models and some Possible Implications for Current World Trading Arrangements', *Journal of International Economics*, 15 pp. 323–48.

Hamilton, C. and Whalley, J. (1988) 'Strategic Options for Developing Countries in the Global Trading System', mimeo (London, Canada: University of Western Ontario).

Hansen, T. and Jaskold-Gabszewicz, J. (1972) 'Collusion of Factor Owners and the Distribution of Factor Output', *Journal of Economic Theory*, 4 pp. 1–18.

Helleiner, G. K. (1977) 'The Political Economy of Canada's Tariff Structure: An Alternative Model', *Canadian Journal of Economics*, 10 (May), pp. 318–25.
Hudec, R. E. (1987) *Developing Countries in the GATT Legal System* (London: Macmillan for TPRC).
Johnson, H. G. (1953) 'Optimum Tariffs and Retaliation', *Review of Economic Studies*, 21, pp. 142–53.
Kreps, D. M. (1984) 'Corporate Culture and Economic Theory', mimeo, Stanford University, May.
Mandel, M. J. (1985) 'Focal Points and Wage Bargaining', mimeo, Harvard University, June.
Marvell, H. P. and Ray, E. J. (1983) 'The Kennedy Round: Evidence on the Regulation of International Trade in the United States', *American Economic Review*, 73 (March), pp. 190–7.
McMillan, J. (1986) *Game Theory in International Economics* (New York: Harwood).
Myerson, R. B. (1986) 'Negotiation in Games: A Theoretical Overview', in W. P. Heller, R. M. Starr and D. A. Starret (eds) *Uncertainty, Information and Communication: Essays in Honor of Kenneth J. Arrow*, vol. III (New York: Cambridge University Press).
Newbery, D. M. G. (1981) 'Commodity Price Stabilization in Imperfectly Competitive Markets', Discussion Paper No. 32 (Washington, DC: Development Research Center, World Bank).
Oye, K. A. (ed.) (1986) *Cooperative Under Anarchy* (Princeton University Press).
Porter, R. H. (1983) 'Optimal Cartel Trigger Price Strategies', *Journal of Economic Theory* 29, pp. 313–38.
Ray, E. J. (1981) 'The Determinants of Tariff and Nontariff Restrictions in the United States', *Journal of Political Economy*, 89 (February), 105–21.
Reidel, J. (1977) 'Tariff Concessions in the Kennedy Round and the Structure of Protection in West Germany: An Economic Assessment', *Journal of International Economics*, 7 (May), pp. 133–43.
Roth, A. E. (1985) 'Toward a Focal-Point Theory of Bargaining', in A. E. Roth (ed.), *Game-Theoretic Models of Bargaining* (Cambridge University Press).
Roth, A. E. (1987) 'Bargaining Phenomena and Bargaining Theory', in A.E. Roth (ed.), *Laboratory Experimentation in Economics: Six Points of View* (Cambridge University Press).
Rubinstein, A. (1987) 'A Sequential Strategic Theory of Bargaining' in T. Bewley (ed.), *Advances in Economic Theory: Fifth World Congress*, (Cambridge University Press).
Schelling, T. C. (1960) *The Strategy of Conflict* (Cambridge, Mass: Harvard University Press).
Smith, A. (1952) *An Enquiry into the Nature and Causes of the Wealth of Nations* Chicago: Encyclopedia Britannica).
Winham, G. R. (1986) *International Trade and the Tokyo Round Negotiation* (Princeton University Press).

12. Reciprocity in Trade: the Utility of a Bargaining Strategy

C. Rhodes

Recent works in international relations theory have focused on the value of reciprocity as a means of achieving cooperation in international policies.[1] They argue that in an anarchic setting in which self-help typifies the behavior of sovereign nation states, the strategy of matching comparable responses to the actions of other nations may educate them over time to cooperate, even in the absence of centralized enforcement. However, little effort has been made to examine the applied value of reciprocity in foreign policy actions. This article empirically confirms that reciprocity is useful in achieving cooperative outcomes.

The study summarized in this article was launched to determine whether a reciprocal strategy can affect another nation's calculation of self-interest so that behavior is modified and cooperation is enhanced. An empirical investigation of the use of flexible reciprocal bargaining strategies in U.S. bilateral trade relations indicates that under certain circumstances reciprocity is an effective means of eliciting cooperation from trading partners. Results demonstrate that this cooperation is usually consistent with the General Agreement on Tariffs and Trade (GATT) norms of liberal trade and dispute settlement, even when it is inconsistent with the GATT principle of nondiscrimimation.[2] This is largely due to common definitions of cooperation shared by trading partners within the GATT regime, which buttresses the theory that regimes also influence behavior.

Because regime cooperation and the responses that reciprocal strategies elicit are intermingled in bilateral relations, it is necessary to define cooperation and reciprocity in the context of world trade norms and actors' expectations. The first part of this analysis is devoted to a discussion of the interplay between GATT regime norms and member nations' mutual expectations when reciprocal strategies are utilized. It includes a taxonomy of the policy choices and outcomes that have been traced in the cases examined in this context. The second part identifies a summary of selected trade disputes to illustrate the patterns that emerged. Finally, the third part utilizes the taxonomy of actions and outcomes in a comparative assessment of the character and efficacy of reciprocity as a bargaining strategy in trade under differing circumstances.

RECIPROCITY AND COOPERATION IN TRADE: DEFINITIONS AND EXPECTATIONS

Bilateral trade relations provide useful cases for examining the efficacy of reciprocal strategies because subjects can be chosen for their interdependence and therefore for their likelihood of continued interaction. This is important in enlarging the shadow of the future so that each actor is well aware that the trading partner may retaliate against uncooperative behavior or may offer benefits when cooperation is secured. As Robert Keohane and Robert Axelrod have noted, in international political economy "retaliation for defection will almost always be possible [because of the interdependent and iterated character of relations in this area], and a rational player, considering defection, has to consider its probability and its potential consequences."[3]

This feature of international trade decisions has influenced trade analysis to apply similar logic to the negotiation of trade agreements. Beth and Robert Yarbrough have recently argued that reciprocity, which implicitly includes retaliation, can facilitate the "successful negotiation" of such arrangements.[4] They are joined by strategic trade theorists, who recognize the opportunities and constraints posed by political intervention in the world marketplace and agree that reciprocity may be the best overall strategy.[5]

Because it is conjectured that international trade cooperation can be facilitated by reciprocity, this issue-area is well suited for empirical examination. While there exists a cooperative framework for international trade in the form of GATT, the absence of enforceable multilateral sanctions makes cooperation under GATT uncertain, and unilateral strategies that might facilitate cooperation are worth investigating.

Moreover, focusing on trade relations under GATT is of value for our purposes in that GATT is a tangible reflection of the normative expectations for cooperation of its major participants. In fact, GATT norms play a significant role in reciprocity in trade. Because reciprocity requires that one must be "nice" as well as "forgiving," the context of trade interactions is very important to an understanding of the expectations of GATT trading partners.[6] Presumably if autarky were the preference of all actors, then reciprocity could neither do injury to others nor offer them benefits. This does not merely mean that interdependence is requisite; it also means that the preference ordering of the actors involved must include the perceived advantages of continuing that interdependence.

Under circumstances in which there is a high potential for future interactions, one would expect that short-term interests would be weighed against long-term interests and that the expectation of punishment or renewal would be taken into account. It is likely, therefore, that the decision between such interdependent actors to cooperate or not to cooperate would depend upon each one's perception of mutual vulnerabilities and interests in the immediate situation as well as over time. A strategy that trains another actor to fear the punishment of retaliation and to seek the reward of continued cooperation may be the most effective form of bargaining leverage in international politics.

Liberal economists successfully convinced the post-World War II generation that free trade encourages economic growth at home as well as abroad. Yet the free trade norm alone has not ensured commitment when adherence to it has conflicted with other interests. The fear that others will retaliate is necessary to strengthen the cooperative commitment. Although GATT members have a strong incentive to pursue liberal trade in exchange for its reciprocation, they also have an incentive to retaliate in response to noncooperation by forcing the uncooperative member to return to liberalism or to offer acceptable compensation. When norms alone fail to constrain harmful behaviour, the threat of retaliation may be a necessary reminder of the punishment that might result.[7]

In fact, GATT itself was founded on two distinct and contradictory principles that were inherited from U.S. trade law and that embody this set of expectations: the principle of unconditional most-favored-nation (MFN) treatment and the principle of balanced treatment. The first principle guarantees equally to all contracting parties benefits granted any contracting party. Although the second ensures mutual and roughly equivalent concessions as the basis for tariff bargaining, it also gives members the right to retaliate when those concessions are withdrawn or when unfair acts are committed. This retaliation may take many forms, ranging from antidumping duties to market closure, depending upon the action disputed and the perceptions of the actors involved. Since GATT rules incorporate these two principles, reciprocity is often a condition of trade arrangements between GATT members even though it contradicts nondiscrimination.[8]

Thus, the general commitment to liberal trade and fairness is embedded in an expectation of balanced treatment and a preservation of state sovereignty.[9] Consequently, because reciprocity and retaliation provide the "carrot" and "stick" for MFN cooperation among GATT members, they are vital enforcement mechanisms. Yet it must be understood that reciprocity is a subjective concept that is determined by the perceptions of the actors involved.

Reciprocity

As Keohane has noted, "Reciprocity refers to exchanges of roughly equivalent values in which the actions of each party are contingent on the prior actions of the others in such a way that good is returned for good and bad for bad."[10] Approximate equivalence is a crucial component of reciprocity because in many situations equivalence cannot be measured and the acceptability of the proposed exchange cannot be predicted. Only in a few situations is equivalence exact and measurable – for example, in certain market transactions or in the extension of reciprocal legal rights. Of necessity, then, equivalence must be recognized as a concept that is subject to the perceptions and particular requirements of the decision makers involved at a given point in time. An exchange of equivalent trade concessions, for example, may be made in mutual good faith, even though the impact of those concessions may vary and from time to time be highly unbalanced.[11]

The key to the concept of equivalence is that as long as both sides consider the exchange to be equivalent, reciprocal treatment is assumed. Only when one side perceives a lack of balance will equivalence again become an issue, and even then in negotiations and agreements the definition of equivalence will be a matter of opinion rather than measurement. Consequently, it is highly possible that while one actor perceives itself as taking reciprocal, retaliatory action to redress a malignant imbalance with another actor, the latter perceives such action as a harmful initiative to alter the previous bargain.

The concept of contingency poses similar problems. As in the above example, there may be instances in which a government takes a retaliatory action which it interprets as being an appropriate response to something another government has wrongfully done but which the latter views as a nonreciprocal deviation from a cooperative relationship. This ambiguity is fairly common under circumstances in which one side sees itself as playing by the rules of the game in a narrow sense while the other side takes a broader view. The trade relationship between the United States and Japan often fits this description. Whereas the Japanese government takes the position that its trade surplus is the result of its nation's genuine competitive ability in comparison with that of others, the U.S. government argues that the trade surplus is only possible because Japan has more open access to other nations' markets than they do to Japan's market.[12] Thus, Japan claims that in its particular trade tactics it is behaving fairly as is expected under the GATT framework, while the United States claims that there is an accumulated imbalance that "delegitimizes" those tactics.

Because such subjectivity is endemic to international relationships, including trade relationships, an investigation of the use of reciprocal strategies may have to rely upon the perceptions of the decision makers involved in identifying and analyzing particular sequences of reciprocal and nonreciprocal actions. This at times means that for a specific set of interactions there may be more than one interpretation of the actions and responses, making formal discrete modeling of the sequence somewhat cumbersome.

Another analytical problem that the condition of contingency presents for modeling is the difficulty of interpreting the actual sequence of the interaction itself. The particular reciprocal strategy itself. The particular reciprocal strategy "tit for tat" outlined by Axelrod prescribes a "policy of cooperating on the first move and then doing whatever the other player did on the previous move."[13] However, it may be that a general policy of reciprocity at times includes nonsequential conciliatory gestures that are designed to provide new momentum for stalemated negotiations. The problem with a strict "tit for tat" strategy is that it can deteriorate into a feud (or in the case of international commerce, a trade war).

Therefore, even if one actor should, according to a reciprocal strategy, continue to defect from cooperation contingent upon its partner's continuing to do so, it may actually be more productive to break the deadlock with a very different accommodative initiative. This is especially true during periods of active bargaining when a settlement of the disagreement at hand would return the trading partners to a cooperative norm. For example, in the steel case described below, the United States broke the deadlock in negotiations by arranging access for European producers to steel pipe contracts for a Texas-California pipeline. This conciliatory gesture had the effect of inducing the European Community (EC) Commission to agree to a compromise with the United States on the inclusion of semifinished steels.[14] Thus, while contingency is a logical component of reciprocity, it should be a condition that is considered broadly for identifying an overall policy rather than strictly demanded in each and every instance of cooperation is indeed the desired outcome.

Cooperation

Cooperation under GATT also takes two general forms. The first form, which is most often associated with GATT, is the institution and maintenance of liberal trade policies. The second form is the compensation of GATT trading partners when liberal actions are taken against them. The cooperative ideal is collective trade liberalization by members in the pursuit of their common well-being as defined by the normative framework of GATT. However, it is recognized that when individual nations cannot maintain their cooperative commitment to liberal trade, there is an expectation that their injured partners must be compensated. If compensation is not forthcoming or if it is considered inadequate, contracting members have the right under specific circumstances to take retaliatory action.[15]

Inherent in GATT cooperation is the expectation that members will recognize the liberalizing efforts of their counterparts and reciprocate. When a dispute arises over the equivalence of the reciprocity or over new illiberal or illegal actions, the parties involved are expected to negotiate a mutually acceptable settlement or to defer to previously negotiated guidelines for compensation. Most disputes are settled bilaterally to the mutual satisfaction of the nations involved, making it unnecessary to refer the dispute to the GATT Contracting Parties for their collective recommendation.[16] Bilateral settlement is encouraged by GATT, which recognizes that the disputants involved must be mutually satisfied before there can be a practical resolution of the matter.

The character of this bilateral cooperation varies from case to case. Some settlements are illustrative of the willingness of trading partners to recognize the "rules of behavior" as defined by GATT and to accept GATT procedures for dispute settlement. There are times, however, when established guidelines are either ambiguous or unacceptable to one or both trading partners and require that disputes be settled by *ad hoc* arrangements that involve case by case negotiation. The nature of cooperation is further determined by the degree to which the mutual interests of the disputants are served by the arrangement. Thus, settlements can be classified as collusive, concessionary, or capitulatory, depending upon the symmetry of reciprocity reflected in the outcome.

A taxonomy of trade policies is provided in Table 1. This classification differentiates between reciprocal and nonreciprocal policies and between cooperative and noncooperative policies. Cooperative and noncooperative outcomes are categorized by association with the policies that produced them according to the degree of reciprocity involved.

For example, in a dispute between nation A and nation B, if the latter merely accommodates the coercive demands of nation A even when nation B has committed no injury to upset the balance of bilateral reciprocity, it is a case of *capitulation*. A cooperative outcome has been achieved, but since it favors nation A, it is not an outcome that reflects mutual interest. It is, in fact, the result of a nonreciprocal response by nation B to injury imposed or threatened by nation A. If nation B had been guilty of some earlier transgression of its own (which had stimulated its trading partner's retaliation) and had been willing to reform its behavior in a cooperative manner, then its action could be classified as a *concession*. The distinction is that a concession is considered to be a reciprocal action predicated on bilateral cooperative expectations, whereas capitulation occurs when expectations of bilateral reciprocity are not at issue. There is one important exception to this generalization. During deadlocked negotiations, it may be

TABLE 1 *Classification of trade policies, actions, and outcomes*

Trade policy	Action	Outcome
Noncooperative		
Nonreciprocal	*Protectionism*: (1) coercive noncooperation (offensive) or (2) domestic protectionism (defensive)	*Noncooperation*: (1) stalemate (acceptance of damages; no escalation) or (2) feud (active escalation of dispute)
Reciprocal	*Retaliation*: punishment	*Noncooperation*: (1) stalemate or (2) feud
Cooperative		
Nonreciprocal	*Accommodation*: (1) capitulatory accommodation or (2) initiatory accommodation	*Cooperation*: (1) capitulation, (2) concession, or (3) collusion
Reciprocal	*Reward*: (1) concessionary reward or (2) collusive reward	*Cooperation*: (1) capitulation, (2) concession, or (3) collusion

constructive for one side to initiate a nonreciprocal cooperative action to encourage the other side to reconsider its position. This *accommodation* may be a vital tactic in an otherwise reciprocal strategy.

When expectations of bilateral reciprocity influence both nations to mutually offer concessions in order to reach a settlement, then *collusion* is the outcome. This form of cooperation has become increasingly popular between nations that do not want to follow established GATT guidelines for liberal trade but do want to maintain their bilateral trade relations. As surplus capacity in sector after sector has made worldwide market competition fierce and politically volatile, nations have become less willing to adhere to a strict interpretation of GATT rules of behavior.[17] Thus, it is quite common for importing nations to seek agreements with exporting nations on restricting the quantity of certain exports to their market. Although Article II of GATT prohibits such quantitative restrictions, the fact that both the importer and the exporter collude to arrange limits on the level of exports to that particular market means that the rule infraction does not in itself cause a dispute.[18] It is, in fact, the cooperative culmination of a negotiated settlement.

Ironically, this form of cooperation between trading nations consists of collusion against the letter of GATT law governing quantitative restrictions.

However, the cooperative norm of GATT, which is to maintain liberal trade or to compensate for deviations from that commitment, is actually upheld by such arrangements. Because the exporting nation benefits from the quota rents that are derived from supply nation.[19] This, combined with continued access to the market in question, gives the exporting country a strong interest in cooperating with the nation seeking restraint.

While the importing nation may use the threat of unilateral market restrictions and the retention of quota rent or tariff revenue to gain leverage with the exporting nation, the fact that it offers the exporter the compensation of quota rent and bilateral involvement in the decision is evidence of its own cooperative effort. Moreover, evidence indicates that this form of managed trade does maintain market access and prevents a serious deterioration in trade flows.[20] Therefore, even though voluntary export restraints are a form of collusion against the liberal ideal of GATT, they may actually be the most politically feasible means of maintaining cooperation for relatively open trade in the face of protectionist pressure.

Noncooperation also contains reciprocal and nonreciprocal forms. When one nation initially deviates from the cooperative norm of liberal trade, it may be for one of two basic reasons. First, it may be merely succumbing to domestic political pressure for protection against foreign imports. This is the most common cause of noncooperation in international trade. Second, it may be taking protective actions to induce another nation to respond. This is both offensive and coercive in purpose. For example, if nation A wants to induce a concession from nation B, regardless of nation B's past cooperation and the reciprocal relationship between the two nations, nation A may resort to coercive threats to extort accommodation. In this case, nation A is aggressively exploiting the vulnerabilities of nation B in an interdependent trade relationship in order to gain an advantage for itself. Because these two forms of noncooperative policy — *domestic protectionism* and *coercive noncooperation* – are not taken in response to another nation's unfair or illegal behavior, they are both categorized as nonreciprocal.

The reciprocal form of noncooperation is *retaliation*, which is specifically pursued as punishment against or compensation for some prior uncooperative action by a trading partner. There are two general types of noncooperative outcomes that might emerge from any given set of noncooperative policies: *stalemates* and *feuds*. In cases of stalemate, the outcomes are typified by acceptance of the damages incurred. There is no escalation, but the dispute is not resolved. Antagonists agree to disagree. However, when feuds occur, there is evidence of active conflict. In such cases, interactions are characterized by retaliation and counterretaliation that escalate into a trade war. While the premise of this article has been that reciprocity (including retaliation) will enhance cooperation, it is recognized that there are hazards associated with its use. There is a risk that the use of retaliation will catalyze such a deteriorating spiral.

This taxonomy allows us to visualize the potential positive and negative attributes of reciprocity as well as the limits and opportunities afforded by other strategies in trade for achieving cooperation. It facilitates the comparative evaluation of reciprocal strategies which follows.

CASE MATERIAL: THE UTILITY AND CHARACTER OF RECIPROCAL STRATEGIES IN TRADE

In order to move from the realm of speculation and actually evaluate the utility of reciprocal strategies as a means of achieving cooperation between nations, the relations of the United States with its three most important trading partners (Canada, Japan, and the EC) were compared in three different trade sectors: steel, automobiles, and wheat flour. Generally, the case material confirms that coercive tactics, whether part of a reciprocal strategy or not, have the effect of inducing a cooperative response from a trading partner.

The United States, Canada, Japan, and the EC are treated as individual rational unitary actors for the sake of abstraction and comparison.[21] It is recognized that decision making involves the intervention of domestic interests as well as international considerations (and their interaction). In the area of trade, in which many domestic actors and institutional arrangements affect the decision outcome, this may be particularly true. Nonetheless, the unitary actor depiction is useful as an analytical simplification which recognizes the constraints and opportunities posed by institutions and subnational actors but which allows us to direct our attention to the bargaining dynamic between trading partners rather than that between governments and domestic interest groups.

The comparative case study approach was chosen in order to establish whether an empirical basis exists for the theoretical proposition that reciprocity can promote cooperation in international trade. Differences in outcome which emerge from the different disputes help us to determine under what circumstances this occurs.

The groups of cases were chosen for several reasons. First, they involve the largest trading partners of the United States, both in terms of imports and in terms of exports (see Table 2). This makes them very important to the United States and indicates that future significant trade interactions will take place. The importance of each partner as an importer of U.S. products as well as an exporter to the United States is evidence of the mutual opportunity and the mutual vulnerability inherent in the relationships.[22] Although asymmetries exist, the potential for the mutual use of the reciprocal trade strategies is available.

Second, although these partners all experience vulnerability to U.S. threats of retaliation, the depth of that vulnerability and the capability to exploit the vulnerabilities of the United States are different. Variations in the use of counter-reciprocal strategies help to account for the ranges of cooperative outcomes that emerge.

Third, industrialized, long-term contracting parties to GATT were purposely selected, since they are all governed by the same set of norms and rules (while there are exceptions for less developed countries) and since they are all highly integrated in the world political economy. This makes the context for cooperation more consistent across relationships and also indicates that continued interaction is expected.

Thus, while GATT offers the most likely context for the appearance of bilateral reciprocity in a collective international framework because of the general norm of reciprocity among members, the trading partners selected are the most likely relationships within GATT to generate date supportive of the hypothesis that reciprocity enhances cooperation. Since these examples do generally confirm that this is true under certain circumstances, this study is the first hurdle in the empirical analysis, indicating that further testing of less likely cases will be worth pursuing.

The sectors of steel, automobiles, and wheat flour were chosen because each suffered from surplus capacity and severe price competition in the international market during the time periods examined and the resulting conflict is readily apparent.[23] Each sector contains sets of individual disputes that form the units of analysis for this study. Although the sectoral trade relationship may continue to be punctuated with discord, the bargaining and settlement of these "encapsulated" disputes provides twenty-three different cases for comparative analysis.

These cases are individually analyzed and reported in detail elsewhere.[24] For the purposes of this article, a few typical sets of interactions will be used to illustrate the value and limits of reciprocity for achieving cooperative outcomes, the behavioral strategies used in these instances, and the ambiguities that plague the analysis of reciprocity. We will look first at an example in which reciprocity was obviously the guiding strategy of both actors, and then we will examine a more ambiguous case.

U.S.–EC Carbon Steel Trade Dispute, 1981–82

The dispute between the United States and the EC centered on charges by U.S. steel producers that EC steel was being exported to the United States with the aid of unfair subsidies. By early summer of 1982, preliminary affirmative countervailing duty determinations were announced in response to a fusillade of petitions against subsidized carbon steel imports. These determinations concerned certain steel producers from EC member countries Belgium, France, Italy, Luxembourg, the Netherlands, the United Kingdom and West Germany.[25]

The EC Commission immediately sought consultations with the U.S. government and threatened retaliation if the countervailing duties were actually imposed. Moreover, it obtained an "exclusive mandate" from member states to conduct negotiations with the United State for a separate agreement that would avert the countervailing duties that appeared imminent under the U.S. administrative procedure (which is consistent with GATT rules concerning subsidies and countervailing procedures).[26]

Throughout the summer and autumn of 1982, negotiations took place between U.S. and EC officials in Brussels and Washington. In the end, the countervailing duty procedure was suspended in favor of a bilaterally negotiated settlement. The agreement resulting from these negotiations "provided that the entry into effect of the arrangement was conditional on the withdrawal of the petitions filed by the U.S. industry in respect of imports originating in the EC and on the termination of all proceedings and investigations concerning [countervailing duties]."[27]

In return, the arrangement provided for voluntary, EC-allocated export quotas on carbon steel. This, it was argued, would remove the "injurious effect" of subsidized imports without interfering with the EC's steel restructuralization policy, which relied on subsidization to temper the effect of reduced capacity. This compromise was particularly attractive to the EC Commission, since it would be in charge of determining which EC producers would be granted which levels of exports to the United States, rather than letting U.S. countervailing duties price some EC steel producers out of the market while not others.

It was vital to the EC Commission's collective steel program that costs of a diminished U.S. market be spread evenly across member states in relation to past market shares. Whereas a voluntary quota administered by the EC would provide this flexibility, U.S. countervailing duties would not. If countervailing duties were imposed, costs would be borne by the most heavily subsidized producers, while more efficient producers (particularly in Germany and the Netherlands) would hardly be affected.[28]

Although placing the extra cost burden on inefficient industries is the normative purpose behind GATT-sanctioned countervailing duties, it was not an effect comparable with the EC steel policy. Therefore, the voluntary restraint appeared a more attractive option.

This compromise was not immediately accepted by the American steel producers, however, who viewed the settlement as not being comprehensive enough because it omitted steel pipe and tube imports. Once the EC Commission agreed to include these items in its export restraint agreement, a final settlement was reached, with the U.S. complainants pledging to the Reagan administration that they would withdraw their countervailing duty suits.[29] The most interesting aspect of the settlement package was that it nowhere included any blame for unfair or injurious trading practices on the part of the EC.[30]

Table 3 illustrates the sequence of interactions in this particular dispute, which culminated in cooperation. Both actors pursued generally reciprocal strategies following the EC's initial export policy. For the United States, the "carrot" side of reciprocity was its willingness to suspend countervailing duty procedures in favor of a settlement more to the liking of the EC Commission, which included compensation for protection plus continued market access. The "stick" side consisted of the threat of countervailing duty retaliation. Similarly, the EC utilized threats of counterretaliation to press the United States into negotiations, but it was willing in those negotiations to offer American producers some protection against European exports to get an amicable settlement.

One of the most interesting aspects of this bargaining interaction was the fact that the threat of counterretaliation by the EC had the effect of persuading the U.S. government to reconsider its own countervailing duty procedure, not because it was legally suspect but because it was politically unacceptable. Cooperation in this case did not mean that either side forfeited its trade-distorting practices. Instead, a mutual understanding was reached that reflected concessions on both sides consistent with the compensatory requirements of GATT, though not with its liberal ideal. Collusion was the outcome.

U.S.–Japan automobile trade dispute, 1980–81

The use of a reciprocal strategy in the U.S. dispute with Japan concerning Japanese car exports to the United States is less straightforward. Faced with

TABLE 2 *Top three purchases of U.S. exports and suppliers of U.S. imports in 1985*

Top three	Amount in US$ millions 1983	1984	1985
Purchasers of U.S. exports[a]			
Canada	$38,244	$46,524	$47,251
EC	44,310	46,976	45,777
Japan	21,894	23,575	22,631
Suppliers of U.S. imports[b]			
Japan	43,559	60,171	72,380
Canada	52,546	66,911	69,427
EC	45,623	59,882	67,818

[a]Exports domestic and foreign merchandise, FAS (free alongside ship).
[b]Imports general imports, CIF (costs, insurance, freight).
Source: U.S. Department of Commerce, International Trade Administration, *1985 Foreign Trade Statistics*, Washington, D.C., 1986.

layoffs due to insufficient demand for American-manufactured automobiles, the United Auto Workers (UAW), joined by Ford Motor Company, filed a request in 1980 for import relief under Section 201 of the 1974 Trade Act. After the International Trade Commission (ITC) held public hearings, it announced that "although the U.S. automobile industry had suffered severe injury, foreign automobile imports were not a substantial cause of this injury."[31] Thus, blocked in their request for Section 201 import relief, the UAW and Ford Motor Company appealed to Congress, asking it to "empower the Administration to negotiate restrictions on the imports of Japanese cars."[32]

During this same period, the Carter administration had been negotiating with the Japanese government to remove its barriers to imports of automotive components, which the United States was producing at competitive rates. After extensive negotiations, the Japanese Diet approved the "elimination of tariffs on 38 automotive parts categories" to take effect on 1 April 1981.[33] Although the American automobile industry viewed this as a step in the right direction toward a more reciprocal trade relationship with Japan, the concessions hardly compensated for the 25 percent market share held by Japanese car producers, who had virtually free access to the American market since the Tokyo Round negotiation.

It is not surprising, then, that after the ITC refused to grant import relief, protectionist legislation was demanded, not only to provide temporary relief for adjustment but also to redress the general trade imbalance in this sector. This was the logic behind several of the protectionist measures being considered by Congress, including a resolution empowering the President to "enter negotiations with foreign governments to persuade them to voluntarily limit their export of automobiles."[34] Armed with the threat that Congress would take action on these measures if no "voluntary" restraint were forthcoming, the Reagan administration entered into negotiations with the Japanese government and secured an agreement on export limits on 1 May 1981.

Rather than threatening retaliation, as the EC did in the carbon steel case, Japan maintained a strategy of grudging but well-intended cooperation. The Japanese government was at pains to note its high degree of good citizenship in the world of trade and its willingness to shoulder part of the cost of the competitive adjustment of its trading partners. Citing its willingness to reduce trade barriers to American-manufactured automobiles and components and to continue "joint capital ventures and other forms of cooperation with the Big Three U.S. automobile manufacturers" as evidence of good faith, the Japanese government emphasized that its accommodative effort was designed to avoid future American protectionism and the deteriorating effects it would have on the GATT regime.[35]

The cooperative outcome was a given as long as Japan accommodated U.S. demands, but its reason for doing this provides a useful comparison with the previous case. While the EC had initiated the option of a voluntary restraint agreement in the steel dispute, in this case the U.S. executive branch introduced the possibility of a voluntary restraint agreement as an alternative to a congressional quota, thus deflecting worse protectionism and offering a compromise. The fact that cooperation resulted from this offer is indicative of the Japanese government's feeling of vulnerability to U.S. market restrictions as well as its desire to maintain a long-term commercial relationship with the United States. Continued access, as well as receipt of the quota rent for Japanese manufacturers (which has proven to be substantial), made voluntary restraint preferable to American-imposed limits.[35] Aware also of the mounting pressure in the United States for more balance in the trade relationship, the Japanese government pursued a cooperative policy in hopes of deflecting demands for stricter reciprocity.

While the resolution of this dispute cannot be attributed to the United States pursuing a reciprocal strategy from the outset, the fact that pressure was building for such a strategy on other trade fronts involving Japan did not go unnoticed in Tokyo. In many respects, the Japanese government recognized the larger reciprocal framework within which this dispute took place – including the GATT framework – even if reciprocity was not the original issue.

The U.S. bargaining strategy in this case raises a difficult analytical problem. While Congressional speeches indicate that one of the motivations behind protectionist legislation against Japanese car imports was the enforcement of reciprocity, it is also clear that there was a good deal of pressure for protection regardless of the reciprocity issue. Therefore, the question arises whether the voluntary restraint agreement was the product of a reciprocal strategy, in which case the U.S. threats of protection were retaliatory, or whether it was simple coercion, in which case the U.S. threats of protection were noncooperative deviations from the norm of reciprocity (coercive noncooperation).

The U.S. threats against Japanese exports could be interpreted as tactics in a larger reciprocal strategy if we accept that the United States was attempting to induce Japan to play a more responsible, cost-absorbing role in world trade in fair exchange for long-standing access to the relatively open markets of the United States. There is some quite convincing evidence to support this interpretation, particularly in regard to later U.S.–Japan interactions concerning this sector.[37] The sequence of events up to May 1981 indicates that a general expectation of reciprocity guided U.S. officials even when specific protectionist pressure appeared to be nonreciprocal in origin. This observation is consistent with Keohane's concept of "diffuse" and "specific" reciprocity. While the particular events leading to the voluntary restraint agreement do not constitute specific reciprocity, in which "partners exchange items of equivalent value in strictly deliminated sequence," they may well fit the concept of diffuse reciprocity, in which equivalence is less precise "and the presence of events is less narrowly bounded."[38]

This case also demonstrates why the mere presence of retaliatory threats in the bargaining process is not an indication of a reciprocal strategy. The threat of U.S. protection against Japanese auto imports was made in response to market conditions favoring Japanese manufacturers, rather than in retaliation for unfair Japanese actions. Under GATT, U.S. unilateral protection in contravention of Article 19 would constitute the first illegal and uncooperative action between the two countries in this particular sequence. Therefore, to threaten such action is coercive protectionism in the first instance, not reciprocity (see Table 4).

This somewhat ambiguous situation raises an interesting observation about coercion and reciprocity in trade. When the U.S. government pressed Japan for voluntary restraints, it was basically responding to domestic protectionist demands that it depart from its established liberal trade orientation in this sector even though there was no determination that the trade practices of Japan were the cause of the domestic industry's distress. The threat of Congressionally mandated import restrictions was clearly a coercive tactic but was less clearly a part of a reciprocal strategy.

However, once Japanese leaders were aware that expectations in the United States were increasingly based upon a definition of reciprocal responsibility in world trade that included Japanese restraint of exports in the absence of import liberalization, the expectation of reciprocity was interjected in the equation. This established a link between the U.S. coercive strategy and Japan's willingness to cooperate rather than retaliate. If Japan had not perceived its position in the world trade regime as vulnerable on the grounds of reciprocal expectations, it may have been less willing to accommodate U.S. demands.

This is not to claim that pressure mounting from the expectations of reciprocity was the determining factor in this case. It is more likely that asymetrical Japanese dependency on the American market and the desire to secure that market into the future were the major motivating factors behind cooperation. Even so, the Japanese hope for being judged as a responsible partner in trade demonstrated a visible uneasiness with the perception abroad that Japan was taking advantage of trade openness that it had not reciprocated.

As in the 1982 voluntary restraint agreement for steel, the U.S.–Japan agreement of 1981 was a negotiated compromise that provided continued market access coupled with quota rent compensation for the limits that were imposed. Despite

TABLE 3 *Sequence of actions in the U.S.–EC carbon steel trade dispute, 1981–82*

(1)	EC subsidizes steel that is bound for the U.S. market.
(2)	U.S. producers file countervailing duty suits in retaliation.
(3)	EC threatens retaliation and demands negotiations.
(4)	U.S. and EC negotiate alternative settlement.
(5)	EC and U.S. reach a compromise, with the U.S. suspending countervailing duty procedures in exchange for voluntary export restraints from the EC.

TABLE 4 *Sequence of actions in the U.S.–Japan automobile trade dispute, 1980–81*

(1)	Japan signs an agreement for automotive component import concessions.
(2)	U.S. threatens unilateral protection against Japanese automobile imports.
(3)	Japan enters into negotiations with the U.S.
(4)	U.S. and Japan reach an agreement on Japanese voluntary export restraints.

protectionist demands and a dip in automobile imports from Japan in the remainder of 1981 and 1982 automobile imports from that country rose consistently until exchange rates affected quantities in recent years.[39] The outcome again was a form of collusion, not mere capitulation on the part of Japan.

U.S.–Canada Automobile Trade Dispute, 1963–65

The U.S.–Canada case is of particular interest in comparison with the U.S.–Japan case, since it demonstrates that even in a highly asymmetrical trading relationship, the weaker partner can utilize its leverage to its own advantage. During the early 1960s, the Canadian automobile industry was in serious trouble. It was grievously uncompetitive, and although it was protected by high tariffs, the Canadian government registered a deficit in automobile trade of $620 million with the United States in 1964.[40] Realizing that the balance of trade in automobile products was increasingly to be in the favor of the United States, the Canadian government initiated a "duty remission program" in which U.S. automobile exporters could garner a larger share of the Canadian market in exchange for increasing their companies' investments in Canadian auto product industries.[41] Begun in 1963, this program would allow "manufacturers to import duty-free a value of autos and parts equivalent to the Canadian content of the increase in their exports of these products over the 1962 base year."[42]

Because Canadian import duties were so high and their remission such a valuable offer, U.S. companies immediately sought a greater share of investment in Canadian operations. This investment effort was further facilitated by the fact that most Canadian automobile assembly and parts companies were already subsidiaries of parent firms in the United States. Initially, it looked like the Canadian scheme to rationalize its automobile industry by enticing foreign investment and guaranteeing Canadian content would be a success.

However, in early 1964, as a direct result of this program, the Modine Corporation of the United States filed a countervailing duty suit against Canadian auto exports, "charging that the tariff remission in the new plan constituted a bounty or grant" in violation of GATT.[41] Knowing that an affirmative ruling on this case would undermine the duty remission program, the Canadian government sought negotiations with the U.S. government for a bilateral agreement on automobile trade. At the same time, the Canadian government also threatened that if a satisfactory agreement was not reached, it "would act unilaterally to restrict the Canadian automotive market to products made in Canada."[44]

The so-called Autopact was to "guarantee a level of Canadian production of automobiles and original equipment parts as a proportion of Canadian consumption of automobiles."[45] If negotiations proved to be successful for the Canadians, then the guarantee of domestic content, which had been the original purpose of the duty remission program, would be exchanged for the mutual elimination of import duties.

The U.S. government viewed the negotiations as a means of avoiding a disruptive confrontation with the Canadians over their duty remission scheme, and it was supported by the U.S. automobile firms involved. However, the ultimate goal of the U.S. government was to achieve a genuine free trade agreement in the automotive sector and to phase out the Canadian content restrictions, which the U.S. understood to be transitional.[46]

The immediate results of the agreement signed on 19 January 1965 were an increase in U.S. investment in Canadian production facilities and an improvement in the balance of automobile trade in the favor of Canada.[47] It was the U.S. position that the agreement would prove to be in the best interests of U.S. manufacturing even if investment and the balance of trade shifted somewhat in the favor of Canada. This view was influenced both by the fact that the U.S. government considered the restrictions in the agreement as transitional and by the fact that the agreement would prevent the unilateral, protective regime threatened by Canada.

The sequence of interactions in this example are shown in Table 5. Not only did Canada initiate the dispute with its duty remission program, but it also won its way with the later threat of counterretaliation against a U.S. countervailing duty determination. The United States (via the Modine Corporation) initially utilized a reciprocal (retaliatory) strategy to counter the duty remission program: however, when it encountered the Canadian counterthreat of closing its automobile market to U.S. access, it negotiated a compromise arrangement. Therefore, Canada's first action was an attempt to unilaterally implement a policy that affected bilateral trade relations. Yet its second action was a retaliatory move in the sequence of reciprocity begun by the United States.

The outcome reflected both Canadian and U.S. interests, especially if we accept the claim by U.S. officials that the restrictions built into the free trade arrangement were to be phased out over time. In exchange for dropping the

TABLE 5 *Sequence of actions in the U.S.–Canada automobile trade dispute, 1963–65*

(1)	Canada initiates a "duty remission program."
(2)	U.S. auto parts industry files a countervailing duty suit against resulting Canadian imports.
(3)	Canada threatens unilateral closure of its market if a suitable agreement is not reached.
(4)	U.S. government agrees with the Canadian content component of the Autopact arrangement.

countervailing duty suit, the United States would receive free access to the Canadian market as long as Canada was ensured a percentage of the production in the integrated transborder industry. Thus, the smaller and more vulnerable trading partner effectively utilized the potential value of its domestic automobile market to induce a favorable agreement with the largest and more powerful state. The U.S. countervailing duty suit made it clear to Canada that it could not take unilateral restrictive action with impunity, but Canada's counterthreat made it clear that it would be in the best interest of the United States to negotiate a solution. Here again, collusion was the outcome of this bilateral interaction.

U.S.–EC Wheat Flour Dispute, 1980–

Although the cases in the automobile and steel sectors generally support the usefulness of reciprocity as a strategy of achieving cooperation, this final example demonstrates its limitations. The outcome of the wheat flour dispute is a feud of noncooperation. The EC consistently refused to alter a policy considered by the United States to be unacceptable to its interests, even when the United States utilized a reciprocal strategy intentionally designed to force the EC to change. The conflict involved wheat flour trade in which the EC maintained a policy of export subsidization to compensate for the artificially higher prices that its farmers receive domestically and that would otherwise make their flour too expensive on the world market. The United States objected to this policy, arguing that it provided an unfair advantage against the more market-oriented U.S. agricultural producers.

In 1981, the United States filed a formal complaint with the new GATT Subsidies Committee about the EC wheat flour export practices. Bilateral negotiations between the two trading partners were launched immediately in an effort to resolve the dispute while the GATT panel examined the case. However, when the EC refused to alter its export policy, the United States took reciprocal action in January 1983 by subsidizing a substantial wheat flour sale to Egypt, a traditional European market. The American strategy was designed to win an important European market away from the EC as a means of leverage to persuade the EC Commission to alter its policy of subsidizing wheat flour exports. The rationale was based on the belief that the EC would change this practice if it realized the costs involved in such a market war.

TABLE 6 *Sequence of actions in the U.S.–EC wheat flour dispute, 1980–*

(1)	EC subsidizes wheat flour exports (a long-standing practice under the EC's Common Agricultural Policy [CAP]).
(2)	U.S. countersubsidizes to seize the traditional EC market.
(3)	EC threatens counterretaliation.
(4)	U.S. sporadically continues the practice of countersubsidizing in combination with market competition.
(5)	EC continues the practice of subsidizing.

EC members protested strongly. Two months later, when the GATT panel made its decision in their favor, the EC threatened retaliation in the form of demands for financial compensation for the market loss inflicted by the recent u.S. concessionary sale to a traditional European market.[48] In June of the same year, the United States filed another complaint, this time targeting European pasta exports. In this case the panel's report was favorable to the United States, but no changes appeared in the EC's policy.[49] From that point on, the U.S. government and the EC Commission have exchanged threats and counterthreats over this issue and have instituted subsidies and countersubsidies, and the rhetoric on both sides has been charged with resentment, frustration, and refusals to compromise.

With no apparent resolution on the horizon but with a general commitment to negotiate agricultural subsidies in the next GATT round and to reduce price supports at home, this conflict presents a very interesting case on the limits of reciprocity as a strategy for inducing cooperative behavior. A number of useful observations can be made about this example and will help to clarify why it differs from the others.

First, the existing normative framework around which expectations of behavior might converge is not only contrary to free trade principles, but it also does not include compensatory provisions. Unlike the previous sectoral disputes outlined, the wheat flour dispute has emerged where no behavioral consensus occurs. The GATT itself has never been adequately developed in the agricultural sector, because national governments from the beginning wanted the flexibility to pursue domestic support policies without having to abide by international rules for free trade.[50] Moreover, because separate, noncooperative agricultural prices have been tolerated from the origins of GATT's existence, independent behavior by nations or, in the case of the EC, by communities is well established.

This means that at least in a benign sense the world community has tolerated the behavior for a long enough period that a "right of use" has lent legitimacy and established expectations that the behavior will continue. Thus, if there has been any convergence of expectation in the past in this sector, it has been focused on the prerogative of individual governments to pursue policies that fit their domestic needs. Contrary to efforts made elsewhere under GATT, past cooperation in these circumstances has consisted of mutual toleration for sovereign idiosyncrasies, not a collective commitment to international guidelines. Although the situation in the wheat flour dispute initially appeared to be a stalemate, it became a feud when the United States, suffering adverse effects from the EC's Common Agricultural Policy (CAP) export subsidy competition, attempted to shape a new bilateral consensus about legitimate, cooperative behaviour rather than accept past patterns of behavior. It would appear from this case that such an ambitious effort is more difficult to achieve than is reform of practices that deviate from a well-established cooperative norm.

Recent attempts to incorporate rules about the use of agricultural subsidies in the Tokyo Round negotiation and in subsequent GATT panel reports have merely resulted in highlighting the ambiguities that exist in the agreements and the reluctance of these two major agricultural traders to agree. GATT panel contradictions, confusion about the meaning of "equitable market shares" and past provisions allowing subsidies on primary products all contribute to confusion over what appropriate behavior should be.

Second, as the CAP has endured and been accommodated in the world community over time, it has also become deeply entrenched in the domestic politics of EC members.[51] This has meant that there are ranks of domestic interest groups within the CAP resisting change. This latter situation reduces the coercive effect that retaliation might have under some circumstances, such as when the policy does not have a strong established constituency. Prying decision makers away from a deeply embedded policy is likely to be much more difficult than inducing a return to previously cooperative behavior. Debate within the EC is evidence that even the reform-oriented leaders are unable to do much in the way of influencing significant change.[52]

Third, the coercive effect of retaliation is also likely reduced in this case by the fact that the United States and the EC are competing for third markets rather than for access to each other's market. In the case of competition from abroad for one's own national market, there is the potential of threatening closure against imported goods; however, when one is competing for a market elsewhere, this ultimate degree of inducement is available only if the retaliating nation links the accessibility of its own market to its demands for reform on other fronts. Thus, the use by the United States of a "tit for tat" matching strategy may have been less effective than some other form of retaliatory strategy that would deprive EC producers of markets they have established in the United States.

Furthermore, because the EC policy is well established and because the U.S. attempt to reciprocate has been an experimental departure from its usual practices, it is likely that in calculating the potential costs of continuing its export subsidy policy the EC may have rightly assumed that it has the political strength to endure U.S. competition for some time, while the United States is embarking on uncertain and politically volatile waters. The Reagan administration's vacillation between countersubsidization and fierce market competition and its inconsistency in executing a matching strategy are evidence that such a calculation has been accurate.[53]

Even so, agricultural export subsidies are on the agenda for the next GATT round of multilateral negotiations, and there is more and more agitation within the EC and throughout the world for agricultural policy reform. While the immediate future holds little hope for a resolution of the conflict, the long-term costs of the export subsidy program (including the additional cost of competing with a U.S. reciprocal policy) may become great enough to eventually force significant change in the CAP and a new cooperative effort in this sector.[54]

AN EVALUATION OF POLICIES AND OUTCOMES

These comparative illustrations of how national governments utilize coercive bargaining strategies to settle trade problems with other countries contribute to our understanding to reciprocity and its efficacy and limitations. The case of the U.S.–Japan voluntary restraint agreement for automobiles and the case of the U.S.–Canada Autopact are illustrative of the ways in which the threat of market closure can be utilized as a coercive, noncooperative tactic to induce an acceptable compromise from the trading partner. In the former example, U.S. pressure for negotiation of a Japanese voluntary restraint agreement was buttressed by the larger contextual expectation that responsibility for export restraint was an unwritten part of Japan's reciprocal commitment to world trade cooperation. However, in the latter example, the initial Canadian policy of duty remissions was clearly a unilateral protectionist effort to press foreign importers into direct investment in Canadian production facilities. In both examples, coercive noncooperation proved to be an effective bargaining tactic with the exporting countries involved, regardless of the overall power relationship.

Even so, two cases examined – the Canadian automobile case and the U.S.–EC carbon steel case – demonstrate that reciprocal strategies may be a useful defense against such coercion. As we saw in the Canadian Autopact case, the fact that a U.S. corporation filed a countervailing duty suit against Canadian imports that benefited from the duty remission program threatened the existence of the Canadian program and raised the issue to the level of intentional bargaining. A counterthreat of Canadian market closure brought the U.S. government onto the scene to represent the automobile industry, and the Autopact agreement was the negotiated settlement. While the U.S. retaliation in the form of a countervailing duty suit did not change the Canadian practice, it effectively put pressure on the Canadian government. In turn, the Canadian counterrelation raised the stakes and made bilateral negotiation more pressing. In this case, the reciprocal strategy ensured a bilateral trade agreement that was preferred by U.S. producers over the loss of the Canadian market, even with the strings that were attached.

The situation in the steel case was similar for the EC. In countering the U.S. reciprocal strategy with its own, the EC Commission induced the U.S. government to suspend the countervailing duty procedures and engage in bilateral negotiations for a compromise settlement. When the United States initiated the threat of retaliation against the EC in this particular instance, it was clearly part of a reciprocal effort to counter the effect of EC export subsidies. While the United States could have executed its countervailing duty retaliation and prevented the EC from benefiting from this practice, it was forced to choose the alternative of an EC voluntary restraint agreement because of the bargaining pressure effected by the Commission. The resulting cooperative arrangement represented a compromise of interests on both sides of the Atlantic.

These examples demonstrate that while one nation may succeed in taking a noncooperative, coercive action against another nation, the best defense against being the victim of such a policy is to pursue a reciprocal strategy oneself. The circumstances of the particular relationship involved may mitigate against such an option, as in the case of Japan, which is especially vulnerable to the trade closure of the United States. However, the tentative evidence demonstrated by the Canadian example indicates that mutual interdependence, even if asymmetrical, can be exploited to one's advantage in order to obtain bargaining leverage.

It is clear at present that neither the United States nor the EC is willing to capitulate to the other side on the issue of agricultural export subsidies. Yet there is a continuing effort to discuss differences, to grapple with domestic price support reform, and to contain the dispute rather than allow it to escalate to other issue areas. The fact that the United States is unable to dislodge the EC from its long-standing policy is due in part to its embedded nature and to the fact that the form of cooperation expected by the United States in this area requires a major departure from this policy.

The comparative examination also indicates that the failure of the strategy may be attributed equally to the way in which reciprocity has been pursued. The successful examples of reciprocity consisted of specific punishments or threats of punishment against the industry involved, such as countervailing duties, quota protection, or market closure. Reciprocity in the wheat flour case consisted of actual matching strategy – that is, doing exactly what the other actor did in the previous move – rather than targeted punishment. Mimicking the EC may have a punishment effect, but it is not as directed or as immediate as the retaliatory actions observed in the other examples, which actually had the potential for preventing the objectionable activity by closing market access or by offsetting subsidy with a countervailing duty.

It does appear that U.S. reciprocity in this area is raising the costs to the EC of maintaining its use of export subsidies, and the calculation of the value of continuing the practice increasingly includes this consideration. However, as long as the United States cannot prevent the practice and can merely match it, the costs may rise, but the practice can continue for some time if these costs are politically acceptable at home. The calculation of EC interest also likely includes an assessment of the will of the U.S. government to continue its matching policy. Thus, the type of reciprocal response and its consistency over time may be as crucial to its success in both a short-term and a long-term measurement as how deeply entrenched the unacceptable practice is. While stalemates may degenerate into feuds, it is also possible that feuds may become so costly that the actors involved will reconsider their noncooperative policies.

In each set of interactions examined, the dispute emerged over a departure from a previous cooperative norm; and in each settled dispute, there was a new, mutually acceptable arrangement in the bilateral relationship. Even in the wheat flour case, the dispute has not spilled over into other trade sectors where reciprocal cooperation continues. Containment was seen in the other cases as well, and this implies that the contextual relationships encompassing the particular bilateral interactions were characterized by "nice" and "forgiving" strategies that were indeed reciprocal.

Collusion was the most common form of cooperation in these cases, even when accommodative policies helped to produce it, as in the Japanese effort to deflect U.S. protectionism against auto imports. In fact, there is considerable evidence that clear-cut concessions resulting from the administrative free trade law, such as antidumping and countervailing duty, have been giving way to collusive arrangements, which are politically more attractive on both sides.

In conclusion, this study shows that reciprocity proved to be an effective means of enforcing a compromise settlement in cases in which the trading partners generally accepted the governing norm of liberal trade (or, in its absence, accepted some compensation for the illiberal actions taken) and in cases in which retaliation had a potential directly harmful effect. Thus, the maintenance of existing cooperative regime norms was enhanced by reciprocity, although specific bilateral arrangements such as voluntary restraint agreements contradicted certain rules of GATT.

NOTES

Earlier versions of this article were presented at the annual meeting of the International Studies Association, Anaheim, California, in April 1986 (where it won the Carl Beck Award) and at the University of Southern California-Claremont Graduate School Conference on the Politics and Economics of Trade in April 1987. I thank Robert Keohane, John Odell, Stephen Krasner, Tom Willet, Thomas Ilgen, Rence Marlin-Bennett, and Tod Shenton for their helpful suggestions and criticisms.

1 See Robert Axelrod, *The Evolution of Cooperation* (New York: Basic Books, 1984); Robert O. Keohane, "Reciprocity in International Relations," *International Organization* 40 (Winter 1986), pp. 1–28; and Robert O. Keohane and Robert Axelrod, "Achieving Cooperation Under Anarchy," in Kenneth A. Oye, ed., *Cooperation Under Anarchy* (Princeton, N.J.: Princeton University Press, 1985), pp. 226–54.

2 Article 1 of GATT commits all signatories to the principle of equal treatment via the unconditional most-favored-nation clause. Yet the Preamble to GATT pledges signatories to pursue balanced, mutually acceptable arrangements. Other provisions allow specific retaliatory and compensatory actions. For a thorough analysis of this inherent set of contradictions, see Carolyn Rhodes-Jones, "The Reciprocity Dilemma: U.S. Trade Policy, Retaliation and the GATT Regime." Ph.D. diss., Brandeis University, 1987, chap. 5.

3 Keohane and Axelrod, "Achieving Cooperation Under Anarchy," pp. 232–33.

4 Beth, V. and Robert M. Yarbrough, "Reciprocity, Bilateralism and 'Economic Hostages': Self-Enforcing Agreements in International Trade," *International Studies Quarterly* 30 (March 1986), pp. 7–21.

5 David Richardson, "The New Political Economy of Trade Policy," in Paul R. Krugman, ed., *Strategic, Trade Policy and the New International Economics* (Cambridge, Mass.: MIT Press, 1986), p. 274.

6 Axelrod, *Evolution of Cooperation*, p. 13.

7 John Jackson, "Dispute Settlement Techniques Between Nations Concerning Economic Relations – With Special Emphasis on GATT," in T. Carbonneau, ed., *Resolving Transnational Disputes Through International Arbitration* (Charlottesville: University Press of Virginia, 1984), pp. 67–68.

8 See footnote 2 above.

9 John Ruggie developed the concept of "embedded liberalism" to explain American

trade policy and GATT. This term aptly describes the persisting American normative view. See John Gerard Ruggie, "International Regimes, Transactions and Change: Embedded Liberalism in the Postwar Economic Order," in Stephen D. Krasner, ed., *International Regimes* (Ithaca, N.Y.: Cornell University Press, 1983).

10 Keohane, "Reciprocity in International Relations," p. 8.

11 In an interview in Geneva in January 1985 with Jan Tumlir, former head of the economics division at the GATT Secretariat, Tumlir argued that national delegation requests for economic measurements of equivalent trade concessions were impossible to fulfil, given the nonequivalence of market conditions, gross national products, export dependence, and a multitude of other variables. Politically, however, a perception of equivalence was crucial to successful negotiations.

12 Stephen D. Cohen, *Uneasy Partnership: Competition and Conflict in U.S.–Japanese Trade Relations* (Cambridge, Mass.: Ballinger Press, 1985), especially pp. 36–45.

13 Axelford, *Evolution of Cooperation*, p. 13.

14 *International Herald Tribune*, 8–9 June 1985, p. 7.

15 For example, Article 19 of GATT, which allows emergency import protection under certain circumstances, provides that affected trading partners may obtain compensation through negotiated arrangements or through unilateral action if negotiations fail. This principle is upheld as well by the "nullification or impairment" provision of Article 23. In instances of dumped or subsidized exports, duties that remove the unfair pricing advantage may be legally applied in retaliation under Articles 6 and 16. See GATT, *Basic Instruments and Selected Documents (BISD)* (Geneva, 1952). Articles 6, 16, 19, and 23.

16 The term "Contracting Parties," when capitalized, refers to the collective GATT membership that takes formal action. References to the contracting parties in general or to one contracting party in particular are not capitalized.

17 Susan Strange and Roger Tooze, eds, *The International Politics of Surplus Capacity: Competition for Market Shares in the World Recession* (Boston: Allen & Unwin, 1981).

18 GATT, *BISD* 1 (Geneva: 1952), Article II.

19 Kent Jones, "The Political Economy of VER Agreements," *Kyklos* 37, no. 1, 1984, p. 89.

20 After voluntary export restraints were placed on Japanese automobiles in 1981, Japanese imports increased from 1,911,525 units in 1981 to 2,603,015 units in 1984. There was an increase for steel as well. After the voluntary export restraint for steel was arranged with the E.C. in 1982, import levels from EC sources increased from 7.3 percent of total U.S. consumption in 1982 to 7.5 percent in 1985. Overall, steel imports grew in the same period from 21.85 percent of consumption to 27.6 percent. For statistics regarding automobiles, see U.S. Department of Commerce, *Official Statistics*, Washington, DC, 1985. For statistics regarding steel, see U.S. Department of Commerce, *Official Statistics*, compiled in U.S. International Trade Commission, *Monthly Report on Selected Steel Industry Data*, Washington, D.C., January 1986.

21 Although the individual members of the EC are the GATT contracting parties, the EC represents their interests collectively with other contracting parties in most cases.

22 Keohane and Nye's useful concept of "vulnerability interdependence" is well illustrated in these cases. See Robert O. Keohane and Joseph S. Nye, *Power and Interdependence: World Politics in Transition* (Boston: Little Brown, 1977), particularly pp. 13–19.

23 There is one exception to this generalization: the U.S.–Canada automobile trade dispute of the early 1960s took place under very different market conditions. The automobile sector has since been a classic example of surplus capacity.

24 Rhodes-Jones, "Reciprocity Dilemma," chaps. 6–8.

25 Hans Mueller and Hans van der Ven, "Perils in the Brussels–Washington Steel Pact of 1982." *The World Economy* 5 (September 1982), p. 262.

26 Frank Benyon and Jacques Bourgeois, "The European Community-United States Steel Arrangement," *Common Market Law Review* 21 (June 1984), p. 340.
27 Ibid., p. 333.
28 Steven Woolcock, "U.S.–European Trade Relations," *International Affairs* 58 (Autumn 1982), pp. 616–17, and Gary Horlick, "American Trade Law and the Steel Pact Between Washington and Brussels," *The World Economy* 6 (September 1983), p. 357.
29 *The Economist*, 9 October 1982, p. 78; and 22 October 1982, p. 52.
30 See *Official Journal of the European Community*, entry no. 1.307/12, for a letter from Commerce Secretary Baldridge to Minister Davignon on 21 October 1982 which includes verbatim the same assurance. See also entry no. 1.307/26. The *Official Journal* is deposited with the Delegation of the Commission of the European Communities, Washington, D.C.
31 Mitsuo Matsushita and Lawrence Repeta, "Restricting the Supply of Japanese Automobiles: Sovereign Collusion?" *Case Western Reserve Journal International Law* 14 (Winter 1982), p. 49.
32 Robert H. Ballance and Stuart W. Sinclair, "Reindustrializing America: Policy Makers and Interest Groups," *The World Economy* 7 (June 1984), p. 206.
33 Robert Hormats, "Auto Parts Industry," *Department of State Bulletin* **82**, no. 2059, February 1982, p. 40.
34 Matsushita and Repeta, "Restricting the Supply of Japanese Automobiles," p. 50.
35 Robert J. Leo, "An Update of the Japanese Export Restraint," *Brooklyn Journal of International Law* 8 (Winter 1982), pp. 159–60.
36 Jones, "Political Economy of VER Agreements," p. 86.
37 See Keith A. J. Hay and Andrei Sulzenko, "U.S. Trade Policy and 'Reciprocity,'" *Journal of World Trade Law* 16 (November–December 1982), pp. 472–73; William R. Cline, "Reciprocity: A New Approach to World Trade Policy?" in William R. Cline, ed., *Trade Policy in the 1980s* (Washington, D.C.: Institute for International Economics, 1983), pp. 121–58, and *Far Eastern Economic Review*, 18 December 1981, p. 43.
38 Keohane, "Reciprocity in International Relations," p. 4.
39 See footnote 20 above.
40 Charles Stedman, "Canada–U.S. Automotive Agreement: The Sectoral Approach," *Journal of World Trade Law* 8 (March–April 1974), p. 176.
41 Gilbert R. Winham, *The Automobile Trade Crisis of 1980* (Halifax, Nova Scotia, Dalhousie University Center for Foreign Policy Studies, 1981), p. 88.
42 Stedman, "Canada–U.S. Automotive Agreement," p. 177.
43 Ibid.
44 Ibid.
45 Winham, *Automobile Trade Crisis of 1980*, p. 89.
46 Carl F. Beigie: *The Canada–U.S. Automotive Agreement: An Evaluation* (Montreal: Canadian American Committee, 1970), p. 1.
47 Stedman, "Canada–U.S. Automotive Agreement," p. 181. A GATT waiver was obtained by the United States to enter into this preferential arrangement with Canada. Canada required no waiver, since it agreed to offer the same opportunity to any other exporters willing to undertake the required investment in Canadian production.
48 GATT, *Panel Report SCM/42: European Economic Community Subsidies on Export of Wheat Flour* (Geneva, 21 March 1983).
49 GATT, *Panel Report SCM/43: European Economic Community Subsidies on the Export of Pasta Products* (Geneva, 19 May 1983).
50 Article 11, Section 2(c) of GATT excepts "import restrictions on any agricultural or fisheries product, imported in any form, necessary to the enforcement of governmental measures which operate (i) to restrict the quantities of the like domestic product permitted to be marketed or produced [or] . . . (ii) to remove a temporary surplus of

the like domestic product." Moreover Article 16 of GATT allows an exception for export subsidies of primary products to the extent that they assist the exporting nation in maintaining an "equitable share" of the market. See GATT *BISD* 1 (Geneva: 1952); and GATT *BISD* 26 (Geneva: 1980). See also Jimmy S. Hillman "Evolution of American Agricultural Trade Policy and European Interaction," in Hartwig de Haen, Glenn Johnson, and Stefan Tangerman, eds., *Agriculture and International Relations: Analysis and Policy* (London: Macmillan, 1985), pp. 159–60; and Gilbert R. Winham, *International Trade and the Tokyo Round Negotiation* (Princeton, N.J.: Princeton University Press, 1986), chap. 4.

51 Brian F. Hall, *The Common Agricultural Policy v: Past, Present, and Future* (New York: Methuen, 1984), pp. 19 and 23–25.

52 *The Economist*, 5 April 1986, p. 54.

53 While the administration pledged the United States to a policy of matching subsidy for subsidy, it also has promised a policy based upon full reliance on market competition to allow prices to find their "natural" level. The development of this latter policy is largely in response to the unexpected costs of agricultural support programs under this administration at a time when the size of the federal budget deficit is an increasing political liability.

54 Recent reports from the EC indicate that more than defensiveness is behind statements about agricultural reform. The reduction of price supports in both dairy and beef production is cited as evidence of a commitment to broaden the effort to wheat and wheat products. See *Europe*, June 1987, p. 15.

13. Toward a Positive Theory of the Most Favored Nation Obligation and its Exceptions in the WTO/GATT System

W. F. Schwartz and A. O. Sykes

Article I of the General Agreement on Tariffs and Trade (GATT), now a part of GATT 1994 in the treaty creating the World Trade Organization (WTO), prohibits discrimination among trading partners with respect to tariffs and other border charges as well as certain domestic taxes. This "most favored nation" (MFN) obligation has been called the "cornerstone" obligation of GATT.[1] It is not without important exceptions, however, including those that permit some discrimination in the protection afforded to declining industries under the "escape clause" of Article XIX, and most importantly the authority in Article XXIV for the creation of preferential trading arrangements known as "customs unions" or "free trade areas."[2]

The normative economics of discrimination in international commercial policy has been a subject of study for many decades, and is reasonably well understood at least for competitive markets. But little work has been done on the *positive* economics of trade discrimination generally, or of the MFN obligation and its exceptions within the WTO/GATT system in particular.

At the outset, it is perhaps useful to set forth the distinction between the positive and normative perspectives. The usual normative analysis of international trade rests on conventional welfare economics. An "optimal" policy will thus strive to maximize the sum of producer and consumer surplus, as well as government tariff revenue if not otherwise distributed to consumers or producers. This maximization can be carried out at a multilateral level to characterize an optimal cooperative agreement among trading nations, or at the national level to characterize optimal behavior by a national government in a non-cooperative setting.

If national governments *in fact* pursued policies to maximize national economic welfare, or nations acting cooperatively *in fact* pursued policies to maximize joint economic welfare, such normative analysis would also provide the basis for positive theory. Yet it is obvious that governments do not maximize welfare as defined in this fashion, whether acting on their own or acting cooperatively. If they did, many if not most tariffs and other trade restrictions would have long ago been abolished unilaterally, as such measures typically lower the sum of producer surplus, consumer surplus, and government revenue in the importing nation. And most tariffs that survived in a non-cooperative environment, such as those imposed by large countries seeking to improve their terms of trade, would have been abolished in international agreement as nations covenanted to eliminate all beggar-thy-neighbor policies. A glance at the history of unilateral policies prior to the formation of GATT, however, and a glance at the trade policies that survive under GATT itself, reveals vastly more protectionism than is plausibly compatible with national or global welfare maximization. Hence, even if economic welfare defined in the conventional sense affords an appealing normative benchmark for policy, trade policy in practice cannot be explained as an effort by governments to maximize that conception of welfare. For this reason, a successful positive theory must diverge considerably from conventional normative theory.

The most promising avenue for positive theory draws the insights of public choice, or what trade theorists term the theory of "political economy." At the national level, trade policies that are incompatible with national welfare maximization arise because not all citizens are equally effective at pursuing their interests in the political process – in particular, the domestic political process assigns disproportionate weight to the interests of domestic producers as compared to those of individual domestic consumers (consuming *industries*, of course, may have considerable political influence). This emphasis on producer interests over consumer interests affects international trade agreements as well, so that nations acting cooperatively tend to enter bargains that are attentive to the mutual interests of their producer groups and perhaps to the revenues of signatory governments, but the welfare of individual consumers remains less emphasized. Put differently, trade agreements reflect a kind of "political" welfare maximization, with the divergence between the political optimum and the conventional welfare optimum attributable largely to the fact that individual consumer interests receive less weight in the political calculus than in the welfare calculus. It is also possible, as we discuss below, that the welfare of some producer groups will receive more weight than the welfare of others.

This framework has proven to have considerable power in explaining the general rise and decline of import tariffs.[3] Prior to GATT, national governments often imposed substantial tariffs, conferring rents on their domestic producers at the expense of consumers. The formation of the GATT, as well as other trade agreements, caused tariffs to fall because the interests of exporters could then be taken into account – governments would exchange mutual commitments to reduce barriers to imports as long as the losses suffered by their import-competing producer constituents (as translated into an impact on votes, campaign contributions, and the like) were outweighed by the gains conferred on export-oriented producer constituents.[4]

We believe that the same general framework should have much to say about other aspects of international commercial policy, including discrimination by nations acting unilaterally and non-discrimination obligations of the WTO/GATT system. To our knowledge, however, little has been done to examine within the public choice framework the unilateral incentive to discriminate prior to the formation of GATT or the reasons why the signatories to the GATT agreement would have chosen to include an MFN commitment qualified by the various exceptions noted earlier.

We argue below that discrimination is, as a unilateral matter, beneficial for a country imposing barriers to international trade only under limited conditions. A desire to raise revenue or to bestow surplus on politically favored trading partners provides a possible motive for unilateral discrimination, but revenue-raising discrimination is difficult to implement, especially over time, and efforts to favor particular trading nations often seem better undertaken through alternative policy instruments. To a considerable extent, therefore, a non-discrimination requirement in GATT merely replicates what countries would often choose to do unilaterally. The MFN requirement of GATT then appears, at first blush, to be superfluous to a significant degree.

This view is too simplistic, however, because a trade agreement such as GATT might nevertheless permit discrimination if it would promote the joint interests of producers on a multilateral basis. It is hardly obvious *a priori* that discrimination systematically harms producer interests – rather, discrimination helps some producers and hurts others. To provide a basis for an agreement banning discrimination the signatories would have to believe that the gains to those producers who benefit from discrimination are, systematically, less important politically than the loss to those who suffer discrimination. We suggest below that this condition holds under some conditions, but not always.

The analysis is further complicated by the fact that the MFN obligation serves as an important part of the rules governing the conduct of multilateral trade negotiations. *Ex ante*, the participants in the negotiations know that all concessions they give under MFN will extend to every other signatory government regardless of their ability to exact a *quid pro quo*. They further realize that they may benefit from concessions extended by others without having to give a *quid pro quo*. *Ex post*, the participants know that the value of any concession they obtain under MFN will not be impaired by subsequent and more generous concessions to other countries. Hence, the MFN requirement is not simply a rule that constrains trade discrimination, but also a rule that shapes the bargaining game in the WTO/GATT system. This latter perspective introduces a range of additional considerations.

Our analysis proceeds as follows. Sections I to III develop some theoretical considerations that bear on the political costs and benefits of discrimination in commercial policy, considering both unilateral and cooperative scenarios. Section IV applies the theoretical analysis to a brief discussion of international practice prior to the formation of GATT, and to three prominent features of the WTO/GATT agreement that implicate the MFN principle: (1) the general prohibition of discrimination in Article I of GATT 1994: (2) the opportunities for discrimination in escape clause actions under the Uruguay Round Agreement on Safeguards; and (3) the exception to the MFN principle for free trade areas and customs unions in Article XXIV of GATT 1994 (hereafter, we refer to GATT 1994 as simply "GATT").

I. THE UNILATERAL INCENTIVE TO DISCRIMINATE

In this section we consider the incentive to discriminate on the part of an individual importing nation that takes the policies of other nations as fixed – that is, the incentive to discriminate in "Nash equilibrium." By hypothesis, trading partners have no opportunity to influence policy directly through offers of concessions or through threats of retaliation. Instead, the interests of trading partners will affect policy only to the extent that the domestic polity "cares" about the well-being of citizens in other countries.

Discrimination to Raise Tariff Revenues

By tariff "discrimination," we mean the imposition of different tariffs on exports from different countries even though those exports are viewed by consumers as perfect substitutes. Market power is necessary to make such tariff discrimination profitable. A "small" country that acts as a price taker in international markets faces a perfectly elastic supply of imports from all sources at the world price. Any attempt to discriminate against one country in favor of another through tariffs will simply cause disfavored suppliers to sell elsewhere, and all imports will then come from the favored sources of supply. For a small country, therefore, tariff discrimination is pointless if the goal is to raise revenue – the effective tariff rate will always be the lowest tariff rate afforded to any supplier.[6]

For "large" countries, however, defined as nations that face an upward sloping import supply curve, it has long been recognized that an opportunity to exploit market power exists. The large country can behave as a monopsonist, using tariffs to extract monopsony rents (in trade parlance to "shift the terms of trade" in its favor). The "optimal tariff" in traditional trade theory maximizes the national welfare of the importing nation in this fashion, taking proper account of its effect on exchange rates and thus on other markets in general equilibrium.[7] From a partial equilibrium perspective, it is analogous to a single price monopsony optimum.

Like other monopsonists, however, large trading nations can potentially do better through price discrimination. Under competitive supply conditions and taking a partial equilibrium view, the ideal form of price discrimination for a national welfare maximizer would involve a distinct tariff for each unit of each imported good equal to the difference between its supply price (given by its location on the import supply curve) and the competitive market price. Such a policy would extract all of the producer surplus from foreign suppliers without causing any distortion in consumption. Much the same policy might also be followed by a nation that was not maximizing national welfare but was instead affording protection to a competing domestic industry. Whatever the desired price in the protected market, the importing nation would simply charge a tariff equal to the difference between that price and the supply price for every unit of imports.

Such a policy would not really discriminate among countries but rather among producers, and perhaps even among different units of output from the same producer. Nevertheless, a loosely analogous form of imperfect price discrimination can be implemented such that goods from each country are charged a different tariff according to supply conditions in that country. For any price that prevails for consumers in the importing nation, an appropriately designed system of discrimination country by country can increase tariff revenue relative to what would otherwise be raised. It is thus potentially useful for any importing nation with market power, whether or not that nation is simultaneously engaged in welfare-reducing measures to protect competing domestic industries.[8]

At some level, the claim that discrimination can increase tariff revenue is obvious. A move from a policy of non-discrimination to a policy permitting discrimination removes a constraint on tariff policy, and optimization subject to fewer constraints can only result in a higher optimum. In general, the optimal system of discriminatory tariffs will tend to impose a greater tariff on exporting nations with a less elastic export supply curve, since producers in those nations will absorb more of the tariff through reduced prices than producers elsewhere.[9]

These observations might seem to suggest that large countries will regularly be tempted to use discriminatory tariffs to raise revenue in the absence of international legal prohibition against it or some credible threat of retaliation. In fact, however, we conclude the opposite, for three reasons.

First, for most products, it is likely that tariff discrimination will induce entry and exit responses over time. In particular, it encourages entry by high-cost producers in nations subject to low tariffs and encourages exit by low-cost producers in nations subject to high tariffs. Even if discrimination increases revenue for a given configuration of foreign producers in the short run, therefore, its effects on entry and exit in the long run can reduce revenue. An importing nation that practices tariff discrimination may in the end find that it is served primarily by high-cost producers subject to low tariffs, whose exports yield little revenue.[10]

To illustrate with a limiting case, consider a long-run competitive setting with constant returns to scale everywhere. There is free entry and exit with international capital mobility. For simplicity, transport costs are zero. Then, with non-discriminatory tariffs, only the most efficient foreign producers (lowest constant unit costs) will sell to the importing nation, all others are driven from the market. Discrimination makes it possible for inefficient producers to survive *if* discrimination is in their favor. Which regime will the importing nation prefer? Suppose that there is some desired home market price p^*, which reflects the degree of protection desired for home market producers, and let the quantity of imports that clears domestic excess demand at p^* be q^*. For any q^*, an importing nation with an interest in raising government revenue will prefer the non-discriminatory tariff structure to one that allows higher-cost foreign producers into the market. The reason is that by purchasing q^* only from the most efficient suppliers, tariff revenue is maximized.[11]

To be sure, an importing nation with perfect knowledge of how tariff discrimination may affect entry and exit decisions can factor that information into its discriminatory policies. It can then design an optimal discriminatory policy, which varies over time, to maximize the present value of the revenue stream. But such a policy would require an extraordinary amount of information.

Indeed, a second reason why profitable tariff discrimination will likely prove difficult, even ignoring entry and exit responses, relates to information problems. As suggested above, successful discrimination requires knowledge of cost conditions in different supplier nations. Individual export prices are, of course, observable, but export supply curves are not. It is by no means obvious how this problem could be overcome at a single point in time, much less how changes in supply conditions could be monitored over time to avert the problem of counterproductive discrimination in the long run.

Third, it is non-trivial to identify the country of origin for imported merchandise, a determination that is plainly necessary to the application of a discriminatory tariff structure. Exporters in countries subject to high tariffs have a strong incentive for fraud, and policing it will not be easy. Mere transshipment may suffice to avoid high tariff rates. And even putting aside deception (or bribery) of customs officials, rules of origin can become immensely complicated and expensive to administer for products that have components from various countries – whether the substantial transformation test, the value added test, or some other test is employed to determine origin, the documentation requirements and litigation potential are great. For this reason, efforts to take advantage of existing tariff preferences, such as those available to Canadian and Mexican exporters under The North American Free Trade Agreement (NAFTA), are sometimes not worth the bother.[12]

We thus suspect that discrimination for the purpose of increasing tariff revenues will prove attractive only on infrequent occasions, even if it might in theory look tempting in a frictionless world. The practical difficulties with the design and administration of a discriminatory tariff for this purpose, coupled with its potential to backfire in the long run, should suffice to discourage it most of the time even in the absence of international legal constraints or retaliation.

Discrimination to Subsidize Particular Trading Partners

We postulate for this case that a country is, for some reason, not indifferent as to which countries earn the producer surplus from sales in its protected market. It wishes to discriminate so as to affect the realization of that surplus by certain favored countries. Perhaps the favored nation is a strategic ally, perhaps it is deemed worthy of assistance for humanitarian reasons, or perhaps it simply has close political ties to officials in the importing nation. Discrimination of this type would consist of relatively low tariffs to favored countries.

While this tactic can be successfully employed to some extent in the short run, what can be accomplished may be more limited in the long run. For example, consider an exporting industry with no home market sales, with constant returns to scale in the long run, and fixed capacity in the short run. The nation to which it exports plans to introduce a tariff preference on behalf of this exporting industry. Starting from an equilibrium with uniform tariffs, the initial tariff preference confers a short-run rent on the favored producers equal to the margin of preference on each exported unit. But in the long run, capacity will expand and the favored industry will increase its exports to its trading partner, driving down the price in its export market to the point that there is no longer any incentive for entry. Consumers in the nation that afforded the preference will at that point enjoy a lower price, but producers in the favored exporting industry will earn no long-run surplus from it.

To be sure, this example assumes away fixed factors, and if long-run supply is less than perfectly elastic a tariff preference can confer surplus that persists. Likewise, it is obvious that preferences can confer short-run surplus on favored suppliers regardless of supply conditions. The harder question is whether such a policy makes sense given in the *alternative* ways of providing assistance to a favored nation. The revenue from a non-discriminatory tariff might be distributed as foreign aid, for example. The analysis in the previous section is pertinent, and suggests that discriminatory tariffs are unlikely to be the cheapest way to assist a favored country. Unless by chance such a policy happened to coincide with an opportunity for revenue-raising tariff discrimination – hard to identify and variable over time as noted – the importing nation seemingly would do better to provide aid directly in the form of cash assistance, at least putting aside any *quid pro quo* for the tariff preferences as our Nash equilibrium assumption requires. Another virtue of cash assistance is that its recipients can be targeted more precisely, whereas the beneficiaries of tariff preferences may not be the ideal beneficiaries of desired subsidies.

Conceivably, subsidies through the device of tariff preferences are somehow less visible or less politically controversial than direct assistance. If so, they may at times be preferable from a political standpoint. One can also imagine that domestic investors expect to take advantage of a tariff preference by investing capital in the favored trading partner, so that what appears to be foreign producer surplus may in fact be converted to domestic producer surplus, and a domestic constituency favoring the preference will exist. This observation might also help to explain why aid would be provided in the form of a tariff preference, the benefits of which can be appropriated partly by a domestic constituency, rather than direct cash assistance to the foreign government.

Furthermore, it is plain that tariff preferences are at times afforded to particular countries, instead of or in addition to direct cash assistance, for reasons that are not readily apparent in relation to any *quid pro quo*. It is difficult to imagine that preferential access to the market of Israel was terribly important to the United States prior to the U.S.–Israel Free Trade Agreement, for example, and of course the U.S. Generalized System of Preferences and the Lomé Convention afford preferential treatment to developing nations without any explicit *quid pro quo* (whether an implicit *quid pro quo* exists would take us afield). Thus, it seems plausible that the desire to subsidize favored trading nations is at times a basis for tariff preferences in practice. We doubt that this possibility has much relevance to trade among the major developed trading nations, however, or that it has much to do with important preferential arrangements such as the European Union and NAFTA.

II. DISCRIMINATION IN COOPERATIVE AGREEMENTS: THE COASEAN CASE

If the incentive to discriminate in commercial policy is limited when the policies of other nations are taken as fixed, it is plainly not so limited when nations have the opportunity to act cooperatively. History is replete with international agreements to afford discriminatory trade preferences (e.g., the Treaty of Rome and NAFTA mentioned a moment ago). Indeed, the United States Constitution (and before it the Articles of Confederation) is in part a preferential trading arrangement, giving trade among the states of the Union a preference over trade with foreign nations. More generally, national boundaries routinely serve, among other things, to define the geographical scope of important trade preferences.

Our goal in this section and the next is to begin to understand the reasons for such cooperative arrangements, as well as the constraints on discrimination that international agreements also embody. We divide the discussion of cooperative arrangements into two segments. In this section, we focus on the policy that nations would covenant to pursue if, counterfactually, bargaining among them was free of all transaction costs and strategic behavior so that they could attain the first-best cooperative optimum from a political standpoint. The assumption of zero transaction costs to the multilateral bargaining process makes this the "Coasean case." In the next section we consider the practical complications associated with large numbers trade negotiations.

It is instructive to begin this section with a brief review of the conventional welfare economics of discriminatory trading arrangements. Discriminatory tariffs may permit higher-cost producers in the nations that benefit from lower tariffs to outcompete lower-cost producers in the nations subject to higher tariffs. This phenomenon, known as "trade diversion," creates deadweight losses that do not occur when all suppliers are subject to the same tariff. Other things being equal, therefore, non-discriminatory tariffs enhance global welfare. Other things being equal, therefore, non-discriminatory tariffs enhance global welfare; a non-discriminatory tariff policy ensures that imports are supplied by the countries that can produce them most cheaply.

Yet, other things need not be equal, for it is readily possible that a reduction of tariffs on a discriminatory basis will improve welfare relative to the maintenance of higher, non-discriminatory tariffs. The reason is that any tariff reduction, discriminatory or otherwise, will allow lower-cost foreign firms to displace higher-cost domestic producers, saving resources in production and lowering prices to consumers – so-called "trade creation." Thus, where the choice is between preferential trade liberalization and no liberalization at all, preferential liberalization can enhance welfare.[13] Furthermore, it is *possible* to construct a preferential arrangement such that an improvement in global welfare is guaranteed. For example, the members of a new preferential arrangement could adjust the tariffs that apply to non-members so that trade with non-members remains the same as before. The welfare of non-members would then remain unaffected, and the members of the preferential arrangement would derive benefits solely from trade creation.[14]

In short, from a conventional welfare perspective, discriminatory arrangements are not first-best, and of course trade barriers of any sort are almost always incompatible with the first-best. But discriminatory arrangements can be a second-best improvement relative to a more protectionist world without discrimination.

Does this conclusion change if one shifts from the conventional welfare perspective to the public choice perspective? In particular, if we hypothesize that each nation is represented by political officials who care less about consumer interests than conventional welfare maximization would require, is it possible that the "first-best" bargain from their perspective would embody trade discrimination? The answer, perhaps not surprisingly, is maybe.

Producer Surplus, Government Revenue, and the Political Calculus

As noted previously, discrimination favors some producers and injures others. But not all producer groups are equally well organized or influential with their political representatives. Trivially, if discrimination would benefit a well-organized and influential producer group in one country at the expense of a producer group in another country that was poorly organized and lacking in influence, then a politically savvy bargain among all concerned might well elect to discriminate in favor of the former group.

If all producer surplus and government revenue counts equally in the joint political calculus, however, it seems that discrimination will not often be attractive. The underlying reason is that, at least in competitive markets, producer groups in the country or countries that would suffer from discrimination, coupled with the treasury of the importing nation itself, have more to lose from discrimination than producer groups in the countries who benefit from it have to gain.

The point is easiest to see in the "long-run" illustration of Section 1, with the free entry and exit and constant returns to scale everywhere. In such a scenario, foreign producer surplus is zero: all foreign producers simply earn a competitive rate of return. The foreign producers are thus indifferent to discrimination,[15] and whatever is politically optimal for the importing nation acting unilaterally is also politically optimal cooperatively. Recall that the importing nation prefers non-discriminatory tariffs here because they ensure that any given quantity of imports is supplied by the lowest-cost suppliers abroad, with the treasury earning a tariff equal to the difference between the home market price and unit cost on each imported unit.

This idea is in fact more general. Consider, in partial equilibrium, an importing nation confronting an arbitrary set of fixed import supply curves for a homogeneous good from various trading partners, and suppose initially that a non-discriminatory tariff prevails that results in some total quantity of imports, call it q^*. Let transport costs be zero for simplicity. Because the tariff is non-discriminatory, marginal imports from each supplier country have the same marginal cost of production. Now suppose that the importing nation shifts to a discriminatory tariff structure while maintaining the same aggregate volume of imports, and thus the same level of protection for its home market producers. Foreign suppliers that benefit from discrimination move up their supply curves into a region of higher marginal cost, whereas other suppliers reduce their exports and move down their supply curves to a region of lower marginal cost. A deadweight loss is created because the aggregate quantity of imports is no longer produced at minimum cost. Further, because the surplus of consumers and producers in the importing nations is fixed (price in the importing nation has not changed), this deadweight loss must fall on the treasury of the importing government, on producer surplus in supplier nations, or both.

Thus, at any level of protection in an importing nation (at any home market price), and under competitive conditions, a non-discriminatory tariff will maximize the sum of foreign producer surplus and tariff revenue for the importing government. It does so by ensuring that trade diversion does not occur, thus preventing the dissipation of surplus through uneconomically high-cost production. If a dollar of producer surplus wherever generated and a dollar of tariff revenue wherever earned all count equally in the political calculus, therefore, a politically optimal cooperative agreement would not tolerate discriminatory tariffs.

There are several corollaries worth noting. First, revenue-increasing tariff discrimination, of the sort considered in Section I, creates a joint loss that an ideal cooperative agreement would eliminate (just as an ideal cooperative agreement would not tolerate non-discriminatory "optimal tariffs"). Second, the countries that form customs unions or free trade areas are reducing the sum of producer surplus and government revenue that would otherwise exist globally if those nations opened up their home markets to the same extent through the cause of non-discriminatory tariffs. Third, and related, if all producer surplus received equal weight in the global political calculus , we might expect a greater degree of trade liberalization under a non-discriminatory tariff regime than under a discriminatory regime. The reason is that non-discriminatory trade liberalization creates more surplus in the aggregate, and thus the sum of postconcession tariff revenue and what trading partners collectively should be willing to "pay" for concessions should rise, making concessions in general more attractive.

Is All Producer Surplus Created Equal?

We have already touched on the standard public choice insight that consumer surplus, much of it belonging as it does to a diffuse and poorly organized interest group, will weigh less heavily in the formation of trade policy than producer surplus. But there are circumstances in which some producer surplus may be expected to "count" less than other producer surplus as well.

In addition to the possibility that some producer groups are more concentrated and thus better organized, as noted above, an important distinction exists between producer surplus that represents an ordinary competitive return on sunk investments and producer surplus that represents a supracompetitive return. When prices fall so low that producers cannot recoup a competitive return on sunk investment, they benefit more from protection to raise their prices, other things being equal. The reason is that an increase in prices to a level that restores a competitive return will not induce entry, and thus the gains from such a price increase will not be competed away by the expansion of domestic capacity. A price increase to a level that yields supracompetitive profits, by contrast, will induce domestic entry under competitive conditions to drive the price back down to a competitive level.

It follows that when returns to sunk investments fall below the competitive level, producers will tend to invest more resources in lobbying or trade protection. Of course, a transitory period of supracompetitive profit will still justify some efforts to secure it, but the gains will be smaller and the amount of resources expended to secure it accordingly lower.[16]

This reasoning works equally well on the export side. An exporter benefits more from a trade concession abroad that allows it to restore its profits to the competitive level than from a concession that produces a transitory period of supracompetitive profit that will be eroded by entry. Likewise, the burden on an exporter of new protectionist measures abroad will tend to be smaller where their consequence is simply to eliminate a supracompetitive return.

We have so far paid no express attention to the interests of workers, who will often share in producer surplus to some (perhaps considerable) extent. In declining industries, workers who have made human capital investments that do not readily transfer to other industries (those with industry-specific human capital) are analogous to firms with sunk costs. Whether recently unemployed because of international competition or merely fearful of becoming unemployed, these workers may constitute a vocal and well-organized interest group favoring protection, doubly so if they are unionized.

By contrast, the workers in an industry that is expanding and already earning a better than competitive return gain less from protection for the same reason that firms gain less – entry will occur and any increase in wages will be transitory. Further, *potential* workers in an expanding industry are more likely to be diffuse and poorly organized, as well as to have their returns limited by the need to make sunk investments up front to realize them. It thus seems likely that workers (and potential workers) in expanding industries will lobby less to obtain home market protection, or for improved access to foreign markets, than workers in declining industries.

These observations may have much to do with explaining the conventional wisdom that declining industries work harder to obtain protection, and with the observation that the most extensive protection in practice is indeed afforded to declining industries (in the United States, such industries as textiles, footwear, and steel). It may also bear importantly on the escape clause exception to the most favored nation obligation in the WTO/GATT system, as discussed in Section IV.

It seems unlikely, however, that the asymmetry in the political efficacy of expanding and declining industries would have much to do with long-term preferential arrangements such as customs unions and free trade areas. For one thing, customs unions and free trade areas embody preferences that cut across all industries in the participant nations regardless of their economic condition. More importantly, such arrangements *liberalize* trade on a preferential basis, and thus will tend to damage import-competing industries, which are more likely to be inefficient and declining, while benefiting export industries that are competitive internationally and thus less likely to be declining. Hence, although the political economy of declining industries may have something to say about occasional industry-specific preferential arrangements such as the old European Coal and Steel Community, and may explain why some preferential arrangements are *unattractive* politically, it seems that we must turn to other considerations if we are to adduce a positive theory of the incentive to create customs unions and free trade areas.

III. THE MOST FAVORED NATION OBLIGATION AND THE MULTILATERAL BARGAINING PROCESS

The previous section considered the question whether determination will arise in a unilateral trade agreement that exhausts all the joint political gains from trade policy. In practice, of course, some of the joint gains may be difficult to realize because of the transaction costs and strategic behavior that arise in large numbers of multilateral trade negotiations. More importantly for our purposes, the most favored nation obligation may affect the transaction costs of negotiation or the opportunities for strategic behavior in bargaining. This section examines such matters, inquiring whether a most favored nation obligation impedes or facilitates the realization of joint gains in bargaining. Once again, the answer is inconclusive, because the most favored nation obligation helps to solve some problem (protecting the value of concessions against future erosion) while exacerbating another (a free rider problem). After setting forth the competing considerations here, we will argue in Section IV that the WTO/GATT system is quite attentive to them, and that some of its provisions may be understood as a roughly optimal accommodation between the costs and benefits of non-discrimination.

The Free Rider Issue

In a multilateral trade agreement governed by the most favored nation obligation, any concession negotiated with a single trading partner or group of trading partners must be extended without condition to all other trading nations. The number of nations entitled to most favored nation treatment in the modern WTO/GATT system now exceeds 120. The obvious danger is that nations will try to free ride on each other during bargaining, with the result that mutually beneficial deals will not be struck.[17]

To illustrate with an obviously stylized example, suppose that political gains from trade are possible if the United States makes a trade concession that would admit an additional one million widgets into the U.S. market – that is, there is exists a set of concessions and counter concessions, including the hypothesized U.S. concession on widgets, that yields joint political gains to the trading community. Based on the analysis of the last section, a non-discriminatory tariff just sufficient to admit 1 million widgets should maximize the sum of U.S. tariff revenue and foreign producer surplus at that level of imports. Plausibly, therefore, this non-discriminatory tariff would lie on the political "Pareto frontier" for the trading community (i.e., it would maximize joint political gains from trade) and would represent a part of the ideal Coasean bargain among all trading nations. Assume so. But if the widget concession would benefit a number of U.S. trading partners, each may be tempted to understate their "willingness to pay" for it, hoping that offers of reciprocal concessions by other nations will suffice to induce the United States to agree to the concession anyway. With each nation so understanding its willingness to pay, it is possible that the United States will elect not to make the concession at all, even though by hypothesis a bargain exists in which the concession is made and all nations benefit.

If this free rider problem becomes acute, there are various options for changing the structure of negotiations to try to reduce it. None of these alternatives, however, is entirely satisfactory. One option is for the nations that might be tempted to free ride on each other to caucus and work out a collective offer for a desired concession. But this procedure is obviously imperfect because each nation will still have an incentive to understate its willingness to pay in formulating the collective offer.

Another possibility is for nations to abandon product-by-product negotiations over concessions and instead agree that every nation will afford tariff cuts in accordance with a mutually agreed formula. Nations might agree, for example, to cut all tariffs by 50%, subject to an exception list – such a procedure has in fact been followed in modern GATT negotiating rounds.[18] The difficult here, of course, is that across-the-board cuts fail to exploit the joint political gains from a more subtle and tailored set of concessions. Moreover, once nations deviate significantly from the formula with their exceptions list, the free rider problem immediately reemerges.

Because there is no complete solution to the free rider problem, there can be little doubt that the most favored nation obligation prevents the parties to large scale multilateral trade negotiations from exhausting all joint political gains.[19] In the absence of a most favored nation obligation, by contrast, free riding of the sort described above would not be present. A country that secured a discriminatory concession would realize the full benefit of it and could look to no other source for the counter concession required to induce it.

A relaxation of the most favored nation obligation might thus permit trading nations to realize greater political gains from trade. To return to our stylized example, suppose that the United States despairs of striking a profitable non-discriminatory bargain and proposes instead to reduce the tariff applicable to Canada only, in an amount sufficient to allow Canada to export an additional 1 million widgets. Canada, by hypothesis, is not the lowest-cost supplier for an additional million widgets, and thus such a discriminatory arrangement will reduce the sum of U.S. tariff revenue and (global) producer surplus. Nevertheless, because no other nation can free ride on the concession to Canada alone, Canada's willingness to pay may rise so much that the concession is now attractive to the United States, even taking into account that its tariff revenue on the million imported widgets will be lower.

Of course, the fact that the bargain is now politically attractive for the United States and Canada does not ensure that it raises *global* political welfare. Rather, the gains to the United States and Canada must exceed the losses to other nations. But this too is certainly possible *measured against a baseline where no deal at all is struck*. Suppose, for example, that Canada is a reasonably efficient producer of widgets, so that the total cost of an additional million widgets produced in Canada is not much greater than the total cost of an additional million widgets produced by the most efficient suppliers elsewhere. Then, most of the producer surplus lost elsewhere is Canada's gain, and U.S. tariff revenue under the discriminatory concession need not be much less than it would have been under the ideal non-discriminatory bargain. The joint gains to the United States and Canada from the discriminatory arrangement may then be nearly as great as would be the global gains from the non-discriminatory arrangement that is infeasible because of free riding, and may considerably exceed the losses caused by the discrimination to excluded nations. Other things being equal, the desirability of discriminatory arrangements would seem to be greater, the more serious is the free rider problem for non-discriminatory arrangements, and the less the amount of trade diversion that results from discrimination.

Focusing narrowly on the free rider issue, therefore, one might ask whether the most favored nation obligation is counterproductive, and whether the multilateral trading system might realize greater joint political gains (and perhaps a greater degree of overall trade liberalization as well) if it were eliminated. The discussion above suggests a danger with eliminating the most favored nation obligation, however, relating to the possibility that preferential arrangements might impose net political losses on the global trading community due to trade diversion. The next section will suggest still further reasons to doubt that eliminating the most favored nation obligation altogether would be desirable.

The Benefits of a Most Favored Nation Obligation in the Bargaining Process

The costs of the free rider problem must be weighed against the costs of two other problems that a most favored nation obligation avoids. A trading regime without a most favored nation obligation creates an opportunity for a subset of trading nations to *threaten* to create a discriminatory arrangement – even one that was not genuinely in their joint interests – unless other nations make concessions to stop it. The possibility of such threats, followed by counterthreats, retaliation, and so on, might make for an uncertain and unstable trading regime that would unravel and threaten the political gains from reciprocal trade negotiations. With the most favored nation obligation in place, by contrast, nations are disabled from making threats to discriminate.

More importantly, the most favored nation obligation protects the value of concessions against future erosion through discrimination. If country A receives a concession from country B and is not entitled to most favored nation treatment from B, then the value of the concession can be undermined if country B later makes an even better concession to country C on the same goods (or close substitutes). Faced with this uncertainty, country A would offer less for the concession in the first place (as would country B for the reciprocal concession), and fewer valuable deals would be struck.[20]

Of course, a blanket most favored nation obligation is not the only conceivable solution to this problem. Another solution might be for each party to a trade agreement to secure, in conjunction with each concession, additional promises limiting the future concessions that a trading partner could subsequently make to its other trading partners respecting the same or similar goods. The transaction costs and information costs of proceeding in this fashion could be extensive, however, especially if the ancillary promises were anything more than a simple most favored nation commitment.

Another option might be to confine all trade concessions to well-defined multilateral negotiating "rounds", with no nation committing to anything until it can review the entire schedule of proposed discriminatory concessions by each trading partner to each of its supplier countries. Once agreement had been reached among all participants as to the various schedules, the concessions would take effect and no further changes in schedules would be permitted until the next negotiating round. A drawback to this approach would again be the information costs of evaluating the consequences of discrimination on a product-by-product basis. It is also unclear how long it would take for negotiations to come to closure under this system.

A third option is to adopt some sort of across-the-board principle to protect the value of concessions against erosion by subsequent and more favorable concessions to others. What principle makes the most sense in this respect? In our view, the most favored nation obligation seems a natural focal point. It is eminently simple to state it – nobody else gets a better deal – and it seems as easy to administer as any alternative that we can imagine. It also has the virtue of preventing trade diversion, and thereby raises the global political gains from trade in many settings. An across-the-board principle with this property and the further virtue of simplicity has much to commend it.

In short, although the free rider problem caused by the most favored nation obligation is no doubt important and an impediment to the realization of joint political gains, the elimination of the most favored nation obligation would create other difficulties. No other solution to these difficulties comes to mind that would have the same ease of administration, and would do more to promote joint surplus on average, than the most favored nation obligation.

IV. IMPLICATIONS

The discussion above indicates that, in a cooperative setting, the most favored nation obligation has its benefits in protecting the security of concessions and in increasing joint political surplus under many circumstances, but also has its costs in the form of a free rider problem and in limiting the opportunities to discriminate in circumstances where it would enhance joint political surplus. Were the nations of the trading community constrained to choose between unflinching adherence to a most favored nation obligation and its total elimination, the choice would not be an obvious one. Yet, as noted in the introduction, the range of options is in fact richer and more subtle, and the WTO/GATT system embodies rules that blend a general most favored nation obligation with a number of significant exceptions. In this concluding section of the paper, it is our thesis that these rules represent a fairly sophisticated balancing of the costs and benefits of the most favored nation obligation.[21]

The Primacy of the Most Favored Nation Obligation in the WTO/GATT System

Article I of the GATT provides that, with respect to customs duties and other charges on goods on international payments for goods, the methods of computation for all such charges, rules, and formalities governing importation and exportation, and domestic excise taxes and product regulations, any "advantage, privilege, favour or immunity" granted by any contracting party to any product originating in or destined to another contracting party "shall be accorded immediately and unconditionally to the like product originating in or destined for the territories of all other contracting parties."[22] By enshrining this most favored nation obligation in Article I of GATT, one of the two articles that requires a unanimous vote for amendment,[23] the drafters made clear that tariff discrimination among trading partners would be the exception rather than the rule.

Although Article I does not cover quotas, an obvious loophole, Article XI of GATT creates a general prohibition on them, subject to exceptions, and Article XIII provides that quotas permitted under GATT shall in general be administered in a non-discriminatory fashion. In particular, whenever quota rights are allocated by country under Article XIII, they should aim "at a distribution of trade . . . approaching as closely as possible the shares that the various contracting parties might be expected to obtain in the absence of such restrictions."[24] The shares of each country may be established by mutual agreement, and otherwise the benchmark is the share of each nation during a "representative period" prior to the imposition of the quota.[25] Because the share of each nation in trade prior to a quota regime will ordinarily have been established under a most favored nation tariff, the requirement that relative shares be preserved under an allocated quota system is a way of approximating what would happen with a tariff increase on a most favored nation basis. It is important in this respect to be sure, but in the absence of detailed information on supply conditions in each country, it likely provides the best feasible approximately to a most favored nation tariff.

Thus, with respect to the traditional instruments of protection, tariffs, and quotas, and with respect to other broader measures and domestic regulatory policies that might serve as instruments of protection, the GATT provides that most favored nation treatment shall ordinarily prevail. Our prior analysis suggests two reasons why. First, as argued in Section II, the most favored nation obligation tends to maximize the joint surplus of exporting producers and importing governments, at any level of protection in the importing nation, by averting the deadweight losses due to trade diversion. We think it likely that this gain in joint surplus should, on average, produce joint political gains as well. Second, as argued in Section III, the most favored nation obligation prevents importing nations from frustrating the expectations associated with trade negotiations under GATT by prohibiting more favorable concessions to other trading partners.[26]

Declining Industries and Short Run Discrimination Under the Escape Clause

In Section II, we considered the possibility that discrimination might make some sense if it confers a competitive return on producers with sunk costs while burdening primarily those exporters with higher than competitive returns who expect to lose them soon anyway because of entry. Discrimination might also be valuable if it remedies an unemployment problem among workers with industry-specific human capital without simply exporting it to similarly situated workers abroad. These observations, we believe, afford a plausible explanation for the permissible scope of discrimination under the GATT "escape clause."

This escape clause, otherwise known as the "safeguards" article, is contained in Article XIX of GATT. It provides that nations may raise trade barriers that they had previously promised to lower when "increased imports" are a cause of "serious injury" to a domestic industry. The authority for renewed protection is limited to the period necessary to remedy to prevent the serious injury.

In a previous paper, one of us argued that this provision can be understood to facilitate the "efficient breach" of promises made under GATT – that is, it defines in a rough way circumstances under which breach of promise should be allowed because the *ex ante* (political) benefits to the breaching party exceed the *ex ante* costs of breach to other parties. In particular, it was argued that "serious injury" is a market for industrial decline, where the returns to sunk investments are below a competitive level and considerable unemployment is usually present. The political gains to protection for such an industry will tend to be larger, other things being equal, for the reasons given above. Likewise, "increased imports" serve as a rough market for situations in which exporters as a whole are expanding and prosperous, so that restrictions on their exports (up to a point) need not drive the return on sunk investment below a competitive level and need not result in the unemployment of workers who have invested in industry-specific human capital.[27] For these reasons, the *ex ante* political costs of trade restrictions to exporting nations under the conditions specific in Article XIX are likely to be less than the political benefits of restrictions to importing nations.

If this analysis is right, a corollary is that discrimination may be valuable under the escape clause. Consider, for example, measures to protect a declining steel industry in a developed nation. Restrictions on exports from similar nations, also with declining steel industries, simply shift the locus of below competitive returns from one declining industry to another, and export unemployment. As a first approximation, there will be no joint gains from such restrictions. Restrictions on nations whose exports are rapidly expanding, by contrast, where returns are high and unemployment is unlikely to result, may remedy dislocation in the importing nation without a causing dislocation and below competitive returns in exporting nations.

This reasoning suggests that a politically savvy escape clause might allow importing nations to impose more substantial restrictions on exports from growing and prosperous exporting nations than on exports from nations with declining industries. An allocation of restrictions based on historical market shares (the Article XII principle) will not achieve this goal in many cases, and an argument might be made for restrictions that take into account not only past market share but the rate of change in past market share, on the premise that exporters with a rapidly increasing share are more likely to be experiencing high returns and are better able to bear restrictions without as much consequent dislocation.

This principle is found in the new Uruguay Round Agreement on Safeguards. It provides that when quotas are used as the protective device and shares are allocated by country, the shares shall ordinarily reflect historical market share during a previous "representative period."[28] The *exception* is where "imports from certain [WTO members] have increased in disproportionate percentage in relation to the total increase of imports of the product concerned in the representative period."[29] That is, discrimination is permissible against those countries whose exports have expanded most rapidly.

Such a principle is difficult to reconcile with any sort of welfare analysis, since the countries whose exports have grown most rapidly are likely to be the most efficient producers. Discrimination against them is then likely to create deadweight losses relative to a non-discriminatory policy achieving the same level of protection. But the joint political returns to discrimination become evident if one posits, as we do above, that lost surplus to firms and workers in declining industries "counts" more in the political calculus than lost surplus in industries earning better than competitive returns.

This rationale for discrimination is time limited, however, and as sunk investments decay there will be joint losses if discrimination induces inefficient new investment. Not surprisingly, therefore, escape clause relief is temporary and is to be phased out gradually over time.[30] Such a policy in a very rough way allows those with sunk investments to recoup a competitive return, while signalling to potential new investors that an expansion of industry capacity to replace depreciated physical and human capital is not worthwhile.

Customs Unions and Free Trade Areas

Our understanding of the rationale for Article XXIV of the GATT, which permits the formation of preferential trading arrangements known as "customs union" or "free trade areas," is less satisfactory. Nevertheless, for reasons that we elaborate below, we believe that Article XXIV crudely promotes joint gains in the face of the free rider problem and does so without undue damage to joint surplus through trade diversion or through undermining the security of concessions.

A "customs union" is a preferential arrangement in which all members adopt a common external tariff (the European Union is the most important example). A "free trade area" is a preferential arrangement in which the members do not adopt a common external tariff (NAFTA is the most important example). Otherwise, both are subject to the same requirements, including the requirement that "duties and other restrictive regulations of commerce . . . are eliminated with respect to substantially all trade" between the members, with allowance for a phase-in period.[31]

At first blush, Article XXIV presents a considerable puzzle. If discrimination is in general counterproductive as a political matter, making the most favored nation obligation an important part of the WTO/GATT system, why should its members create an exception that allows discrimination as long as it is conducted on a sufficiently massive scale (i.e., with respect to "substantially all" trade)? We have some tentative thoughts to offer.

Recall that, aside from occasional circumstances in which producer groups receive unequal weight in the joint political calculus (such as circumstances covered by the escape clause), the major potential drawback to the most favored nation obligation is the free rider problem. Although negotiations can be structured to try and reduce it, it cannot realistically be eliminated and thus it is likely to prevent trading nations from exhausting on a multilateral basis all the joint political gains from reciprocal trade concessions. The first-best political optimum is thus unattainable.

Under these circumstances, as argued earlier, preferential trading arrangements may make some (political) sense as a second-best alternative. But there are also problems with preferential arrangements for reasons also noted earlier – they tend to dissipate political surplus through trade diversion that affects producers and national treasuries, and they tend to undermine the security of trade concessions. The trading community at large thus confronts a difficult problem. It is in the joint interest of all trading nations to permit preferential arrangements when they result in a second-best improvement on the joint political optimum that is attainable with the most favored nation obligation in place. But it is also in the interest of the trading community to prohibit preferential arrangements that result in a lower level of political welfare for the trading community as a whole – that is, to prohibit them when the costs to those who are excluded from the preferential arrangement exceed the gains to those who are part of it. These costs will tend to be greater, as noted, the greater the degree to which the preferential arrangement causes trade diversion, and the greater the degree to which it upsets the expectations associated with prior trade concessions.

To put it more succinctly, preferential arrangements create externalities – a loss of surplus for excluded producers associated with trade diversion and frustrated expectations. Sometimes these negative externalities are so great that a preferential arrangement is a net loss for the trading community as a whole, and sometimes the externalities are small enough that the gains to members of the preferential arrangement exceed the losses to outsiders. Ideally, GATT should discourage the former arrangements and permit the latter.

How can the trading community ensure that any preferential arrangement is a source of joint gains? An obvious way would be to require that nations entering a preferential arrangement provide "compensation" to those excluded from it. We do not imagine that such compensation would take the form of money, but rather the form of compensatory trade concessions. Officials in nations whose exporters were harmed by discrimination against them would secure new trade concessions to benefit the same or other exporters, thus restoring their original level of political support.

A glance at Article XXIV reveals, however, that it does not contain a general requirement of compensation. It does provide that if (a) the members of a customs union establish a common external tariff rate for a good that exceeds the tariff rate on the same good imported into some member of the union prior to the formation of the customs union, and (b) that member had promised not to raise its tariff in a previous trade negotiation, then other countries adversely affected by the breach of this promise are entitled to compensation.[32] But this compensation requirement has no applicability when the external tariff rates of a customs union do not exceed any of the tariff rates previously promised by its members, and it says nothing about compensation for loss of trade caused not by an increase in the external tariff but a decrease in the internal tariff. Likewise, for free trade areas, there is no requirement of compensation at all since the members of the free trade area ordinarily do not change their external tariffs. In short, when trade diversion results simply from the formation of a preferential arrangement (i.e., from the lowering of trade barriers internally rather than from an increase in trade barriers externally) or from an increase in the external tariff that does not violate a prior commitment, compensation is not required.

The compensation requirement may in fact be somewhat broader because, as noted in Section III, a preferential arrangement can undermine the expectations associated with prior trade concessions to non-members, even if there is no express breach of a prior commitment. Such a frustration of expectations, even without a violation of the letter of the agreement, can in theory constitute a "non-violation of nullifaction or impairment" of benefits owing under the agreement, for which the aggrieved party would be entitled to some redress.[33]

We are reluctant to make too much of this point, however, because we are not aware of any prior complaint under GATT that was predicated on the notion that a preferential arrangement under Article XXIV caused a non-violation nullification or impairment. Even if such complaints are possible in theory, therefore, it seems much too strong to suggest that in practice the threat of such complaints will suffice to ensure joint gains from preferential arrangements. We are forced to conclude, therefore, that nothing in the structure of the agreement requires effective compensation to those injured by preferential arrangements.[34]

If there is no general compensation arrangement in place to ensure joint gains, another possible mechanism for discouraging undesirable preferential arrangements is retaliation, whether in trade policy or elsewhere. The threat of retaliation could be strictly implicit, and credible given the repeat play nature of the interactions among members of the WTO/GATT system. Whatever the legal rules in place, GATT members might then anticipate that preferential arrangements that cause undue losses to non-members through large amounts of trade diversion will become subject to some sanction down the road.

In addition, it is important to remember that Article XXIV contemplates preferences that *liberalize* trade relative to the most favored nation baseline, not preferences that restrict it, Preferential arrangements that reduce trade barriers *and* that reduce joint surplus for the trading community as a whole will also tend to be costly for the parties to the preferential arrangement, because the deadweight cost of trade diversion will be borne to some considerable degree by governments who are party to it. If the United States reduced tariffs on Canadian widgets to zero, and Canada is an inefficient producer of widgets so that the result is high-cost widget production in Canada that survives only because of the preference, who has gained? The U.S. government has foregone the tariff revenue on widgets from other sources. Canadian producers may not have gained much to offset this loss if most of their price advantage relative to other foreign widget producers is dissipated through higher costs. To a considerable extent, therefore, the loss in tariff revenue for the U.S. Treasury may be a gain to no one. By contrast, when a preferential arrangement is trade creating (i.e., it encompasses low-cost producers who would supply the importing nation under a most favored nation tariff reduction), the loss to the importing nation's treasury is more likely to be a gain to the producers of the preferred trading partner, because they do not dissipate it through higher costs. And, even if they compete away the gains over the long run, at least consumers in the importing nation derive a benefit as prices decline. Thus, one might argue, the costs of trade diversion to nations that are parties to preferential arrangements will discourage them from entering arrangements to *liberalize* trade if the preferences would result in a lot of trade diversion.

But both of these arguments prove too much from our perspective. If implicit threats of retaliation or the potential reduction in internal surplus due to trade diversion sufficed to ensure joint gains from discriminatory policies, there would be no need for a general most favored nation obligation. The parties to GATT could leave themselves free to discriminate, at least in the direction of *lowering* existing barriers, knowing that inappropriate discrimination would be unprofitable.

We are thus led to suspect that the key to a complete understanding of Article XXIV is the "substantially all" requirement – the rule that precludes preferential arrangements unless they *eliminate* trade barriers on virtually *everything*. It is this requirement, perhaps coupled with the considerations noted above, that tends to ensure that preferential arrangements do less harm to those excluded than they benefit the members.

To explain why, consider first the problem of trade diversion, and suppose that there were no "substantially all" requirement (i.e., that the MFN requirement were effectively non-existent). Now imagine that the United States and Canada are discussing the possibility of giving each other trade preferences. It seems quite plausible that the government of the United States might be willing to give a trade-diverting preference to politically powerful Canadian producers in a single industry, even though the loss of tariff revenue exceeded their gain in surplus, in return for a similar preference extended by Canada to a politically powerful U.S. exporting industry. Such a deal might be struck despite the net loss to the trading community as a whole because the nations who lose from it are diffuse and do not come forward with any counterproposal.

Now imagine that the "substantially all" requirement is in place. It is no longer possible to exchange a pair of concessions (or several pairs) affecting only politically powerful industries. Rather, barriers to trade must be eliminated across the board for all industries, many of which are poorly organized or are otherwise ineffective in the political process (perhaps they had cast their lot with the party out of power). Suppose further that such an arrangement between the United States and Canada would cause a lot of trade diversion, so that for the reasons given above, the gain in producer surplus in the two countries is considerably smaller than the joint loss of tariff revenue. On these assumptions, the two governments would be foregoing considerable tariff revenue in many industries where there was little political surplus being generated as a result.

In short, if the agreement creates a lot of trade diversion, the joint political surplus generated per dollar of foregone revenue seems likely to be less when the two nations are constrained to eliminate tariff preferences across the board. It is thus harder to imagine nations going forward with preferential arrangements that cause a lot of trade diversion if they are forced to eliminate all trade barriers.

Absent much trade diversion, of course, preferential arrangements can easily generate more producer surplus than they cost participant governments in tariff revenue, because trade-creating preferences cause production to shift from high-cost domestic producers to lower-cost foreign producers. On average, therefore, the political surplus generated per dollar of foregone tariff revenue will be greater as trade diversion grows smaller. This leads us to expect that across-the-board preferences may well prove attractive, even if some of the beneficiaries are not terribly well organized and if trade diversion is minimal. For these reasons, the "substantially all" requirement seems a potentially valuable device for discouraging trade diversion in preferential arrangements. This observation may help to explain why, in the empirical economic literature on preferential arrangements under GATT, the conclusion seems to be that trade creation usually exceeds trade diversion.[35]

The other concern that we have identified about preferential arrangements relates to the frustration of expectations. Here, too, the "substantially all" requirement may play an important role. Were nations free to grant trade-liberalizing preferences at any time on only part of their trade, one might anticipate preferential deals springing up all the time. Their formation would simply require a circumstance in which political leaders in two nations were willing to exchange preferences on as few as two products. Nations whose negotiated concessions might be undermined by preferences would then face a high degree of insecurity about their future value.

When preferential arrangements require across-the-board elimination of trade barriers, by contrast, they will ordinarily be preceded by an extended period of negotiation and publicity. The U.S.–Canada Free Trade Agreement, for example, was contemplated by the Trade Act of 1974, even though it did not take effect until 1988. The negotiations over the addition of Mexico, to form NAFTA, occurred over a period of 4 years during the early 1900's.[36] It is also suggested that the formation of the European Community was anticipated by the drafters of GATT in 1947.[37] Other trading nations are perhaps unlikely to be surprised by the formation of these arrangements, therefore, and can to some extent factor their probable effects into their own offers of concessions during GATT negotiating rounds that occur closely proximate in time. And, if political officials have a sufficiently short time horizon (if you like, a sufficiently high discount rate), the fact that trade negotiations have only a few years notice of a pending preferential arrangement may not matter much – their concern may be mainly with the frustration of expectations in the short term.

Lastly, relating both to the trade diversion problem and the frustration of expectations problem, the "substantially all" requirement ensures that any damage to the broader trading community because of new preferences will not occur piecemeal. This fact, coupled with the likelihood that other nations will have years of advance notice, enhances the ability of export interests that would be harmed by the preferences to organize in opposition. They can then better prevail on their governments to use diplomatic suasion and perhaps even threats of retaliation to discourage a preferential arrangement that causes a great degree of trade diversion or otherwise frustrates expectations under the GATT bargain. Were smaller scale preferences to be permitted, by contrast, those harmed by them would face the problem of constantly monitoring for any change in policy that would create them. Even then, if the damage to exporting interests were small enough, it might be difficult to motivate government officials to take any action to avert it.

We concede that this analysis is tentative, and that Article XXIV is at best a crude device for facilitating preferences that benefit the parties to them more than they hurt others. It is no doubt possible to imagine that at times Article XXIV might fail to ensure joint gains to the trading community at large from across-the-board preferential arrangements, and that it may at times impede narrower preferences that would yield joint gains despite their narrower coverage.

It is equally clear that the "substantially all" requirement is applied rather loosely as a legal matter, and that many preferential arrangements have entered into force despite the retention of a number of trade barriers within them, at least for an extended period of years.[38] Nevertheless, it is our thesis that the "substantially all" requirement of Article XXIV was designed to balance the potential gains from preferences in the face of the free rider problem with the costs that can result from trade diversion and the frustration of expectations. And, although we do not suggest that Article XXIV is the best that can possibly be done to permit discrimination only when it is jointly valuable, it is instructive that Article XXIV has survived so long in the GATT bargain, with little movement toward changing it.[39] It is also instructive, as noted above, that existing preferential arrangements may be dominated by trade creation as an empirical matter. These facts suggest that Article XXIV has served the political interests of the GATT community rather well on balance, and that its structure may indeed reflect a degree of political savvy heretofore unacknowledged.

V. CONCLUSION

Our analysis demonstrates that in designing the institutional framework in which joint gains may be realized through the exchange of concessions reducing trade barriers, essentially three considerations must be taken into account: (1) uncertainty with respect to future changes in trade barriers that would affect the value of concessions granted or received in a multilateral negotiation; (2) the free rider problem that arises when a concession inures to the benefit of a participant in the multilateral negotiation, whether or not the participant provides the *quid pro quo* for the concession; and (3) the political weight that attaches to different constituent interests, and the effects on their surplus that will result from trade diversion when nations discriminate in their commercial policies.

The generally applicable most favored nation requirement protects the expectations of participants in multilateral bargaining by forbidding subsequent more favorable treatment of other participants and avoids the deadweight loss resulting from trade diversion. It does so, however, at the cost of preventing nations from discriminating when it might be valuable to benefit certain politically powerful producer interest groups (such as declining industries) and at the cost of substantial incentives for participants in multilateral negotiations to attempt to free ride.

The escape clause responds sensibly to the first of these problems at least for a potentially important class of cases. Other institutional features serve to reduce the incidence of free riding but at a cost of reduced certainty with respect to future actions that may impair the value of concessions and result in trade-diverting discrimination. One of them is Article XXIV, which allows trade liberalizing preferences as long as they apply across the board to most of the trade between the parties to the preferential arrangement. We have argued that Article XXIV strikes a fairly sensible balance between the need to overcome the free rider problem on the one hand, and the need to ensure that the global community as a whole does not suffer from preferential arrangements on the other. It is, however, substantially imperfect, and the fundamental question about Article XXIV is whether it goes too far or not far enough in allowing discrimination. We are not prepared at this point to suggest a course for reform of Article XXIV, yet we also do not wish to leave the reader with the impression that we endorse every detail of the existing law and practice of Article XXIV as the best that the trading community can do. The issue of whether a superior institutional solution can be devised is an interesting one and is a potentially fruitful area of further research.

NOTES

This paper is condensed from another paper of the same title that will appear in *Economic Dimensions in International Law*, forthcoming from Cambridge University Press. We have benefited immensely from the comments of Alan Deadorff, and we wish to thank the Scaife Foundation for financial support of this project.

1 See The Most Favored Nation Obligation. Executive Branch GATT Studies, No. 9. The Most-Favored-Nation Provision, p. 133. Subcomm. on Int'l. Trade, Senate Comm. on Finance, 93rd Cong. 2nd sess. (1974).

2 Others include the reservations for various service sectors under the General Agreement on Trade in Services, the exceptions in Article I for certain historical trade preferences such as those of the British Commonwealth, qualifications to the MFN requirement for quantitative restrictions under Article XIII, and the authority under a GATT waiver for preferential treatment toward developing countries such as that afforded by the U.S. Generalized System of Preferences.

3 See Ronald Jones and Anne Krueger, eds. *The Political Economy of International Trade*, (Cambridge, MA: Blackwell, 1990); Jagdish Bhagwati, *Political Economy and International Economics*, ed. Douglas Irwin (Cambridge, MIT Press, 1991).

4 See Robert Baldwin, "The Economics of the GATT," in *Issues in International Economics*, ed. Peter Oppenheimer (Stocksfield, England: Oriel, 1980): Alan Sykes, "Protectionism as a Safeguard: A Positive Analysis of the GATT "Escape Clause" with Normative Speculations, 58, *University of Chicago Law Review* 255 (1991); Beth Yarbrough and Robert Yarbrough, *Cooperation and Governance in International Trade* (Princeton: Princeton University Press, 1992).

5 Actually, under GATT, discrimination is defined as the imposition of different tariffs on "like" products from different sources. It is possible that products may be "like" even though they are not perfect substitutes in the economic sense. We have more to say about the "like product" issue in the second part of Section IV.

6 We recognize that if goods from different countries are *imperfect* substitutes, the government may wish to use different tariffs because the elasticity of demand for them differs – the literature on optimal taxation addresses such matters. See e.g. Jean-Jacques Laffont, *Fundamentals of Public Economics* (Cambridge: MIT Press, 1988) Ch. 7. Discrimination of this sort might be viewed as tariff discrimination in GATT if the goods subject to different tariffs were sufficiently similar as to be considered "like products." Because we think it unlikely that the elasticity of demand would often differ much for products that are "like" for GATT purposes, however, we do not dwell on that possibility – as the second part of Section IV will discuss, products must ordinarily be very close substitutes to be considered "like" under Article 1.

7 See Alan Deardorff and Robert Stern, "Current Issues in U.S. Trade Policies: An Overview," in *Trade Policies in a Changing World Economy*, ed. Robert Stern (Cambridge: MIT Press, 1987).

8 See also Konstantine Gatsios, "Preferential Tariffs and the Most Favoured Nation Principle: A Note," 28 *Journal of International Economics* 365 (1990). Gatsios considers an imperfect competition model with two supplier firms located in different countries, and no domestic industry in the importing nation. The importing nation seeks to maximize its welfare, and in general discrimination is required to do so: Starting from an initial position of non-discrimination, there is a marginal gain to imposing a higher tariff on the supplier with lower cost who has a higher volume of imports initially, and a lower tariff on the higher-cost producer. Such a small change in tariffs raises revenue but leaves the quantity of imports and thus consumer surplus unchanged.

Another instructive paper on this topic is Andrew Caplin and Kala Krishna, "Tariffs and the Most-Favored-Nation Clause: A Game Theoretic Approach," I *Seoul Journal of Economics* 267 (1988). Section III of their paper considers the Nash equilibrium for a tariff game between three nations each seeking to maximize national welfare. They conclude that a legal prohibition on tariff discrimination has ambiguous welfare implications that depend on parameters.

9 To illustrate, suppose that an importing nation has two supplier nations for a homogeneous good, with distinct upward-sloping import supply curves from each supplier nation, $S_1(p)$ and $S_2(p)$. A domestic industry also produces the good, with an upward sloping curve $S(p)$. It does not export. Domestic demand is given by $D(p)$. Suppose further that the government desires a certain price to prevail in its domestic market, call it p^*. The government need not be committed to national welfare maximization, so that p^* may well represent the target price for an inefficient protectionist regime. The only assumption required for this illustration is that the government prefers to raise more revenue from tariffs rather than less.

The government can set a different tariff on goods from its two supplier countries, denoted t_1 and t_2. The condition for market equilibrium to prevail at the target price p^* is thus $S_1(p^*-t_1) + S_2(p^*-t_2) = D(p^*) - S(p^*) \equiv Q(p^*)$. Tariff revenue is denoted by R, and we assume that the government desires to maximize tariff revenue $R = t_1S_1(p^*-t_1) + t_2S_2(p^*-t_2)$ subject to the constraint that p^* prevail in equilibrium.

With a little algebra, the first order conditions imply that $S_1/S_1' - t_1 = S_2/S_2' - t_2$, with the arguments of each function evaluated at p^*. From this condition, it is obvious that $t_1 = t_2$, if $S_1(p) \equiv S_2(p)$, and generally not otherwise.

For example, take the case of two import supply curves of constant elasticity: $S_1(p) = c_1p^{e1}$; $S_2(p) = c_2p^{e2}$. Substituting into the first order condition above implies:

$$(p^*-t_1)/e_1-t_1 = (p^*-t_2)/e_2-t_2$$

Plainly, we cannot have $t_1 = t_2$ unless $e_1 = e_2$. Likewise, $e_1>e_2$ implies $t_1<t_2$, and vice-versa. The last result shows that the tax should be higher on the supplier country with less elastic supply. Intuitively, the supplier country with the less elastic supply absorbs more of the tariff through a reduction in its export price and thus more of the revenue comes out of its product surplus.

10 A related point is made in Jav Choi, "Optimal Tariffs and the Choice of Technology: Discriminatory Tariffs vs. the Most Favored Nation Clause," 38 *Journal of International Economics* 143 (1995). Choi considers a model in which two exporting firms in different countries can make costly investments to reduce their marginal costs. The importing nation maximizes national welfare through either a discriminatory or non-discriminatory tariff. The optimal non-discriminatory tariff does less to penalize a firm for reducing its costs than a discriminatory tariff, so that both firms end up with lower costs absent discrimination, to the benefit of the importing nation in the long run.

11 For example, let p^* be 20, let unit cost (and thus price) in country A be 10, and let unit cost in country B be 15. Suppose that the demand for imports at a price of 20 is 100 units. The government can achieve this with a uniform tariff of 10, which results in imports only from country A at a price to the consumer of 20, raising revenue of 1000. It could also achieve this with a tariff of 5 on imports from country B and a tariff of more than 10 on imports from A; all imports would come from B, the price to the consumer would again be 20, but revenue would be only 500. With a discriminatory tariff of 5 on imports from B and exactly 10 on imports from A, the equilibrium is indeterminate, but plainly this tariff structure can only reduce tariff revenue relative to uniform tariff of 10.

12 See John Jackson, William Davey, and Alan Sykes, *Legal Problems of International Relations*, (3rd ed. Sections 8.3, 10.3) (Minneapolis: West, 1995).

13 See Richard Lipsey, "The Theory of Customs Unions: A General Survey," 70 *Economics Journal* 496 (1960).

14 See Murray Kemp and Henry Wan, "An Elementary Proposition Concerning the Formation of Customs Unions," in *Three Topics in the Theory of International Trade: Distribution, Welfare, and Uncertainty* (Amsterdam: North Holland, 1976).

15 We assume implicitly that discrimination does not affect the competitive rate of return in exporting nations. This rate of return may change slightly in response to commercial policies abroad, particularly in nations that do not have access to capital at a "world" price, but it seems reasonable to suppose that any such effects are small in general and can be ignored in thinking about the political calculus.

16 David Friedman, *Price Theory*, 2nd ed. (Cincinnati, OH: South-West Publishing, 1990), pp. 546–550.

17 This issue has attracted some formal attention in the literature. Caplin and Krishna, *supra*, note 8, pp. 281–84, formalize the free rider idea in a model where two countries bargain over concessions, knowing that a third country will benefit from them under the most favored nation principle. Not surprisingly, the model confirms that free riding results in fewer concessions. Ludema, by contrast, constructs a Rubinstein style model in which the free rider problem is solved by a sophisticated first mover who constructs the initial offer so that the other two players are just indifferent to accepting it and as a result do so immediately because delay will do them no good. The agreement achieves the Pareto frontier, because the first mover has an incentive to propose a bargain that attains the frontier, that party will appropriate all the surplus over the other two parties' threat points. Ludema thus argues that the free rider problem attributable to the most favored nation obligation is easily exaggerated. See Rodney Ludema, "International Trade Bargaining and the Most Favored Nation Clause," 3 *Economics and Politics* 1 (1991). We are quite skeptical, however, because the assumptions of the Rubinstein style game – perfect information, strict "rationality" in the response of other players, and exogenously given "rules" (such as the order of play) – seem highly unrealistic.

18 Jackson, Davey, and Sykes, *supra*, note 12, Section 8.2.

19 Although it is difficult to quantify the extent of the problem as an empirical matter, a study by Finger suggests that there has indeed been a tendency in the GATT system for concessions to be focused on products traded heavily between the parties to the bargain and less heavily with outsiders (what he calls "internationalization"). J. Michael Finger, "Trade Liberalization: A Public Choice Perspective," in *Challenges to a Liberal International Economic Order*, eds. R. C. Amacher, G. Haberler, and T. Willet (Ann Arbor, MIBooks on Demand, 1979).

20 Such concerns afford a familiar rationale for most favored nation clauses in labor contracts – the UAW promises Chrysler that it will receive a wage contract no less favorable than that afforded to Ford and GM. Otherwise, Chrysler would fear that an

early agreement with UAW would make it vulnerable to being placed at a competitive disadvantage.

21 Our theoretical discussion implies that nations unilaterally would engage in only limited discrimination in their commercial policies, and that discrimination to raise revenue, in particular, would be quite rare. It would, of course, be informative to see if this implication is consistent with historical experience. We argue that historical experience bears out the theory in an expanded version of this paper, to appear in *Economic Dimensions in International Law*, forthcoming from Cambridge University Press.

22 GATT, Article I(1).

23 See GATT, Article XXX.

24 GATT, Article XIII(2).

25 *Id.*

26 The practical application of the most-favored-nation obligation requires nations to define the class of products to which the obligation not to discriminate extends. The GATT itself invokes the phrase "like product" and prohibits discrimination between like products from different trading partners. The scope of the "like product" in a given instance may be open to disagreement and to manipulation. Proper interpretation of the phrase requires a balance between a broad conception of "likeness" aimed at averting disguised discrimination based on contrived, narrow product categories, and a narrow conception aimed at limiting the scope of the free rider problem. We discuss these issues in detail, and the GATT solution to them, in the expanded version of this paper that will appear in *Economic Dimensions in International Law*, forthcoming from Cambridge University Press.

27 See Sykes, *supra*, note 4.

28 See Uruguay Round Agreement on Safeguards, Article 5.2(a).

29 *Id.* Article 5.2(b).

30 *Id.* Article 7.

31 GATT, Article XXIV(8).

32 GATT, Article XXIV(6).

33 See Jackson, Davey, and Sykes, *supra*, note 12, Section 7.3(C).

34 It is worth noting that a compensation requirement might create problems of its own – in particular, the familiar problems associated with bilateral monopoly and hold-up situations. If the parties to a preferential arrangement that increases joint surplus cannot appropriate much of the net gain, their incentive to create it diminishes.

35 See generally, Robert Lawrence, *Regionalism, Multilateralism and Deeper Integration* (Washington: Brookings, 1995). Lustig, Bosworth and Lawrence, eds, *North American Free Trade: Assessing the Impact* (Washington, D.C.: Brookings Institution, 1992); Gary Hufbauer and Jeffrey Schott, *North American Free Trade: Issues and Recommendations* (Washington, D.C.: Institute for International Economics, 1992).

36 Jackson, Davey, and Sykes, *supra*, note 12, Section 10.3(b).

37 See John Jackson, *World Trade and the Law of GATT* (NY: Bobbs Merrill, 1969), p. 580.

38 See Jackson, Davey, and Sykes, *supra*, note 12, Section 10.2(b).

39 It is noteworthy that much of the tension associated with Article XXIV has been caused by the enlargement of the European preference area and the right of compensation claimed by outsiders when the common external tariff was raised above the tariffs previously in place in member States. See Jackson, Davey, and Sykes, *supra*, note 12, Ch. 10. This suggests why a compensation requirement may not be the way to police undesirable preferential arrangements – the resulting bilateral monopoly problem may do a good deal of harm to trading relations.

14. Evaluating Alternative Formulae for Reducing Industrial Tariffs

R. M. Stern

One of the major objectives of the Multilateral Tariff Negotiations (MTN) convened under GATT auspices in February of 1975 is to achieve substantial reductions in industrial tariffs. Since there are various alternative formulae available for reducing tariffs, it is necessary in the preparation for and actual conduct of the negotiations to develop criteria that can be used to evaluate different formulae. The purpose of this paper accordingly is to outline the important issues that should be considered in the evaluation process.[1]

I. OBJECTIVES OF TARIFF REDUCTION AND QUALIFICATIONS TO THE CASE FOR TARIFF REDUCTION

The tradition theory of tariffs focuses on the excess *production costs* that tariffs entail by diverting domestic resources to the protected industries and on the *consumption costs* that are borne by consumers due to higher domestic than world prices. The case for tariff reduction rests accordingly on diminishing or eliminating these costs. While it may well be true that tariff reduction leads to greater efficiency in resource use and enhances consumer welfare, this conclusion cannot be taken for granted. There are many qualifications that must be taken into account before a final judgement can be rendered. It is useful to consider these qualifications because they may bear upon the evaluation of alternative tariff formulae.

We may note first that the traditional theory of tariffs is premised on the existence of competitive market forces with respect to both goods and productive factors. If, as seems realistic, market imperfections exist, reducing or eliminating tariffs will not necessarily enhance economic welfare because productive factors may not move readily to alternative and more efficient uses with the tariff change. The *a priori* case for tariff liberalization may thus be deceptively simple. This means that careful factual studies of the effects of liberalization will have to be made before any positive or negative conclusions can be drawn.

Second, the traditional theory abstracts from the structure of tariffs, which from observation is known to be escalated in most countries from the raw materials stage to finished products. While the theoretical analysis and measurement of the effects of tariff structure have been subjects of debate among academic economists in recent years, there is no denying that resource movements are influenced by differential tariff rates on factor inputs and final products. Tariff reduction or elimination must therefore be looked at in terms of the tariff structure that will emerge and how resource movements will be affected. Again, it is conceivable, depending upon the distribution and depth of the tariff cuts with respect to the stages of processing, that protection could be increased rather than diminished.

Third, the traditional theory does not consider for what reasons tariffs were originally introduced. While historically, revenue needs were once paramount, many countries have since attached a positive social value to tariffs as a means of promoting their industrialization and of favoring some producing groups over others. The traditional production and consumption costs of tariffs may thus be rationalized in this light. Tariffs are not the best means of achieving these objectives, however, as compared with "first-best" measures such as domestic tax-subsidies that can be implemented without distorting resource use and creating consumption burdens. Tariffs are nevertheless a fact of life and, so long as governments are reluctant or politically unable to use domestic measures for accomplishing domestic objectives, there may be resistance to reducing or eliminating tariffs. But if tariff liberalization can be undertaken in a multilateral framework and concessions balanced among countries, mutual benefits may be realized. This may partially explain why countries are so concerned with reciprocity in tariff bargaining.

Tariffs and other trade barriers have also often been introduced to increase the level of employment and to ameliorate payments imbalances. However, it has come to be increasingly realized that these macroeconomic problems can be more effectively dealt with by domestic monetary and fiscal policies and exchange-rate flexibility. By this same line of reasoning, the macroeconomic impact of tariff liberalization should not create unusual difficulties if domestic stabilization policies are effectively pursued and the balance of payments is equilibrated with requisite exchange-rate adjustments.

The formation of customs unions and other preferential arrangements can be accommodated readily in the light of the discussion so far. One cannot say that customs unions are good or bad from the standpoint of economic welfare; this judgement depends upon the balance between the effects of trade creation engendered by the increased accessibility of markets within the member countries and the effects of trade that may be diverted from low-cost nonmember suppliers to higher-cost member countries as a consequence of the preferential tariff changes. In addition, the behavior of preferential groups can be understood in terms of the positive benefits that they may attach to common policies even when these policies may be inimical to welfare in the rest of the world. What the foregoing means is that the case for trade liberalization is strongest when preferential arrangements may on balance result in trade diversion. However, liberalization may be limited when preferential groups seek common objectives and use trade policy for these purposes even though domestic tax-subsidy measures would be less damaging with respect to efficiency and welfare.

The traditional theory of tariffs assumes that the markets for goods and for productive inputs will adjust instantaneously in a frictionless manner. Realistically, however, adjustment takes time and productive factors may experience unemployment in the wake of an exogenous event such as a reduction of tariffs. The answer here is not necessarily to forego or to decelerate the tariff liberalization. Rather, programs of adjustment assistance can be utilized to ease the burden of adjustment. The macro-economic pursuit of full employment policies will certainly make it easier to handle these adjustment problems.

Finally, the traditional model may give insufficient weight to the dynamic forces set into motion by previous tariff policies and by potential future changes in these policies. These forces can cut both ways. That is, tariff protection can lead to greater efficiency in resource use if a phenomenon like learning by doing results in lowering per unit costs of production. Alternatively, protection may foster inefficiency and create vested interests that may be powerful enough to resist the competitive shock to which they would be exposed by tariff reduction. It is difficult to know which of these effects will predominate, although there should not be much problem in assessing the costs of inefficiencies that protection may engender through time.

The foregoing markets should not be construed to negate the benefits to be derived from tariff reduction or elimination. Rather, what should be emphasized is that the realization of benefits is by no means a foregone conclusion once account is taken of various market imperfections, the structure of tariffs, the positive social value that governments may attribute to protection and to preferential groups, time lags in the adjustment process, and the influences of dynamic forces. Many of these factors do not lend themselves readily to empirical measurement so that assessments of the effects of tariff changes cannot be completely definitive. Assessments must nevertheless be made in order to formulate alternative policies and to provide some indication of the likely import that will result from the policies actually implemented. This article now turns to the important issues that arise in the choice and evaluation of alternative formulae for reducing industrial tariffs.

II. CRITERIA FOR CHOOSING THE EVALUATING ALTERNATIVE TARIFF FORMULAE

Depth of Cut

The first question to be considered is whether there exists an optimal tariff-cutting formula. In theory, such a formula would be for all countries to eliminate their tariffs completely so that goods would move freely. In this case, domestic and world prices of goods would be commensurate, making allowance of course for transportation and related costs. One would also have to insure that countries did not behave monopolistically in world trade so as to turn the terms of trade in their favor.

An argument could be made that countries can just as well gain by unilateral removal of their tariffs. While there is perhaps some truth in this, the benefits from unilateral tariff removal may be equivocal, particularly if adjustment costs are encountered due to the difficulty in moving resources from one industry to another. But, more importantly, there is little incentive for unilateral removal once account is taken of the reasons why countries have resorted to tariffs in the first place. Thus, a movement to completely free trade in industrial products either on a multilateral or unilateral basis is most unlikely in view of the commitments that most countries have already made to varying levels of protection.

The choice of a tariff-cutting formula then becomes a subject for negotiation among countries. In this regard, it might be argued that the most preferable formula is the one that moves the participating countries closest for the free trade point of zero tariffs. The depth of cut would accordingly provide one criterion in choosing among alternative formulae. However, in itself, the depth of cut is an incomplete criterion because it provides no indication of what the *economic* consequences of the cut may be. One therefore needs other criteria that will reflect these consequences more directly.

But it should be noted that even to assess the depth of cut is no simple matter, since it requires some method of weighing the existing tariffs and the cuts that are made according to the different levels of aggregation of the tariff classification. Unfortunately, there are no computationally feasible weighing schemes that are neutral for different aggregation levels so that one may be forced to rely upon tariff averages that are subject to an unknown degree of inaccuracy. In order to deal with this problem, alternative weighting schemes can be constructed, the most common ones being to use a country's own imports or "world" imports as weights. Both of these schemes are utilized in the GATT Tariff Study,[2] and it would be desirable therefore in designing an evaluation process for tariff formulae to be able to calculate both measures in order especially to ascertain if there are any peculiarities in a country's own import weights that reflect idiosyncrasies in its tariff schedule.

Other Statistical and Economic Criteria

In addition to depth of cut, there are other statistical measures that can be readily calculated. These include: (1) frequency distributions of tariffs by *ad valorem* groupings together with measures of tariff dispersion based upon the standard deviation or coefficient of variation; (2) trade coverage according to the various levels of existing tariffs and of alternative post-negotiation tariffs; (3) tariff-revenue losses associated with alternative tariff cuts based on existing trade; and (4) preferential tariff margins before and after alternative tariff cuts.

These various statistical measures will provide different perspectives concerning the magnitude and distribution of alternative tariff cuts. But, in themselves, they do not convey much information that is *economically* useful. What is required accordingly are estimates of the effects of alternative cuts upon the level and industrial composition of a country's trade, output, and employment. These effects can be analysed in terms of the direct impacts of the tariff cuts, holding other things constant such as the exchange rate and domestic price level. Alternatively, allowance can be made for these secondary effects.

Macroeconomic Effects

The simplest model that can be used to estimate the trade impact of tariff changes is one in which it is assumed that a country both produces domestically and imports given products, and that it faces a constant world price for imports. The domestic price will then be equal to the world price plus the tariff. If the world price is set equal to unity, the domestic price will then be equal to one plus the *ad valorem* tariff. Assuming further that the tariffs do not completely prohibit imports, any reduction in tariffs can be expressed as a ratio of the change in the tariff to one plus the tariff. This ratio will be an approximation of the extent to which the tariff reduction lowers the domestic price of imports. One then needs to determine how responsive the quantity demanded of imports will be to the price change, that is, what the price elasticity of import demand may be, and how responsive domestic supply may be.

The measurement of demand and supply elasticities involves many difficult problems of statistical methodology and the proper specification of empirical data. Numerous studies have been made in recent years and it may now be possible to determine a range of empirically plausible demand elasticities for particular commodity classes and countries.[3] The estimation of supply elasticities is another matter altogether, however, and there is comparatively little information on what these elasticities may be. In any event, assuming that one had the relevant information on elasticities and on the ratio of domestic consumption and of domestic production to imports, it would be possible to determine how imports would change in response to alternative tariff reductions, how tariff revenues would be affected, and what the effects on economic welfare would be. One would then be able to choose among tariff formulae based upon the estimated welfare effects. It might be mentioned parenthetically that the estimated changes in tariff revenues, based on this simple model, would be of concern only to the importing country since the price to foreign suppliers is assumed to remain constant.

In actuality, the situation will be more complicated since world prices will not be constant. It would then be necessary to know both the elasticity of domestic and foreign demand and the elasticity of domestic and foreign supply in order to estimate the effects of alternative tariff reductions on imports, tariff revenues, and economic welfare. The information requirements of an exercise like this cannot unfortunately be satisfied given the existing state of knowledge. One may be forced then to revert to the existing state of knowledge. One may be forced then to revert to the simpler model outlined above, although even here the information base is limited. This suggests that assumed values may have to be relied upon for many of the relevant elasticities in evaluating alternative tariff formulae. It would be desirable accordingly to experiment with different assumptions concerning these elasticities and to determine how sensitive the results might be.

In estimating the effects of tariff reductions on imports, one was abstracting from the effects on exports. Unfortunately, the export effects are more complex, for what is needed here is information especially on the market shares of different countries in exports to particular destinations together with knowledge of the degree to which different countries' exports substitute for one another as the result of relative price changes. One approach that can be followed is to adapt a world trade model so that the country and commodity impacts of tariff changes can be estimated. While models exist that can be used for this purpose, they have not yet been perfected to the point where they can handle fairly low levels of aggregation. The best that may be done with these models is to stimulate the effects of alternative tariff cuts for the major one-digit SITC commodity groups, certain particular commodities within these groups, and for total trade. These exercises, although limited, might nevertheless be useful in providing insights into the trade-balance implications of tariff changes and into the possible impacts on national GNP and employment levels.

In view of the relatively small changes in import and export prices likely to result from most tariff reductions together with the presumptions that the concessions will be balanced unilaterally and staged over a given number of years, the macroeconomic impacts on total output and the level of employment will be small in magnitude and therefore manageable using overall domestic monetary and fiscal stabilization measures. However, while the aggregate effects of tariff reductions may be relatively small, there may be substantial changes in output and employment in individual industries. One must therefore be concerned with these microeconomic changes for they embody the allocative shifts that bring about the realization of the welfare gains from tariff reductions as well as the associated costs of adjustment.

Microeconomic Effects

Since tariffs drive a wedge between domestic and world prices, they tend to divert resources from industries that are relatively more efficient to those that are less efficient. If one views the spectrum of a country's industrial structure in terms of comparative advantage, the most efficient export industries will be at one end and the least efficient import-competing industries at the other end. As an aid in tariff negotiations, it would thus be helpful if industries could be arranged from the most to the least efficient in order to identify the ones that would expand or contract in response to tariff reductions. Unfortunately, this may be very difficult to do.

The main problem is that comparative advantage is a multidimensional phenomenon, which is a fact that has become increasingly well documented especially in studies of the determinants of the commodity composition of trade in manufactures of the U.S. and other industrialized countries.[4] These studies have evolved in the past two decades beginning with simplistic models in which the structure of trade was to be explained in terms of a country's endowments of physical capital and the labor force. As the models were brought closer to reality, they have been broadened to include a country's: (1) endowment of human capital; (2) technological characteristics as reflected in the employment distribution of highly skilled individuals and expenditures on R & D; (3) innovative character as reflected in the introduction of new and improved products and processes; (4) ability to exploit economies of scale; and, finally, (5) the level and structure of tariffs and other impediments to trade.

With the present state of knowledge, one could say, for example, that U.S. industries that are net exporters can be characterized as: employing relatively large amounts of human capital; being technologically dynamic in terms of the skill attributes of their employees, relative expenditures on R & D, and innovativeness; perhaps realizing economies of scale; and probably not hampered seriously by foreign tariffs. U.S. net importers would then reflect the obverse of the foregoing economic characteristics together with the existing domestic tariff levels and structure. Knowing that U.S. net exporting and net importing industries can be characterized as just noted is an important accomplishment. It does not follow, however, that a country's industries can be arrayed on some scale from the most to the least efficient.

Such a ranking might be possible if a unidimensional indicator of comparative advantage could be constructed. It has been suggested in this regard, especially by Keesing,[5] that a measure of human capital or skill mix might be used. While this is plausible to a certain extent, it is important to note that the human capital-skill factors have accounted for less than half of the observed variation in industry trade balances for fairly aggregate 2-digit data in studies that have been made for the U.S. And it is noteworthy further that when 3-digit and 4-digit data were used, the explanatory power of the human capital-skill factors was diminished considerably.[6] It would be undesirable therefore to rely heavily on unidimensional rankings of industries. If this conclusion is correct, it might be asked whether the parameters from a multiple regression analysis could be utilized to indicate the relative importance of certain variables. This would be possible in a statistical sense, but, unfortunately, there is no way to combine this information to obtain industry rankings as such.

The difficulties in ranking industries by some specified criteria do not of course vitiate the principle of comparative advantage and the gains from trade. As mentioned earlier, one might choose among alternative tariff-reduction formulae on the basis of estimate changes in economic welfare subject to certain specified assumptions about secondary effects and parameter values. However, if the interest lies in the microeconomic aspects of tariff reductions, it is necessary to work within a framework that will yield estimates of the impacts on output and employment by industry.

For this purpose, the changes in imports and exports due to the tariff reductions must be combined with information on industry output and employment. What is especially important here is to determine the extent to which industry output will contract or expand in response to the price changes that are brought about by the tariff reductions. As already mentioned, however, very little is known about the magnitudes of these supply responses so that it may be necessary to experiment with different assumed values. Once the output changes are estimated, information is needed on the labor-output coefficients for the industries directly affected and for the indirect labor effects that may be experienced from changes in related industries. These labor-output coefficients can be obtained from input-output studies that are broken down by industry. The main difficulty here is that the coefficients themselves are subject to change through times as relative input prices are altered, but there exist procedures to estimate the changes in these coefficients.

Using these data and relationships between output and employment, estimates can then be made of changes in employment due to the tariff changes. Separate calculations can be made of the unemployment that may occur as certain industries are forced to contract due to increased imports and of the increased employment due to the expansion of export industries. Presumably, if full employment policies are pursued, the workers that may become unemployed due to the tariff changes will more readily find alternative employment. There may nevertheless be a substantial time lag before this adjustment is completed. The size of these adjustment costs will depend upon the number of workers involved, their average wages, and the duration of their unemployment.

While there may be a significant margin of error in the calculations of the adjustment costs due to the uncertainty of the elasticity and labor-output parameters, these calculations should none the less be indicative of the industries that appear to be the most vulnerable to competition from increased imports. In these instances, it may well be that short-run adjustment costs could exceed the welfare benefits that may ensue from the tariff reductions so that these industries may be treated as exceptions in any general negotiating formula. The issue then becomes one of designing policies for the excepted industries that will minimize the costs of transition, for example, by lengthening the time period for the stages of tariff reduction or to assure that appropriate adjustment assistance will be forthcoming.

The foregoing analysis relates only to the direct impact of the tariff cuts on the sectors in question. It might be desirable therefore, depending on the information available, to take into account the effects on other producing sectors and the effects on the country's exchange rate to the extent that the tariff changes result in a positive or negative effect on the country's trade balance.

It is possible and, in any case, probably necessary to simplify some of the foregoing steps because of lack of information. This is especially true, as noted, with respect to the absence of systematic and reliable data on demand and supply elasticities. This suggests therefore that a good deal of "guesstimation" will be required in analysing and in attempting to quantify the *economic* effects of tariff reductions. As things stand at present, using the GATT Tariff Study, it is a straightforward exercise in computer programming to determine the effects of alternative formulate for tariff reductions on the level and composition of tariffs. This is a most important first step since the depth of cut and the consequent estimated price changes provide the raw materials for determining what the economic effects of the reductions may be. It is of interest therefore to assess what has been done thus far in the evaluation process and to offer some comments on other possible directions.

III. THE EVALUATION PROCESS

Statistical Analysis

The most pertinent work that has been done on alternative tariff formulae is by the Office of International Trade Policy in the U.S. Commerce Department. Among the various tariff formulae they have considered are: (1) the "maximum authority" under the Trade Reform Act of the U.S.; (2) various illustrative formulae suggested by the GATT Tariff Study Working Party in which the degree of tariff reductions depends upon the initial height of the tariff, according to a particular algebraic formula; (3) the British formula in which there are several rounds of reduction, with each reduction equalling the initial height of the tariff; (4) the Japanese formula in which percentage tariff reductions would vary within initial tariff intervals, with the object of achieving a certain degree of harmonization of rates among countries; (5) the U.S. harmonization formula that seeks to take into account the difference between the Most-Favored-Nation tariff rate and the lowest existing preferential rate; and (6) the lowest Brussels Tariff Nomenclature (BTN) average formula in which the tariff would be reduced to the lowest average rate of a country within a predetermined group of countries. These formulae by no means exhaust the possibilities, which seem limitless considering the many permutations and combinations imaginable.

In any event, it is relatively easy, on the basis of the GATT Tariff Study, to determine the percentage tariff reductions that would result for the major negotiating countries if any of the foregoing formulae were to be implemented. The percentage cuts will vary naturally by country, depending on the height and distribution of the individual tariff rates and the weights used for the purposes of aggregation.

Given the tariff reductions, it is then possible to estimate the losses in tariff revenues on existing trade, and more importantly, the import-price reductions that may occur due to the tariff change. Then, using some guesstimate(s) of the price elasticity of import demand, the increase in imports due to alternative tariff reductions can be estimated. It is also possible to determine how a country's exports might change, assuming that market shares will remain constant following the tariff reduction. The net change in trade can then be calculated.

It is noteworthy that the U.S. and EC-9 have appreciably different proportions of industrial imports subject to duty, due to there being zero tariffs on intra-EC trade in industrial products. This fact has occasioned interest in a harmonization formula, such as (5) above, that would be designed to reduce the degree of preference afforded to intra-EC as compared to external-EC trade. Such a formula would presumably be applicable to other preferential arrangements, such as the Automotive Products Trade Agreement between the U.S. and Canada. The premise of the harmonization formula is that existing preferential arrangements have on balance led to more trade being diverted than created. As mentioned earlier, there is no *a priori* basis for determining whether a preferential arrangement leads to greater trade creation or trade diversion. Only detailed factual studies can answer this question. Several studies have indeed been made of the effects that the EC formation has had on trade in industrial products, and the consensus seems to be that trade creation has substantially exceeded trade diversion.[7] While it is possible that the EC enlargement could change this conclusion, there is no clear indication as yet. It would appear therefore that there is not much basis for arguing in favor of such a harmonization formula. Furthermore, it must be realized that the EC's common external tariff is one of the basis components of European union.

In comparing the different formulae, there is an issue of what is permissible in terms of existing legislative authority and what individual countries will in fact accept. Since the U.S. will play a dominant role in the negotiations and since the permissible reductions written into the Trade Reform Act (TRA) are quite substantial, this suggests that the TRA maximum authority might be used as a standard of comparison for other formulae. If the TRA maximum authority were in fact fully implemented, indications are that it would be but a short additional step to complete removal of industrial tariffs by the major industrialized countries.

Finally, the statistical analysis might suggest that, depending on the formula, countries will experience different changes in their balances of trade. This in itself should present little cause for concern since the exchange-rate effects would probably be relatively small. By the same token, countries might attempt to counterbalance the estimated changes in their trade balance with other possible concessions on NTBs or on agricultural imports in the course of the negotiations.

LDC Trade

One important issue that has yet to be addressed in the evaluation process concerns the impact of tariff reductions on trade with the LDCs. It will be realized that in the Kennedy Round there was concern that the reductions negotiated were more favorable to the advanced countries than to the LDCs, and that there was apparently some basis for this conclusion. With the institution of the Generalized System of Preferences (GSP), the LDCs may take the view that multilateral negotiations will tend to undermine their preferential margins. This would be true in an arithmetic sense, although there is no reason to believe that, considering the way the GSP has been implemented, the LDCs have in reality received much benefit.[8]

Nevertheless, since the LDC interests deserve serious consideration, more attention should be given to evaluating alternative tariff formulae from their standpoint. The first step would be to identify products that are presently and potentially important LDC exports to the advanced countries, to determine existing tariff levels on these goods, and to estimate what the effects of alternative reductions might be. Some attention could also be given to changes in effective tariff rates on imports from LDCs. However, if the principle is followed of making sizable nominal-tariff reductions on final products of interest to the LDCs, substantial reductions of effective tariff rates would be bound to occur. It would not be necessary therefore to gather all of the information on input coefficients that would be required to calculate effective tariff rates.

Unit of Account

A further issue concerns the unit of account that should be used in the evaluation process. This was not a problem during the Kennedy Round negotiations because there were not important changes in exchange rates. The difficulty now is that the level and composition of trade in the U.S. and elsewhere have been subject to change due to differential rates of inflation and exchange-rate variations.

It is not clear that there is any completely satisfactory way to resolve this issue, but reasonable compromise may be to base the unit of account on a basket of currencies comprising the SDR. The basis problem concerns the reference period and the weights that are to be assigned to the changes that occur. Put simply, tariffs could be weighted according to the composition of trade that existed in some past reference period when exchange rates were unchanged and international rates of inflation comparable. Alternatively, the most recent period available could be used as a reference. The difficulty is that, in the interim, the composition of trade may have been altered due to relative changes in inflation and in exchange rates. A compromise solution would be to take the average of the two reference periods.

A decision must be made then as to the units in which the changes are to be measured. If, for example, U.S. dollars or German marks were used, one would obtain somewhat different results because these currencies have not remained fixed *vis-à-vis* each other and with respect to other major currencies. The most reasonable approach that suggests itself is to use the SDR as the unit of account and to relate each country's exchange rate to it, using as weights the relative importance of individual countries in world trade. This procedure would not circumvent the problem of how to compare changes through time when the composition of trade used for weighting purposes is changing. But if the weights changed slowly, the discrepancies in measurement would not be substantial in the short run. If this reasoning is correct, there is no need to get bogged down in debate over whether to see the U.S. dollar or some other national currency or currencies as the unit of account.

The fact that there have been substantial realignments of trade in recent years in response to differential inflation and changes in exchange rates would be a further reason for using world-trade weights for purposes of tariff averaging and for evaluating the effects of alternative tariff-cutting formulae. The advantage of world-trade weights would be to neutralize the differences among countries with respect to the manner in which their foreign trade has responded to inflationary and exchange-rate developments.

Much of the concern over the unit of account to be used for the trade negotiations stems from the preoccupation with balancing concessions in terms of effects on the level of imports of the negotiating countries. What is more fundamental, however, is the effect that tariff reductions will have on domestic income and the level and composition of employment.

Income and Employment Effects

As was mentioned earlier, the macroeconomic effects of tariff changes on trade flows and GNP can be estimated in a manner analogous to what has been done for changes in exchange rates. For example, the Project LINK model of the world economy would be capable of accomplishing this task.[9] However, neither this model nor presently existing models designed to analyse changes in trade flows would be able to provide much information on tariff impacts by industry.

Work is in progress at the University of Michigan and elsewhere on partial equilibrium and general equilibrium models designed to measure impacts at the industry level for the major negotiating countries.[10] The advantage of these models is that they are systematic and self-contained, although subject of course to certain simplifying assumptions. They can be implemented on the basis of empirically-estimated relationships, or when such relationships cannot be measured adequately, assumed and hopefully plausible guesstimates can be employed. Since it is the domestic economic effects at the industry level that are of importance for tariff reduction, it would be desirable to extend the evaluation process along these lines.

The Michigan and related models are well suited for this task because they cut across industries and across countries. Since tariff levels and changes are important determining variables in the models, it should be possible to stimulate the TRA maximum authority and any of the other tariff formulae mentioned earlier. This would require processing the necessary underlying data and calculating the empirical relationships involved before performing the various simulations of alternative tariff reductions. This could be speeded up, however, if hypothetical, but hopefully plausible, values of some of the parameters of the models could be used when needed. The outcome of such analysis will not of course be totally precise but should nevertheless provide the negotiators with indications of the potential industry impacts that are the crux of the negotiations themselves.

Presumably each party in the negotiations will conduct its own investigations and will alter its negotiating position based on its evaluation of the domestic impacts of the tariff changes. Since it is this assessment that is at stake in determining how beneficial or costly tariff concessions may be to each country, it should be clear that issues like tariff dispersion, preferential margins, and the unit of account are of secondary importance.

Conclusion

The statistical analysis of alternative tariff formulae based upon the GATT Tariff Study is already far along. Given that the TRA maximum authority is quite substantial and that it sets an upper bound on the U.S. negotiating position, this formula can serve conveniently as a reference point for analysing other alternatives.

The evaluating process needs to give more attention to LDC trace. This should not be with reference to the GSP, but rather to the opportunities that would benefit the LDCs from multilateral reductions in tariffs on finished goods that they are capable of exporting.

The choice of a unit account can be handled in terms of a basket of currencies comprising the SDR. Using world-trade weights for this purpose and for tariff averaging should minimize the differential impacts among countries of varying rates of inflation and changes in exchange rates.

The final consideration relates to the evaluation of the impact of tariff reductions on employment by industry in the negotiating countries. Since it is these *domestic* effects that are the crux of the negotiations, the evaluation process should be brought more directly to bear on their measurement.

NOTES

This paper is an outgrowth of a memorandum prepared on a consulting basis in the summer of 1974 for the Office of the Special Representative for Trade Negotiations in

Washington, D.C. I am indebted to Geza Feketekuty and his staff for helpful comments.

1 Many of the issues to be discussed are pertinent also to the evaluation of alternatives for reducing or eliminating nontariff barriers on both industrial and agricultural products. However, it would be necessary for analytical purposes to convert the NTBs to tariff equivalents, which is often rather difficult to do. We shall therefore confine our attention here to tariffs.

2 See GATT, *Basic Documentation for Tariff Study*, Geneva, 1974. Underlying this documentation are computer tapes containing information on post-Kennedy Round (1972) tariffs and imports by country of origin for 1970 and 1971 for each of the major industrialized countries and the European Community as a group.

3 In this regard, see Robert M. Stern *et al.*, *Price Elasticities in International Trade: A Compilation and Annotated Bibliography of Recent Research*, London: Macmillan, forthcoming.

4 For an interpretive survey of this research, see Robert M. Stern, "Testing Trade Theories", in P. B. Kenen (ed.), *International Trade and Finance: Frontiers for Research*, Cambridge: Cambridge University Press, 1975.

5 See Donald B. Keesing, "Estimating the Gains from Trade for Purposes of Tariff Negotiations", Office of Management and Budget, Washington, D.C., May 1973, mimeo.

6 See William H. Branson and Helen B. Junz, "Trends in U.S. Trade and Comparative Advantage", *Brookings Papers on Economic Activity*, No. 2, 1971, pp. 285–338; and William H. Branson, "U.S. Comparative Advantage: Some Further Results", *Brookings Papers on Economic Activity*, No. 3, 1971, pp. 754–9.

7 See Bela Balassa, "Trade Creation and Trade Diversion in the European Common Market: An Appraisal of the Evidence", *Manchester School*, June 1974, pp. 93–135.

8 See, for example, Richard N. Cooper, "The European Community's System of Generalized Tariff Preferences: A Critique", *Journal of Development Studies*, July 1972, pp. 379–94.

9 The LINK model is described in many different publications. See, for example, R. J. Ball (ed.), *The International Linkage of National Economic Models*, Amsterdam: North-Holland Publishing Co., 1973; and Keith Johnson and Lawrence R. Klein, "LINK Model Simulations of International Trade: An Evaluation of the Effects of Currency Realignment", *Journal of Finance*, May 1974, pp. 617–30.

10 See Alan V. Deardorff and Robert M. Stern, "Partial Equilibrium Estimation of the Effects of Trade Liberalization", paper presented at the Winter Meetings of the Econometric Society, San Francisco, 28 December 1974; and Edward E. Leamer and Robert M. Stern, "The International Specialization of Labor", in process. Robert E. Baldwin of the University of Wisconsin, Madison, is also working on the trade and employment effects of alternative tariff reductions.

15. The Most-Favored-Nation Clause

J. Viner

COMMERCIAL TREATIES, since the sixteenth century and even earlier, have commonly contained the most-favored-nation pledge, which in its general form provides that each of the contracting countries shall grant to the other any privilege or favor in commercial matters which it has hitherto granted or may subsequently grant to any third country. In the latter half of the nineteenth century its use became general and, with minor exceptions, international tariff relations, if on a friendly basis, were in accordance with the most-favored-nation principle. The pledge, if it was unconditional in form, constituted a mutual guarantee of equality of treatment as between foreign countries. Even before 1914, however, there was no unanimity as to the merits of the principle. One country in particular, the United States, adhered to it only with qualifications which deprived it of most of its virtues, and France always tended to find the obligations which it imposed irksome, because, in so far as Germany was concerned, they were commonly regarded as not voluntary because permanently embodied in the Frankfurt Treaty of 1871, a treaty representing to France the terms of peace dictated by a victor to the vanquished after a disastrous war. The Great War, which divided a great part of the world into two hostile camps, and which imposed upon the non-belligerents the onerous necessity of carrying out a role of neutrality of degrees of benevolence to the belligerents which never met the latter's expectations, contributed still further to deprive equality of treatment of some of its nineteenth-century attractiveness and to lend reinforcement of a chauvinistic sort to the objections which had long been made against the most-favored-nation principle on economic grounds. Was it reasonable to adhere to a principle which, when the war ended, would prevent you from giving to your Allies, and to those neutrals who had been well-disposed towards you during the great struggle, any better treatment than that which you would feel disposed to extend to the enemy countries and the less friendly neutrals?

On grounds such as these the Allied countries, at their Economic Conference held in Paris in 1916, and under French leadership, agreed in general terms to an ambitious post-war programme of systematic discrimination in economic matters. Countries were to be classified in different categories on various grounds intelligible only in terms of wartime psychology, and to each category a different level of tariff treatment was to be applied. When peace finally came, however, England had lost her enthusiasm for the project; the United States, which had never had any part in it, was vigorously opposed to it; and France was left to proceed alone on the lines laid out in 1916 if she so desired. President Wilson, influenced largely by his early recognition of the dangers and the evils involved in the continuation of economic hostilities after the military arms had been laid down, attempted, in the third of his famous Points, to obtain general acceptance of the most-favored-nation principle as an established principle of international law. He only succeeded, however, in securing the adoption, as Article 23 of the Covenant of the League of Nations, of the empty because ambiguous and indefinite formula pledging all the member countries to grant each other "equitable treatment."

French dissatisfaction with the most-favored-nation principle survived the end of the war. On December 15, 1918, M. Clementel, French Minister of Commerce, declared that "the Government has denounced all commercial conventions which embody the most-favoured-nation clause. That clause will not reappear. It will never again come back to place itself at cross purposes with our efforts. It will never again poison our tariff policy." But France found the process of getting rid of the most-favored-nation clause more difficult and more costly than she had anticipated. To some of the low-tariff countries she continued provisionally to grant most-favored-nation treatment after their conventional rights to such treatment had been cancelled. With other low-tariff countries France negotiated short-term extensions of pre-war most-favored-nation treaties. Even in the new treaties negotiated after the war she found it necessary to incorporate the most-favored-nation clause, because other countries were unwilling to grant her any concessions as long as she reserved the right to render nugatory the concessions which she gave in return by granting to third countries even better terms on the same commodities. At first, these post-war pledges of most-favored-nation treatment were limited in their application to commodities specifically listed in each treaty, or to concessions granted to third countries limitrophe with the other signatory and therefore likely to be its chief competitors in the trade with France. While reluctant to concede an unlimited pledge of most-favored-nation treatment herself, France, however, insisted upon getting such a pledge in her favor from the countries with whom she negotiated commercial treaties. But only small countries to whom the French market was of great importance and whose own markets were not, individually, vital to French export trade, were weak enough in bargaining power to be unable to refuse acceptance of arrangements on this unequal basis. In some cases, moreover, the inequality was more apparent than real and in withholding the unlimited pledge France was saving appearances only, since the commodities listed as subject to the pledge covered all the trade, actual or prospective, that was of any consequence. The great commercial nations were even less yielding, and to secure commercial treaties with them France was obliged to grant to Germany, Italy, Belgium, and Switzerland unlimited pledges of most-favored-nation treatment. Within a few years the wartime plans of France to free herself from the obligations of the most-favored-nation clause had quite definitely proved unrealizable, at least for the time being.

But although the most-favored-nation principle still survives, it is no longer accepted as a matter of routine that the tariff relations between friendly countries should be governed by that principle, and departures from the principle are at the present moment more widespread and more important than at any time in the last century. It is quite apparent also that the idea of its general abandonment, which before the war was rarely encountered, is now receiving serious consideration in many quarters. The most-favored-nation principle now appears to be definitely on the defensive, and, while it has shown great survival power in the past, there is no ground for assurance that a concerted attack on it in which a number of countries participated simultaneously would not put an end to the dominance of the principle of equality of treatment in tariff matters. It is worth while, therefore, to examine the objections which have been made against the most-favored-nation clause, and to compare its merits and defects with those of the principles which have been suggested as possible substitutes.

There has been a common tendency to expect more of the most-favored-nation clause than it can contribute. In a world in which each country is engaged in feverish attempts to acquire economic advantages at whatever cost to other countries, the most-favored-nation clause is not more than a mildly moderating factor in the process of pursuit of prosperity by means of multiplication of the barriers to trade. It does not in any direct or concrete way promote free trade. It is not even certain that its general tendency is to make tariffs lower, instead of higher, than they would be in its absence. Its one contribution to both economic welfare and international amity is that it proscribes discrimination in the tariff treatment of foreign countries.

On economic grounds a number of objections can be made against discriminatory tariffs which do not apply, or apply only in much less degree, to uniform tariffs of even a higher average level. A tariff that is high, but uniform in its treatment of imports regardless of their origin, may divert trade from the channels which it would follow if allowed freely to choose its own path much less than would a more moderate tariff which applies different treatment to imports according to their country of origin. Suppose that under free trade country A would find it to its advantage to import a particular commodity from B, and that even with a high duty it is still not possible to produce the commodity at home at a profit to its producers, so that it continues to be imported from B. While the tariff reduces the volume of trade, it does so only as a revenue measure, and still permits the commodity to be produced there where it can be produced most cheaply. Suppose, now, that the duty is reduced by half on imports from a third country, C, and that by virtue of this preferential treatment C can undersell B and capture A's trade. The result of the discrimination in favor of C is that the commodity, which could be most cheaply produced in B and would be produced there even if A had a high tariff, provided it was non-discriminatory, is now produced in C, where the conditions for its production are comparatively unfavorable. The reduction in duty, because it is discriminatory and not uniformly extended to all, operates as a deterrent instead of a stimulus to the optimum allocation of the world's resources in production.

In so far, moreover, as country A follows a discriminatory tariff policy, it is impossible for the producers, even those in countries that are treated with special favor, to plan safely and intelligently how best to meet the future needs of its consumers, for at any moment the entire economic foundation of their trade may be destroyed by the withdrawal of the preferential treatment or by the grant of even more favorable terms to a competing country. Even uniform tariffs are a sufficiently disturbing factor to the stability of industries dependent on foreign markets for the disposal of their products, for an increase in the tariff may suddenly shut you out of an important market to the advantage of domestic producers. If in addition there is the further danger that preferential tariff treatment may at any moment be given to a competitor in a third country, production for export tends to become a hazardous occupation indeed.

The economic injury resulting from a discriminatory tariff policy, moreover, is not confined to the country subjected to the unfavorable discrimination but extends to the country which is following a discriminatory policy. The hazards which result therefrom to the industries in foreign countries which supply its markets with their products, by impairing their financial stability and acting as a check to their development, lessen their capacity to serve its needs efficiently and cheaply. There are more direct disadvantages, moreover, to the discriminating country. To abstract from the question of the comparative merits of protection and free trade, let us assume that the discriminating country, A, does not itself produce the commodity in question, that it can be produced by countries B and C, and that imports into A are free of duty if from B, but dutiable if from C. What are the consequences for A of the remission of duty on B's product, while C's product remains dutiable?

There are several possibilities under these circumstances, depending upon B's capacity to supply A with its needs. Suppose that B can produce as cheaply as C and in quantities sufficient to satisfy A's wants even at the price which would prevail if imports from C were also free of duty. The duty on C's product will then have no adverse effect on A, unless the producers in B combine to take advantage of their privileged position by exacting from A a price higher than C's price by all or part of the duty on C's product. Next, suppose that B cannot produce sufficient to satisfy A's wants, and that imports from C will continue to some extent in spite of the discriminatory duty on its product. The price in A will then be C's price plus the amount of the duty on C's product. But duty will be collected only on imports from C, and the producers in B will get a price for their product equal to C's price plus the duty. As compared with free import the consumers in A will be paying on all its imports a price higher approximately by the amount of the duty, against which there will be as an offset only the customs revenue collected on the imports from C. As compared with a uniform duty on imports from both B and C, the consumers in A will be paying the same price, but A will be losing the customs revenue which otherwise would have been collected on imports from B, and which now goes as a subsidy to B's producers at the expense of A's national treasury.

That discriminatory duties work in practice in this way was shown inductively in a study made by the writer some years ago for the United States Tariff Commission of the effect of the preferential free admission of Hawaiian sugar into the United States prior to the annexation of the Hawaiian Islands in 1898, and of the preferential reduction of the duty on Cuban sugar from 1903 on. In each case, as long as it continued to be necessary for the United States to import full-duty sugar in order to meet the needs of domestic consumption the American price was the world price plus the *full* duty, and the effect of the preferential remission of duty was simply that the producers in the favored territories got, at the expense of the American customs revenue and without any discernible benefit to the American consumer, a substantial bounty which amounted, through the years, to surprisingly large sums of money.

Another advantage, though of less importance, of equality of treatment in tariff matters is that it renders unnecessary the exact determination of the origin of imports, and makes customs administration simpler, less expensive, and less burdensome to commerce. But the economic disadvantages of discriminatory tariffs, important though they unquestionably are, are much less serious than their contribution to international ill-will. Abundant experience shows that public opinion reconciles itself with amazing speed, especially in times of prosperity, to high foreign tariffs, provided that they do not discriminate in favor of third countries, but that its resentment against tariff discriminations, even when small in amount and of little commercial importance, tends to be bitter and enduring. Whether it is rational or not, moreover, the resentment against tariff discrimination tends to be just as strong when your own country is doing likewise as when the discrimination from which you suffer is wanton and unprovoked. When two countries discriminate against each other in tariff matters, we have a "tariff war" which has in it most of the ingredients necessary to prepare the way for the more serious type of war. Tariff discriminations are not only economically injurious to both parties, but they are extremely dangerous, especially when directed against powerful nations.

Let us turn now to the case which its opponents have made out against the unconditional most-favored-nation clause. It is sometimes claimed that the use of this clause, instead of tending to lessen the barriers to international trade, on the contrary tends to add to them. Whereas country A, it is argued, might be willing to grant reductions of duty to country B if there were no obligation to extend them immediately to all other countries, it is less likely to be willing to do so when subject to the obligation resulting from the most-favored-nation clause of generalizing the concession to all countries with whom it has commercial treaties. But grounds have already been presented above for holding that it is in the interest of a country to generalize its concessions, and the objection against the unconditional most-favored-nation clause often made in the United States, and in recent years also in Europe, that it is an obstacle to the negotiation of arrangements providing for the exchange of exclusive concessions, mistakes the chief virtue of the clause for a defect.

A more plausible objection is that the most-favored-nation principle is particularly ill-suited for dealing with countries with prohibitively high single-schedule tariffs, who rely on their most-favored-nation treaties to bring them all the concessions which other countries engage reciprocally to grant to each other, but are under no real pressure to make any concessions in return. There is no ground for doubt, in fact, that much of the present wave of criticism of the unconditional most-favored-nation principle in Europe arises out of dissatisfaction with the position in which the European countries find themselves in the present state of their tariff relations with the United States. The latter country has a single-schedule tariff of skyscraper altitude. Presumably because of the most-favored-nation treaties or agreements which it has with most countries, it benefits from the reductions in duty which result from the tariff treaties which European countries negotiate with each other. But it grants nothing in return except equality, i.e., equally bad treatment to all. Surely, say the critics of the most-favored-nation principle, this is not an equitable situation. Perhaps not. But it would be foolish to attribute either the existent situation or the absence of more widespread tariff retaliation against the United States to such temporary and terminable things as the most-favored-nation agreements with the United States. In any case, the remedy for a situation such as the one described, if there is a remedy, is to be found not in the abolition, among the countries which do extend to each other reasonable or at least endurable tariff treatment, of equality of treatment with all its mutual advantages, but in withdrawing from most-favored-nation obligations towards countries whose tariffs are regarded as going beyond reasonable limits. Whatever may be the proper methods of dealing with a tariff drunkard, quarrelling with and abusing one's sober neighbors is surely not one of them!

Resting on similar reasoning, and subject to a similar rejoinder, is the argument that the most-favored-nation clause hinders effective tariff bargaining in dealing even with countries who would be prepared to make concessions from their general tariff if it were necessary in order to secure counter-concessions from other countries. If country A has already made substantial concessions to countries B and C and is not prepared to reduce its tariff any further, or if the concessions that it has already made to B and C cover all the commodities that are of interest to D and E, these latter countries, relying upon the fact that the most-favored-nation clause will automatically bring them the concessions that A has already granted to B and C, will stand fast and refuse to yield anything in return. In most cases, however, D and E would find that the concessions that A has made to B and C do not altogether meet their needs, and that additional concessions, of special interest to themselves, can be obtained only if they give some compensation in return. In any case there is available an adequate remedy for this state of affairs, and one already systematically practised by some countries, and especially Germany, before the war, namely, the association of the most-favored-nation pledge with the negotiation of mutually satisfactory tariff treaties. By having all commercial treaties, including their most-favored-nation clauses, expire simultaneously in so-called *Kometenjahre* and renewing them only upon the successful negotiation of new tariff arrangements, a country can fully protect itself against any loss in its bargaining power with reference to country D resulting from the grant of concessions to B and C. If this procedure is followed, the right to receive most-favored-nation treatment in another country becomes a privilege to be enjoyed only if one's own tariff is made acceptable to that country, and the use of the clause becomes an aid instead of a hindrance to successful tariff bargaining.

It is frequently claimed that the increasing tendency towards "specialization" of tariffs, or the detailed classification of commodities for tariff purposes with a consequent multiplication of the number of tariff items, operates to deprive the most-favored-nation pledge of all significance, since concessions can then be granted in such terms as to make them inapplicable to the products of third countries. Such is no doubt the theoretical tendency of the progressive specialization in tariffs which has been under way in most countries in the last thirty years. But so far as I am aware none of the many writers who have made of this tendency the basis for serious objection to the most-favored-nation practice has presented convincing evidence that in practice tariff specialization has actually impaired in any substantial degree the effectiveness of the most-favored-nation clause. With monotonous uniformity such writers present as the sole concrete demonstration that specialization is intended to, and in operation does, have this result the following unimportant item in the German conventional tariff of 1902, resulting from a tariff treaty with Switzerland:

> Large dapple mountain cattle or brown cattle reared at a spot at least 300 metres above sea level and having at least one month's grazing each year at a spot at least 800 metres above sea level.

If it were a common practice to carry tariff specialization to this extreme length, the most-favored-nation clause would lose its significance, and while it would still not be capable of doing any harm it would at least be without possibility of doing much good. But the fact that all the writers who use this argument against the most-favored-nation clause cite this trivial item and it alone as tangible evidence in support of their position justifies scepticism that tariff specialization has been carried to any such absurd lengths either by Germany or by other countries. The fact that no formula is proof against bad faith and that in the last resort reliance must be had on the mutual exercise by both parties of a reasonable degree of common honesty is, unfortunately, a defect from which international treaty relations suffer in common with all other species of human relations. Perhaps some measure of assurance against this type of abuse can be secured through the general inclusion in most-favored-nation pledges of a provision such as the following in the protocol of the commercial treaty of 1923 between Great Britain and Germany:

> The Treaty of Commerce and Navigation signed this day being based on the principle of the most-favored-nation, both Parties to the Treaty undertake to give the widest possible interpretation to that principle. In particular . . . they undertake to abstain from using their respective Customs tariffs or any other charges as a means of discrimination against the trade of the other, and to give sympathetic consideration to any cases that may be brought to their notice in which, whether as a result of the rates of Customs duties or charges themselves or of arbitrary or unreasonable Customs classification, any such discrimination can be shown to have arisen.

In recent years, when there has been much talk of the possibility of establishing customs unions in various parts of Europe, it has been urged as an objection to the most-favored-nation principle that it presents an obstacle to the elimination of trade barriers and even of political boundaries by the method of customs union. As a rule, customs unions probably constitute a forward step towards freer trade, since such unions are commonly established or proposed between neighboring countries, and the trade which would result if the tariff wall is removed between two adjoining countries is likely to be trade which in large part would persist if the duties on imports from third countries were also abolished. But whatever the merits of customs unions, those who desire them would be reasonable in objecting to the most-favored-nation principle if it stood in the way of their establishment. Such, however, is not the case. A country which foresees even the faint possibility that it may some day wish to enter into customs union with some particular country or countries usually takes the precaution of inserting in its commercial treaties a provision exempting tariff arrangements resulting from such union from the obligations of the most-favored-nation clause. Similar freedom of action is secured also by virtue of the "limitrophe" or adjacent country clause contained in many commercial treaties, which provides that concessions which may be granted to neighboring countries, or to specified countries with which there are close geographical or historical or economic relations, shall not be subject to the obligations imposed by the most-favored-nation principle, even when such arrangements fall short of complete customs union. So abundant are qualifications of this type in present-day commercial treaties that there are few really conceivable customs unions which could not be immediately established without violation of any existing most-favored-nation pledge. It would usually be a simple matter to secure the revision or termination of any treaties which did stand in the way of such union. (Some writers even assert, although I believe wrongly, that the most-favored-nation pledge is not applicable to arrangements resulting from the establishment of customs unions even when the pledge contains no express exemption of such arrangements from the obligations which it imposes.) In actual experience, moreover, few of the special tariff arrangements with neighboring countries which are dreamt of ever obtain realization, and of the very many clauses which have been introduced into commercial treaties in the last century providing for the exemption from most-favored-nation obligations of any customs-union arrangements, scarcely any have ever been invoked. I have not been able to find a single instance in the past in which the most-favored-nation clause proved to be a serious obstacle to the consummation of a customs union which was otherwise within the realm of practical politics.

The discussion so far has had reference only to the unconditional form of the most-favored-nation pledge. There is another form of the pledge, however, the "conditional" or "American" form, and in some quarters it is argued that it has greater merits than the unconditional form. The conditional form was invented by American statesmen and was introduced by the United States in her first commercial treaty, the treaty with France of February 6, 1778. Article III of that treaty contained the most-favored-nation clause in what had hitherto been its standard form, but it was followed by the proviso that if either party should grant any favor to a third country, the other party "shall enjoy the same favor, freely, if the concession was freely made, *or on allowing the same concession, if the concession was conditional.*" Under the conditional pledge, in other words, the obligation is to extend without specific compensation any concessions made to third countries without compensation, and to extend for equivalent compensation any concessions made to third countries for compensation. With a few exceptions due to inadvertence or ignorance on the part of the American negotiators, the United States, until 1923, uniformly used the conditional form, and even when she used the unconditional form she insisted upon interpreting it in the conditional sense. Latin-American countries and Japan, following the American example, also used the conditional form, but since they had single-schedule tariffs and made no special concessions to other countries, they rarely, if ever, had occasion to invoke the conditional provision. In Europe the conditional form was widely used from 1820 to 1860, but there also the general prevalence of single-schedule tariffs, the rarity of special tariff concessions, and the common practice of generalizing such concessions as were made irrespective of the existence of treaty obligations to do so, resulted in there being few instances of the application of the conditional provision.

For reasons which will later be made clear, the American State Department in 1923 adopted the unconditional form and proceeded to negotiate a completely new set of commercial treaties, in which the unconditional pledge of most-favored-nation treatment was to be substituted for the conditional pledge. There was thus presented the interesting phenomenon of a new enthusiasm in Europe for the conditional form of the most-favored-nation clause coinciding in time with the abandonment of that form by the country which for almost 150 years had been its chief and almost sole exponent. The abandonment by the United States of the conditional practice, it should be noted, however, was not complete. The United States tariff act of 1922 contained a number of "contingent duties," or duties whose amount depended on the amount of duty imposed by other countries on similar commodities imported from the United States. These duties, although unquestionably inconsistent with unconditional most-favored-nation practice, continued to be applied even after the change in policy proclaimed by the State Department. In the new tariff act of 1930, also, such duties are to be found.

The chief argument urged in support of the superiority of the conditional over the unconditional pledge, and the consideration which led to its original adoption by the United States is the argument, already familiar to us, that it is manifestly unfair that a country should be in a position to claim without compensation concessions which other countries have secured only by giving concessions in return. Such a claim can be established, as we have seen, under the unconditional practice, but under the conditional practice you can get what other countries have paid for only by paying the same price. This sounds equitable, but it works badly in practice.

In the first place, a country cannot follow the conditional practice towards some countries, and the unconditional towards others. The existence of a single unconditional most-favored-nation pledge in a country's treaties makes all the other pledges, whatever their form, unconditional in effect. Suppose that A has most-favored-nation treaties with countries C, D and E, of which C and D are conditional and E unconditional, and that A grants to B, for compensation, a reduction in tariff duties. C and D cannot claim from A the benefit of this tariff reduction for their own commodities on the ground that it has been given to B, unless they offer compensation for the reduction equivalent to that given by B. But E can claim the reduction unconditionally, and once it has been given to E freely, it must then be extended freely to C and D also. Whatever disadvantages the conditional practice may have, therefore, will apply to the tariff relations with all countries, whether these have been satisfactory to A or not, and it will not be possible to extend unconditional most-favored treatment to some countries while withholding it from others.[1]

Secondly if all the treaties into which a country enters contain the conditional pledge, then in actual operation the situation will be little, if at all, different from its granting no most-favored-nation pledges whatsoever. A conditional pledge by A to B is a pledge to extend freely to B what has been given freely to any third country, C, and to grant to B upon the same compensation what has been granted for compensation to any third country, C. Now countries rarely make concessions freely, unless to serve their own purposes, and in such cases they make them general. Such concessions would be obtained, therefore, even by a country which had no commercial treaty whatsoever with A, unless A, for some reason, wished deliberately to discriminate against that country alone. The obligation to grant freely to B what is granted freely to C is therefore of little significance to B. Even of less value to B is the obligation on the part of A to grant to B for equivalent compensation what is granted to C for compensation. The task of determining equivalence of compensation would always be difficult and necessarily a matter for negotiation. If A did not wish to extend the concession to B, it could always deny the equivalence of the compensation offered by B to that given by C. Moreover, if B is prepared to offer A substantial compensation for the extension to itself of the concessions granted by A to C, it does not need, and will not be aided by, the treaty right to have such offer considered by A. The conditional most-favored-nation practice, therefore, if universally followed, would in effect be simply a polite way of not practising most-favored-nation treatment at all.

This was virtually the situation for the United States while it followed the conditional practice. Dealing mainly with countries who were extending unconditional most-favored-nation treatment to other countries, the United States received, by virtue of her conditional most-favored-nation treaties, everything which she would have received if they had all been unconditional. But she gave nothing in return. If she gave special concessions for compensation to a particular country, she either refused outright to grant them on any terms to a third country, or she extended them to third countries on the basis of special bargains struck with them and wholly irrespective of whether these countries had any most-favored-nation rights or not. With a few minor and unintended exceptions, no country ever received any privilege in the United States in tariff matters by virtue of its most-favored-nation treaty with that country.

To those many statesmen and writers who regard a tariff concession which is confined to one country as more favorable economically for the country granting it than would be the same concession extended to most or all countries, the position of the United States under the conditional practice would seem ideal. Why then did the United States abandon its traditional policy which seemed to work so well? The sudden reversal of American policy was due to the recognition by a few American officials that the situation was changing adversely to the United States in several respects, and that it was likely that the attempt to persist in the conditional practice would result in serious difficulties. In the first case, it had for some time become increasingly difficult for the United States to secure the renewal of old or the negotiation of new treaties on the conditional basis, and she was without commercial treaties and subjected to serious tariff discrimination in several important countries. Secondly, other countries were threatening to adopt for themselves the conditional practice, and the principal advantages of that practice for the United States, as the American protectionist saw them, would disappear as soon as other countries also followed it. Thirdly, American export trade had changed in character, and was now more liable to, and capable of being more seriously injured by, foreign tariff discriminations than had formerly been the case. In the past the United States was chiefly an exporter of raw materials and foodstuffs, which foreign countries could not do without, and which in their own interests they admitted free of duty or at low duties irrespective of American tariff treatment of their own products. The situation was now radically different. American exports consisted now in large and steadily increasing proportions of manufactured commodities, and foreign countries were able, and to an increasing degree, willing, to impose heavy and discriminatory tariffs on such commodities. It had become more important and also more difficult for the United States to secure a guarantee of unconditional equality of treatment from other countries, and as long as the American tariff was higher than that of most other countries and as tariff bargaining involving reductions from that tariff was practically out of the question because of constitutional difficulties, it was vital for her to secure pledges for most-favored-nation treatment which were not in any way qualified, and especially which were not conditional upon the grant by the United States to foreign countries, in return for their minimum tariff rates, of compensation equivalent to that paid for them by third countries. There is no likelihood that the United States will ever again be able to operate as advantageously, even in appearance, under the conditional principle as she did before the War. Nor is it at all likely that any other country can reproduce the advantages which the United States then enjoyed: of being practically alone in following the conditional practice; of being able to secure from most countries the signature to treaties which under these circumstances operated conditionally for the United States but unconditionally for them; of being an exporter in the main of commodities which, because of their nature, were not liable to tariff discrimination; and of being, in spite of her high tariff, so important a market that few countries dared seriously to retaliate against her no matter how severe were the tariff burdens which she imposed upon their products.

The only other instance of any importance in which a country succeeded in maintaining apparently successful tariff relations with other countries while following the conditional practice, is afforded by the experience of Sardinia under Cavour in 1851. In that year Sardinia succeeded in negotiating with a number of countries tariff treaties which brought her important concessions, although Sardinia, in addition to the specific concessions which she granted in return, pledged herself only to conditional most-favored-nation treatment. These countries, apparently, did not regard the danger that Sardinia, by granting to third countries concessions still greater than those given to themselves, and to which they would have no claim, would render nugatory the concessions which they received, to be sufficiently great to render tariff arrangements with her on the conditional basis unacceptable. But before the year was over Sardinia found it necessary, in order to induce Austria to come to terms, to grant her a pledge of unconditional most-favored-nation treatment. As has been pointed out above, the grant to even a single country of unconditional most-favored-nation treatment would have the effect of making all the other treaties unconditional in their mode of operation. If, therefore, there was any net result for Sardinia in negotiating the earlier treaties on the conditional rather than the unconditional basis, it was probably that she did not secure as favorable terms from these other countries as she would have been able to secure if she had offered them an unconditional pledge in the first instance.

The unconditional most-favored-nation pledge is far from being a universal remedy for the ills which beset international economic relations, and for the most serious of them, exaggerated tariffs, it affords no relief whatsoever. It merely affords a guarantee that those countries bound by it and entitled to its benefits will receive and extend among themselves equality of tariff treatment, whether that equality is on a high or a low level. This guarantee of equality of treatment, however, is a valuable contribution to both economic prosperity and international goodwill, and in an age when such contributions are exceedingly rare in the field of commercial policy, there should be serious hesitation before anything is done which in any way impairs the strength of the guarantee.

NOTES

1 A form of conditional pledge could be devised, however, which would permit of conditional practice towards some countries and unconditional practice towards others. The conditional pledge could provide for the extension freely and without compensation only of such concessions made to third countries as originally, in the first instance of their being made, were granted without return compensation being received. A country C receiving such a pledge could not demand the gratuitous extension to itself of concessions made freely to E, if these concessions had originally been made to B for compensation. A clause of this type has never been used or suggested, however, as far as I know, and the objections to the conditional practice which follow would apply to this form in equal or even in greater degree.

16. Negotiating the Abolition of Non-Tariff Barriers

L. A. Winters

1. INTRODUCTION

Just as all the world is against sin, so all the world is against non-tariff barriers (NTBs) to international trade – well, at least against everybody else's sin and non-tariff barriers. Similarly, just as the world has yet to discover a way of eliminating sin, it has a long way to go on removing NTBs. This paper explores one possible procedure for translating good intentions into good behaviour, describing the consequences of applying past GATT negotiating techniques on tariffs to the removal of NTBs. Adopting the neomercantilist criterion that most countries use in assessing trade negotiations – i.e. stressing market expansion rather than economic welfare – the paper identifies substantial "gains" to both industrial and developing countries from NTB negotiations. Although this approach has little to do with economic efficiency, it does represent a strong stream of thought among policy makers and has, in the past, been a principal motivation bringing countries to the negotiating table. Since they rely on well-tried procedures and a realistic assessment of what countries actually want from trade talks, negotiations of the sort described here offer a feasible route towards significant trade liberalization.[1]

The time is particularly ripe for examining strategies for negotiating non-tariff barriers. In 1981 over 25% of industrial countries' imports were subject to commodity specific governmental border measures. By 1983 the figure had reached 27% and it has probably continued to grow since then. At the same time, the international community is now preparing for a new round of trade talks, in which NTBs will figure prominently. The present paper is not offered as a blueprint or agenda for these talks, but seeks to illustrate the attractions to countries of entering negotiations. In particular, by considering negotiations between developing and industrial countries it shows that the former group could win significant concessions by negotiating equally with, and offering reciprocal concessions to, their richer neighbours. This is in strong contrast to the tenor of many "North-South" analyses in which developing countries are presumed to require "special and differential treatment", so that they offer little of no reciprocation for industrial countries' liberalization.

2. NON-TARIFF BARRIERS – THE BACKGROUND

Strictly speaking, a non-tariff barrier is any measure other than a tariff that reduces international trade. It includes any discrimination against imports arising from, for instance, import quotas, excessive customs documentation, health regulations, input subsidies, government purchasing practices, retailing agreements, or tax holidays, see, for example, Yeats (1979). While there is much anecdotal evidence about the whole range of NTBS, no comprehensive data exist on such a scale.

Recently, however, UNCTAD (1983) has compiled a thorough and detailed survey of a sub-set of NTBs – governmental, product-specific border measures on imports – a smaller sub-set of which is analysed in Nogués, Olechowski and Winters (1986) – henceforward referred to as NOW. Dealing only with NTBs on which sound and internationally comparable data are available, NOW consider five groups of measures:

(i) Quantity Controls – prohibitions, quotas, conditional and discretionary import authorizations.
(ii) "Voluntary" Export Restraints (VERs), including the Multi-Fibre Arrangement (MFA) on textile trade.
(iii) Decreed Pricing Systems – variable levies and minimum price agreements.
(iv) Quasi-tariffs – seasonal tariffs and tariff-quotas, excluding those in which the lower tariff rate is explicitly concessional (e.g. as in the Generalised System of Preferences).
(v) Monitoring Measures – anti-dumping and countervailing duties, anti-dumping and countervailing investigations, and import surveillance.

NOW treat the last group as NTBs because the criteria permitting the application of import duties are often looser than are those permitting redress in corresponding domestic anti-trust actions (Dickey, 1979); because filing anti-dumping and countervailing duty actions has a protective effect independent of the outcome of the action (Finger, 1981); and because surveillence is often explicitly protective in intent (e.g. EC Council Regulation 288/82, see EC, 1982).

Table 1 summarises some of NOW's results. It reports the shares of total imports of particular categories of goods that are subject to NTBs. These shares – known as coverage ratios – give no information on the degree of protection, just its extent; the analogous figure in tariff analysis is not the tariff average, but the ratio of dutiable to total imports.[2]

Table 1 shows the extensive NTB protection offered to industrial countries' agriculture – especially in the trade between themselves; it also shows the large number of quantitative restrictions and price arrangements on such trade. Manufacturing as a whole is less prone to NTBs, but particular sectors fare as badly as agriculture. Textiles is the prime example, where over half of developing countries' exports to industrial countries are controlled. It is notable that so-called "voluntary" export restraints and monitoring measures are more common on imports of manufacturers, especially those from developing countries. Imports of oil were also formally subject to NTBs in many countries in 1983 – e.g. France, Norway, Switzerland and the USA. In most cases, however, the recent declines in oil consumption mean that the licencing and quota arrangements are no longer binding. Overall, 27% of industrial countries' total imports are subject to at least one of this limited range of NTBs. On imports from developing countries

TABLE 1 *The coverage of non-tariff barriers on industrial countries' imports (Industrial Countries;* 1983 barriers; 1981 trade)*

(I) By class of Measure	*All Imports of Goods*[bc]	*Agriculture from Industrial Countries*	*Agriculture from Developing Countries*	*Manufacturing from Industrial Countries*	*Manufacturing from Developing Countries*
Quantity Controls	8.6	23.5	20.8	3.2	5.4
Voluntary Export Restraints	3.0	0.0	0.0	3.9	12.1
Decreed Prices	1.7	13.1	11.1	0.8	0.6
Quasi-tariffs	1.3	5.9	5.9	0.8	1.0
Monitoring Measures	14.8	4.8	3.1	7.5	8.6
All above[d]	27.1	40.5	31.2	14.5	21.3

(II) By Commodity Group	*All Sources*[c]	*Industrial Countries*	*Developing Countries*
All products	27.1	21.0	34.3
Fuels	43.0	59.5	51.9
Agriculture	36.1	40.5	31.2
Manufactures	6.1	14.5	21.3
of which:			
Textiles	44.8	23.3	57.2
Footwear	12.6	3.5	17.3
Iron and Steel	35.4	34.3	31.4

[a] Australia, Austria, EEC(10), Finland, Japan, Norway, Switzerland, USA.
[b] Including Minerals and Fuels.
[c] Including imports from centrally planned economies.
[d] This row is less than the sum of those above because some commodities are subject to several measures.
Sources: Nogués, Olechowski and Winters (1986).

the figure is 34%, and on imports from the major developing country borrowers 35%.[3]

Non-tariff barriers are costly because they frustrate the economic gains available from free trade. In part the losses are the same as those associated with tariffs. Thus importing countries tend to consume less and/or produce more of the restricted goods than is optimal given their real resource costs, whilst exporting countries suffer income losses as they are forced to produce goods other than those in which they have greatest comparative advantage.

There are, however, also a number of additional costs associated with particular NTBs. First, certain NTBS – e.g. VERs and monitoring measures – discriminate geographically and thus frequently cause trade diversion, the displacement by an unrestricted high-cost supplier of a restricted low-cost one. Indeed, recent research by Hughes and Krueger (1984) and by Hughes and Newbery (1986) suggests that this has been one of the major effects on developing-industrial country trade: as successful developing country exporters have been excluded from OECD markets, they have been at least partially replaced by other suppliers and have themselves moved into other markets and ranges of goods.

Second, quotas and VERs often prevent market adjustment in response to external and internal economic changes; thus they tend to become more restrictive as domestic demand grows and more costly as comparative advantage changes.

Third, NTBs tend to be less uniform across commodities and thus more distortionary than tariffs. For example, in the 1960s restrictions on cotton trade stimulated trade in man-made fibres which were then uncontrolled. Similarly, the recent US restriction on imports of cars from Japan merely limited the number of cars admitted; this led to high-quality expensive cars substantially displacing cheaper cars in the import bundle, Feenstra (1985).

Fourth, when quotas or VERs constrain imports, the rights to import or export into the restricted market become valuable; this often leads traders to expend real resources to obtain them. Such "rent-seeking" is clearly socially wasteful. Krueger (1974), for example, in her seminal work suggests that rent-seeking on import licences could have absorbed up to 5% of Indian GDP in 1964, and up to 15% of Turkey's in 1968; Mohammed and Whalley (1984) suggest 4% for India in 1980–81.[4]

Finally, the lack of transparency and the high degree of official discretion in their administration make NTBs a very much more uncertain barrier for exporters to overcome. This discourages international specialization.

It is difficult to quantify the costs of NTBs precisely, but several studies estimate rough orders of magnitude for importers' costs. For example, Hindley (1985) estimates that the UK wastes at least £80 million per year through her VER on video cassette recorders; even on the most favourable assumptions this amounts to at least £80,000 per job saved in the European industry. Morkre (1985) estimates that US quotas on textile imports from Hong Kong cost over $300 million p.a. – some eighteen times any possible benefits. Tarr and Morkre (1984) estimate that the US VER on Japanese car imports cost around $1 billion p.a. The World Bank (1986) summarises a number of studies of agricultural protection most of which arises from NTBs: typical estimates are of annual economic losses of around $15 billion, $4 billion and $4.5 billion in the EEC(10),

Japan and the USa respectively. Fuller surveys of NTBs and their costs include Anjaria *et al.* (1985), Hamilton (1985), World Bank (1985), and, on agriculture, World Bank (1986).

Economic theory offers three broad sets of qualifications to the foregoing partial equilibrium analysis of the costs of NTBs. First, a recent stream of research summarised in, e.g., Dixit (1984) and Richardson and Grossman (1984) shows that under certain assumptions NTBs can be welfare-improving in oligopolistic markets. No empirical evidence has been published yet, but it is inconceivable that the simple goods exported by developing countries could fit the required assumptions. Second, the general equilibrium effects of protection can be complex but significant. However, to the limited extent that they have been explored for NTBs, they tend to reinforce the view that NTBs are costly, see, e.g. Dixit and Grossman (1984) or Spencer and Brander (1983). Third, the general theory of second best argues that the partial elimination of distortions can not be guaranteed to increase welfare. The simplest application of this theorem – namely to trade diversion – is not relevant here, because the proposals below serve to undo existing discrimination rather than to increase it, but the theorem does apply to the extent that not all NTBs and other distortions are eliminated. However, it is impossible to believe seriously that existing NTBs generally offset other incurable distortions, and so for all practical purposes the second-best argument may be discounted.

3. NEGOTIATING SCHEME[5]

Given the costs that NTBs entail, it is surprising that so many should exist. A full discussion of this issue is not appropriate here, but among the most important explanations are a general antipathy towards economic change – Corden's (1974) so-called Conservative Social Welfare Function – and the ability of particular interest groups to mobilise this antipathy in order to gain protection from outside pressures at the expense of the rest of the population. Almost all public discussion of trade policy is conducted in terms of injury to producers and the neomercantilist notions of market loss and market access, rather than with the economist's ideas of the consumer gains from cheap imports and the efficient use of resources. This paper argues, however, that even if policy-makers do think in such terms, some progress could be made towards the removal or reduction of NTBs by applying the techniques of negotiation evolved in the early GATT Rounds of tariff talks.

In all the rounds of GATT tariff negotiations prior to the Kennedy Round countries negotiated tariff reductions bilaterally, and then extended any reductions – "concessions" – to all members of the GATT through the Most Favoured Nation Clause. The interaction of this latter clause with members' mercantilist instincts led naturally to the organization of talks along so-called "principal supplier" lines. Participants measured the benefits of a negotiating round by the extent to which, *ex post*, it resulted in increased access to partners' markets, and the costs by the extent to which it opened up their own market. Since these were unknown *ex ante*, however, countries came to value their negotiating stances on the basis of how much actual trade was subject to the tariff barrier in question. Now if any concession that country *A* obtained from country *B* in bilateral talks was to be thrown open to all *B*'s other partners, *A*'s "benefit" from that concession relative to *B*'s "cost" would be greatest if *A* was *B*'s principal supplier of the good concerned. This clearly suited *A*, but it also suited *B*, for by these means *B* obtained the greatest leverage over *A* per unit of its own "cost". By symmetry, *A* would offer concessions on *B*'s principal exports, and so talks would concern only mutual principal supplier trade. With this mercantilist definition of costs and benefits, principal supplier negotiations maximized the benefit/cost ratio for each bilateral commitment. In Finger's (1979) terminology, they maximized the *internalization ratio* – the ratio of internal benefits (to the negotiating parties) to total benefits. By so maximizing the incentive to negotiate trade liberation, the GATT was able to hitch the mercantilist tractor to the welfare-maximizer's plough.

This paper applies the principal supplier rule to the negotiation of the removal of a subset of the NTBs discussed above – those which directly control the quantity of imports (quantitative restrictions). Assuming that a sample of developing and industrial countries swap concessions on quantitative restrictions (QRs) on every product for which each is the other's principal supplier, it presents the mercantilist calculus of the previous paragraph. For such negotiations it calculates the *trade coverage ratio* – the share of total trade affected by negotiations – and the *internalization ratio*. Broadly speaking, these statistics define the scope and incentive for negotiations.[6]

A significant difference between tariffs and QRs is that the latter are much more frequently discriminatory. Formally the removal of a QR applied to only one country generates an internalization ratio of one – all the benefit accrues to the (single) supplier subject to restriction. This increases the attractions of negotiations to that supplier, but of course, it correspondingly generates no beneficial external effects. One approach to discriminatory QRs is to count only the imports from the restricted supplier in the coverage and internalization statistics calculated. This would tend to give higher internalization ratios and lower coverage statistics than the more conservative path adopted here. In the present exercise discriminatory and global QRs are treated identically. Thus for a discriminatory QR, just as for a global one, we enter imports of the good from the principal supplier in the numerator of the internalization ratio and total imports in the denominator. Similarly we enter total imports in the numerator of the coverage ratio. There are two reasons for preferring this approach. First, it prevents our exaggerating the incentives for individual countries to negotiate. Second, it is a more accurate reflection of the realities of international trade, for, if the principal supplier of a good is subject to a QR, there is a pretty strong message to other producers that "self-restraint" would be advisable. In other words if the principal supplier is regulated de jure, there is a strong presumption that other major suppliers feel constrained de facto.

4. THE DATA[7]

The need for comparable data on both industrial and developing countries' NTBs makes it necessary to use data that are inferior to NOW's in several respects.

First they are drawn from interpreters' official reports of their own import restrictions. Such "self-reporting" leads to considerable understatement of the number of barriers; on the other hand, however, because all the restrictions included in the data-set have been reported to the GATT, they have been officially acknowledged to exist and are therefore more likely to be negotiable.

Second, we are obliged to restrict our attention to what the GATT refers to as commodity-specific quantitative restrictions on imports – quotas, licenses, state-trading and minimum price arrangements. This is a considerable reduction on the set of NTBs shown in Table 1 above. For example, it excludes the Multi-Fibre Arrangement (MFA), as well as variable levies, surveillance measures and countervailing and anti-dumping duties. Moreover, the self-reporting of barriers leads to the omission of nearly all voluntary export restrictions.[8]

Third, the data on QRs and on imports are available only at the four-digit level of the Common Customs Classification Nomenclature and the Standard International Trade Classification (Revised) respectively. Thus for each country we distinguish only around 700 commodity groups in which trade actually takes place.

Fourth, only a few countries can be covered. We consider QRs in the "Big Three" industrial countries: the European Community (as of 1983), Japan and the United States.[9] For developing countries we include all as potential principal suppliers, but only eight as importers: Argentina, Brazil, Chile, Hong Kong, Korea, Pakistan, the Philippines and Singapore. This is the subset of major developing country exporters for which reasonable QR data were available.

As in NOW, the trade data refer to 1981 and the QR data to 1983. They suggest that about 7% of industrial countries' imports are subject to barriers compared with 27% in Table 1. Thus the present exercise deals only with the tip of the protectionist iceberg. For the developing country sample, the corresponding coverage ratio is about 8%.[10]

5. THE NEGOTIATIONS

Bilateral principal supplier negotiations entail pairs of countries negotiating over pairs of commodities for which each is the other's principal (i.e. largest) supplier. For instance, Brazil is the United States' principal supplier of heavy iron and steel plate, while the United States is Brazil's principal supplier of, *inter alia*, farm tractors. Each flow is subject to a QR, and thus fruitful bilateral negotiations are feasible. While we consider a few such specific examples below, this paper is not designed to list all such potential negotiations. Rather, we wish to assess the overall scope and benefits of talks on QRs. We start, therefore, by assessing how much of various countries' trade would be potentially negotiable under industrial country-developing country principal supplier rules, without worrying about precisely who talks to whom, or whether all negotiations between particular pairs of partners could generate complete reciprocity.[11]

Potential Industrial Country Concessions

About 3.4% of "Big-Three" imports from developing countries have a developing country as the principal supplier and face at least one QR. Nearly all the affected goods are either primary agricultural commodities or simple manufactures. If the "Big-Three" negotiated on each of these import categories with the relevant developing country principal supplier, up to $2.7 billion of the latter's exports could be liberalized; after Most Favoured Nation extension, these concessions would cover $8.4 billion of developing countries' exports and $10.0 billion of world exports (see Table 11). Thus for developing country exporters, the bilateral internalization ratio – the ratio of the principal suppliers' trade to total trade in the concession categories – would average 27 percent, but the internalization ratio for developing countries as a group would be 85 percent. The former is rather lower than similar ratios in the early GATT rounds, but the latter evidences the strong community interest of developing countries as a group.

The coverage statistics understate the gains to developing countries of "Big-Three" liberalization. First, almost all the QRs considered here, apply to goods in which developing countries have a comparative advantage and high elasticities of supply; thus their removal would likely permit a strong growth of exports. Developing countries captured many of the market access gains from the Kennedy and Dillon Rounds despite the concessions generally being oriented toward industrial countries' interest. One would expect an even stronger growth of developing countries' exports from the "tailor-made" negotiations described here. Second, our QRs exclude the MFA and all VERs. The former is highly restrictive, while the latter are heavily concentrated on developing countries' exports – see Table 1. NOW shows that at least a further $12 billion of 1981 exports from developing to "Big-Three" countries are covered by the MFA and VERs. If these were included in the negotiations, the developing country group coverage ratio would rise to at least 8.3%. Finally, industrial countries have many non-tariff barriers other than QRs, and if these were included, the coverage of negotiations could increase even further.

Potential Developing Country Concessions

For lack of data we can not analyze QRs in the whole of the developing world, so we consider a sample of eight major developing country markets, accounting for about 20% of developing countries' total imports, see Section 4. The estimated coverage of QRs varies strongly between markets, at least partly because of different reporting conventions and coverages. For example, data on QRs on industrial goods are largely missing for Argentina and the Philippines, and several countries maintain general (rather than commodity-specific) restrictions which we cannot handle here. Thus our data represent an underestimate of QRs in the developing world. However, even if we take them at face value, 20 percent of our sample countries' imports from the "Big-Three" are subject to QRs. In terms of potential negotiations, these QRs affect $8.08 billion of "Big-Three" principal suppliers' exports, and, after extension by the Most Favored Nation clause, up to $12.44 billion of total "Big-Three" exports and $15.02 billion of world exports (see Table III). Thus the bilateral internalization ratio for "Big-Three" exporters would be 54 percent and the "Big-Three's" group internalization ratio 83 percent.

TABLE II *Potential Industrial Country Concessions*[a] *("Big-Three" imports (1981) with a developing country principal supplier which faces a QR)*

	$ billion	*As percentage of total affected imports*
Imports from principal suppliers	2.67	27[bc]
Imports from other developing countries	5.77	58[c]
Imports from all other countries	1.56	16
Total imports	10.00	100[d]

[a] 1983 quantitative restrictions applied to 1981 imports.
[b] Bilateral internalization ratio for developing country negotiator.
[c] The sum of these items is the developing country group internalization ratio.
[d] Column does not sum due to rounding.

Generalizing these calculations to all developing country markets will obviously increase the absolute amount of trade covered by negotiations, but will not have a predictable effect on either the coverage or internalization ratios.

Country Specific Negotiations

As well as these averages, specific bilateral negotiations between our sample countries can be explored. Working at a higher level of commodity aggregation – and thus increasing the various coverage statistics relative to the previous discussion – Winters (1985a) identifies several feasible negotiations. Some concern very small trade flows: for example, Argentina is Japan's principal supplier of horsemeat and Japan is Argentina's principal supplier of certain iron and steel goods; however, mutual trade in these goods is only about $40 million and total imports about $100 million in each direction. The Philippines appear to face QRs on more of its (principal supplier) exports ($733 million) than it imposes on its (principal supplier) imports ($318 million), but this probably reflects the incomplete coverage of the Filipino QR data. Nonetheless, negotiations on the barriers to Filipino trade that we can identify could liberalize up to $2.640 million of world trade. Unlike the Philippines, Korea and Pakistan report (for 1983) much heavier restrictions on their imports from principal suppliers than they face on the export flows for which they are principal suppliers; thus they have much to offer in negotiations. Exactly the opposite applies to Hong Kong and Singapore, which have zero and one QR respectively. Chile is similarly nearly free of QRs if one ignores its general import and foreign exchange licensing system, but even if one does not, it would not be very active in negotiations because it is only rarely a restricted principal supplier to a "Big-Three" country.

TABLE III *Potential Developing Country Concessions*[a] *(Sample country imports (1981) from a "Big-Three" principal supplier which faces a QR)*

	$ billion imports	*As percentage of total affected imports*
Imports from principal suppliers	8.08	54[bc]
Imports from other "Big-Three" countries	4.36	29[c]
Imports from all other countries	2.58	17
Total imports	15.02	100

[a] 1983 quantitative restrictions applied to 1981 imports.
[b] Bilateral internalization ratio for "Big-Three" negotiators.
[c] The sum of these items is the "Big-Three" group internalization ratio.

Brazil offers scope for substantial and balanced principal supplier negotiations. $540 million of Brazilian exports to the USA and $1,820 million of USA exports to Brazil would be covered, each extending, through the Most Favored Nation clause, to around $3,100 million of world trade. For the United States' exports this represents a very attractive internalization ratio. Brazilian–European Community trade offers similar scope, with over $1,000 million of mutual trade in each direction covered, extending to over $8,000 million of world trade in all. In all these cases developing countries would be offering concessions on imports of more sophisticated manufactures and asking them on exports of primary or simple manufactured goods.

6. DISCUSSION

This analysis suggests that negotiations between developing and industrial countries on QRs are feasible. Recalling our limited set of barriers, coverage ratios of 8.3% and 20% are worth negotiating over; the coverage ratio for all tariff reductions and bindings by industrial countries in the Tokyo Round was only 18%, GATT (1979). The average individual internalisation ratio for developing countries is, at 27%, rather small by historical standards, but both our treatment of discrimination and our tight definition of principal suppliers serve to reduce it. Moreover, the high group internalization ratios offer considerable incentive to sets of countries to negotiate. To reap these, developing countries do not necessarily have to form a coalition, but merely agree that all will join negotiations seriously. This is not necessarily an easy agreement to reach, however, for, unlike the game played once negotiations have begun, it admits strategic bargaining and blocking coalitions among developing countries; besides it is difficult to commit to and monitor the "seriousness" of negotiations. Thus some side-payments, e.g. agreements over intra-developing country trade, may be necessary in order to reach agreement to negotiate. However, most countries should find it in their mercantilist interests to take part in the trade round, and it would certainly be easier for them to agree as a group to enter bilateral principal supplier negotiations than it would to form a developing country coalition to negotiate directly with the industrial countries. Thus the proposals here do not appear unrealistic on that score.

Once negotiations are agreed there remain a number of serious questions that must be addressed before progress can be made. Some of these are specific to the proposal described here, but many are significant for any scheme to negotiate QRs.

The principal supplier approach runs the risk that negotiations will dry up before all QRs have been negotiated, for it is possible that, while all principal supplier trade-flows are free of restriction, other flows are not. This is relevant only for discriminatory-flows, and is anyway unlikely to be serious because NTBs tend to be imposed on the major trade-flows. More worrying is the case where a constrained principal supplier runs out of concessions to offer, a possibility that besets any negotiations based on reciprocity. It was partially overcome in the tariff rounds by heavily protectionist countries making deeper and wider cuts, although this is much easier to arrange in multilateral than in the bilateral negotiations proposed here. A further partial solution is to relax the definition of the "principal supplier" to include countries with lower market shares, and thus to bring more countries into the set of possible negotiators on a particular trade flow. Extending the definition would also raise the coverage ratios by allowing developing countries to negotiate on more goods.

A related difficulty is that occasionally a developing country may feel that it actually gains from a QR in one of its markets. For example, its quota may boost its market share or allow it to earn artificial scarcity rents. Information is very scarce on this dimension of NTBs, but in general, even under QRs, the largest suppliers appear to be relatively efficient producers, and thus the most likely to gain from increased import liberalization. If this were a problem, however, it too could be tackled by relaxing the definition of "principal supplier".

Cheating would also have to be overcome. That is, countries would wish to ensure that the negotiated reductions in QRs were permanent and not offset by increases in other measures. This could be achieved by supporting the reductions with a series of "bindings" – commitments not to increase protection from negotiated levels – as was done in the early GATT Rounds. It is true that as an economy grows, a fixed QR becomes more restrictive, but over the short run for which bindings were originally made (about two years) this is not a serious problem. Similar worries about the reversal of negotiated concessions pervaded the earliest tariff rounds: bindings were made for only two years, at which point a new round of talks would review the domestic acceptability of the concessions made and, if necessary, renegotiate the package. As it turned out, the benefits of earlier concessions so outweighed the perceived costs after two years, that renegotiation was replaced by the negotiation of further liberalization.

If designing bindings is technically more difficult for QRs than for tariffs, it may be that negotiations could be conducted by converting NTB into tariffs and then negotiating reductions in these. However, this would not overcome another difficulty that is often said to face future negotiators. It is often argued that the ordinary tariff bindings were agreed because negotiators knew they could fall back on "safeguard" QRs if liberalisation proved too painful. Present import barriers, on the other hand, are said to represent the "last ditch" and therefore will not be readily bound. Even if this were true, it would not reduce the benefits of 'bound liberalization", but merely make negotiations more complicated. However, it is only partly true. There is no reason to suppose that negotiators could not agree mutual bindings that allowed some sort of emergency protection. For example, tighter GATT rules for compensation or retaliatory "unbindings" could be agreed if necessary.

A further danger facing any formal scheme of negotiation that trades "concessions" is that it discourages unilateral liberalization between rounds, and may even encourage the imposition of bargaining QRs. This would be a powerful argument against our proposal if the present system of "informal unilateral liberalization" worked, but the recent growth of NTBs suggests that the risk of formality would be well worth taking. It does, however, suggest that trade talks could usefully be scheduled to occur more frequently than the present once per decade.

A thorny political problem with any attempt to remove existing QRs is their legality, or lack of it, under the GATT. Some readers of earlier drafts of this paper have argued that those QRs which are legal under the GATT are effectively non-negotiable precisely because they have been officially sanctioned. Others have argued that it is QRs which are *illegal* under the GATT that are non-negotiable because, being illegal, they should be abolished with no counterpart being offered! Given sufficient political will it would be perfectly possible to negotiate all QRs, legal and illegal, together, so one might interpret protestations about legality is mere manoeuverings to improve countries' initial positions in any future formal negotiations.

Alternatively, however, this difference of opinion could be taken to illuminate a rather more serious shift in the role of the GATT since the 1950s. Having evolved as a means of generating trade liberalization, the GATT turns out in this view to hinder it.[12] As a legal instrument the GATT was originally a tool of, and quite subordinate to, the political process of freeing international trade. Now, however, its legal forms and technical procedures tend to dominate attitudes towards liberalization, see Finger (1984). Thus whereas initially the protectionist compromises in the GATT articles seemed unimportant, because the spirit of the law ruled, now they are critical, because the letter of the law predominates. Liberalization was always a difficult process because it affected the distribution of income within a country, but now the fact that the GATT legitimizes certain QRs makes it doubly so. First, countries are reluctant to surrender their "legal rights to protection", particularly in negotiations with "villains" who have imposed illegal QRs. Second, there is a (mistaken) view that negotiating legal and illegal measures together somehow undermines the standing of the GATT. Thus there arises a sterile debate about legality that both diverts attention from the harmful nature of *all* QRs and permits laggards to hide their reluctance to liberalize behind a veil of legal rectitude. Moreover, it is wrong to suppose that merely bringing QRs into conformity with the GATT would foster liberalization. The GATT was never the moving force behind trade liberalization, but just the instrument through which liberal political aims were given practical expression. Without that political will, no amount of legal or technical discussion will yield significant fruits, whereas with it, the intermediate step of "legalization" would be unnecessary.[13]

This interpretation suggests two conclusions. First, significant trade liberalization will be possible only if the political environment for it improves. In particular this involves the emergence of domestic political coalitions – possibly of consumers and exporters – to overcome the resistance to liberalization from import-competing sectors. By showing the mercantilist attractions of negotiations, this paper aims to encourage that process. Second, in devising safeguard clauses and binding agreements account must be taken of the long-term dangers of inertia and legal precedent: exceptions to liberalization should both decay automatically and be explicitly temporary.

7. CONCLUSIONS

This paper has explored the feasibility of establishing industrial country–developing country negotiations on the abolition of QRs. While there are many difficulties to overcome, it has been suggested that principal supplier negotiations could be sufficiently attractive to policy-makers to generate some progress. We do not claim optimality for the principal supplier rule, but rather argue that by establishing an acceptable and feasible scheme we have taken a first step towards devising more efficient modes of organization.

Turning to the detailed results of the paper, we have shown that the early GATT procedure of bilateral principal supplier negotiations between developing and industrial countries offers considerable scope for mutual "concessions" on QRs. At least $20 billion of developing countries' exports could be freed from restrictions under such a scheme. While concessions would have to be made in return, there is no reason to believe that they would be excessive. Moreover, both Finger's (1979) evidence on the Kennedy Round and the "Big-Three's" current rhetoric suggest that the dispensation granted to developing countries under the GATT, by which they are not required to make reciprocal concessions, will be quite unable to deliver any such gains in market access.[14] Thus even on mercantilist grounds, let alone on those of economic welfare, developing countries have a strong incentive to negotiate with the industrial world over the removal of non-tariff barriers. One caveat is in order, however. Meaningful developing-industrial country negotiations will have to range over the whole spectrum of commodities: if the industrial world insists on excluding agricultural products and simple manufactures from discussion, then there is very little room for mutual concessions, and both sides will return home empty-handed.

NOTES

This research was carried out while the author was an economist in the Development Research Department of the World Bank. The views expressed are those of the author and should on no account be attributed to the World Bank or its affiliated organizations. I am particularly grateful to J. Michael Finger for suggesting this study and for his constant advice and encouragement. Thanks are also due to B. Balassa, V. Corbo, J. Falkus, I. Frank, D. Greenaway, O. Kalantzopoulos, A. Krueger, J. Nogués, A. Olechowski, P. Williams, M. Woll, the participants of seminars at the Centre for Economic Policy Research and the International Economic Study Group, the Editors, and the referees for discussions of earlier details of the papers, and to Jackson Magargee and Meg Winters for typing. None of these people can be held responsible for any remaining infelicities.

1 The use of the neomercantilist approach represents not our own assessment of the benefits of trade liberalization, but rather an assumption in the positive economic exercise of deciding whether trade liberalization could actually come about.

2 If anything coverage ratios tend to understate restrictiveness, for the tighter an NTB, the lower the imports it affects. NOW seek to alleviate this problem by using 1981 imports to weight together 1983 NTBs, and also by sometimes using world trade instead of own-imports as weights.

3 The UNCTAD data are compiled from official statutory instruments and reports; both they and the import data used by NOW to analyse them are defined at the tariff-line level – that is on the definitions of goods actually used by customs staff to apply them. Thus unlike previous estimates of the extent of NTBs – e.g. Cline (1984) and Balassa and Balassa (1984) – they are not subject to an upward bias from commodity aggregation.

4 A useful survey of the theory of rent-seeking and related DUP (Directly Unproductive Profit-seeking) activities is Bhagwati, Brecher and Srinivasan (1984).

5 The remainder of this paper summarises Wintes (1985c).

6 The mercantilist calculation is made, not because it measures the benefits of liberalizing trade, but in order to show that trade liberalization could be attractive even from a mercantilist point of view.

7 Further details of the data and methodology are available in Winters (1985a).

8 The narrowness of the definition of QRs is regrettable but inevitable. The precise details of the MFA required for this sort of exercise were not available to us (the GATT treats the MFA under a different protocol from other barriers), while no information on non-QR NTBs was available for developing countries. Since this work was completed it was learned that the data set excluded European Community restrictions on imports from Eastern Europe and possibly also some conditional import authorizations on agricultural imports.

9 The EEC is treated as a single entity, netting out intra-EEC trade. Principal suppliers are defined by countries' exports to the whole Community. The set of commodities with a developing country principal supplier is then matched with individual member countries' QR data (including both national and Community restrictions) to calculate individual coverage and internalization ratios. Finally these last are aggregated (weighted by imports) into aggregate EEC figures.

10 While industrial countries' trade policies are rather stable, developing countries' are not. Thus this last figure can not be readily extrapolated to other years.

11 In the early tariff rounds "principal supplier" was defined rather more broadly than here to include all major suppliers. Under such a definition, if it could have been operationalized, the internalization ratios would have been considerably larger than reported here, and the coverage ratios somewhat larger. In other words, negotiations would have looked even more attractive than they do below.

12 I mean here the GATT as a legal instrument, *not* the Secretariat.

13 Similar arguments apply to reforming the GATT. No currently viable reform would achieve anything in the absence of political will, whereas with political will, the present structure would be quite adequate.

13 Finger (1979) found that those developing countries which participated fully in the Kennedy Round received far greater concessions on their exports than those that did not.

REFERENCES

Anjaria S. J., Kirmani, N. and Petersen, A. B. *Trade Policy Issues and Developments*, Occasional Paper No. 38, The International Monetary Fund, Washington D.C., 1985.

Balassa, B. and Balassa, C. "Industrial Protection in the Developed Countries", *The World Economy*, 1984, pp. 179–196.

Bhagwati, J. N., Brecher, R. A. and Srinivasan, T. N. "DUP Activities and Economic Theory", *European Economic Review*, vol. 24, pp. 291–301, 1984.

Cline, W. *Imports of Manufacturers from Developing Countries: Performance and Prospects for Market Access*, Brookings Institution, Washington, D.C., 1985.

Corden, W. M. *Trade Policy and Economic Welfare*, Oxford University Press, Oxford, 1974.

Dickey, W. L. "The Pricing of Imports into the United States," *Journal of World Trade Law*, vol. 13, 1979, pp. 238–256.

European Commission *The Official Journal of the European Communities*, EC, Brussels.

Dixit, A. K. "International Trade Policy for Oligopolistic Industries", *Economic Journal Supplement*, vol. 94, pp. 1–16, 1984.

Dixit, A. K. and Grossman, E. M. "Targetted Export Promotion with Several Oligopolistic Industries", NBER Working Paper 1344, NBER, Cambridge, Mass., 1984.

Feenstra, R. C. "Voluntary Export Restraints in US Autos, 1980–1984", mimeo, National Bureau of Economic Research, Summer Workshop 1984.

Finger, J. M. "Trade Liberalisation: a Public Choice Perspective", *American Economic Review*, vol. 64, 1974, pp. 291–303.

Mohammed, S. and Whalley, J. "Rent-Seeking in India: its Costs and Policy Significance". *Kyklos*, vol. 37, 1984, pp. 387–413.

Morkre, M. E. *Import Quotas on Textiles: Welfare Effects of US Restrictions on Hong Kong, An Empirical Analysis*, Federal Trade Commission, Washington D.C., 1984.

Nogues, J. J., Olechowski, A., and Winters, L. A. "The Extent of Nontariff Barriers to Imports of Industrial Countries", Staff Working Paper No. 789, The World Bank, Washington, D.C. 1986.

Spencer, B. J. and Brander, J. A. "International R & D Rivalry and Industrial Strategy", *Review of Economic Studies*, vol. 50, pp. 707–722, 1983.

Tarr, D. G. and Morkre, M. E. *Aggregate Costs to the United States of Tariffs and Quotas on Imports*, Federal Trade Commission, 1984.

UNCTAD "Nontariff Barriers Affecting the Trade of Developing Countries and Transparency in World Trading Conditions: the Inventory of Non-tariff Barriers", TD/B/940, UNCTAD, Geneva, 1983.

Winters, L. A. "Non-tariff Barrier Negotiations Between Developing and Industrial Countries: Coverage and Internalisation Ratios", Development Research Department Discussion Paper No. 119, The World Bank, Washington, D.C., 1985a.

Winters, L. A. "The Prevalence of Quantitative Restrictions – Some Evidence from the GATT', mimeo, International Economics Division, Development Research Department, The World Bank, Washington D.C., 1985b (Restricted).

Winters, L. A. "Negotiating the Reduction of Nontariff Barriers", mimeo, International Economics Division, Development Research Department, The World Bank, Washington D.C., November 1985c.

World Bank, *Trade and Development*, Paper Presented to The Development Committee. The World Bank, Washington D.C. 1985.
World Bank, *The World Development Report 1986*, The World Bank, Washington, D.C. 1986.
Yeats, A. J. *Trade Barriers Facing Developing Countries*, Macmillan, London, 1979.

17. Reciprocity

L. A. Winters

> Reciprocity: Mutual or correspondent concession of advantages or privileges, as forming a basis for the commercial relations between two countries (1782). *The Shorter Oxford English Dictionary*.

Negotiations, almost by definition, are about reciprocity. They entail the search for mutually acceptable outcomes when action by one party without reciprocal action by the other would be unacceptable. That is, negotiations involve the reciprocal exchange of concessions that neither party would wish to make in isolation.

Reciprocity in trade negotiations comes in many guises, ranging from the simple bilateral swapping of tariff reductions, through multilateral reciprocity, to qualitative reciprocity in which mutual concessions are made in the design of agenda or of codes of practice. Although reciprocity is difficult to define, several conventions grew up during the early GATT Rounds to make it operational – such conventions as the use of trade coverage to measure it and the adoption of principal-supplier modes of negotiation to arrange it. This chapter describes these conventions and shows that, although the Kennedy and Tokyo Rounds sought to broaden the basis of negotiation, reciprocity still dominated their outcomes. Qualitative reciprocity is already evident in the agenda for the Uruguay Round. And reciprocal principal-supplier negotiations could give developing countries the means to free their exports to industrial countries from quantitative restrictions.

RECIPROCITY AND MERCANTILISM

Reciprocity provides a means of reducing trade restrictions any time a government believes that it has an interest in maintaining its barriers, but a larger interest in removing those of its trading partners. It is thus as relevant to the negotiation of "optimum tariffs" (see below) as it is to today's neomercantilist protectionism.

Today's protectionism is neomercantilist in that it stresses output and employment more than consumption and leisure. It typically concentrates on the effects of international trade on competitive producers of an imported product rather than on the users of the product, be they final consumers or other industries. The main reason for this is that competitive producers' interests are less diffuse and more readily quantifiable than other interests, and thus tend to be more powerfully represented in policymaking. Moreover, actual producers carry more weight than merely potential producers. Thus the political pressures on governments are toward maintaining or increasing the output of existing goods and firms rather than toward wider objectives even on the production side. The result is that most of the public discussion of trade policy is about the injury to producers and the mercantilist notions of market loss and market access – not about the economists' notions of the consumer gains from cheap imports and the efficient use or resources.

The economists' view almost invariably leads to the prescription of free trade, but even the mercantilist view can lead in that direction once a role is admitted for reciprocity. A country may liberalize its imports if other countries, by liberalizing theirs, allow it to increase its exports in line. This was clearly expressed in the discussions surrounding the U.S. Reciprocal Trade Agreement Act of 1934. The preceding slump and protectionism had cut U.S. exports substantially, and Cordell Hull argued that U.S. negotiators would be able to win improved access and increased exports to foreign markets only by offering reductions in the massive Smoot-Hawley tariff. The United States concluded twenty bilateral and explicitly reciprocal tariff agreements under the act. Presidents Kennedy and Nixon used similar arguments to launch the Kennedy and Tokyo Rounds.

RECIPROCITY AND GATT

The 1934 Act largely determined the US. attitude to the proposed International Trade Organization and to GATT. Thus the preamble of GATT refers to "entering reciprocal and mutually advantageous arrangements directed to the substantial reduction of tariffs and other barriers to trade." Its articles do not, however, define reciprocity or specify how reciprocal negotiations may be arranged. Doing either of these things is no easy matter. The present director-general has said that "Reciprocity cannot be determined exactly; it can only be argued upon." (GATT Press Release no. 1312, 5 March 1982). Dell – an unrepentant mercantilist – writes: "What it means is obscure and subjective and, in the end, may be determined simply by what is politically acceptable" (1986). Nonetheless several procedures have grown up since 1947 to operationalize the concept in the GATT negotiations.

A fundamental feature of GATT is the most-favored-nation (MFN) clause. This clause complicates the operation of reciprocity because it requires that concessions – tariff reductions – granted to one supplier be extended to all others. So, while the country with which a concession is negotiated might be expected to offer a reciprocal concession in return, other suppliers can be free riders. They can wait quietly in the wings until the concession is eventually delivered without ever having to reciprocate. This complication, coupled with the mercantilist view of the benefits of trade liberalization, led naturally to the development of a principal-supplier pattern of negotiation.

Mercantilist governments measured the benefits of a negotiating round by how much it increased their access to partners' markets, and the costs by how much it opened their own markets. Since these were unknown beforehand, however, and since actual producers were far more influential than potential ones, countries came to value their negotiating stances by the amount of actual trade subject to the tariff barrier in question.

If any concession that country A obtained from country B in bilateral talks was to be thrown open to all B's other partners, A's benefit from the concession relative to B's cost would be greatest if A were B's principal supplier of the good concerned. This clearly suited A, but it also suited B, for by these means B obtained the greatest leverage over A per unit of its own "cost." Similarly, A would offer concessions on B's principal exports, and so talks would concern only mutual principal-supplier trade. With this mercantilist definition of costs and benefits, principal-supplier negotiations maximized the benefit-cost ratio for each bilateral commitment.

Finger refers to the benefit-cost ratio as the internalization ratio (1979). It measures the extent to which the countries that make concessions are also the countries that receive concessions. It thus reflects the extent to which the benefits of improved market access are kept internal to the negotiations rather than allowed to spill over to other, external, non-negotiating countries. Unless internalization ratios are kept high, there is little incentive for countries to negotiate concessions. And as with any other activity in which the actors cannot appropriate a high proportion of the gains, the amount of negotiation will be suboptimal from a global point of view.

Principal-supplier negotiations occurred under the U.S. Act of 1934, but the negotiating rules of the early GATT Rounds (1947–62) gave them a special status (see below). Moreover, to the extent that there were spillovers to free riders, GATT also helped to internalize their gains. The reason is that GATT allowed all bilateral negotiations to be conducted and agreed on simultaneously – and ensured that each set of negotiators had details of the requests and offers made in the other sessions (Curzon 1965). So, by maximizing internationalization and seeking to internalize any externalities that did arise, GATT maximized the incentives to negotiate and so hitched the mercantilist tractor to the welfare-maximizer's plow.

Internalization ratios, calculated for each set of bilateral negotiations, reflect a dimension of simple bilateral reciprocity: the extent to which a country granting concessions gains from the reciprocal concessions offered by its negotiating partner. As noted above, given the modes of measurement adopted, these gains appear largest for a principal-supplier country. For the first six GATT rounds, Finger (1979) showed that the average bilateral internalization for U.S. concessions reached as high as 74 percent in Geneva 1956. He also calculated group internalization ratios for the sets of countries participating in each round. These ratios reflect multilateral reciprocity: how much the benefits of concessions by the negotiating parties were kept among themselves, even if they could not all be restricted to the principal suppliers. In 1947, 84 percent of U.S. imports in categories in which the United States cut tariffs came from the twenty-two other participants in the trade talks. In the next two rounds, group internalization was lower, but by the Dillon Round it reached an astonishing 96 percent. This multilateral reciprocity was a clear advantage of concentrating the bilateral talks in a single round.

Reciprocity governs the coverage of concessions and their size. Although the binding of low tariffs as initially intended to be equivalent to cutting and binding higher ones, this intent was never fully accepted. Thus, after 1952, negotiators sought reciprocal coverage of tariff cuts. Within the set of reductions, balance was also sought in the average depth of cuts, but less was made of this dimension of reciprocity publicly because it was less readily measurable.

The principal-supplier procedure was perfectly natural in the mercantilist context, but it was buttressed by the GATT articles and the negotiating rules for the various rounds. These rules presumed that only principal suppliers would request concessions and allowed countries to dismiss requests from other suppliers – except, for example, where the principal supplier was not negotiating or where each of several partners requested a concession and was prepared to reciprocate for it. The articles do not mention principal suppliers in the context of negotiating new concessions. But Article XXVII grants the one or two principal supplier(s) the right to negotiate, along with the country that originally won a concession. The reason is that the withdrawal of a concession is likely to impinge hardest on the principal supplier regardless of the country that originally received the concession.

RECIPROCITY AND OPTIMUM TARIFFS

Economic theory admits one unambiguous welfare-maximizing case for import restrictions – the optimum tariff. If a country is large enough to influence the world price for its imports, it may raise its welfare by taxing imports and so reducing the prices that foreign suppliers charge. This is not the prime motivation for modern trade intervention. Witness, for example, the use of voluntary export restraints (VERs), the use of protection by very small countries in very competitive markets, or the prominence of output and jobs in the public debate about protection. But even if optimum tariffs were widespread, the techniques of tariff negotiation would be much the same as now. Although the optimum tariff raises the importer's real income, it cuts the exporter's by more, so reciprocal reductions would be attractive. Moreover, since the welfare gains from changes in the terms of trade are roughly proportional to the amount of trade and the change in price, deals would naturally be assessed by reference to their trade coverage, internalization, and depth of cut.

THE KENNEDY ROUND

Because the world has so many trading countries, internalization is difficult to achieve – the more so bilaterally than multilaterally. The proportion of total imports the successive GATT Rounds covered fell from 78 percent in 1947 to between 7 and 12 percent in the 1950s and early 1960s. Moreover, as the number of countries participating in negotiations grew, it became progressively more complex to conduct bilateral trade talks while still keeping track of the implications for multilateral reciprocity. Thus in the Kennedy Round a general tariff-cutting formula was adopted – the linear rule, by which all tariffs were to be cut by the same proportion.

In principle, a linear cut makes multilateral reciprocity both certain and automatic. If all countries cut all tariffs by, say, 10 percent, each participant receives a 10 percent concession on both its total exports and total imports. As it happened, however, zero tariffs upset this symmetry (just as they would any scheme based on reciprocity in tariff cuts rather than levels). So did the absence from the table (or the exemption from reciprocity) of most trading countries. Even more seriously, nearly all countries submitted long lists of exceptions to the linear cut. These lists defined the agenda for subsequent negotiation. And although the lists were initially discussed multilaterally, all the crucial bargains were made bilaterally.

During the negotiations countries added to and subtracted from their exception lists to achieve internalization and reciprocity. The clearest example of internalization concerned the U.S. exception of petroleum imports. "The Americans, on the basis of previous GATT procedure, claimed that items primarily supplied by nonparticipants need not be considered in the reciprocity debate" – and although this view was never formally agreed it, it eventually prevailed de facto (Preeg 1970, p. 88). Reciprocity entered most critically in the debate over the American Selling Price customs valuation of benezenoid chemicals. This practice granted U.S. producers very high levels of protection, and the Europeans were desperately anxious to abolish it. But because the practice was contrary to those prescribed by GATT, the Europeans argued that the United States should abandon it unrequited. This the United States refused, and the issue remained deadlocked until Europeans finally responded with significant concessions in the chemicals sector.

The episode shows the dangers of sectoral negotiating groups and of excessive legalism in trade negotiations. The Kennedy Round established special groups for five industrial sectors in which negotiations over exceptions looked likely to be very difficult. Those for paper and pulp and for chemicals succeeded but those for steel, textiles, and aluminium did not achieve much. Similarly the special groups for agriculture – grains, dairy, and meat – were disappointing. Each group faced its problems, but a common theme was the difficulty of achieving reciprocity in the sector. Sectoral negotiation enhances the bargaining power of producers, and because most sectors have relatively unbalanced trade, net exporting countries have little to offer net importers in return for the latters' concessions. Effective reciprocity requires cross-sectoral deals, and indeed the whole Kennedy Round would have foundered but for the director-general's last-minute compromise exchanging concessions in steel, agriculture, and chemicals.

The American Selling Price fell into what Dam calls a "legal half-light" (1970, p. 343). It was clearly contrary to GATT Article VII but legally defensible under the grandfathering clause of the Protocol of Provisional Application because it existed before 1947. Any harm that it did to Europe was independent of its morality or legality. So the rigid positions that legalism encouraged during negotiations were as irrelevant to the main point as they were dangerous to the outcome.

The Kennedy Round signified the ascendancy of multilateral over bilateral reciprocity, but reciprocity was still king. For example, the main claim of the official U.S. summary of the round was that it entailed granting concessions on \$8.5 billion of 1964 imports (\$6.4 billion from major participants) and receiving concessions on \$8.1 billion (\$6.7 billion) of exports (United States 1967). Moreover, U.S. concessions affected 70 percent of U.S. imports from other major negotiating partners, 49 percent of those from other industrial countries, 33 percent of those from fully participating developing countries, and just 5 percent of those from other developing countries (Finger 1979). Of the concessions to fully participating developing countries, 77 percent were on goods for which these countries were the United States' principal supplier (United States 1967). These figures suggest substantial returns to reciprocal participation.[1]

THE TOKYO ROUND

The tariff negotiations of the Tokyo Round also adopted a general rule with exceptions. Considerable debate surrounded the choice of rule. The major participants sought advantages not so much in the coverage of concessions (as before, the exceptions lists took care of this) but in the depth and variance of the cut. The EEC had long expressed concern over the dispersion of U.S. tariff rates, which coupled a low average with occasional very high rates. The issue had been prominent in the early stages of the Kennedy Round and lay behind some of the bilateral exceptions negotiations. But in the end, the EEC made little headway with it. In the Tokyo Round, therefore, the EEC proposed a non-linear formula that involved small average cuts but that reduced high rates much more than low ones. The United States preferred a substantial proportionate cut – and Japan, a linear rule. Japan, however, had recently reduced its tariffs unilaterally, and it also argued that the Kennedy Round's bound rates (not actual rates) should provide the base lines for the formulas. After two years a compromise was struck: the Swiss formula (between the U.S. and EEC proposals) was applied to Kennedy Round rates.

The ensuing exceptions and sectoral negotiations followed a pattern similar to that of the Kennedy Round. For example, the EEC withdrew concessions that it felt the Japanese had not justly reciprocated. The final reductions and bindings covered some \$155 billion in world trade and entailed average costs on industrial goods (relative to the Kennedy Round's bound rates) of 29 percent, 31 percent, and 49 percent for the EEC, United States, and Japan, respectively (GATT 1980). The average Japanese cut relative to actual tariffs was about 25 percent (Deardorff and Stern 1985).

The innovation of the Tokyo Round was its set of agreements on nontariff barriers. Although there were a few reciprocal reductions in specific nontariff barriers – as there had been in the Kennedy Round – progress in formulating codes of practice was significant. The major agreements covered customs valuations, government procurement, and subsidies and countervailing duties. The major failure concerned with safeguard actions.

Three facets of reciprocity were evident in these agreements. First, a qualitative reciprocity by which concessions in the negotiation of one code – such as U.S. application of a material-injury criterion in the countervailing duties code – was traded against those in another – such as European agreements on agricultural barriers and subsidies. Second, quantitative reciprocity applied within certain codes: the sets of institutions subject to the government procurement code were chosen at least partly to ensure similar import coverage across countries. Third, the benefits of some codes were restricted to the contracting parties that signed and therefore applied them – such as those on countervailing duties, technical standards, government procurement, and civil aircraft. Whether or not such discrimination is consistent with GATT – and there is some debate on this – it clearly reflects a form of bilateral reciprocity. Such "rules reciprocity" has figured in American debate since 1980 – the "new reciprocity" (Cline 1983). Like any reciprocity based on levels of protection, rather than changes in protection as the GATT tariff negotiations have been, its danger is that some parties will increase the restrictiveness of their measures.

Perhaps even more than the negotiation of tariffs, the negotiation of codes also shows that reciprocity provides the means but not the only motive for trade negotiations. Governments may find that the codes proposed in a GATT Round are in the national interest independent of whether other countries sign them. For example, the codes may bolster the government against special interest groups or enforce the more accurate collection of economic statistics. Nonetheless, the governments may find it impossible for reasons of domestic politics to adopt such codes in the absence of external pressure and reciprocity. In these cases, reciprocity is a means not an end, and the formality and binding nature of GATT agreements become an important part of the process.

THE URUGUAY ROUND

The stamp of reciprocity already marks the Uruguay Round. The ministerial declaration makes explicit mention of property rights, agriculture, tropical products, tariff escalation, and textiles and clothing. And negotiations on services will proceed in parallel with those on goods. This scope is broad enough to permit qualitative reciprocity. Even from the initial statement, it is clear that some progress on textiles and tropical products will be necessary if developing countries are to concede anything on services and property rights. Similarly the United States is suggesting that developing countries should make concessions on services in return for rollbacks and standstills on goods. Such details require, however, that reciprocity be viewed over the whole range of products and trade barriers. In this respect, clause B(iii) of the Punta del Este Declaration – "balanced concessions should be sought *within* broad trading areas and subjects" (emphasis added) – is potentially dangerous.

Even within groups, there is scope for qualitative reciprocity. The former might arise, for example, over the provision of services. Industrial countries are requesting the "right to establish" service outlets in developing countries. And this might be balanced by granting developing country nationals the "right of temporary immigration" to provide certain services in industrial countries. Given the likelihood that some code on services will emerge, developing countries will do better to offer and request concessions and join the negotiations than to sit

TABLE 1 *Potential industrial country concessions*[a]

Item	Big Three imports (1981) with a developing country principal supplier that faces a quantitative restriction	
	Billions of dollars	As a percentage of total affected imports
Imports from principal suppliers	2.7	27[b,c]
Imports from other developing countries	5.77	58[c]
Imports from all other countries	1.56	16
Total imports	10.00	100[d]

a. 1983 quantitative restrictions applied to 1981 imports.
b. Bilateral internalization ratio for developing country negotiator.
c. The sum of these items is the developing country group internalization ratio.
d. Column does not add up to 100 due to rounding.
Source: Author's estimates.

on the sidelines and wonder why the resulting deal excludes or disadvantages them. Moreover, as noted above, developing countries may well perceive domestic advantages to a services code independent of the concessions it causes industrial countries to grant them.

Reciprocity will also be important in the goods markets. As an illustration of its potential, I have examined the possible outcome of principal-supplier negotiations between developing and industrial countries over commodity-specific quantitative restrictions on imports (Winters 1987). GATT defined these restrictions as including quotas, licensing, state-trading and minimum price arrangements, but excluding the Multifiber Arrangement (MFA), as well as variable levies, surveillance measures, and countervailing and antidumping duties. Moreover, because the data rely on countries reporting their own import barriers, nearly all voluntary export restrictions are omitted. The scope for concessions is described in tables 7.1 and 7.2.

About 3.4 percent of Big Three imports from developing countries have a developing country as the principal supplier and face a quantitative restriction. Negotiations on the affected import categories with the relevant developing-country principal suppliers would liberalize up to $2.7 billion of the latter's

TABLE 2 *Potential developing country concessions*[a]

Item	Sample country imports (1981) from a Big Three principal supplier that faces a quantitative restriction: Billions of dollars	As a percentage of total affected imports
Imports from principal suppliers	8.08	54[a,b]
Imports from other Big Three countries	4.36	29[c]
Imports from all other countries	2.58	17
Total imports	15.02	100

a. 1983 quantitative restrictions applied to 1981 imports.
b. Bilateral internalization ratio for Big Three negotiators.
c. The sum of these items are the Big Three group internalization ratio.
Source: Author's estimates.

exports. After most-favored-nation extension, these concessions would cover $8.4 billion of developing countries' exports and $10.0 billion of world exports. So, for developing country exporters, the bilateral internalization ratio would average 27 percent, but the group internalization ratio for developing countries as a group would be 84 percent. The first ratio is rather lower than similar ratios in the early GATT Rounds; the second shows the strong community interest of developing countries as a whole. The coverage ratio also looks rather low, but it would be substantially higher (about 8.3 percent) if the MFA and VERs were included and higher still if other barriers were included.

The data on developing countries' quantitative restrictions are very crude and probably underestimate their prevalence. But even taking them at face value, 20 percent of the sample countries' imports from the Big Three are subject to such restrictions. In terms of potential negotiations, these restrictions affect $8.1 billion of Big Three principal suppliers' exports, and after extension by the most-favored-nation clause, up to $12.4 billion of Big Three exports and $15.0 billion of world exports. Thus the bilateral internalization ratio for Big Three exporters would be 54 percent, the group internalization ratio for them 83 percent. Generalizing these calculations to all developing country markets would obviously increase the absolute amount of trade covered by negotiations, but would not have a predictable effect on either the coverage or internalization ratios.

These calculations show that restricted principal-supplier trade flows exist in insufficient number to render negotiations worthwhile and to allow developing countries bargaining power to prise open industrial countries' markets. Some difficulties will have to be overcome before negotiations can be concluded, however. Some bilateral disparities may be troublesome – for example, Hong Kong has no quantitative restrictions but is a principal supplier of several Big Three imports. And occasionally a principal supplier may not wish to remove a discriminatory quantitative restriction in one of its markets. These problems could be cured by relaxing the definition of the principal supplier or by having developing countries presenting joint requests for concessions. Moreover, both changes would bring this exercise closer into line with past GATT practice and increase the reported internalization ratios. Methods for binding quantitative restrictions will have to overcome their scruples at negotiating GATT-consistent and GATT-inconsistent barriers together. (They are, after all, equally deleterious from either a mercantilist or a welfare point of view.) Nonetheless, the figures in table 7.1 and 7.2 do suggest that if no better modes of negotiation for quantitative restrictions can be devised, significant progress could be made by falling back on the well-tried technique of principal-supplier requests and negotiation.

These calculations also show that developing countries have considerable scope to negotiate market liberalization from industrial countries in the Uruguay Round, if only they will reciprocate. Moreover, Finger's findings about the Kennedy Round and the current rhetoric in American and European capitals suggest that reciprocity provides by far the most promising route for improving market access for developing countries' exports.

NOTES

1 Strictly, these figures show only that participating developing countries gained something, not that participants gained more than they would have done without participation – or that nonparticipants gained less than they would have done with participation. But unless the participation decision was very highly correlated with potential gains, the latter is a reasonable conclusion. (See Chapter 10 for more on the interpretation of these results.)

REFERENCES

Cline, William R. 1983, "Reciprocity: A New Approach to World Trade Policy?" in W. R. Cline, ed., *Trade Policy in the 1980s*. Washington, D.C.: Institute for International Economics.

Curzon, Gerard, 1965. *Multilateral Commercial Diplomacy*. London: Michael Joseph.

Deardorff, Alan V., and Robert M. Stern, 1986. *The Michigan Model of World Production and Trade*. Cambridge, Mass.: MIT Press.

Dell, Edmund, 1986. "Of Free Trade and Reciprocity," *The World Economy*, 9 (June): 125–40.

Finger, J. Michael, 1979. "Trade Liberalization: A Public Choice Perspective." In R. C. Amacher, G. Haberter, and T. D. Willet, eds., *Challenges to a Liberal International Economic Order*. Washington, D.C.: American Enterprise Institute.

GATT Secretariat. 1980. *The Tokyo Round of Multilateral Trade Negotiations: Supplementary Report*. Geneva.

Preeg, Ernest H. 1970. *Traders and Diplomats*. Washington, D.C.: Brookings Institution.

United States Office of the Special Representative for Trade Negotiations. 1967. *Report on United States Negotiations*. Vol. I, *General Summary*. Washington, D.C.

Winters, L. Alan, 1987. "Negotiating the Removal of Non-tariff Barriers." *Oxford Economic Papers*, forthcoming.

18. Two-Edged Sword: Demands of Developing Countries and the Trading System

M. Wolf

> The separate economic blocs and all the friction and loss of friendship they bring with them are expedients to which one may be driven in a hostile world, where trade has ceased over wide areas to be cooperative and peaceful and where are forgotten the healthy rules of mutual advantage and equal treatment. But it is surely crazy to prefer that.— Lord Keynes, House of Lords, British Parliament, December 18, 1945.

With these words, delivered shortly before his death, Lord Keynes defended the Financial Agreement with the United States, the Lend-Lease settlement, Bretton Woods, and the commercial policy proposals that led ultimately to the General Agreement on Tariffs and Trade.[1] As a result of his efforts and those of many others, an open world economy was recreated after World War II. That achievement is now under threat. Yet if it was "crazy" then to remain wedded to controls over trade and payments, when liberalization was a painful experience still to be undergone, how much more crazy would it now be to throw the achievement away?

The liberal economic order was established after World War II by the industrial market economies. These countries continue to bear the principal responsibility for both its maintenance and its further strengthening. Not only does it reflect their economic philosophy, but commercial and financial transactions involving their citizens still account for by far the greater part of international exchange.[2] It is undoubtedly the failure of the industrial countries to live by the rules to which they themselves had earlier agreed that presents the greatest present danger.[3]

This failure, grievous though it is, is not the subject of this chapter, which is instead the role of developing countries—past, present, and prospective—in the trading system. More precisely, the chapter deals with the consequences of demands which Robert Hudec of the University of Minnesota, a leading authority on the GATT, has described as follows:

> The developing country bloc has sought two kinds of change in general. It has urged the developed countries towards a greater "legalism"— more effective enforcement of developed country obligations, and adoption of new developed country obligations for the particular benefit of developing countries. On the other hand, the bloc has worked just as hard to remove inconvenient GATT obligations controlling its own conduct.[4]

The desire of developing countries to create a world in which one group of countries has most of the obligations and another most of the rights is long-standing. It goes back to the discussions that led to the Havana Charter of 1947. As Kenneth Dam has remarked,

> It was the U.S. position that the less-developed countries could best develop by participating fully in a multilateral nondiscriminatory system with the lowest possible levels of tariffs and no quantitative restrictions. This position proved totally unacceptable to the less-developed world, which sought both affirmative commitments by all member countries to further the process of economic development, and, more important, specific exceptions to many of the prohibitions of the Charter in order to permit the less-developed countries to follow an independent commercial policy. The reigning view in less-developed countries was that economic development . . . required the creation of import substitution industries. It was asserted that such industries could flourish only behind high tariff walls supplemented . . . by quantitative restrictions.[5]

In effect, developing countries have engaged in a sustained assault on the liberal international trading system, including the principle of nondiscrimination, embodied in article I of the GATT. They have argued that "equal treatment of unequals is unjust" and have urged, instead, that there be discrimination in favor of developing countries. Thus, they began pressing for the following:

> to be excused in multilateral trade negotiations from making reciprocal tariff reductions, which they formally secured in part IV of the GATT, added in 1964,
>
> to be accorded tariff preferences in the markets of developed countries for their exports of manufactures and semimanufactures, which they formally achieved in the "waiver" of the most-favored-nation (MFN) clause, granted in 1971, sanctioning the Generalized System of Preferences (GSP), and
>
> to be afforded "special and more favorable treatment . . . in areas of the negotiation where this is feasible and appropriate," which they formally obtained in the Tokyo Declaration setting out the terms of reference for the multilateral trade negotiations of 1973-1979.

These and other developments over the past quarter of a century have resulted in a very considerable divergence in the formal application of GATT principles and rules to the trade of developing countries, on the one hand, and to that of developed countries, on the other. As the Brandt Commission report has correctly stated; "The Tokyo Round agreement has recognized that preferential treatment of developing countries should be accepted as a permanent feature of the world trading system rather than as a temporary exception."[6]

It is the principal purpose of this chapter to argue that the United States was correct in its original view and that the demands of developing countries, however understandable in origin, were mistaken and were indeed damaging to the sustainability of the liberal trading system where they were not directly damaging to developing countries themselves. In effect it argues that the demand for special treatment has proved a two-edged sword.

Certain caveats are in order. The discussion is concerned largely with the international trading system and focuses on the diplomacy of international rule making. Thus, two closely related issues are treated only in passing—world trade itself and optimal policy for a single country— although the relation between both of these and the rules of the trading system is considered when necessary. Second, the question of commodity-price stabilization is not discussed. The focus is on market access, namely the terms and conditions on which citizens or organizations of one country may enter into transactions with those of another. Furthermore, with few exceptions the discussion deals with the traditional GATT concern: trade in goods. Third, although the topic of "graduation" (as it has come to be called) is related to that of this chapter, the discussion below concerns more than graduation. The idea of graduation presumes a world of two distinct status groups, the problem then being how to manage the transition of countries between the two. The discussion below questions whether a world of two distinct groups is desirable in the first place. Fourth, the heterogeneity of the group referred to as "developing countries" must be recognized. There can be no serious prospect that all developing countries will make the recommended commitment to the liberal international order. In practice, the countries that might make such a commitment are the more advanced market economies. There are therefore difficult questions concerning negotiating tactics, which can only be touched upon below. Finally, although the emphasis here is on what developing countries have done to damage the liberal trading system and might do to restore it, this does not imply that the developing countries bear the main responsibility for either that damage or that restoration. The principal responsibility rests with the industrial market economies.

REASON FOR ACTION

The trading system is already under serious threat, with numerous "dead spots" in the GATT code and the proliferation of restraints outside its purview.[7] The protectionist pressures revealed by the almost calamitous GATT ministerial meeting of November 1982 are very strong.[8] In consequence, it may well be that even a strong commitment by the most successful developing countries to the principles of the liberal trading system will not reverse the trend. Nevertheless, there is no reasonable alternative for them. The collapse of the liberal international order, with attendant consequences for financial flows to developing countries, is most threatening to those rapidly growing countries that require a smooth accommodation by the rest of the world to their growth. Thus, it is the importance of the task, rather than the probability of success alone, that should determine their actions.

THE UNDERLYING CONCEPT OF GATT AND THE INTERESTS OF DEVELOPING COUNTRIES

Rules of the international economic order exist to bind governments and restrict their actions, in order to allow agents, wherever located, to make long-term plans in a stable policy environment and so participate fully in an integrated world economy. In this way extensive economic specialization across national frontiers is made possible. These international rules therefore help to ensure the survival of an international economic system based on market principles.

The Essence of the Trading System

In order to achieve their desired goal in international trade, those who framed the GATT decided that the commercial policies of participating states should have four fundamental attributes: nondiscrimination, liberalism, stability, and transparency.[9] The tariff was selected as the sole instrument of commercial policy because it is intrinsically transparent, easy to negotiate, and fully compatible with the market. Tariff bindings were agreed in order to give economic agents the security to invest on the assumption of long-term market access. Restrictions on the circumstances and ways in which protection could be increased (including articles and codes on nontariff measures) were also intended to ensure stability and transparency. Finally, it was agreed that trade policies would not retain the desired attributes without acceptance of the principle of nondiscrimination. In this view the authors of the GATT were influenced by the experiences of the 1930s. The same principle, nondiscrimination, ensured that global benefits were derived from liberalization by a relatively small number of countries.

None of the four basic elements was newly invented in the GATT. On the contrary, they were also the central elements of the trading system that grew out of the Cobden-Chevalier Treaty of 1860 and led to the great expansion of world trade of the second half of the nineteenth century. The similarity between that period and the period after World War II was, therefore, no accident.

The rules of the international trading system were not designed to achieve free trade. It was accepted that individual countries were bound to differ on this issue and that many would wish to reserve the right to protect. At the same time, it is politically difficult to sustain greater liberalism in one democratic country than in another when they are in apparently similar circumstances. Moreover, since mercantilist prejudices are strong, it is virtually impossible to liberalize unilaterally. Reciprocal bargaining over trade barriers therefore became in practice the principal instrument of general trade liberalization. Even though it is an effective technique of liberalization, the emphasis on reciprocity is also a source of fragility, tending (as is now clear) to generate conflicts and resentments where no economic justification exists.

From the point of view of the world order as a whole, adherence to the rules by major market economies is much more important than adherence by smaller countries. If Sri Lanka were to pursue free trade one year and autarky the next, the upheaval would be a legitimate concern for its own citizens but would be of little importance to the rest of the world. The same is not true for the European Community or the United States. They face consequences and therefore constraints— entirely beneficial ones from the point of view of their own long-term interests—that do not affect others to the same degree.

The most important role of large market economies in world trade is as the major open markets on which all can rely and in which global supply and demand can be balanced relatively smoothly. If a major market is suddenly cut off from the rest of the world, especially by quantitative controls, the impact of global supply and demand fluctuations will be felt more sharply in the remaining open markets. Partly for this reason, such protection tends to spread rapidly. If, however, all major markets are controlled, no exporter can enjoy predictable market access. All trade becomes subject to permanent negotiation and is in consequence determined by political rather than economic considerations. Exporters will then come to depend on ex gratia favors by governments of importing countries, and potentially efficient investments will inevitably be curtailed and development prospects impaired. Thus, adherence to the rules by the governments of the major economies makes possible a global public good: a reasonably stable, yet dynamic, world economy.

It is possible, therefore, to consider the trade policies of any country (or group of countries) from two perspectives. For a country, looked at in isolation, the question is whether the government's policies allow for efficient international specialization. This is the classic problem in international trade theory, and the current view is that—except where the aim is to exploit monopoly power (a dangerous game)—the best trade policy is simply free trade.[10] From the point of view of outsiders, however, the question is whether the country's policies contribute to a harmoniously functioning international economy. What are required for this, especially in the case of large economies, are simply the stable, transparent, and liberal policies that the GATT attempted to ensure.

The Interest of Developing Countries in the Adherence of Other Countries to GATT Principles

Developing countries are individually fairly weak and are latecomers to economic growth. The value for the weak of the binding of the strong by international rules has been brought out clearly in the following remarks, in which Sidney Golt, formerly deputy secretary in the Department of Trade and Industry in the United Kingdom government, explains how the GATT originated in a reaction against the abuses of power in commercial relations that characterized the 1930s:

> . . . a significant element [of the justification for the GATT system] was the view of the body of international rules, customs and practices as not only governing the relationships of the strong countries towards each other, but also as safeguards for the weaker powers in the international system.... There was to be no repetition of what was seen as a particular evil of the 1930s—the operation of bilateral bargaining through which a strong country, by the sheer use of its commercial power and, even more objectionably, its political power, imposed its own desired patterns of trade upon a weaker trading partner.[11]

Equally, it has been the historical experience that in periods of liberalism—the second half of the nineteenth century and after World War II—dynamic latecomers have performed better than established economic powers. A liberal world economy does not, of course, guarantee the success of any economy, but it does at least ensure the accommodation of others to it. In an open, nondiscriminatory market, the more competitive suppliers will automatically shoulder aside the less competitive suppliers. This automatic accommodation is particularly important for small countries, for which trade is certain to be a central element for growth, but even a large country like Japan could hardly have achieved its extraordinarily rapid growth after World War II in a more restrictive environment.

For each individual developing country it is also desirable that other developing countries follow the rules. It is true that industrial countries are the world's largest market, accounting for 64 percent of world imports in 1981, but developing countries themselves accounted for 25 percent.[12] Secure and predictable access to these markets would undoubtedly be a boon for the development of each country.

Optimal Trade Policy, the GATT, and Reciprocity

If it is accepted that any given country would want other countries to adhere to basic GATT principles, what of its own policies? In general, there is no conflict between optimal, unilateral trade policy and GATT rules. Indeed, a country following an optimal policy would avoid taking advantage of virtually all the loopholes in the GATT, especially such devices of "administered" or "contingent" protection as the escape clause.[13] There are three areas in which conflict can arise. Two of these— export subsidization and infant-industry protection—pose trivial problems, but the last—reciprocity and GATT mercantilism—creates much greater difficulty.

Developing countries claim the need to be free to subsidize exports. The principal justification is that of offsetting the effects of their own protection. This justification could, of course, be made unnecessary by a compensated devaluation and lowering of import barriers. Furthermore, in practical terms the Code on Subsidies and Countervailing Duties, negotiated during the Tokyo Round of Multilateral Negotiations, allows developing countries to subsidize exports if the subsidies are not used "in a manner which causes serious prejudice to the trade or production of another signatory."[14] At the same time, the code grants substantial freedom to employ domestic subsidies.[15] Similarly, there is plenty of room in the GATT (probably too much room) for infant-industry protection (under article XVIII).

A more substantial problem is that of reciprocity, the principal technique of trade liberalization under the GATT. Four issues arise:

> An optimal trade policy would approximate free trade, but a country following a policy of complete free trade has, as Hong Kong and Singapore know well, no bargaining power whatsoever.
>
> Small countries have, in any case, limited bargaining power, and they tend therefore to obtain modest reductions in trade barriers on products of direct export interest to them, especially when tariff negotiations are carried out under the "principal supplier" rule.[16]

> To the extent that the GATT performs the role of a weak constitutional constraint on trade policy, the failure of reciprocity for small countries works both ways. Just as small countries know they can get rather little in return for tariff "concessions," they know also that retaliation against withdrawal of "concessions" by them is unlikely. *De minimis non curat GATT*. Thus, the fear of retaliation is of modest help to the government of a small country wishing to pursue liberal policies and to resist domestic pressures for protection.
>
> The GATT, like other constitutional arrangements, has an educational function. Unfortunately, its mercantilist language concerning tariff "concessions," combined with the language of its escape clauses, all of which emphasize the cost of increased imports, teaches the wrong lesson: that, as Gustave Flaubert once put it, "imports are the canker at the heart of trade." For this reason, membership in the GATT is of little help in explaining the value of an efficient trade policy.

It may be concluded that small countries will have at best limited influence on the trade policies of others via GATT mechanisms; that the more efficient their policies, the smaller their direct leverage; that GATT mechanisms will provide only modest assistance to them in achieving an efficient trade policy; and that such a policy will involve a liberalism that goes well beyond that of the GATT.

Nevertheless, the notion of reciprocity is not useless for developing countries. Collectively, developing countries (even the group of more advanced developing countries) have substantial weight in world trade. If they can coordinate their offers and the withdrawal of offers, they can hope to influence the trade policies of others. Moreover, most developing countries now have trade policies that are much more illiberal even than those consistent with GATT principles. For them there is no contradiction between offering "concessions" on trade barriers and simultaneously moving toward more efficient policies.

DEVELOPING COUNTRIES' DEMANDS AND THE EROSION OF THE GATT SYSTEM

Although the central principles of the GATT are strong and sensible, it had to be constructed with a multitude of loopholes. The GATT permits the renegotiation of bound tariffs (article XXVIII), imposition of (nondiscriminatory) emergency protection against competitive imports (article XIX), protection for balance-of-payments reasons (article XII), countervailing action against dumped or subsidized goods (article VI and the code on subsidies and countervailing duties), formation of customs unions and free-trade areas (article XXIV), and the imposition of quantitative restrictions against agricultural imports (article XI).

Unfortunately, the industrial countries have found it increasingly difficult to live by even this enfeebled system. Their great achievement was the progressive liberalization and binding of tariffs in a series of seven multilateral negotiations. When the Tokyo Round tariff cuts are completed, the weighted average MFN tariff of industrial countries on all industrial products will be only 4.7 percent.[17] Meanwhile, however, there have been the following major derogations and failures.[18]

The principle of nondiscrimination has been seriously eroded. Preferential trade arrangements, including the European Community's agreements with associates and arrangements among developing countries that fall far short of satisfying the conditions of article XXIV, have proliferated. In addition there has been a renewed trend toward bilateralism with the growth of "voluntary" export-restraint agreements, negotiated mainly with Japan and the advanced developing countries. As the principal authors of the GATT had anticipated, this mushrooming of discrimination has proved increasingly incompatible with the maintenance of stable, transparent, and liberal trade policies.

The growth in discrimination has been associated with the failure of the provision in the GATT (article XIX) that permits the imposition of emergency protection against import surges, but only on a nondiscriminatory basis. Governments have found "voluntary" discriminatory arrangements a more attractive alternative.

Whole industries have been excepted from liberalization. Since the early 1950s, trade in temperate-zone agricultural products has been effectively removed from GATT governance. From 1961, a plurilaterally agreed-upon system of discriminatory restraints against developing countries' exports of textiles and clothing has been in force, and these restraints have become increasingly restrictive over time. Since 1977, there has been a rapid movement toward a not dissimilar system of restraints on trade in steel. Trade in automobiles appears now to be on the verge of similar global cartelization.

The reciprocity technique of trade liberalization has meant disproportionately small liberalization of trade in products of immediate interest to developing countries.[19]

A complex system of "administered" or "contingent" protection has been built up in industrial countries, as a substitute for tariffs, through exploitation of the loopholes present in the GATT and corresponding domestic laws.[20]

Finally, the process of multilateral consultation and collective judgment has fallen into disuse. The formal process of dispute settlement has proved an ineffective replacement, especially where complaints of small powers against the great are concerned.[21]

Many of these exceptions, especially those involving resort to discriminatory protection outside the purview of the GATT, were the result of an accommodation to protectionist pressure that might otherwise have threatened the achievement of tariff liberalization. Such trimming of the sails has not been unsuccessful; certainly the liberal framework of trade policy has endured in a way not experienced in the 1930s. Nevertheless, the damage being done by the cumulation of individual exceptions, each justifiable on its merits to practical men— damage in terms of increased uncertainty, misallocation of resources, and failure to adjust—threatens to overwhelm the open trading system. Moreover, since adjustment at the margin is resisted most, developing countries are likely to be the most damaged by the growth of the discriminatory protection that is the principal symptom of decay.

The Demands of Developing Countries and the Responses of Industrial Countries

As a result of the above trends, developing countries have found it easy to agree—quite rightly—that constraints on industrial countries in the GATT are feeble and that their practice has fallen short of even these far-from-exalted standards. They have attempted, therefore, to impose a sterner discipline. For example, spokesmen for developing countries have demanded tighter and more specific definition of the concepts of injury and market disruption, which are central to various GATT clauses and codes, to the textile arrangement, and to domestic law.[22] Similarly, they have demanded in the hitherto abortive discussion of the code on safeguard protection that procedures be made more open, that duration of safeguard protection be limited, and in other ways that the right to safeguard protection be circumscribed.

Developing countries have gone still further. They have demanded of industrial countries discrimination in their own favor, the principal result being the GSP. Moreover, they have consistently argued that the fetters to be placed on industrial countries are inappropriate for themselves since they need greater sovereign discretion.

So automatic has become acceptance of this double standard that it is even to be found in an excellent pamphlet by Carlos F. Diaz-Alejandro and Gerald K. Helleiner, who state: "These lessons [of economic history] maintain their relevance in 1982. They should strongly discourage departures from the broad principle of *non-discrimination* in commodity trade, except for transitional preferences for LDCs . . . and customs unions formed by those countries."[23]

While developing countries have won a number of formal concessions in the GATT, it has also become increasingly the practice of industrial countries to discriminate against the more successful among them. In effect, industrial countries have been prepared to grant the appearance of compliance with developing countries' demands while denying the reality. They fear the consequences of dynamic growth of new competitors, but they are willing to offer the carefully controlled favors of what Harry Johnson once described as neo-neo-colonialism, thus dividing developing countries into disruptive goats, against whom discriminatory protection is appropriate, and less successful sheep, for whom favors can be done. It is because of the supposedly more favorable treatment accorded to all, in principle, but the less favorable treatment accorded to the more successful, in practice, that the problem of graduation has become so vexed. A country has little incentive to graduate into hostile and discriminatory, rather than equal, treatment.

An interesting historical example of industrial countries' divide-and- rule tactics was the Brasseur plan for selective preferences in favor of developing countries, advanced by the Belgian representative at the 1963 GATT ministerial meeting.[24] It was in part a response to years of sustained pressure for a general liberalization of barriers facing developing countries, just as was the vague rhetoric of part IV of the GATT.[25] Preferences—a side issue at best—then became a principal concern of the United Nations Conference on Trade and Development of 1964.[26] Unfortunately, developing countries were willing to take the bait. They had doubted the appropriateness of liberal trading policies for themselves from the beginning. Equally widespread was their belief that special favors and concessions were needed if their exports were to grow.[27]

In consequence, developing and industrial countries' attitudes present a mirror image. Both fear the general application of universal and liberal rules vis-à-vis one another, and both are prepared to accept derogations from such universality, hoping thereby either to obtain special favors, as in the case of developing countries, or to avoid liberalism toward the more dynamic developing countries, as in the case of industrial countries. In the process, a Gresham's Law of negotiations has come into effect: Bad (or marginal) issues have driven out good.

Consequences of Developing Countries' Demands

What is the value of the concessions that developing countries have obtained? This question can be treated under four heads: the economic effects of industrial countries' preferences, the effect on industrial countries' attitudes, the effect on the body of trade rules, and the effect on developing countries' policies.

The literature on the economic consequences of preferences is vast and cannot be reviewed here in any detail.[28] Three conclusions can legitimately be drawn from it, however: that the dramatic growth of developing-country manufactured exports after 1960 (at a volume growth rate of close to 13 percent a year) was not due to preferences, that trade creation has probably been a larger source of the benefit from preferences than trade diversion, and that the greater part of the benefits go to relatively advanced developing countries such as South Korea and Brazil.

Industrial countries regard this as an ex gratia favor to an arbitrarily defined group of countries. For this reason the preferences are neither generous enough nor secure enough to have the impact on infant industries that had been hoped for.[29] It is also to be noted that the difference between the effects of preferences and equivalent general liberalization consists of trade diversion. Not only is diversion a small part of the benefit to developing countries, however; it is also the part that is threatened by further general trade liberalization. Moreover, because the preferential element (as opposed to the liberalization per se) works by promoting exports in which other suppliers have a comparative advantage, this element of the GSP is unlikely to stimulate development in line with the global comparative advantage of the developing country itself. It is therefore just insofar as the benefit derives from the preferential element that it is most dubious. In effect, preferences are a combination of general liberalization, desirable to both parties, and an inefficient form of aid.

Not only are preferences—the most visible benefit derived from the peculiar position of developing countries—of doubtful value, but they join with other demands in exercising a damaging effect on industrial countries' attitudes toward trade with developing countries. From these demands astute citizens of an industrial country (the majority of whom are, after all, not economists) would draw the following conclusions:

> Imports from developing countries are not so much a mutual benefit as a favor, that is, a form of aid, granted (or owed) to the developing countries.

This "aid" goes to the "wrong" countries (the "dominant" suppliers, as they are called in the case of the Multifiber Arrangement) not to the more deserving.

The "injustice" should be cured by doling out trade opportunities, like aid, to the least successful, while holding back the successful.

The rules that industrial countries are enjoined to obey are not likely to be in their interest, since rapidly growing developing countries claim that they are a hindrance to development, but again a favor owed to developing countries.

In sum, the effect is to undermine the belief that liberal trade is a matter of mutual advantage, or of unilateral advantage to the industrial countries. Rather, the impression is that it is a burden on the industrialized countries. It is not surprising, therefore, that in more difficult times the industrial countries have been less willing to bear such a "burden."

I now turn to the system of trade rules. It is evident that a completely arbitrary distinction between countries has been introduced. Industrial countries "know a hawk from a handsaw" and can see that the difference between Hong Kong and Holland is much smaller than that between Hong Kong and Haiti. In light of the arbitrariness of the distinction between developed and developing countries—an arbitrariness that has meant that developing countries could only be defined by self-designation—it is surprising neither that further categories appear de facto or de jure (such as the category of "countries in transition," against whom discriminatory protection is justified) nor that "graduation" has become an issue of contention.

It is partly because of the arbitrariness of any dividing line between countries that the frequency made proposal that international rules be universal but not uniform is likely in practice to create rather than resolve difficulties. Moreover, these difficulties will grow as the process of ever finer differentiation continues (being aimed at each stage at removing injustices created at the previous one). It should be remembered that the principle of equal treatment before the law is not justified by the proposition that all people are identical; on the contrary, it is justified by the opposite proposition, that differences among people are so many and various that criteria for a just differentiation can never be universally agreed upon. Furthermore, in the absence of such criteria no authority can safely be entrusted with the arbitrary power of differentiation. Exactly the same arguments apply to rules governing the behavior of states.

A difficulty has also been introduced into the liberalization process itself by the GSP (and other preferences). The fruits of trade diversion cannot be enjoyed if barriers fall more generally. As a result, developing countries became a voice against tariff liberalization during the Tokyo Round of multilateral trade negotiations.

Finally, there are damaging effects on developing countries. Contrary to earlier views, limitless protection is not in the interests of individual developing countries. It is also not true that governments find it any easier in developing countries than in industrial countries to exercise unlimited sovereign discretion wisely and without falling prey to special interests. The release from all external constraints on their policies, however weak, combined with the constant preaching that the ideas embodied in those constraints are damaging, has allowed developing countries to construct restrictive regimes that can be liberalized only with great difficulty and that strangle their own growth.

One of the most damaging licenses for developing countries has been that to construct protectionist preferential trading arrangements. Because of the large element of trade diversion inherent in these schemes, they have proved fragile.[30] Worse, they have proved a diversion from consideration of the need for more comprehensive liberalization. Latin American countries, for example, have put great effort into such schemes but have labored to produce a mouse: In 1979 trade in manufactures within the Latin American Free Trade Area (LAFTA) was $4.7 billion, about a third of the gross manufactured exports of Hong Kong alone.[31]

Assessment of Developing Countries' Demands

Enough has been said to cast doubt on both the premise that equal treatment of unequals is unfair and the demand that rules be universal but not uniform. What these mean in practice is, first, that developing countries are permitted to pursue policies damaging to themselves. As Ian Little has recently put it, "In the trade field . . . [developing countries] beg to be allowed to hurt themselves."[32] In this respect, therefore, the demand for special treatment is similar to a demand by a pedestrian for the "right" to jaywalk and so step under a bus. Second, developing countries obtain a benefit in the form of preferences that appears to be valuable but actually amounts to a particularly inefficient and inequitably distributed form of aid. In the process, they have weakened the commitment of industrial countries to the liberal trading system and so contributed to the pressures that lie behind many of the derogations and failures of the GATT system. Thus, while developing countries are certainly not mainly responsible for the erosion, they have played their part. They have done so, most fundamentally, by their assault on the simple and powerful concept of a body of liberal principles universally applied.

THE ROLE OF DEVELOPING COUNTRIES IN RESTORING THE OPEN TRADING SYSTEM

Developing countries can make a contribution to a restoration of the open trading system. There are indeed many reasons why they should now be prepared to make such an effort. First, it is no longer possible to ask only for derogations from GATT principles in their favor, in the expectation that the basic framework of liberal trade will be unaffected. At the GATT ministerial meeting of November 1982 it was impossible to agree on more than "to make determined efforts to ensure that trade policies and measures are consistent with GATT principles and rules and to resist protectionist pressures."[33] No more compelling witness to the fragility of the system could be supplied. Second, developing countries are the newcomers and therefore depend most on a liberal trading system that accommodates their growth. Third, developing countries have shown themselves well able to expand manufactured exports, now equal in value to their primary commodity exports (excluding fuel), provided their own trade policies do not tax these exports excessively and there exists reasonably unrestricted market access.[34] Automatic accommodation to their growth (or, in other words, secure market access) is, therefore, their greatest interest in trade negotiations. Fourth, it has proved unnecessary—indeed costly—for them to enjoy limitless freedom to follow import substitution policies. Fifth, the colonial period is now slipping into the past and should no longer be allowed to dominate attitudes. Finally, even if a special status were desirable in itself, it can be achieved only at the price of victimization of the successful. There is little likelihood that industrial countries will grant special privileges to some countries without also victimizing others (or even the same countries in different circumstances).

As Harry Johnson once wrote, "One of the few genuine issues, and the one most subject to obfuscation, is purely and simply that of allowing the developing countries to sell freely what they are good at making."[35]

A Lead by Developing Countries

What is needed is that the developing countries, or as large a group of them as possible, affirm their belief in the value of the open trading system and show their willingness to abide by its disciplines (preferably, even if industrial countries fail to do so). This would involve a commitment to replace quantitative restrictions by tariffs and to liberalize tariffs to a substantial extent over a specified period of time, a willingness to abide by GATT articles and codes in essentially the same way as industrial countries (thus accepting a minimum standard of international discipline on commercial policies), an insistence on the applicability of unconditional nondiscrimination in all countries' trade policies, and a willingness to engage in North-South negotiations over such a restoration and over complementary liberalization of industrial countries' barriers against them.

The recommended path does not depend on any precisely formulated notion of reciprocity, over which a fruitful discussion of present difficulties can only founder. What is demanded is the sort of commitment that can change the context in which discussions occur, thus breaking the logjam created by present mistrust and the cumulation of past errors.

Objections to Liberalization

Strong objections have been made to these arguments for liberalization by developing countries. The principal point has been that developing countries already import all they can and, with their high level of indebtedness, can certainly not import any more.[36] In order to deal with these arguments, it is useful to distinguish two issues: long-term specialization in international trade and adjustment to liberalization in the short term.

With regard to long-term specialization, it is simply untrue that developing countries already import all they can, if by that it is meant that developing countries cannot export (and, therefore, import) more.[37] Protection against imports is a tax on exports. *Ceteris paribus,* the more protectionist a country, the lower both its exports and imports in relation to gross domestic product (GDP). Since many industrially advanced developing countries are highly protectionist—Brazil, India, and Mexico, for example—and some became still more so after 1973, there is no good reason to suppose that they are unable to increase exports.[38] Thus, after a period of adjustment to the reduction in protection, a perfectly sustainable rise in trade can occur.[39]

The real problem is that of the period of adjustment. Developing countries themselves can do much to facilitate adjustment, largely by ensuring adequate incentives for exports.[40] Nevertheless, with the present recession and the debt problem outside support will be helpful. This should be raised as an international issue. Finance of an adjustment program that will make developing countries more creditworthy is in the interest of both the industrial market economies and the debtor countries.[41] There is a precedent for financial assistance in support of the liberalization of the trade policies of protectionist countries: the Marshall Plan.

Finally, the desired adjustment is possible only if increased exports are accommodated in world markets. Thus, domestic liberalization and strengthening of the liberal trading system go hand in hand, the former helping and at the same time depending on the latter. There is indeed one respect in which they are virtually the same: Concerted liberalization by developing countries will give an automatic increase in access to the world's most dynamic markets, those of one another.

Relation to Optimal Trade Policy

A commitment to liberalization in accordance with GATT principles is, therefore, not against the interests of developing countries, but at the same time it is only a first step toward an efficient trade policy. In view of the starting point of most developing countries, there need be no conflict between the two, but developing countries would be wise to go further than the GATT and not avail themselves of its many loopholes. A useful step might be to incorporate the gains from trade into domestic decisions on emergency protection and countervailing duties, as Michael Finger of the World Bank has recommended.[42]

An Opportunity for Progress

In sum, developing countries have the opportunity to make a commitment that is likely simultaneously to improve the efficiency of their own trade regimes, increase trading opportunities for the whole world as they open their markets, enhance the legitimacy of the liberal trading system in industrial countries, and, one hopes, reduce the barriers of industrial countries against them. That opportunity should be seized.

ISSUES IN INTERNATIONAL TRADE NEGOTIATIONS

Within the context of the change in policy recommended above, a number of detailed issues in international trade negotiations can be considered. Two of these will be reviewed at some length: safeguard protections and tariffs. Brief comments will then be made on other issues before I turn to the question of tactics.[43]

Selective Safeguards

The Tokyo Declaration, which set the terms of reference for the Tokyo Round negotiations, called on governments to review the operation of article XIX. In doing so they made a concerted effort to negotiate a safeguards code, but it foundered on the European Community's proposal that the code should provide for the imposition of "emergency" protection on a "selective" basis—that is, against imports of a particular product from one or a few countries identified as the cause of "serious injury" to the corresponding domestic industry in the importing country. This proposal encountered determined opposition from the developing countries and from Australia, Canada, and a number of small developed countries. Although the review of article XIX was concluded and thus no amendments were possible, the issue has been kept on the books as unfinished business.

Whether the principle of selective application of emergency protection would have been accepted will not be known; matters never got that far. The negotiators concentrated on the criteria that would determine the "exceptional" circumstances in which selective action might be taken. It was suggested that the dangers of departures from the principle of nondiscrimination could be mitigated by laying down careful restrictions on the use of the privilege. However, agreement could not be reached on clearly defined criteria for what was in effect an escape clause within an escape clause.

The effort to write into GATT law a provision for selective safeguard action might be said to have been an effort to make informal quantitative restrictions formally acceptable within the GATT. This amounts to writing a rule that violates the basic principle of nondiscrimination. Developing countries were absolutely right to resist this proposal as can be seen from inspection of the arguments advanced for it.

The first line of argument was to ask why all exporting countries should suffer from the imposition of emergency protection under article XIX, when the "injury" or "market disruption" is caused by just one or two inordinately competitive suppliers. The argument rests on a belief, entirely inconsistent with the market principles of the GATT, that every producer has a right to be free of irresistible competitors. The economics is also doubtful; if a particular industry suffers from a comparative disadvantage, saving it from the competition of one overseas supplier is unlikely to be enough; the problem will arise again with imports from another supplier. In the case of textiles and clothing, for instance, selective action against Japan led to subsequent problems with imports from Hong Kong, Taiwan, South Korea, and, increasingly, Thailand, the Philippines, and other countries.

The second line of argument acknowledges that "voluntary" export-restraint agreements (VERs) and "orderly" marketing arrangements (OMAs) are undermining the GATT system but suggests that the best way to come to grips with them is to bring them into the legal glare of the GATT. If everybody agrees that VERs and OMAs are the problem, however, why not agree to stop using them? In any case, legalization is neither a sufficient nor a necessary condition for reporting discriminatory trade restrictions.

The developing countries are right to reject selectivity because such legalization of discrimination would be still worse than the present chaos. There are, after all, certain advantages to unofficial VERs. The exporters can capture some of the scarcity rent, and the very illegality of VERs offers them bargaining power. The restricted suppliers have also done well—at least so far—in diversifying into new products and upgrading the quality of their exports. Meanwhile, unrestricted suppliers are given a new export opportunity. Thus, one or two VERs in a sector just are not very effective as a protectionist device in terms of the objectives of the importing country.[44] What is disastrous—and also almost impossible to liberalize—is a comprehensive, global system of bilateral restraints, as in the textile arrangement. The case of textiles shows, however, that it is the proliferation of protection that is threatened by official sanctioning of discrimination, and that such a proliferation is also unlikely to be controlled by the fine words written into any code.[45]

This does not mean that VERs are undesirable. Any discriminatory restraint creates powerful interests opposed to liberalization, not only in the protecting country but also among unrestricted suppliers. It should be remembered, for example, that developing countries have not been averse to being protected from one another in this way. It is in the general interest of developing countries, however, to curb such discrimination and to support proposals for achieving full international notification of VERs and for the creation of a safeguard surveillance committee in the GATT, not only to publicize informal restrictions but also to discuss methods for removal of all quantitative restrictions. Such a position by developing countries would have more force if they were willing to commit themselves to a removal of most of their own quantitative restrictions at the same time.

Tariffs, Tariff Escalation, and Preferences

Developing countries have been concerned about the relatively high level of tariffs against their exports and especially about tariff escalation against the processing of commodities. They have also been pressing for preferential tariffs in their favor by industrial countries as well as for freedom to create preferential trading arrangements among themselves.

A radical solution to the deadlock over tariffs would be to suggest that the cuts negotiated in the Tokyo Round continue until the tariffs reach zero. Developing countries should also accept that the preferential element in the GSP amounts to a form of aid, which will be generously given only to those obviously in need of assistance. They should suggest, therefore, that, so long as tariffs last, the benefits of the GSP be granted, without any of the present restrictions in the various schemes, to all countries that are eligible for IDA credits (except perhaps India and China).[46] In time the tariff cuts would dispose of most of the concern about tariff escalation, leaving only the difficult problem of industries that have been excepted from the tariff cuts, which would require separate negotiation. Alternatively, there could be a negotiation solely about the structure of protection, which aimed at equalizing effective rates of protection. In order to induce such a general lowering of tariffs (or at least their restructuring) the advanced developing countries would accept the immediate loss of GSP privileges and commit themselves to some liberalization of their own barriers to imports.

While reviewing their tariff policy, developing countries should consider whether they would not be much better off if their preferential liberalization with respect to one another, actual and proposed, were instead put on a nondiscriminatory basis.[47] Alternatively, the costs of trade diversion and the consequent fragility of these arrangements could be reduced by negotiating a reduction of the external barriers of the preferential trading arrangements. This is exactly what the European Community did during the Dillon, Kennedy, and Tokyo Rounds of Multilateral Trade Negotiations.

Other Issues

There are other issues in which developing countries have a stake.

The codes negotiated during the Tokyo Round have yet to prove their worth. They could, in any case, be only the beginning of a continuous process of consultation and negotiation, which means that everything depends on the implementation of the agreements reached. Since the agreements were signed, a number of difficulties have arisen. There has been considerable disappointment over the number of countries that have become parties to particular agreements. At the same time, some of the agreements, particularly the one on subsidies and countervailing measures, could usefully be clarified and strengthened. In this process, developing countries should reconsider the desirability for them of the exemptions from various disciplines that they won. There is, accordingly, a need for the different GATT codes of conduct on nontariff measures to be reviewed in order to identify problems inhibiting their implementation on the broadest possible basis.

Although the dispute-settlement procedures of the GATT were reviewed during the Tokyo Round negotiations, they need to be further improved in order to enjoy the confidence of signatory countries, chiefly to raise the level of objectivity. In this respect, panels of inquiry appointed to look into disputes should be drawn from a roster of independent experts in whom signatory countries have confidence. Their first task should be to adjudicate on the legal position of the matter in dispute before setting about conciliation between the parties. In addition, the GATT secretariat should be empowered to intitiate inquiries. One issue on which changes cannot be made is that of enforcement of panel findings. The only realistic sanction is a clear finding that a government is in breach of international law.

Special consideration has to be given to the long-standing problems of integrating agriculture and textiles into the world economy by extending the rules of the GATT, and general trade policy, to both sectors, where deeply entrenched policy regimes are in place. In the cases of textiles and clothing the establishment of a safeguard surveillance committee would permit the export restraints imposed on developing countries to be treated as part of the general body of quantitative restrictions to be liberalized, requiring a conscious decision not to renew the MFA (on the understanding that trade liberalization is virtually impossible in an arrangement confined to a single sector).

There are a number of new issues on the table, of which the most important is trade in services. This American priority has been treated with hostility by developing countries, and one can readily understand their concern. It is certainly not the most important problem facing the GATT; nor can one avoid the fear that services could, like the GSP, prove another case of Gresham's Law of negotiations. Nevertheless, the intensity of American interest can prove tactically useful, since developing countries should be able to obtain something in return for a willingness to discuss the issue.

Tactics

It is not possible to discuss tactics in detail, except to note that leadership in the reconsideration of demands that go back for a generation will inevitably depend on a few countries at first. Unanimity will not be achieved. Advanced developing countries must play the central role.

At the same time, all developing countries need to recognize the futility of continuing to propose disciplines for industrial countries that they reject in their own case. They can also usefully consider the leverage that their imports from industrial countries give them. If a number of developing countries can cooperate, they can be a powerful group; in 1979 Indonesia showed such power on its own when it retaliated against the United Kingdom's intention to limit Indonesia's exports of clothing.[48]

Since the negotiations must focus not only on tariffs but also on the liberalization of quantitative restrictions of various kinds, as well as on codes of conduct, standard GATT techniques of reciprocal bargaining are likely to fail. The very different economic sizes of the partners in a North-South negotiation is also likely to prove a difficulty in this regard. Thus, it is important to avoid getting lost in the arid search for precise reciprocity.

What is required is agreement on action in parallel rather than on the basis of a strict *quid pro quo.* Given a common recognition of the errors of the past and of the domestic costs of those errors, each party should commit itself to abandoning some important and politically sensitive restrictions. A historical precedent for such an approach is the liberalization of quantitative restrictions under the program organized by the Organization for European Economic Cooperation (OEEC) in the 1950s.[49] In this program each country committed itself to a progressive increase in the proportion of trade that would be liberated from quantitative restrictions. The lesson of the OEEC program for relations between industrial market economies and developing countries today is that it embodied a mutual commitment to liberalise without the necessity for agreement on equivalent reductions in the rate of protection or on equivalent lists of product categories to be affected. What is needed, then, is a reciprocal commitment that will serve as a lubricant for agreement rather than as a determinant of the form of that agreement.

THE NEED FOR AN OPEN WORLD ECONOMY

What is at stake? The argument set out above rests on certain fundamental premises: that trade in millions of commodities among well over 100 countries cannot be "managed" except on the basis of universal, liberal principles followed by at least the governments of major trading nations; that if the rules fail and trade is "managed" on the basis of constant bureaucratic intervention the world economy is likely to fail, just as would a horse whose movements were dictated by a committee of jockeys; and finally that in the process of dividing up the trade "pie" in accordance with what bureaucrats and politicians would consider to be "fair shares," politically weak but economically dynamic newcomers would lose the most. Heedless of the latter danger, however, developing countries have left to industrial countries the responsibility for the order as a whole, demanding only exemptions, privileges, and derogations for themselves. Their demands have worked as a two-edged sword, cutting away at the trunk of the order whose branches they wished to trim.

One is reminded of the myth of Midas, who desired that everything should become gold at his touch and ended by turning to gold even his own food. The developing countries love the idea of liberalism for others but hope to make the liberal system still more golden with privileges and exemptions for themselves. In the process they have threatened to deprive their food of its nourishment.

Historically, the major threat to an open world economy has been posed by the emergence of powerful new economies. That emergence has been associated with opposite reactions. Established powers, on the one hand, have been tempted into devising various schemes of exclusion. Meanwhile, the newcomers have been reluctant to adopt the discipline of the existing order, which they suspect or see to be rigged against their interests. With the established powers no longer committed to an order in which their position is declining in relative terms, and with the new powers resentful of "free trade imperialism" or (more frequently) indifferent to their responsibilities, commercial friction and attendant financial difficulties have contributed to two major collapses in this century.

The problem of the smooth accommodation of newcomers is now as acute as ever. The present group of industrial countries accounts for no more than a fifth of the world's population. Their share in world economic activity is declining and is likely to continue to do so. New powers will emerge and, indeed, are emerging. The industrial countries should rid themselves of the illusion that it will be possible to sustain liberal trade among themselves while keeping these intrusive newcomers at bay. At the same time the newcomers—the developing countries—should rid themselves of the notion that liberal trade is the obligation of the rich but a luxury for the poor.

If both sides can recognize their common interest in ordered economic relationships, solutions to the outstanding problems of the world economy should not be difficult. If they do not do so, the international economic order will have failed again, but the wreckage of a third breakdown in this century may not even admit of another chance of reconstruction. To choose that, as Lord Keynes remarked in 1945, would indeed be "crazy."

ACKNOWLEDGMENTS

Parts of this chapter draw on Kenneth Durham et al., *Words Are Not Enough: a Report on the Perils of Protectionism,* Special Report No.2 (London: Trade Policy Research Centre, 1984). I wish to acknowledge the stimulating comments made by participants at the conference, especially those of Ambassador B. L. Das, Ambassador M. Dubey, Professor Carlos Diaz-Alejandro, Professor Gerhard Fels, Dr. Vijay Kelkar, Professor V. R. Panchamukhi, Dr. Jan Pronk, and Dr. André Sapir. I acknowledge the helpful comments of Dr. Jan Tumlir, director of economic research and analysis at the GATT Secretariat, and of Professor Jagdish N. Bhagwati.

NOTES

1 See Richard N. Gardner, *Sterling-Dollar Diplomacy: the Origins and Prospects of Our International Economic Order,* 2d ed. (New York: McGraw-Hill, 1969), chap. 12, esp. pp. 234-235.

2 In 1981 61 percent of world exports and 80 percent of world exports of manufactures came from the industrial market economies. See *International Trade 1981-82* (Geneva: GATT Secretariat, 1982), table A24.

3 For discussions of the EC's trade policies, see Martin Wolf, "The European Community's Trade Policy," in Roy Jenkins (ed.), *Britain and the EEC* (London: Macmillan, 1983); and Jan Tumlir, "Strong and Weak Elements in the Concept of European Integration," in Fritz Machlup, Gerhard Fels, and Hubertus Müller-Groeling (eds), *Reflections* on a *Troubled World Economy: Essays in Honour of Herbert Giersch* (London: Macmillan, for the Trade Policy Research Centre, 1983). See also Jan Tumlir, "International Economic Order: Can the Trend be Reversed?" *World Economy* 5 (March 1982): 29-41.

4 See Robert E. Hudec, *The GATT Legal System and World Trade Diplomacy* (New York: Praeger, 1975), p. 208.

5 See Kenneth W. Dam, *The GATT: Law and International Economic Organization* (Chicago: University of Chicago Press, 1970), pp. 225-226.

6 See Independent Commission on International Development Issues, *North-South: A Program for Survival* (Cambridge: MIT Press, 1980), p. 183.

7 For a discussion of the substantive breakdown, see Robert E. Hudec, *Adjudication of International Trade Disputes*, Thames Essay No. 16 (London: Trade Policy Research Centre, 1978), pp. 15-21.

8 For a discussion of the GATT meeting at ministerial level of November 1982, see

Lydia Dunn et al., *In the Kingdom of the Blind*: A *Report on Protectionism and the Asian-Pacific Region*, Special Report No. 3 (London: Trade Policy Research Centre, 1983), chap. 1.

9 Liberalism cannot be defined precisely. In this context what is meant is, first, permitting markets rather than discretionary, administrative intervention to allocate resources and, second, setting protectionist instruments at levels that permit a steady expansion of world trade.

10 The case for free trade, while allowing for other interventions, is set out in a simple manner in W. M. Corden, *Trade Policy and Economic Welfare* (Oxford: Clarendon Press, 1974). This important argument was made in Jagdish Bhagwati and V. K. Ramaswami, "Domestic Distortions, Tariffs and the Theory of Optimum Subsidy," *Journal of Political Economy* 71 (February 1963): 44-50. See also James E. Meade, *Trade and Welfare* (London: Oxford University Press, 1955), and Harry G. Johnson, "Optimal Trade Intervention in the Presence of Domestic Distortions," in Robert E. Baldwin et al., *Trade, Growth and the Balance of Payments: Essays in Honour of Gottfried Haberler* (Chicago: Rand McNally; and Amsterdam: North-Holland, 1965).

11 See Sidney Golt, *Developing Countries in the GATT System*, Thames Essay No. 13 (London: Trade Policy Research Centre 1978), p. 10.

12 These data are from *International Trade 1981-1982* (Geneva: GATT Secretariat, 1982), table A24.

13 For a discussion of such administrative systems of protection, see J. M. Finger, H. K. Hall, and D. R. Nelson, "The Political Economy of Administered Protection," *American Economic Review* 72 (June 1982): 452-466.

14 See *Agreement on Interpretation and Application of Articles VI, XVI,* and *XXIII of the General Agreement on Tariffs and Trade* (Geneva: GATT Secretariat, 1979), article 14(3).

15 Ibid., article 14(7).

16 For this point, see Alexander J. Yeats, *Trade Barriers Facing Developing Countries* (London: Macmillan, 1979), chap. 4. See also *The Tokyo Round of Multilateral Trade Negotiations,* Supplementary Report by the Director General of the GATT (Geneva: GATT Secretariat, 1980), Annex B.

17 Yeats, table 4.

18 For a fuller discussion of the various derogations from the GATT, see Durham et al., *Words Are Not Enough.*

19 This does not mean that such trade liberalization was not of benefit to developing countries. On this see J. M. Finger, "Effects of the Kennedy Round Tariff Concessions on the Exports of Developing Countries," *Economic Journal* 86 (March 1976): 87-95.

20 On this see Finger, Hall, and Nelson, "Political Economy."

21 On this see Golt, *Developing Countries,* p. 11; and Hudec, *Adjudication.*

22 See, for example, R. Figueredo, "Multilateral Trade Negotiations," TD/ B(XXIII)/ SC.I/Misc./ (Geneva: UNCTAD, 1981).

23 See Diaz-Alejandro and Gerald K. Helleiner, *Handmaiden in Distress: World Trade in the 1980s* (co-published by: North-South Institute, Ottawa, Overseas Development Council, Washington, and Overseas Development Institute, London, 1982) p. 15. See also p. 21.

24 See Dam, GATT, p. 248.

25 Ibid., chap. 14, esp. p. 237.

26 Ibid., p. 249.

27 On these attitudes, see Karin Kock, *International Trade Policy and the GATT, 1947-1967* (Stockholm: Almqvist & Wiksell, 1969), pp. 223-235.

28 On the GSP see, for example, Robert Baldwin and Tracy Murray, "MFN Tariff Reductions and Developing Country Trade Benefits under the GSP," *Economic Journal*

87 (March 1977): 30-46; Murray, *Trade Preferences for Developing Countries* (New York: John Wiley, 1977); André Sapir, "Trade Benefits under the EEC Generalised System of Preferences," *European Economic Review* 15 (March 1981): 339-355; and Sapir and Lars Lundberg, "The U.S. Generalised System of Preferences and Its Impact" (paper presented at a conference on the Structure and Evolution of Recent U.S. Trade Policy sponsored by the National Bureau of Economic Research and held in Cambridge, Massachusetts, December 3–4, 1982).

29 See Golt, *Developing Countries*, pp. 26-29, for the underlying reasons for these limitations.

30 See Constantine Vaitsos, "Crisis in Regional Economic Cooperation (Integration) Among Developing Countries," *World Development* 6 (June 1978): 719-769. For a discussion of the history of regional cooperation among developing countries in the context of the GATT, see Kock, *International Trade Policy*, pp. 247-260.

31 Data are from *Yearbook of International Trade Statistics 1980* (New York: United Nations, Special Table C).

32 See lan M. D. Little, *Economic Development: Theory, Policy and International Relations* (New York: Basic Books, for The Twentieth Century Fund, 1982), p. 370.

33 From "Ministerial Declaration," restricted GATT Doc. W 38/4, Geneva GATT Secretariat, November 29, 1982, 7(i).

34 Apart from the well-known successes, Hong Kong, Singapore, South Korea, and Taiwan, there has been rapid growth of manufactured exports from Brazil and other countries in Latin America; from other East Asian countries (Malaysia, the Philippines and Thailand); from Sri Lanka; and from Mediterranean countries (Morocco, Tunisia, and, recently, Turkey). India has also achieved substantial progress in the past fifteen years or so. On some of the more recent success stories, see Oli Havrylyshyn and Iradj Alikhani, "Is There Cause for Export Optimism? An Inquiry into the Existence of a Second Generation of Successful Exporters," *Wellwirtschaftliches Archiv* 118 (1982): 651-63.

35 See Harry Johnson, "Commercial Policy: What Is There Left?" *Journal of World Trade Law* 9 (May-June 1975): 346.

36 These arguments were put forward by several participants at the conference in New Delhi.

37 It is perhaps not surprising that this pessimistic view was advanced in New Delhi. As I have observed of Indian trade policy in another context, "The degree of specialization is assumed away as a policy option, but is rather the outcome of the desire for self-sufficiency." See Wolf, *India's Exports* (New York: Oxford University Press, for the World Bank, 1982), p. 58.

38 On the trade policies of newly industrializing countries after the oil shock, see Bela Balassa, "The Newly Industrializing Developing Countries after the Oil Crisis," *Weltwirtschaftliches Archiv* 117 (1981): 142-94, which discusses Argentina, Brazil, Colombia, Chile, India, the Republic of Korea, Mexico, Singapore, Taiwan, Israel, Uruguay, and Yugoslavia.

39 A particularly striking example of the response of exports to import liberalization was provided by Chile in the 1970s. Whatever other problems emerged in the Chilean economy, the growth of nontraditional exports was remarkable. See on this T. G. Congdon, "Apertura Policies in the Cone of Latin America," *World Economy* 5 (September 1982): 140-41.

40 There is a vast literature on the optimal adjustment to liberalization. A concise discussion of the options is in Balassa, "Reforming the System of Incentives in Developing Countries," in *Policy Reform in Developing Countries* (Oxford: Pergamon Press, 1977), esp. pp. 25-26.

41 The issue of official support for transition to outward-looking policy is discussed in Anne O. Krueger, "Loans to Assist the Transition to Outward-looking Policies," *World Economy* 4 (September 1981): 271-281.

42 See J. M. Finger, "Incorporating the Gains from Trade into Policy," *World Economy* 5 (December 1982): 367-377.

43 Another and much fuller discussion of issues raised in this section is in Isaiah Frank, *Trade Policy Issues of Interest to the Third World,* Thames Essay No. 29 (London: Trade Policy Research Centre, 1981).

44 On the ineffectiveness of most protective devices, especially VERs, see Baldwin, *The Inefficacy of Trade Policy*, Essays in International Finance, No. 150 (Princeton: International Finance Section, Department of Economics, Princeton University, 1982).

45 On the evolution of the textile arrangements toward ever greater restrictiveness, see Donald B. Keesing and Martin Wolf, *Textiles Quotas against Developing Countries,* Thames Essay No. 23 (London: Trade Policy Research Centre 1980), chaps. 2, 3.

46 It is true that the suggested categorization is also arbitrary. If the goal is however, to ensure that preferences will serve their purported function of stimulating infant exports from the developing countries that need most help, the suggestion seems reasonable. Alternatively, the GSP could be limited to countries with exports of manufactures below a certain level. These are the only sorts of categorization that will lead industrial countries to remove their many restrictions on the use of the GSP, which is desirable if bureaucracy is to be minimized and indeed if the GSP is to be really beneficial for anyone. Nevertheless such *ad hoc* arguments based on political feasibility can never be entirely persuasive. The issue of eligibility for GSP treatment is therefore a vivid example of the difficulty of developing and sustaining a set of clear, generally acceptable and logically compelling rules that are not uniform for all.

47 There is plenty of reason to doubt the value to developing countries of most schemes for preferential liberalization of trade among themselves. A discussion of these issues is in Martin Wolf, *"Fortress Europe"* and *"Collective Self-reliance"*, Weltwirtschaft und Internationale Beziehungen Sonderdrucke 5 (Hamburg: Deutsches Übersee Institut, 1983). A critical examination of UNCTAD's scheme for a global system of trade preferences among developing countries is in Rolf J. Langhammer, "Problems and Effects of a Developing Country Tariff Concession Round on South-South Trade" (paper presented at a conference on South-South versus South-North Trade: Does the Direction of Developing Country Exports Matter? sponsored by the World Bank under the research project on the Direction of Developing Country Exports and held in Brussels, February 28-March 1,1983).

48 See Gerard Curzon, "Neo-protectionism, the MFA and the European Community," *World Economy* 4 (September 1981): 261.

49 See Gerard Curzon, *Multilateral Commercial Diplomacy: the General Agreement on Tariffs and Trade and its Impact on National Commercial Policies and Techniques* (London: Michael Joseph, 1965), pp. 157-165.